Form and Object

Speculative Realism

Series Editor: Graham Harman

Since its first appearance at a London colloquium in 2007, the Speculative Realism movement has taken continental philosophy by storm. Opposing the formerly ubiquitous modern dogma that philosophy can speak only of the human-world relation rather than the world itself, Speculative Realism defends the autonomy of the world from human access, but in a spirit of imaginative audacity.

Editorial Advisory Board

Jane Bennett
Nathan Brown
Levi Bryant
Patricia Clough
Mark Fisher
Iain Hamilton Grant
Myra Hird
Adrian Johnston
Eileen A. Joy

Books available

Quentin Meillassoux: Philosophy in the Making by Graham Harman
Onto-Cartography: An Ontology of Machines and Media by Levi R. Bryant
Form and Object: A Treatise on Things by Tristan Garcia, translated by Mark Allan Ohm and John Cogburn
Adventures in Transcendental Materialism: Dialogues with Contemporary Thinkers by Adrian Johnston
Form and Object: A Treatise on Things by Tristan Garcia, translated by Mark Allan Ohm and John Cogburn
The End of Phenomenology: Metaphysics and the New Realism by Tom Sparrow

Forthcoming series titles

Romantic Realities: Speculative Realism and British Romanticism by Evan Gottlieb
Fields of Sense: A New Realist Ontology by Markus Gabriel
After Quietism: Analytic Philosophies of Immanence and the New Metaphysics by John Cogburn

Visit the Speculative Realism website at www.euppublishing.com/series/specr

Form and Object

A Treatise on Things

Tristan Garcia

Translated by Mark Allan Ohm and Jon Cogburn

EDINBURGH
University Press

For Patrick, my father, and Antonio, my grandfather

Forme et objet: Un traité des choses by Tristan Garcia © Presses Universitaires de France, 2010, 6, avenue Reille, F-75014 Paris

English translation © Mark Allan Ohm and Jon Cogburn, 2014

Edinburgh University Press Ltd
The Tun – Holyrood Road
12 (2f) Jackson's Entry
Edinburgh EH8 8PJ

www.euppublishing.com

Typeset in 11/13 Adobe Sabon by
Servis Filmsetting Ltd, Stockport, Cheshire,
printed and bound in Great Britain by
CPI Group (UK) Ltd, Croydon CR0 4YY

A CIP record for this book is available from the British Library

ISBN 978 0 7486 8149 5 (hardback)
ISBN 978 0 7486 8150 1 (paperback)
ISBN 978 0 7486 8151 8 (webready PDF)
ISBN 978 0 7486 8152 5 (epub)

Contents

Part II: Thing and World

Part III: Being and Comprehending

Book II: Objectively

List of Figures

Acknowledgements

To Agnès, who I thought about and who thought about me. This book was born of ten years of intellectual and affective companionship with her.

To my parents, Monique, Denis, Patrick, and Domenica, who taught me to think;

to Antoine;

to Rose;

to Yves.

I deeply thank the following for their works, which have influenced this book, and for their personal or professional assistance which allowed me to write it:

Quentin Meillassoux, Sandra Laugier, Francis Wolff, and Alain Badiou.

I also thank my professors, Patrick Dupouey and Michel Nodé-Langlois.

For all the lively discussions with children, adolescents, and adults who made their way into these pages, this book owes much to Benoît Anceaume, Julie Rainard, Alice Boussicaut, Flore Boudet, Élodie Fuchs, Mathieu Bonzom, Arnaud Despax, Vivien Bessières, Martin Dumont, Ivan Trabuc, Élise Dardill, Martine Robert, Martin Fortier, and Benoît Caudoux.

Translators' Introduction

As a novelist, Tristan Garcia has received widespread recognition and awards, including the *Prix de Flore*. But it is his most recent philosophical work, *Forme et objet: Un traité des choses*, that secures his place as one of the most significant systematic philosophers in contemporary France.

Garcia's philosophical prose is lucid, in general presenting no special problems for the translator. However, a few key technical terms and phrases are so central to his system that any non-idiomatic English translation would invariably mislead the reader. Thus, explaining our translational choices requires some presentation of the system itself.

In English, 'comprehension' almost always denotes an epistemic state where one or more people *understand* some object or proposition. But this is *not* the case with respect to Garcia's use of '*compréhension*'. For Garcia, one object comprehends another object whenever the second object can be said, *in any way*, to be contained in or encompassed by the first object. The closest English language usage occurs in mathematical set theory, where an axiom of comprehension defines new sets in terms of the properties of their members. But even the set-theoretic notion is merely one instance of Garcia's broader concept. Consider:

> Comprehending is having something inside itself. Comprehending is also comprehending an element by being a set; comprehending one quality by being a substrata of qualities; comprehending someone by appreciating or paying attention to this someone; assimilating a way of thinking or an idea; having a part when one is a composite; or comprehending a temporal, historical, or evolutionary moment in a longer timespan. (i.iii.i, §14)[1]

The idea of comprehension is of central import to Garcia's system for two reasons. First, for Garcia being is nothing other than the inverse of comprehension:

> Being is *being comprehended*. Comprehending is *being been* [*être été*]. The active sense of one is the passive sense of the other. (i.iii.i, §3)

Second, combining this view of being with Garcia's liberal account of comprehension yields a rich ontology where anything that has a determination is something.

In Book I, Part I, Chapter I, Section 15 Garcia produces a set of strikingly original arguments for ontological liberality. He considers in detail six distinct strategies that metaphysicians typically employ to deny that some putative kind of thing is really an object: logical, linguistic, epistemic, cultural, religious, and moral/political. Each strategy denies that something has what Garcia calls a 'minimum-of-whatness' (i.i.i. §16), that is, a minimum determination.[2] Thus, for each case he opposes the claim that a particular category does not pick out objects by attending to how determinations are made within objects of that category. For example, in response to the logician who denies that there are true contradictions, Garcia notes that we can differentiate contradictory entities; the squared circle is necessarily circular while the non-white white is not.

If he is successful at blocking a priori attempts to banish whole kinds of entities from the realm of objects, Garcia must still fight the type of reductionism that attempts a posteriori to explain away one kind of entity in terms of another. Such explanatory violence often proceeds from below, trying to reduce an object to the entities that compose that object:

> Reductionism reduces what things are to what composes these things. Physicalist or materialist reductionism reduces things to the matter that composes them. Evolutionary or naturalist reductionism reduces a living organism to the evolutionary processes of which the living organism is a result. (i.iii.ii §11)

Or they can proceed from above, explaining away the object in terms of things that the object helps compose:

> Other types of reductionism capture the chain of being from the other direction, and reduce a thing to what it is, that is, to what it is

in. Social reductionism reduces a social element to its function in the social whole. Historical reductionism reduces a historical event to the history within which it obtains its place. (i.iii.ii §11)

Following Graham Harman's usage,[3] we can say that Garcia's system is an instance of 'object-oriented ontology' because his central ontological operations are motivated by the attempt to understand what objects must be like if they are to resist reduction from below and from above. Unlike Harman, though, Garcia actually defines the objectivity of an object in terms of this very resistance.

A thing is nothing other than the difference between *that which is in this thing* and *that in which this thing is*. Unless one guarantees this double sense, there are no thinkable things. Every reductionist who claims to deduce that which this or that thing is from that which composes this or that thing only succeeds in dissolving the very thing that they claim to account for. (I.)

Articulating the way this double sense plays out with respect to objects of human interest (beauty, truth, goodness, death, etc.) will be the central motif of Book II. However, before engaging in regional ontology, Garcia's differential model of being must immediately face a question. If an object is the difference between that which it comprehends and that in which it is comprehended, can an object comprehend itself?

The negative answer to the possibility of what Garcia calls 'compactness' (*le compact*) is deceptively simple. If an object just is the difference between that which comprehends it and that which it comprehends then nothing can comprehend itself. 'Difference' here is like subtraction. Since, prima facie, there is no difference between an object and itself,[4] an object for Garcia is just the difference between that which the object comprehends and that which comprehends the object, so a self-comprehending object would subtract itself from itself and be nothing.

This answer is deceptively simple because while there are clearly no compact objects in Garcia's ontology, 'compactness' also names a tendency towards which some things move. And Garcia enumerates central instances of this tendency: philosophers trying to think of things as 'in themselves', the shy person's attempted withdrawal into herself, the saint who would merge with the universe, the introspective psychologist pursuing a perfect kind of self-consciousness, and so on. Objects tend towards the compact, but never reach it, because doing so would result in annihilation.

Readers of Book II will find out just how much of the human condition rests on this impossibility. Indeed, it is so central that Garcia uses the concept to articulate his anti-reductionism.

> Reductionism consists in refusing to consider the irreducibility of that which is a thing to that which it is.
> The cost of reductionism is the conception of a compact point. (i.iii. ii §11)

Reductionism effaces the difference between that which is comprehended and that which is comprehending, rendering the object itself, which is this difference, nothing.

After articulating the negative grounds for rejecting reductionism, Garcia still must construct a positive metaphysics that explains how objects resist their own annihilation. At the very outset of this task he must confront two more categories at opposite ends of being: no-matter-what and something-other-than-a-thing. These are the most technically demanding concepts in the book.

Translation is difficult here because (just as Heidegger did with '*Nichts*') Garcia uses the French phrase '*n'importe quoi*' in both a quantificational ('for any x') sense and in a more name-like sense (analogously to Heidegger's 'the anything'). Failure to attend to the way this is licensed by his ontology will lead the English reader to see inconsistencies in the text that are not there and also miss the philosophical depth of Garcia's discussion.

The English language reader will be prone to think there is a contradiction in part because, on the one hand, Garcia claims that something can never be no-matter-what – that nothing can be no-matter-what. For example:

> Something is never no-matter-what. I could not find something in the world which would be no-matter-what. (i.i.i §9)
> That nothing is no-matter-what means that there does not exist any object, event, god, or idea that would be 'no-matter-what'. (i.i.i §10)

But then, on the other hand, no-matter-what can be something:

Nonetheless, no-matter-what is not nothing. On the contrary, no-matter-what – that is to say, 'equally this *or* that *or* any other thing' – is something. (i.i.i §13)

Garcia is saying both that no-matter-what is something and that nothing is no-matter-what. And he continues:

From this we can claim that it is incompatible to be something and to be no-matter-what. Everything which is not no-matter-what is something. (i.i.i §16)

Again, how can one simultaneously maintain (1) that it is incompatible to be something and to be no-matter-what, and (2) that no-matter-what is something?

To answer this question we must go back to Garcia's concept of comprehension. For Garcia, any object that includes another *in any way* can be said to comprehend that other object. Thus:

The first major consequence of interpreting 'being' as the inverse of 'comprehending' derives from the product of an 'antisymmetric' relation. It may seem that being is the sign of a symmetric identity relation: if *a* is *b*, then *b* is *a*. No! Being is antisymmetry par excellence: if *a* is *b*, then *b* cannot be *a*. Being means nothing other than this unidirectionality [*ce sens unique*]. (i.iii, p. 124)

By carefully attending to comprehension's antisymmetry we can show the seemingly contradictory claims to be consistent.

First, consider the claim that nothing is no-matter-what. Here, take 'nothing' in the quantificational sense and no-matter-what as name-like. Thus, all things are such that they do not enter into the no-matter-what – or, equivalently, all things are such that the no-matter-what does not comprehend them.

Given that being is being comprehended, and that this is antisymmetric, if nothing is no-matter-what, then (for Garcia) no-matter-what is not nothing. This means, quantificationally, that no-matter-what is something.

Now let us recover our pre-Carnapian innocence and think of the quantificational phrase 'something' as name-like. To make this as clear as possible, talk of 'the something'. Then to say that no-matter-what is something is to say that no-matter-what enters into the something and that the something comprehends no-matter-what.

So let's consider the claim that no-matter-what is something with 'no-matter-what' understood quantificationally. Then, to say that no-matter-what is something is to say that anything is something, or as he sometimes puts it 'anything can be something'. Like Meinong, or perhaps more so, when Garcia says 'anything' he really means *anything*.[5] For Garcia, any existent or nonexistent, possible or impossible, imaginary or real, consistent or inconsistent thing is a thing.

But why should one accept this aspect of Garcia's ontology? Remember that for Garcia to be is to be determined. From this, everything that he says about the no-matter-what follows logically. All one must do is consider an entity that lacks all determination, and note that lacking all determination is itself a determination. For Garcia, the no-matter-what names precisely this determination of lacking all determination. Consider a representative passage:

> When this clementine is something, it is not that clementine or something else. No-matter-what, we have said, is this *or* that *or* its opposite *or* something else. No-matter-what is something, anything.
>
> A clementine is not this *or* that *or* its opposite *or* anything else. It *matters* that a clementine be something, that is, that it can be this or that, but that it absolutely cannot be this or that or anything else. If a clementine is no-matter-what, then it is not a matter of a clementine. (i.i.iii §7)

For a clementine to be something it must be determined in some way, but no-matter-what's only determination is that it lacks all determination.

In order to articulate what is arguably the most resolutely anti-reductionist metaphysical system in the history of thought, Garcia puts forward the bold Meinongian claim that anything (no-matter-what) is something. While critiquing specific forms of reductionism inconsistent with this claim, he argues that all that is necessary for being something is possessing some determination. But then what about the concept of just being anything? For this concept to be maximally inclusive it must lack any determination whatsoever. But 'lacking any determination whatsoever' is itself a determination. So it would seem to both lack and possess determinations.

One might say that this no-matter-what is itself thus a contradictory entity, but Garcia's model of being provides a way out of the paradox. Consider all of the things that lack all determinations. By describing the collection in this way, we provide a determination, so everything in this 'collection' is both determined and not determined. So, on the assumption that this is a contradiction we should reject, we now know that nothing is in this collection. But now we have a 'thing' such that nothing is (in) this thing! Moreover, this thing is something, as it has a determination, being the collection of all things that have no determination.

Enthusiasts of mathematical set theory will recognise here the sense in which no-matter-what, qua thing, is similar to the empty set. However, the derivation (which one can fully formalise using an unrestricted second-order comprehension axiom)[6] of this object is, as far as we know, entirely original with Garcia.

With all of this on the table, we can see how Garcia's radical anti-reductionism thus rests on two key claims: (1) no-matter-what can be something, and (2) an object is just the difference between that which it comprehends and that which comprehends it. But if this were the end of the story, Garcia's ontology would easily fall prey to the traditional problem faced by relationist metaphysicians such as A. N. Whitehead, Bruno Latour, and the British Hegelians (Bernard Bosanquet, F. H. Bradley, and J. M. E. McTaggart). Simply put, if the identity of an object depends on its relations to other objects, then one or two things typically follow. The first danger, presented as a virtue by Whitehead and Latour,[7] is that the metaphysics is inconsistent with an object being the same object through any kind of change. Consider Garcia's differential model as applied to the translators of this book. When we first entered the swamps of Louisiana, new things comprehended us. But then if we are merely the difference between the objects that compose us and those things that comprehend us, we became new objects the first time we were subject to the stare of a preternaturally still alligator lurking among the bald cypress knobs.

The second danger, presented as a virtue by the British Hegelians,[8] is in tension with the first. If the first danger is that the ontology is committed to too many objects existing (the translators prior to moving to Louisiana and the translators in Louisiana as separate objects), the second is that the ontology is only committed to one object. For, if the identity of every object is determined by its relation to all other objects, whose identity is also determined by their relations to everything else, then the only thing with intrinsic properties is the totality of these relations.

Garcia's claim that each thing is alone in something-other-than-a-thing is his third most important just because its truth, along with his philosophy of time, helps one navigate between the Scylla of Whitehead's actual occasions and the Charybdis of Bradley's absolute. While objects just are differences, for Garcia these very differences are independent things alone in the world.

> To be in the world is to be outside itself in something-other-than-a-thing. Every thing enters, as an object, into a manifold of 'big things' ['*grosses choses*']: relations, domains, definitions, determinations, sets, and so on. Every thing always belongs to these big things with other objects. But insofar as every thing enters into things, it also enters into something-other-than-a-thing – into that which is not a thing, which we shall call the world. The world is not a reality that pre-exists things, of which one could say that the world is this or that. The world is nothing other than what every thing enters into equally. The world is what enters into nothing. (i.i.iii)

We will not try here to assess whether Garcia's gambit is successful.[9] Rather, we just note that its success would represent a fundamental advance in the history of metaphysics, a relational ontology which is both non-holistic and such that objects remain self-identical over time.

Why does Garcia call his world something-other-than-a-thing? As with no-matter-what's similarity to the empty set, we must again consider mathematical set theory. Garcia's world is just like a 'proper class' in some versions of set theory[10] in that while things can be members of it, it cannot be a member of anything. But why is this? Since Garcia explicitly defends inconsistent objects, the normal mathematical reason that the set of all sets leads to contradiction via Russell's Paradox is not enough.[11] No, the real problem is that a set of all sets would be a member of itself (since it is a set that contains *all* sets), and thus be compact. Since an object is just the difference between that which it includes and that which includes it, the set of all sets would actually be nothing.[12]

Book II is largely an extension and application of the ideas of Book I's pure ontology, developing regional ontologies of an astonishing number of discrete kinds of objects. In the context of what we've said here, two things should be noted. First, Garcia's attempt to avoid the Scylla of Whitehead's actual occasions is dependent on the philosophy of time articulated in Book II. Second, the manner in which the differential ontology is embodied in these kinds ends up obliterating the dialectic between Nietzsche and Hegel that philosophers such as Andrew Bowie find to have been reiterated over and over again in contemporary continental philosophy.[13] If Garcia is successful, then we have principled grounds for refusing final Hegelian syntheses without in any way giving in to Nietzsche's anti-metaphysics. One must try to explain a phenomenon such as adolescence from below, following the history of biological explanations. One must also try to capture it from above, with progressive sociological myths involving adolescence and the adolescent. But adolescence itself actively *resists* its own compactness, its own annihilation through reduction, and one cannot understand adolescence itself unless one understands the history of this resistance.

While Garcia must introduce other productive technical concepts (particularly that of intensity) to make sense of the full range of topics discussed in Book II, the resistance predicted by the differential model is a constant. And the contradictions that result between explanations from above and below, and from successive explanations trying to catch up with the object's resistance, are never resolved. *Pace* contemporary Nietzscheanism, this has nothing essential to do with our epistemic or conceptual limitations, real as those may be. That is, objects *really are* such agents of resistance. But as readers of Garcia's Coda will come to realise, it is not clear whether there is any consolation here. There is never a Hegelian synthesis. Nor could there be . . .

Mark Allan Ohm and Jon Cogburn
Baton Rouge, Louisiana
June 2013[14]

With the exception of the notes that follow, all notes are Garcia's own unless otherwise indicated in brackets. Garcia's sources were checked with their English-language originals, or translations when available. Some translations have been modified. All translated citations that did not have English translations at the time of writing are the translators' own. French terms occasionally appear in brackets in the body of the text, and certain terms and phrases were corrected or clarified at Garcia's request. Bilinguals may consult the original for comparison.

Notes

1. We read '(i.iii.i, §14)' as 'Book I, Part III, Chapter I, Section 14'. With one exception, each chapter in Book I begins with numbered sections, followed by one to three sections of commentary. The chapters in Book II do not begin with numbered paragraphs, and are divided into named sections. So '(i.i.iii)' will cite material in the post-numbered commentary in Book I, Part I, Section III, and '(ii.ii.A)' will cite material in Book II, Chapter II, Part A. For material in the Introduction we use '(I.)'.

2. As with the example of a clementine that follows, Garcia makes this point very clearly elsewhere. See Garcia's 'Crossing Ways of Thinking: On Graham Harman's System and My Own'.

3. See especially Harman on over- and undermining in the opening sections of *The Quadruple Object* as well as the discussion of speculative realism and object-oriented philosophy in the translators' own 'Actual Qualities of Imaginative Things: Notes Towards an Object-Oriented Literary Theory'. Garcia explicitly mentions Harman in the Introduction and then discusses his philosophy much more extensively in 'Crossing Ways of Thinking: On Graham Harman's System and My Own'.

4. We would be remiss if we did not note that this is a little too quick. In Chapter XII of Book II, Garcia's account of beauty allows things to be more or less themselves, with the beautiful object being maximally itself.

5. However, it should be noted that Garcia distances himself from Meinong and various neo-Meinongian currents. See Garcia's 'Après Meinong. Une autre théorie de l'objet'.

6. The translators do this rigorously in 'Garcia's Paradox', presented at the 2013 Notre Dame *Translating Realism* conference. Second-order versions of the standard natural deduction introduction and elimination rules are required. For example, the derivation from the fact that an arbitrary object lacks all determinations ($\forall P \neg P(b)$) to the conclusion that it does have a determination $\exists P(P(b))$ is simply an instance of second-order existential introduction.

7. For a rather profound discussion of this point with respect to Latour, see Harman's *Prince of Networks: Bruno Latour and Metaphysics*. In 'Object-Oriented France: The Philosophy of

Tristan Garcia', Harman explicitly raises the worry with respect to Garcia.

8. Bradley's *Appearance and Reality* is perhaps the canonical text arguing in this fashion. Much of what is still called 'deconstruction-ism' in American humanities departments is just Bradley's arguments about the individuation of objects applied to word meanings.

9. Again, we note Harman's worry about whether Garcia is success-ful. The issues are deep, and as we go on to remark above, crucially involve the interplay between Garcia's philosophy of time and the formal model of things alone in the world.

10. NBG (Neumann-Bernays-Gödel) set theory quantifies over proper classes. However, even in the more standard Zermelo-Fränkel set theory, sentences with free variables must be (meta-linguistically) thought to name proper classes. For a withering critique of both forms that has strong overlap with Garcia's defence of true con-tradictions, see Graham Priest's *In Contradiction* and *Beyond the Limits of Thought*.

11. To be clear, Quine's 'New Foundations' has a universal set and is probably consistent. However, if Priest's arguments against the restriction strategies of standard set theory are valid they would also apply against the kind of type-theoretic restrictions in set theories of this type. In this context, one must also consider the tradition of non-well-founded set theory, which avoids Russell's Paradox via restricted comprehension while still allowing sets to be members of themselves.

12. There are real opportunities for the ambitious formal ontologist here. Since Garcian objects are in part determined by the things that comprehend them, a Garcian set theory would be inconsistent with the standard axiom of extensionality (cf. Nicholas Goodman's 'A Genuinely Intensional Set Theory'). In addition, one would need to look at formal accounts of mereology, since on the issue of unit sets not being identical with their members, versus the way mereology treats join, Garcia's comprehension is much more mereological. There are axiomatisations of mereology where the join relation is irreflexive, antisymmetric, and (unlike set-theoretic membership) transitive, exactly as is Garcia's comprehension. A successful for-malisation would capture the important truths of comprehension, and also shed light on the relation between standard set theories and the new intensional mereology. We don't know whether the formalism would need to be dialetheist just because it is possible to be a dialetheist, but (analogous to the manner in which one might

view glut semantics, perhaps via a guerilla reading of Priest's notion of classical recapture) to avoid substructuralism by taking true contradictions to impose pragmatic restraints on the use of consistent formalisms.

13. See Bowie's *Schelling and Modern European Philosophy*. Recent English language philosophy that genuinely enters into Habermasian dialogue with the German Idealists follows Bowie in critiquing recent philosophy as mere recapitulations of Nietzsche's complaints, but *pace* Bowie are not ready to consign metaphysics to the wide Sargasso Sea of positivism and phenomenology. See especially Iain Hamilton Grant's *Philosophies of Nature after Schelling* and the object-oriented Hegel developed by Robert Stern in such works as *Hegel, Kant, and the Structure of the Object* and *Hegelian Metaphysics*.

14. We would like to thank Ridvan Askin, Eric Bjella, Graham Bounds, Levi Bryant, Emily Beck Cogburn, Jenny Daly, Paul John Ennis, Tristan Garcia, Patrick Gamez, Fabio Gironi, Graham Harman, Adrian Johnston, Carol MacDonald, Rebecca Mackenzie, Raphaël Millière, Louis Morelle, Leah Orth, and Dawn Suiter. Orth served as Cogburn's research assistant during the summer of 2012 and helped check the initial translation of the book's Introduction. Beck Cogburn, Garcia, and Harman each read and annotated complete drafts. Daly, MacDonald, Mackenzie, and Harman have been helpful and attentive throughout. Garcia himself has been unfailingly helpful and solicitous. An unexpected source of joy has been just how much philosophy we have personally learned from Harman and Garcia while thinking through their responses to our missives concerning the translation. Our greatest hope is that this is reflected appropriately both here and in what follows.

Series Editor's Preface

Tristan Garcia's *Form and Object* is one of the most promising works of systematic philosophy to emerge from France since the turn of the century. Thanks to the heroic labour of translators Mark Allan Ohm and Jon Cogburn, we are able to publish an English version of this sophisticated book soon after its original appearance in French, late in the autumn of 2011.[1]

A brief biographical introduction will help set the stage for the treatise itself. Garcia was born in Toulouse on 5 April 1981 to academic parents, but spent his formative years in Algeria. His philosophical originality blossomed early in a manner that led him to difficulties in the conservative French academic system; only later did Garcia find a handful of supporters, with Alain Badiou and Quentin Meillassoux most prominent among them. Later, he wrote his doctoral thesis under the formidable Sandra Laugier. Yet Garcia was already prominent as a literary figure before his public breakthrough as a philosopher. His 2008 debut novel *La meilleure part des hommes* won the prestigious Prix de Flore, and was later translated into English as *Hate: A Romance*.[2] Since that celebrated entrance, Garcia's literary career has continued alongside his already prolific philosophical output, which began early with a little-known treatise *L'Image*, which appeared in 2007.[3] In 2011 Garcia published *Nous, animaux et humains*, a surprising work on a surprising topic: Jeremy Bentham. That was followed just months later by *Forme et objet*, an astonishing achievement for a philosopher of just thirty years old.

Form and Object consists of two parts – or 'Books' as Garcia terms them. Book I (entitled 'Formally') might be described as an austere formal ontology of everything that is. The difficult terrain of this first book is made easier by Garcia's lucid, friendly, modest style of prose. He uses the term 'thing' to describe whatever is in some way. While this sort of 'flat ontology' has been familiar since the time of Alexius Meinong (1853–1920), Garcia has argued elsewhere that Meinong's supposed flatness is not flat enough.[4] He has also claimed that my own distinction between real and sensual objects does not do justice to the initial flatness of reality.[5] For Garcia, each thing is equally solitary with respect to that which it is not: namely, the world. But if the thing is whatever exists without respect to anything else, we can also speak of *objects*, or entities insofar as they are composed of other objects and enter into the composition of further objects. This process continues until we reach the universe, which unlike the world is a 'big thing' composed of all the things that are. The object is neither that which is in it, nor that in which it is, but rather the *difference* between these two extremes. Garcia holds that there is no thing-in-itself outside this difference, since this would make the thing 'compact', his central polemical term (which is luckily the same word in English as in French). After a painstaking analysis of such terms as 'thing', object', 'world', 'universe', and 'form', Garcia concludes that such analysis is necessary but ultimately not very rich. For this reason, as if he were purposely reversing the order of Hegel's *Phenomenology of Spirit* and *Science of Logic*, Garcia turns to a reflection on numerous concrete shapes of human and cosmic existence.

In this spirit, Book II (entitled 'Objectively') is a more reader-friendly progression through various specific topics. Here the distinction between the 'formal' (which pertains to thing/world) and the 'universal' (which concerns object/universe) is the engine of Garcia's dialectic, propelling him through sixteen chapters that lead seamlessly from one to the next, discussing such themes as time, life, culture, art, history, gender, and economics.[6] Central to Book II is Garcia's tantalising concept of 'intensity', by virtue of which an object can be more or less intense, meaning more or less *itself*, despite the ostensibly non-judgemental flatness of Garcia's earliest pages.

Though Garcia occasionally speaks of his debt to Speculative Realism, he is considerably younger than the Generation X founding figures of the Speculative Realist current. Indeed, Garcia can be viewed as the first 'Millenial' philosopher in the continental tradition, or even the first 'post-Speculative Realist'. His vast reading and cognitive elegance add up to a book that will be read widely throughout the Anglophone world and might even create a school of its own.

Graham Harman
Ankara
August 2013

Notes

1. Tristan Garcia, *Forme et objet: Un traité des choses* (Paris: Presses universitaires, 2011).
2. Tristan Garcia, *Hate: A Romance* (London: Faber & Faber, 2010).
3. Tristan Garcia, *L'image* (Paris: Atlande, 2007).
4. See Garcia's April 2012 Paris lecture, 'Après Meinong: Une autre théorie de l'objet', available online at <http://www.atmoc.fr/seances/> (last accessed 15 September 2013). Scroll to the bottom of Séance 23 and click 'Texte de l'exposé' for a PDF file.
5. Tristan Garcia, 'Crossing Ways of Thinking: On Graham Harman's System and My Own', *Parrhesia* 16 (2013), pp. 14–25.
6. For a summary of these rich discussions, see Graham Harman, 'Object-Oriented France: The Philosophy of Tristan Garcia', *Continent* 5.1 (2012), pp. 6–21.

Introduction

Our time is perhaps the time of an epidemic of things.

A kind of 'thingly' contamination of the present was brought about through the division of labour, the industrialisation of production, the processing of information, the specialisation of the knowledge of things, and above all the desubstantialisation of these things. In Western philosophical traditions, things were often ordered according to essences, substrata, qualities, predicates, *quidditas* and *quodditas*, being and beings. Precluding anything from being equally 'something', neither more nor less than any other thing, thus becomes a rather delicate task. We live in this world of things, where a cutting of acacia, a gene, a computer-generated image, a transplantable hand, a musical sample, a trademarked name, or a sexual service are comparable things. Some resist, considering themselves, thought, consciousness, sentient beings, personhood, or gods as exceptions to the flat system of interchangeable things. A waste of time and effort. For the more one excludes this or that from the world of things, the more and better one makes something of them, such that things have this terrifying structure: to subtract one of them is to add it in turn to the count.

This work was born from a feeling which it simultaneously attempts to uphold, illustrate, and rationally respond to: there are more and more things. It is increasingly difficult to comprehend them, to be supplementary to them, or to add oneself to oneself at each moment, in each place, amidst people, physical, natural, and artefactual objects, parts of objects, images, qualities, bundles of data, information, words, and ideas – in short, to admit this feeling without suffering from it. The goal of this work is to bring those who do not yet share this feeling to admit it, and to propose to those who already admit it a way of ridding oneself of it. This involves the construction of a new model of the division of things – of things around us, of things in us, and of us among things.

*
*   *

This treatise is for those of us who love things, but who struggle in the face of their accumulation. It aims to put a thought to the test: a thought *about things* rather than a thought *about our thought about things*. Whoever expects philosophy to teach them something about knowledge, consciousness, or individual and collective subjectivity more broadly, must be forewarned: they may be disappointed. Here we will return as little as possible to this way of thinking. However, this doesn't mean that we will abstain from it altogether. By entering into this work, the reader must agree not to immediately ask for its conditions – in other words, by asking: Where does an object come from? By whom and how? By what right, in what culture, and by what cognitive processes? If the model of things described in the following pages is valid, it ought to be retroactively applicable to any subject, consciousness, and condition of thinking, provided one has the patience to judge it at the end and not at the beginning.

Philosophies of intentionality, consciousness, language, and action that try to address our relations to things fail insofar as they begin by establishing a relation aimed at objectivity. The goal of objectivity is soon abandoned and never attained. For whoever believes that thought commences by aiming at the 'things themselves' always ends up eclipsing things, which were the ends, and siding with this movement of thought, knowledge, and action, which were merely the means.

By beginning this way, whoever bets on thinking primarily about our knowledge or consciousness of things produces an object of thought that they identify with a relation. Henceforth, on this view, each thing that will be an object of thought can only be recognised if it resolves itself within the relation. Just as Konrad Lorenz's geese are 'imprinted' – in the early ethological sense of the term – by the first living creature they see as a maternal object, philosophers who begin with human thought are imprinted by this method. What these philosophers primarily assume as an object of thought will forever remain the form of this object. This will be the imprint of what philosophy can and ought, if it is consistent, to accept consequently as being 'something'. It would be absurd to believe that philosophy could make its primary object consciousness as 'consciousness of', and consequently to discover 'things themselves' other than as given by, for, and with the consciousness of these things, henceforth *imprinted* in it.

Therefore, it is in our best interest to initiate a way of thinking that attaches itself to things – rather than to this or that type of relation directed at things – in such a way that desire, will, mind, or subjectivity can be conceived as objects. A thought about things, marked at its birth by the imprint of objectivity, will no longer recognise anything except things. For this way of thinking, a subject is always an object, though that object may be a determined, modified, or intensified object.

The question is therefore: is it better to begin by thinking about our access, which will never have access to things, but only to our conditions of access, or to begin by thinking about things, which, if we do not want to cheat, obtains the thinghood in every possible mode of subjectivity?

The second solution deserves our approval for at least three reasons.

First, we have been incapable of doing otherwise, since we are caught reflecting on things from adolescence. Everything that proves to be a thing appears to us behind the mask of its thinghood. But this reason only holds a posteriori – and only because we have reluctantly entered a certain state of mind. This reason is singular.

Second, our time is plagued by the metaphysics of access. The twentieth century – to which this treatise in some way proposes to bid adieu – was a period of theorising our methodological *access* to things, rather than theorising about *things* as such. For example, our theories of methodological access talked about formal language and ordinary language; the phenomenology of consciousness and the phenomenology of perception; the opening of being; the structure of the unconscious and the structure of myths; normativity and processes of subjectivation; self-reflection and critical consciousness. But the pendulum was bound to swing the other way. This reason is historical. While writing this treatise, such a historical shift was not always acceptable, and will not endure, since we must also think about the conditions of givenness and of the representation of things. This historical reason is only a particular reason.

Third, we must understand that by initially thinking about things we are not prevented from conceiving of our thought, language, and knowledge as things equal to things thought, said, and known. On the other hand, by initially thinking about our relations to things, we systematically fail to accomplish our original goal, the things themselves; this way of thinking loses its objective en route and falls short of its target. Its sole objective is to give a descriptive account of our methods of aiming at things through consciousness, language, representation, or action. But by thinking about things, we make no promises that we cannot keep, whereas a second-order thought about our thought about things, for example, promises an access to things that it ultimately denies the existence of. To the extent that philosophies of access exchange objects for conditions of their enunciation, things become estranged from their own composition as objects. This is a universal reason.

Personal, historical, and other arguments lead some to first consider that which is 'something', rather than the position, production, or formation of this 'something'.

Does this treatise present a defence of 'realism', since it considers things rather than our access to these things? If one thinks that reality consists merely of possible, impossible, imaginary, or virtual kinds of things, then I think we can answer negatively. No preference is given here to any one special kind of thing, since each kind is neither better nor worse than another kind. *Real* things do not matter to us here. Real *things* matter to us – and, for this reason, other kinds of things as well.

*

* *

Our project finds common ground among those who are developing an 'object-oriented metaphysics', abandoning what Graham Harman calls 'philosophies of access',[1] and who are interested in a 'flat ontology' of things.

In Manuel DeLanda's rereading of Gilles Deleuze's philosophy, the idea of a 'flat ontology'[2] was used to describe theories that do not order worldly entities hierarchically – either in accordance with the substantiality of entities, or based on transcendental principles – but that attribute an equal ontological dignity to each individuated thing. Like in some of Éric Chevillard's novels, every difference between things – an atom, a dead person, a tree trunk's roundness, a football team, the laws of gravitation, or a half of the word 'word' – systematically involves intensive differences, subject to variation.

In fact, we begin this treatise with an investigation of a flat ontology, or the possible ontology of a flat world, where things are devoid of any kind of intensity. The world explored in Book I is the world in which any thing, *sensu stricto*, is equivalent to another thing. Relativists will not breathe easy in this world. This book's central claim is that no classical determination – including the property of being non-contradictory, of being individuated, or of having identity or unity[3] – is contained in our concept of the most unrestricted, emptiest thing and in the most formal possibility of a 'thing'. We consider as inessential all that may characterise a thing until we have properly identified what defines it as a thing, and not as a *consistent* thing, *individual* thing, or *one* thing. We thus aim at neither the being of unconditioned things,[4] nor at that of undetermined things, but rather at the being of *de-determined* things.

Our approach goes to extremes to prove that it is possible to describe the non-trivial qualities of a world of things lacking all qualities. Once the possibility of a description of such a flat world of de-determined things is accepted, we must still prove its necessity, or at least its utility.

The goal of this de-determination is to have at one's disposal a cross-sectional plane of every container and every order which maps the topography of the physical, biological, animal, and human universe; artefacts; artworks; economic networks of production, exchange, and consumption; class, gender, and age differences.

This flat world must make use of necessary divisions, of a referential plane in relation to which the concrete relations of everything that has a determined content could be thought, questioned, and judged.

In short, our project attempts to generate a formal world of de-determined things. But it does not in the least aestheticise or consider this formal world as a refuge of ontological solitude independent of the modern and democratic accumulation of objects. We must understand that only the possibility of considering the flatness of things will enable us to locate ourselves among values, intensities, classes, order and chaos, the maelstrom of everything that inter-comprehends itself inside out [*s'entre-comprend sens dessus dessous*] – all that we comprehend and all that comprehends us. The cross-sectional plane of things without qualities is the final life preserver we cling to as we drown in the flood of all that accumulates, submerses us, continually replenishes the horizons of knowledge and action, and moves us away from the world, from the totality of what is, which we dare not and know not how to imagine.

Since we have the impression that there are too many things (to see, know, or take into account), our thought, life, and actions become paralysed by the apprehension of objective complexity. This impression overflows with factors, networks, and relative positions which divide, intersect, overlap, and contradict each other, like so many injunctions that one cannot follow by simply remaining faithful or coherent (to whom? to what? one hardly knows any more).

The formal plane of thought enables us to cut short all epistemic, experiential, or enacted accumulation through simplicity; its impoverished surface makes possible *this* or *that* as 'something', neither more nor less.

Unlike the 'flat ontologies' proposed thus far, we do not restrict ourselves to a plane of individuated and non-hierarchised entities, having recourse to the concepts of 'interaction' or 'emergence' to explain the appearance of totalities and organisational structures. We combine our *formal* ontology of equality with an *objective* ontology of inequality.

If this treatise presents an ontology of a flat world, its sole aim is to then propose an encyclopedia and topography of the universe and objects, of practical problems of division, and of the valuation of cosmological, biological, anthropological, cultural, artistic, social, historical, economic, and political domains. Far from concluding with a description of a formal world where differences between things have been reduced to zero, this book aims to assemble a description of a flat world of things that can match the antagonistic reconstruction – between universalism and relativism – of the magnitudes, values, depths, variations, and interests of present objects, accumulated endlessly, and contested by several methodological approaches.

*
* *

In hindsight, these contemporary theoretical problems first appeared to us chaotically and in isolation: the status of the ultimate components of matter and the ultimate form of the universe; the alternative between presentism and eternalism in ontologies of time; the emergence of life; the conflict between vitalism and biochemical reductionism; evolutionary theory's division of life into species; and the difference between human and other animal species (dissolved by naturalism in the particular and strengthened by humanism in the universal). We can add to these contentious issues – the division of matter, life within matter, animality within life, and humanity within animality – the conflicts concerning the division of humanity's artworks, artefacts, and organisms into intensities, values (beautiful, true, and good), classes (of origin, of ideas, of social interests), genders (masculine and feminine), and ages. How does one divide a persistent thing or something becoming into different objects? How does one refrain from turning these objects into substances, making them compact, as if they existed in themselves? Conversely, how does one not dissolve them into pure eventiality,[5] potentiality, or becoming? Quite simply, how does one retain *things* – neither too closed on themselves, nor too transient?

We understand that the problem is always the same: that we divide cosmological space-time, the evolution of life, humans, and other animals; that we wonder what distinguishes artworks from other objects; that we classify things according to their value, gender,[6] or time. We must determine whether the concept of things is still possible – things which neither solidify into substances nor vanish into pure potentiality.

How should we proceed?

*
* *

The challenge of this book is to be neither determined by a positive content nor structured by an analytic or dialectical method.

The price to pay for this approach is that it may be judged to be naïve, simple, and fallible, built upon no positive knowledge, adhering to neither humanity nor society, neither history nor nature. The argument does not arrange the universe of all things according to an eminent object which would comprehend them all together. Instead, it seeks its own architecture. It does not put forward a satisfactory explanation, a narrative where *everything* organises itself humanly, naturally, socially, historically, and so on. Here, in the last instance, things will never lie in a household altar of this kind – without actually being an entirely vacuous narrative.

Articulated by no logic, admitting neither the law of non-contradiction nor the a priori conditions of rationality, our argument may also risk seeming to an analytic philosopher, unconscious, inconsistent, without infrastructure, or as refusing to admit what is implicitly its own infrastructure.

Lastly, we refuse to dialectically arrange contradictions. For a dialectician, our theory may appear to go nowhere, to sink into relativism, to make everything and anything possible, to prove to be inconsistent and, worst of all, flat, since it does not hierarchise things formally.

In the last analysis, our theoretical compass will be the conviction that *no thing is reducible to nothing*, which resists both analysis and dialectic. Such a proposition means both that no thing can be absolutely reduced to nothingness – because that thing is dead, past, false, imaginary, nonexistent, or contradictory, for example – and that no thing is absolutely reducible to any other thing. Every analytic reduces the possibility of being something to some logical, rational, or pragmatic conditions. Every dialectic reduces the possibility of being something to its mediation by another thing. Instead, we demonstrate our commitment to that solitary something in each thing that can never be reduced to anything else. This irreducibility is the 'chance' of each thing, and the ground for dismissing both analytic and dialectical ways of thinking. We reject ways of thinking that reduce things exclusively to natural, social, or historical things.

We are situated, and hope to situate the reader, in light of this single idea: we must be aware that no thinkable thing can be reduced to nothing, and that thought itself cannot reduce anything to nothing.

This book tries to retain the ontological *chance* of each thing by considering each disposition of things as a direction of the circulation of being, justifiable so long as it is neither impossible nor makes itself impossible.

*

* *

In order to clarify this idea, we represent possible distribution channels of being.

The first model consists in conceiving of being as circulating from things which do not exist by themselves: predicates and accidents. Let us allow the quality of an entity to be represented by an arrow projecting being, which the quality has, onto the being of an entity that the quality describes. If I aim at the being of some redness, the texture of denim, and some cut or pattern in the form of an hourglass, I can imagine three arrows carrying the being of redness, the being of denim, and the being of the form of an hourglass towards a fourth arrow: a dress which is red, denim, and in the form of an hourglass. And yet the dress is not predicated on anything, while the redness, denim, or form of an hourglass are predicated on the dress. The dress directs the circulation of being into itself, into its *self*. At the end of its flight, the arrow of the dress aims at nothing other than itself. In this substantial model of the distribution of being, the being of some secondary entities flows towards the being of primary entities which flows in a closed channel. Being's channel is blocked by the in-itself, which acts as a necessary buffer against its circulation. A thing, in the strict sense, is thus constituted by the distribution channel of a self-sustaining being, and of beings sustained by this primary being. These qualities are like tributaries of a river – substance – flowing towards its own ocean and its own source. In this essentially ancient and classical way of dividing things – from Plato and Aristotle to Kant and Hegel, and implicit in Confucianism and Samkhya – there is clearly a hierarchisation between what is carried towards something other than itself and this other thing which serves as its ontological support, supporting its proper being.

The second model consists not in distributing being substantially, but vectorially. One thus conceives of trajectories of being, identified with events, facts, powers, intensities, or intentionality.

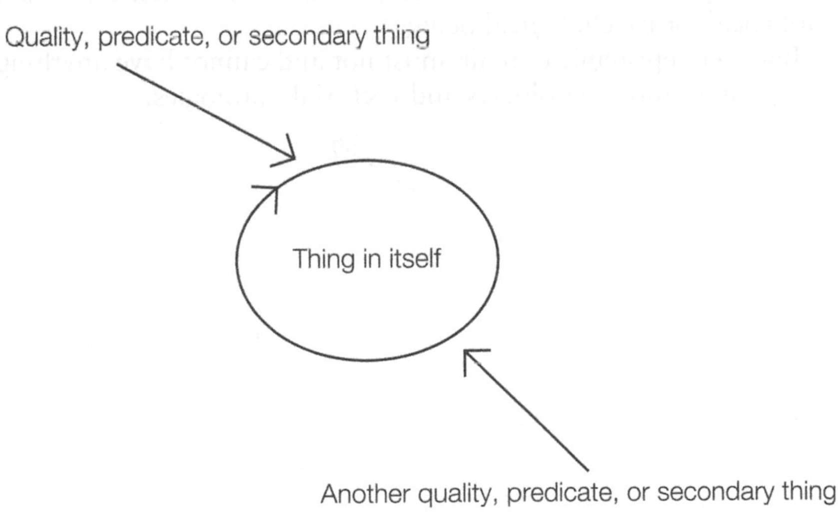

Quality, predicate, or secondary thing

Thing in itself

Another quality, predicate, or secondary thing

Figure 1: The substantial channel of being

These vectors of being are primary. They carry, support, and displace being, but without ever obtaining an end point or objective consistency. In such a representation, what is in the world is not identity but difference, trajectory, becoming, a continuous projection of being which never leads to a compact being, closed upon itself. There is no in-itself. Being is never like the flight of a boomerang. Nothing is self-contained or sealed. The ontological plane is open and extends through flows, forces, and becomings. To account for the apparent existence of things, of identifiable and re-identifiable stable entities, this model views the possibility of determining figures at the intersection of different trajectories. These figures are sealed, like the sides of a triangle made of plumes of transient smoke emitted from three aeroplanes scanning the sky. An observer may have the impression of perceiving a triangle in the sky, a determined figure inscribed in the conjunction of three different events or trajectories. In this essentially contemporary vectorial model (found in certain Nahua philosophies of Mexico, Nietzsche, Bergson, and evolutionary theory), things are considered as secondary effects, constructions, or illusions at the intersection of several events or vectors of being.

Every epistemic domain – from cosmology to sociology (which divide spatio-temporal events or individuals into domains) and from biology to psychology (which define species within evolving processes or subjects among effects, actions, and reactions) – tends to secretly rely on models of the circulation of material, social, biological, or psychological being.

But every epistemic domain must not and cannot have anything *except* substantial ontologies and vectorial ontologies.

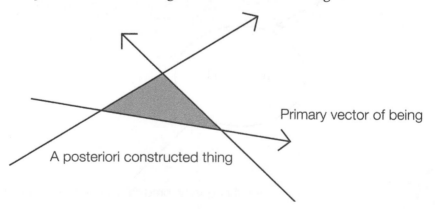

Figure 2: The vectorial channel of being

Each division of things is accompanied by the development of some distribution channel of being. And if we want to divide things in a flat world in order to section off the accumulation of objects (which prevents us from being and from comprehending the world), we must find a non-substantial and non-vectorial way of allowing the being of things to circulate. Substantiality tends to compact being in the final stage of its process, overdetermining self-saturated things or things in themselves. The pure eventiality of the vectors of being tends to dissolve and disseminate being, and transforms things into effects, illusions, or secondary realities. Our concept of a thing fits neither the first nor the second model. The first produces a thing which is too much of a thing, which is 'compact', while the second generates a thing which is not enough of a thing, which is only a construction or ephemeral projection. Our aim is the following: to conceive of a model that is neither too strong nor too weak, and to represent things that are really in the world without being in themselves.

The only solution consists in constructing the following trajectory: being enters into a loop wherein being is not projected in itself, but cast outside itself. In our model, an arrow points inside to a circle – a thing – and then from this circle a second arrow points outside.

Being comes inside a thing and being goes outside it. A thing is nothing other than the *difference* between being-inside [*l'être entré*] and being-outside [*l'être sorti*]. Accordingly, the channel of being is never blocked. Inside a thing, a thing is never itself. A thing is not in itself, but outside itself. Nonetheless, being is not eventially 'pollinated' by vectors, but has an objective end-point. Things correspond to the circle indicating the gap, difference, and inadequacy between the entering arrow and the exiting arrow, and are inscribed or *imprinted* in the world.

To reinscribe things in the world is to situate them outside themselves (as substances) and outside us (as subjects). It is to arrange them outside themselves (their self and ourselves) in the world. The price to pay for this arrangement is a circulation of being that systematically distinguishes two senses [*sens*] of things: *that which is in a thing* and *that in which a thing is*, or that which it comprehends and that which comprehends it.[7]

Take, for example, a block of black slate, a random rectangular sample taken from a site of continental collision. Few people will deny that this block is a thing. One can of course point out that it

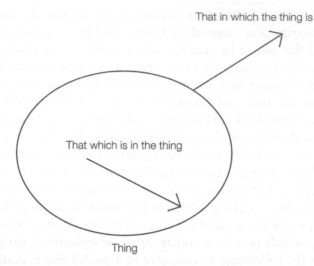

Figure 3: The thingly channel of being

is necessary to have an active subjectivity to divide or distinguish this block of matter lying on the ground of dusty soil, in order to perceive it as such. But this slice of black slate possesses certain qualities of cohesion and of solidity that allow one to dissociate it from its environment, handle it, transport it, and consider it quite simply as 'something'. What is it composed of? It contains quartz, clay-like minerals, mica, some traces of feldspar. And all these components themselves have a certain atomic structure. But in a wider sense, they also enter into the constitution of the rock as 'thing': its rectangular form, the irregularities of its surface, the porphyroblasts coated with pyrite, its sombre color, its delicate texture, its weight, its fragility, and all the primary or secondary qualities by which we can recognise the black slate.

We say that this is *all that is in this thing*, all paths of being that lead to the constitution of this black slate in my hand.

Yet, *that in which this slate is* can never be inferred from *everything that is in this slate*. From everything which composes it, I will not obtain the slate's location in the world, the relations in which it inscribes itself, the fact that it is now in my hand, the function of a weapon that it can exercise if someone attacks me, its place in the landscape or in the series of slate pieces scattered alongside this valley. That which it is, this unique thing which exists in the world, and I hold in my hand, is outside itself. The slate can in fact enter into the composition of the side of a mountain, a roof, or a collection of rocks. As a whole, it then becomes a part of another thing, and it is no longer a question of *that which is in the slate*, but of *that in which this slate is*.

A number of things are in this black slate. The black slate on its own can enter into the composition of a number of other things. Therefore, the black slate is not in itself. It is not a substance on which various qualities are predicated – for example, its weight or its colour. No more is it an ephemeral entity, not existing in itself, constructed by my thought, senses, or action, from events or becomings (some variation in the matter's density, some effects of geological transformation, a trajectory of luminous rays). No, the black slate is a relation, inscribed in the world, between the being that enters the world and the being that goes outside it, and that enters in turn into another thing (into the soil, landscape, classes of other objects, my perception, or the world in general).

A thing is nothing other than the difference between *that which is in this thing* and *that in which this thing is*. Unless one guarantees this double sense, there are no thinkable things. Every reductionist who claims to deduce that which this or that thing is from that which composes this or that thing only succeeds in dissolving the very thing that they claim to account for. We attempt to accomplish the exact opposite of this: to guarantee things as invaluable differences embedded in the distribution channels of being of the world. To complete our task, we set out to discover the meaning which circulates among things, between that which composes them and that which they compose, inside or outside us, with or without us.

* *
*

This meaning that we call for, and that thought seeks, is not salvation. It is not the possibility of holding onto the essential, necessary, or genuine self after the end of life, or in our damaged social existence.

Some ways of thinking seek salvation. Here we seek to redeem nothing: not the soul, not personhood, not the body, not thought, not a community, not the proletariat. A thing among things, this treatise attempts to save neither me nor you; between things there is no salvation whatsoever.

The meaning we seek is not reducible to a mere signification, a language game, a body of practices, or a normative system. Whoever calls for a semiotic meaning of things or a return to the *description* of their signification, to the ways in which we name or make use of things, or to our linguistic, social, or cultural practices will be disappointed. The promise of thought is not kept. I seek a meaning of things outside us, and I have returned to what takes place between us.

Salvation is the hope of situating oneself outside things (escaping annihilation, death, oblivion, inauthenticity, alienation, reification). Signification is the disappointment of never managing to abstract things from the relations that we maintain with them. Salvation situates us outside of things, while signification precludes things from being situated outside of us.

I do not wish for the salvation of my soul, my body, human beings, my ideas, or my individuality. I do not ask for the (linguistic, cultural, historic) signification of things – our way of referring ourselves to them, of constructing their significance, of using them, of exchanging them, of making them significant among us, for us, and by us. No, I simply search for a meaning of things, whether this is the meaning of me, of you, or of a piece of black slate.

In truth, this meaning – neither completely existential nor completely semiotic – is simply the possibility of passing from one thing to the other. It is the possibility and necessity of never being reduced to a thing that would be nothing else, that would be in nothing else, and that would not exist in and by itself – whether one calls that matter, nature, history, society, God, or an individual. As if one could reduce the black slate to being nothing but a material thing or a natural thing or a social thing. As if one could then consider matter, nature, or society as things outside appearances, absolute, remaining in themselves. This ghost of 'compactness', which will be the adversary of our whole adventure of thought, will only disappear on one condition: for each thing to make sense, it must have *two* senses. Nature or history as things contain many things (first sense), but they are contained by things other than themselves (second sense).

*
* *

If one wants to formulate this undertaking in a single equation, it would be this: how do we obtain universality and maintain the sense of relativity at the same time? The price of this twofold commitment both to universalism and to the sense of relativity will be the abandonment of ecstatic becoming and of self-saturated things. In Book I, we must conceive of things emptied of themselves, without identity and de-determined. In Book II, we must conceive of things replenishing each other and ordered encyclopedically. Therefore we must learn to see double, formally and objectively, so that thought advances through a formal step and an objective step.

The structure of the treatise shows us how we can consider these two steps. Setting aside the Coda, which marks the collapse of the whole, the entire treatise is carried out in two books, which complement and respond to each other in sixteen chapters. The first book's formal system demands some confidence from the reader, for it is deliberately devoid of references or citations from the history of philosophy, although it tackles classical questions (for example, the One, the Whole, Being). This book combines affirmative and numbered propositions and full-page argumentation alongside descriptions of the flat world. The second book's objective system is based on first book's forms, but it puts them to the test in connection with various determined and ordered objects – structures of the universe, an individual's death, definitions of life, animality, art, and the economy – by adopting a more discursive style, strengthened by explicit and much more common references.

Whether your way of spontaneously relating to things is *formal* or *objective*, you are free to read this treatise in one way or the other to give meaning to the progress of philosophy.

Notes

1. In other words, ways of thinking that recognise 'that philosophy can be concerned only with our access to things' (Graham Harman, *Tool-Being: Heidegger and the Metaphysics of Objects*, p. 123). Quentin Meillassoux prefers to speak of 'correlationism' to describe the theoretical primacy accorded to the *relation* between thought (or any other directed position: consciousness, perception, intuition, Merleau-Pontian 'flesh') and its correlate, to the detriment of each side of the terms in relation. See Quentin Meillassoux, *After Finitude*.
2. Manuel DeLanda, *Intensive Science and Virtual Philosophy*, p. 47.
3. The entire treatise strives to refute W. V. O. Quine's famous slogan, 'no entity without identity' (W. V. O. Quine, *Ontological Relativity and Other Essays*, p. 23). It also seeks to refute Leibniz's claim in his letter to Arnauld that 'what is not truly *one* being is not truly one *being* either' (G. W. Leibniz, *Philosophical Essays*, p. 86). The aim

of this book is to actively demonstrate, through the construction of a coherent model, that there can and must be something less determined than such an *identifiable* entity or than being *one*: each 'thing' as it is 'alone in the world', and not comparable or compared with other things. Therefore, we maintain that solitude is less than unity and identity, and that it does not imply acceptance (any more than refusal) of the law of non-contradiction.

4. In the German idealist tradition – for example, early Schelling – to be unconditioned is to be what cannot be transformed into a thing. The thing (*das Ding*) is conditioned (*be-dingt*) by something other than itself.

5. [Translators' note: We translate the French neologisms '*événementialité*' and '*événemential*' as 'eventiality' and 'evential' (comparable to 'substantiality' and 'substantial'), to be distinguished from 'eventuality' and 'eventual'. They should be understood in the sense of 'pertaining to events' rather than in the sense of contingent, possible, or probable future events or outcomes.]

6. [Translators' note: The French '*genre*' may be translated in a variety of ways, depending on the context: (1) as 'genus', often in mathematical, scientific, or philosophical contexts; (2) as 'gender', in both the grammatical sense and in the sense of the relations between the masculinity and femininity of persons; (3) or as 'genre', in aesthetics, arts, and letters. The occurrences of '*générique*' are translated most often as 'gendered', though occasionally as 'generic'.]

7. [Translators' note: We have rendered the French '*sens*' most often as 'sense', but also in some cases as 'meaning', and rarely as 'direction'. Readers should also note that Garcia distinguishes '*sens*' from '*signification*'. Garcia's correspondence with us has undoubtedly helped to clarify these matters, and we have tried to maintain consistency as much as possible at Garcia's request.]

Book I

Formally

Part I

Thing

I. No-Matter-What

1. Two questions define the limits of our reflection. First, what is everything composed of? Second, what do all things compose?

The first question concerns the nature, identity, or mere definition of what concerns principles, what is primary, primitive, or elementary, or the irreducible component of everything that is. If a wall is made of bricks, an organism of cells, a sentence of words, a word of letters, an atom's nucleus of particles bound by forces, then what *whole* are they made of? Of matter, substances, heterogeneous multiplicities, the structures of our understanding, our cognition, our language, a god's will, mind, or appearances without reality?

2. The second question aims not to identify the ingredient or fundamental ingredients of the world, but rather to understand the state of the composite of everything that may always act as a component. If one drafts a list of all existent, possible, imaginable, conceivable, apparent, past, present, concrete, and abstract things, what form can account for the totality of everything that is? Is it a physical universe, a space-time continuum, multiple dimensions, multiverses, possible worlds, the course of history, the course of evolution, the limits of my culture, my social perspective, the inherited structures of my capacities for reasoning, an infinity, a Klein bottle, a transcendent, unthinkable, inexpressible form that is inaccessible to representation, the name of God, the

twists and turns of my brain, ecstasy, or a poor pile of very small things?

3. Not only does the first question refer to the second, and vice versa, but each question proves to be both the condition and the reverse of the other. From the idea of a whole or world, one can only wonder what composes this whole or world. From the idea of things, of this or that, of a plurality of objects, entities, or events, one can only wonder what they ultimately compose, the form and contour of their sum. Each of the two questions presupposes the existence of concepts – either the concept of 'whole', or the concepts of 'thing', 'element', or 'unity' – that the other question renders uncertain, or at least transforms into a problem, by establishing as certain what the first question holds up as a problem to solve. The characteristic feature of these two initial questions – 'what is everything composed of?' and 'what do things compose?' – is to present the *explanans* of the first problem as *explanandum* of the second, and vice versa.

4. Between these two questions an infinite series of intermediary questions is assembled regarding the membership of *this* or *that* in such and such body, idea, value, culture, society, history, and so on. If it is a question of knowing if such a thing *is* this way or not, if it *can* be, *must* be, or ought to *act* this way or not, then every possible question – the who, what, where, when, why, and how – consists in determining one (or more) 'something(s)' within a world, totality, horizon, or universe of reference. These questions and the responses they demand arise from a determination of things that *matter* to us; thus, what things matter to us. Most of our life consists not in saying, doing, seeing, or understanding no-matter-what, but rather in establishing differences of importance. In this way, we limit every thing to a sphere of belonging: our interest in intimacy, familial life, our country, social class, culture, artworks, beauty, love, sexuality, sports, knowledge, practical experience, nature, animals, ideas, and so on. Within each of these possible spheres of interest, some things always *matter* more than others. Some things belong to this domain, group, or 'microcosm' in an eminent or exceptional manner.

5. Most of existence consists in defining, paying attention to, and defending what matters.

6. The most important questions in existence are nevertheless framed by two seemingly uninteresting questions: 'what is everything composed of?' and 'what do things compose?'. These two problems admit a response if and only if one considers not merely what matters, but *no-matter-what*.

7. In order to respond to the first question – 'what is it that composes everything?' – it is necessary to not only take into consideration what composes the physical, natural, social, or psychological world, but *every* world. In other words, it is necessary to pay *equal* attention to everything that is something, whatever it is. Social entities compose the social world, living entities compose the living world, physical entities compose the physical world, but what could be the component of the world *tout court*, namely, of everything that is, without any determination or particularity?

8. Take – or do not take – no-matter-what. We understand by 'no-matter-what' this *as well as* that, so that nothing is a priori excluded from it.

To have access to the idea of 'no-matter-what', it is absolutely necessary to not only consider every material object, but to take into account *equally* each object and each of its parts, each word, each idea, each event, and each quality in the same way as the physical substrates to which this quality can be attributed, each moment, each possibility as well each reality, each good, each evil, each truth, or each false proposition, the totality of things, and likewise a contradiction, an impossibility – it doesn't matter. By considering as absolutely insignificant that which things can be, that which can be something appears to us: *no-matter-what*.

'No-matter-what' is neither an entity nor the repository of some quality, determination, or particularity that would be established by way of a principle. 'No-matter-what' is nothing other than the expression of the refusal to attribute some importance, whether to what this is, or to what that is, or to what everything perhaps can be. 'No-matter-what' is not this *more* than that, and it is not this *less* than that.

'No-matter-what' is uninteresting; it is, in the end, only the possibility of not attributing importance to the 'what'.

9. Something is never no-matter-what. I could not find something in the world which would be no-matter-what.

10. That nothing is no-matter-what means that there does not exist any object, event, god, or idea that would be 'no-matter-what'. The characteristic property of something is precisely to never be no-matter-what, but to be *some* what. Something is *in this way*, something is systematically *this*, because this is not *that*. The characteristic property of something is to be incapable of being *equally* all that is.

Let us imagine something which could be all that is, which could be red *and* blue *and* of all colours *and* of all moments *and* of all places, which could be contradictory, omnipresent, omniscient, and omnipotent. This something would certainly not be no-matter-what, because then it would be this *and* that *and* all things ad infinitum, whereas the characteristic property of no-matter-what is to be this *or even* that *or even* another thing *or even* yet another thing, without one knowing what it is, and without this determination mattering in any way. A thing which could be all things and which could have all qualities – a contradictory thing which could be this *and* the opposite of this – would fail to be no-matter-what. No-matter-what is not the totality of all things, but rather no-matter-what thing, anything.

11. To have access to no-matter-what, I can only think at the same time, or rather on the same plane, in the same relation, of all that is differentiated. This is because nothing is no-matter-what – that is, not equally this *and* its opposite, but equally this *or* its opposite *or* yet another thing. No-matter-what does not depend on the conjunction of something and its opposite, but rather on the possibility of being indifferently this or its opposite, or yet *any other thing* than this or its opposite. No-matter-what is what can be indifferently this or something which is not this, or even this *and* something which is not this – nothing prevents no-matter-what from being a contradiction, but nothing forces it to be contradictory either; it doesn't matter.

12. Nothing precedes no-matter-what that would embody this role or don this mask. There is neither a reality nor a possibility that one could call 'no-matter-what', which would express this quality, which would act as a potential support for this identity.

13. Nonetheless, no-matter-what is not nothing. On the contrary, no-matter-what – that is to say, 'equally this *or* that *or* any other thing' – is something.

It is necessary to understand this sentence in at least two ways.

In the first sense, no-matter-what – the possibility of being equally this *or* that *or* its opposite without *this* or *that* mattering; the radical unimportance of 'that which it is' – is not nothing. It is something, which means quite simply that it is. One can know it, evoke it, talk of it, discuss it, argue about it (which we are preparing to do). It is neither a *flatus voci* nor a vacuous concept. Moreover, it is the very proof that nothing is absolutely nothing, that nothing is never a non-being which could take on the deceptive appearance of a being, that nothing is never a groundless idea. Everything that is – even if it is vacuous, false, nothing, or groundless – is *something*. The problem is understanding *in what sense* it is something. To think of an object as complex and elusive is precisely to discover how to grasp it.

In the second sense, the assertion that 'no-matter-what is something' marks the permeability of all the barriers by which one can claim to protect and limit the import of *that which is something*. In fact, one cannot prevent anything from being quite simply 'something', even if it is something illusory, a chimera of the human mind, or a mirage.

14. Give me something, and this will never be no-matter-what. However, you can give me no-matter-what thing. Nothing that you give me can avoid being something.

15. Several anthropocentric strategies deny the possibility that no-matter-what can be something.

We can discern at least six clear strategies that reduce the extension of possible things, though other strategies certainly exist.

The first strategy is *logical*. It consists in the assumption that contradiction is impossible. Consequently, a contradictory proposition can never have unity and be 'something'. This strategy is of Aristotelian origin, but takes on various guises in the history of classical metaphysics, especially in Cartesian metaphysics.

The second strategy concerns *language* and reflection on language. By claiming that some things are functionally or structurally inexpressible, one implies that to be capable of saying things, it is necessary that the conditions of expressibility of these things cannot themselves be said. In the twentieth century, the early Wittgenstein and the logical positivists exploited this strategy specifically. But it is also a long-standing poetic strategy; the means by which I say things (language, speech, meaning) are not themselves expressible by way of things said.

The third strategy is *epistemological*. It unfolds via the transcendental concept. The transcendental concept is the condition of possibility of the knowledge of things, but which cannot itself be an object of knowledge of the same order, the knowledge of things. Kant and Kantianism embody this strategy most successfully. Most epistemologies employ this strategy in some manner.

The fourth strategy is *cultural*. It consists in making taboos function. Taboos are relations to entities that cannot be named, that cannot be made to appear as something, and that can only be defined negatively as what is impermissible. Émile Durkheim defines taboos as 'the institution in virtue of which certain things are withdrawn from common use'.[1] Western ethnography, ethnology, and anthropology paradoxically contributed to this strategy's relativism by making it universal in its form and by giving access to a cultural diversity of ways of being and ways of prohibiting reification. Taboos are, in this way, absolutely variable from one human group to another.

The fifth strategy is *religious*. The idea of sanctity corresponds to the conception of entities that are more than something, or that cannot be grasped or aimed at by the heart or mind as things. These 'more-than-things' demand our care and respect.

The sixth strategy is *moral and political*. It consists in establishing insurmountable natural differences between things and certain goods, sentient subjects, human persons, values, works, or ideas, which must not be reified or lowered to the level of things, like other things, without risking the irreversible collapse of all values and dignity. Marxism, in a critical fashion (of alienation, of reification), has illustrated this just as well as classical liberalism (in a contractual fashion, and by differentiating various types of justice, various relational possibilities to goods and persons). Today, universal humanism and animal ethics clearly embody this spirit by distinguishing human beings, or the set of sentient, suffering beings, from other things.

16. Let us take an example borrowed from the logical strategy: the squared circle. This contradiction in terms, which cannot be an

object of intuition or of knowledge, is not really a thing. How can one successfully combine two contradictory things, a circle and square, into one something? I can imagine quickly hopping from circle to square and from square to circle, rounding the square's angles and squaring the circle's perimeter, but, apparently, I will never obtain an object which could be *both* circle *and* square, together, 'at the same time [and] in the same respect'.[2]

Nonetheless, one might claim that a squared circle is *no-matter-what*. But this is not the case, for the squared circle really, negatively, has properties by default. I can at least claim that the squared circle is not triangular. I can affirm that it is not three-dimensional. I can easily think that it is not pentagonal. In other words, even if I will never successfully unify the concept of the squared circle – which is not an idea, but the contradictory intersection of two ideas – I can determine what this intersection is not. I can always distinguish it from other things and not confuse it with other distinct contradictory ideas. One contradiction is always different from another contradiction; that is, it is not the case that every contradiction is *the same* contradiction. Although their inferences may be identical (since *ex falso quodlibet* – from a false proposition, anything follows), all contradictions must remain themselves individuated, otherwise one would necessarily confound not merely the propositions that one can draw from a squared circle and from a circle without circumference, but also the squared circle and the circle without circumference themselves. Now, the former and the latter do not contradict the possibility of the circle *in the same way*. How is it possible to think that completely identical things do not refer to an identical possibility in the same way – specifically, by preventing it? A minimal difference remains between the squared circle and the circle without circumference.

Is this the same for a contradiction such as a white that one could claim to be both black and 'non-white'? Is the white which is not white and 'non-white' also distinct from the city which is not a city and 'non-city'?

It seems that a minimal quality distinguishes a non-white white from a non-city city. I know at least that the city which is not a city is both a city *and* not a city – that is, it must simultaneously have these two qualities in order to remain the contradictory idea that it is. Whereas I do not know whether the first white in the white which is not white is a city or not a city. The non-white white can equally be a city *or* not be a city. Conversely, a city which is not a city can be white *or* not be white, but I cannot claim that it is both white *and* non-white.

This does not invalidate the logical 'principle of explosion'. If it is true that this is white, and if it is true that this is not white, I can infer that this is a city as well as that this is not a city, and *ex contradictione sequitur quodlibet* – from a contradiction, anything follows. But it is precisely this *quodlibet*, this anything, this *no-matter-what*, that interests us here. For *no-matter-what* has a predetermined power of indetermination that makes it the foundation of every thing, and not the spectre of the end of every distinction between things – which is the reason why most logics have so far either dismissed it or exploited it as a straw-man or foil of rationality.

Now, if no-matter-what can follow from a contradiction, a contradiction is nonetheless neither no-matter-what nor no-matter-what contradiction. How could a contradiction remain contradictory if it was not determined, even in a minimal way? If a contradiction was itself any thing, then it would also be something non-contradictory, and therefore cease being contradictory. A contradiction must have a determination *a minima* in order to remain the contradiction that it is. If what is white and non-white could be absolutely no-matter-what, it could be exclusively white, and therefore not be contradictory and not be no-matter-what. What is white and not white *must* be white and not white, and *can* be a city, *can* be a non-city, *can* be a city and a non-city. What is a city and not a city *must* be a city and not a city, but *can* be white, or not, or be white and not be white – it doesn't matter. Whoever identifies a contradiction with 'no-matter-what' fails to understand what makes this contradiction *one* contradiction, *this* contradiction, and not all contradictions, or even all things at once.

In other words, a difference between two absolute contradictions exists. What is essential to one contradiction – what makes it the contradiction that it is – may be had *or* not had by another contradiction, though the latter would not be affected by it. What makes one contradiction the contradiction that it is, is not exactly the same as what makes another contradiction the contradiction that it is.

If a contradiction is an entryway to the no-matter-what, it is never itself *no-matter-what*, but a *minimum-of-whatness* [*minimum de quoi*]. All that matters to us here is this: a contradiction cannot be identified with 'no-matter-what', and therefore any thing.

It is not because the squared circle is not a concept that it is not *some* thing. If the squared circle or a white and non-white thing are not quite no-matter-what, they are clearly something. Perhaps they are something contradictory, impossible, or with no form of unity. They are no less *some* thing (poor and uninteresting, no doubt).

From this we can claim that it is incompatible to be something and to be no-matter-what. Everything which is not no-matter-what is something.

17. Let us take another example, this time borrowed from the cultural strategy which restricts what can appear as 'something' for a human group. A taboo corresponds to what I cannot think, say, or express in any way. But other taboos always exist. Every taboo is therefore different from others in such a way that a taboo is never *no-matter-what* taboo, but, rather, a very particular taboo. The prohibition, while preventing what is prohibited from being a thing, a practical, discursive, or thinkable object, distinguishes what is prohibited and makes it particularly important as a thing. Taboos exist in order to some day be lifted, for by prohibiting this or that from being objects, we in fact make them objects. The more they are prohibited, the better they are defined, delimited, and determined.

Nothing forms an object better than a long-standing cultural status of concealment and prohibition.

18. The case of sanctity is fundamentally different. There can very well exist something sacred that does not conceal something predetermined, but invents or embodies a new object of thought, of faith, of worship, constituted as sacred. What is sacred does not always precede sanctity: it is possible to begin by considering that 'there is' something sacred, namely, a system that is exceptional to the rule of things, until sanctity has itself become an object (of reflection, of meditation, of hope).

Sanctity is clearly not no-matter-what, since it appears as 'what matters more than any other thing'. However, not being no-matter-what, it must *also* be something. Sanctity is nothing other than the creation of an exception to the system of all that is something. It is constantly in the position of being included in the

system that by its very nature it must go outside of, in a contradictory way that is the very condition of a believer's inner life. If
sanctity is not something, nonetheless it is not any thing, since it
is necessarily something (which must avoid this status to remain
what it is).

19. The theory that it is the structure of language and the inex-
pressibility of non-things that makes possible the expressibility of
things is the same in poetics as in formal, logical languages. Either
an inexpressible is something that cannot be said (for some reason,
in which case other inexpressibles exist for other reasons), or an
inexpressible is what cannot be said (and nothing else). In the first
case, an inexpressible is not any inexpressible. It is a *certain* inexpressible among other inexpressibles. In the second case, an inexpressible is a non-expressible in general. Therefore, it is neither an
expressible nor no-matter-what, nor any thing (since it is *neither*
an expressible *nor* expressible things). It is therefore something.

What cannot be said can at least be shown, sung, drawn, imagined, glimpsed, and so on. The limits of a language are only ever
the limits of things *said*.

20. As for the limits of my knowledge, or its conditions, it
always seems that to know the limits of what I do know comes
back to knowing the limits of what I do not know. Now, to know
the limits of something is to know its unity, contour, and determination. Not only can I make something of what escapes my
knowledge, but I cannot even avoid making something of it *on the
outside*.

If I walk alongside a property that I am not allowed to go into,
drawing up a blueprint of its walls, I certainly don't have access
to whatever is in this mysterious place, but I can still map the
perimeter of the estate. I can visualise the form of what escapes
me, the outline of its inclusion in the world. I know therefore *that
which* this property *is*, its form, without knowing *that which is*
this property, namely, what is inside the residence.

In other words, although I can never enter the mansion, I know
at least that the mansion is *something* in the world, whatever it
encloses. Although I cannot know or claim to know what comes
inside and goes outside [*l'aller-retour*], or what is between that
in which this thing is and that which is in this thing (between the
property's location on the outside and its exploration on the inside

once its doors are open), I must know that it is something, in the absence of knowing *what* is this something.

The surrounding walls of knowledge do not give me access to the castle of transcendence. But they do not prevent me from identifying and locating what I do not know. 'What I do not know' is clearly something, neither all nor nothing nor any thing.

21. There is a strong belief that human persons, sentient creatures with values, works, and ideas, must not be considered as things. But how do I respect, protect, or control that which is *not* something for me? What is this respect, this consideration for what is priceless, this appeal to dignity that one hopes to gain by making an exception of an object – a person, human being, animal, or artwork – from the world of objects? One must understand a human person as a thing like other things in order to be capable of respecting a human person. A human person is no more and no better something than a duck, a pebble, a dust particle, a chair, a word, or the sky. One must know how no-matter-what is something in order to perceive and defend objective differences between things. Reification – the reduction of our world to a world of things – is not an evil, the dehumanisation, desensitisation, or disenchantment of the world, but the precondition of a human understanding of the differences between things. A system of exceptions in the world of things is never an 'ethical' or 'just' system, but rather a metaphysical system of the determination of inequalities between things, of 'more-than-things', which cannot be elements of this system.

To establish what distinguishes some things from other things and our possible actions towards them, we must still conduct the test and consider them all equally as things.

Every moral system of distinction between things and what cannot be something is doubly condemned: first, by distinguishing what must not be something and by reifying it (the 'human person'); second, by denying the possibility of placing all things on an equal footing, which is the very condition of their comparison and of their relative importance.

To know why I do not pay equal attention to another human being, a mosquito, a piece of gravel, a word, and a quarter of a leaf is not a matter of principle. It is, in the strict sense, a matter of interests. What is interesting and what is not interesting? It is the question of knowing what matters to us, what matters to life, and to *human* life, because from the formal point of view of no-matter-what everything is equal.

22. No-matter-what is that which is something. We cannot prevent anything from being something. If one finds, conceives of, or imagines that which can be something (whether this is contradictory, impossible, sacred, prohibited, bad, false, past, to come, nonexistent, perverse, out of reach, useless, and so on), then one will have access to no-matter-what.

And it is this no-matter-what which interests us here.

23. One will ask if this 'no-matter-what' is real, a mental construction, a mere extrapolation of the possible from what actually is, or some misleading linguistic effect. No-matter-what is neither real nor abstract, nor both of these at once. No-matter-what is quite simply the plane of *equality* of what is real, possible, nonexistent, past, impossible, true, false, or bad. It doesn't matter. It concerns the possibility of being *either* real *or* possible, *or* real and possible, *or* neither real nor possible, *either* constructed *or* given, *either* natural *or* artificial, *or* natural and artificial, *either* true *or* illusory, of not being all of these at once, but of equally being able to come under (or not) one of these determinations, any determination.

24. That no-matter-what is something indicates nothing other than the possibility of a flatness: that by which everything is *equally*.

25. Every logic, knowledge, and human action has opposed a certain depth to this flatness: the most and the least important of things, for and through life.

To Matter

A thing that matters is a thing to which some *value* is attributed. Values include beauty, ugliness, truth, falsehood, goodness, evil, practicality, impracticality, or any of the chromatic shades that we systematically dye these values: pretty, pleasant, disgusting, cynical, dangerous, and so forth.

Now a value, any value, positive or negative, always appears as a means of forcing a thing to be what it is more than another thing.

To value a thing is to transform the strictly *extensive* character of every thing into an *intensity*. In this way, a beautiful thing – more beautiful than another thing – is a bit more of a thing than an ugly thing; a true relation between two things is a bit more of a relation than a false relation. A value is what affects the being of a thing by fundamentally making it intensive: beauty affects the thing, truth the relation between things, good the relation of a thing to the world. The importance of a thing is always accentuated or attenuated by its own value; what is beautiful is *more* something. There is *more* between two things which maintain a true relation than between two things whose relation is false. What is good augments the world *more* than what is bad.

To matter, for a thing, is therefore to have either more or less value. In the world of importance, every thing is comparable to itself and to other things: it is more this and it is less that. Things, insofar as they matter, a little or a lot, are continuities from the less to the more, from the more to the less; they expand and contract – they are elastic and comparable with each other – through the relations that objects maintain between each other. The true relation between two things extends, and thus exceeds, the false relation because it is truer.

In fact, we act with things, appreciate them, perceive them, and think about them insofar as they matter to us and they matter to something other than us (to our environment, to the future, to other species, to our ideas, to a god, and so on). But the world of important things lacks the flat world in which each thing is neither more nor less than a thing. This world is not the 'foundation' of things insofar as they matter to us, but, as it were, their 'gauge' or datum line in relation to which it must be possible that some things matter and that they matter to us more than others. In order for some things to matter more than others, whether they are more beautiful (for us or in relation to some idea that we have of them) or more ugly, more true or more false, better or worse, it is necessary that a plane exists on which no thing is either more or less a thing than another. This plane is situated neither beyond nor below our values, which we could disregard, ought to attack with a hammer, or completely deconstruct. This plane is nothing other than the plane of reference of what matters to us.

The flat world, where no thing is more important than another, supposes neither an abstraction nor a reduction, neither asceticism nor critique, neither genealogy nor deconstruction, but a simple *levelling.* The flat world is neither more nor less real than the planes on which what matters to us plays out, where things are exchanged, where we give them or receive them, where there are so many variable intensities.

This is the flat world of the *no-matter-what.*

That No-Matter-What Became Something

If the twentieth century passed on to us one lesson, it is that *no-matter-what* could be something.

Material objects were shown joined together by ideas, qualities, or values, parts overtaken by their whole, wholes by their parts, the aristocratic by the popular, profane things by sacred things. Before, one denied making *something* of them. The hierarchy that ordered the scale of differences between a thing and its qualities, for example, was reduced to nothingness. The various qualities of a thing became things in the same way as the thing that they were qualities of. Previously, red was subordinate to the table it coloured. Then red became a *something* in the same way as a table. During the modern passage to abstraction (in a Rothko canvas or a Klein monochrome, for example), painting set out to represent redness without representing a table, giving to this colour a status of *something* possibly independent, in the same way that a table or chair were substances. A quality, a word, a concept, a judgement, an opinion – the more nothing is *nothing*, the more nothing is *everything*. The more nothing is a less-than-thing, the more nothing is a more-than-thing, and everything is simply something.

Everything that created an order separating things from what is not completely a thing, or from what is a more-than-thing, has disappeared. As a general rule, everything which was a more-than-thing, everything that constituted a 'totality', like God, the world, the soul (the Kantian Ideas, which are both less than knowable things, since they are impossible to intuit, and more than knowable things, since they are the groundwork for practical reason), man, life, being *qua* being, history, or sociey, were in one way or another *objectivised*. In other words, one made an object of them, and one deconstructed the claim of each to be non-reifiable. It was possible to make an object of a human person, as has been theorised since the Enlightenment, just as it was possible to make *something* of God, consciousness, or life. And everything based on metaphysical arguments that seemed to benefit from a status of a more-than-thing was gradually lowered to the level of a mere thing: *something*, not everything and not nothing.

One could argue that consciousness is not something because all things are given to us *in* consciousness. In this way, Husserl defined consciousness as the 'residuum of the destruction of all things'.[4] But society and history made consciousness a something like other things.

One could argue that history wasn't something because all things took place *in* history. But history was also constructed as something in consciousness, or in a particular society, which elevated it to the rank of myth, according to the ethnologist. And, rather than the higher form of all things, history was also found to be something, which one could moreover be wary of, in which even the claims of history were necessarily historicised.

Like Marx and Engels in *The German Ideology*, one could argue that society was not-All, that it was not something, but the condition of all that was given as something for us. However, in the naturalist view, society also appeared as a particular thing, determined, for example, by the more general evolution of life and of animality. Society had a beginning, conditions of appearance, limits, and therefore the status of a finite object.

One could argue in the same way about man, God, being, the will to power, or life (in *Creative Evolution*, Bergson explained why life is not a *thing*). But in modernity, all these *more-than-things* saw their claim humiliated. Something other than themselves always reified them, exposing their limits, determinations, and particularities, before subsequently reducing them to the rank of a particular thing, in an infernal chaos of thought. Everything that made things was made a thing, as if the executioner was condemned to be executed by an executioner, forced to be subjected to the same fate.

On the one hand, what was considered a less-than-thing – what appeared to depend on substantial things or on material things – ended up acquiring a status independent of a mere 'something'. On the other hand, everything that seemed to be a more-than-thing was lowered to the rank of thinghood. The twentieth century left us what could be called a flat world, in which any *criterion* of a thing seemingly no longer subsists, and in which this thing is no longer constructed by different ordered degrees that a metaphysics would be in the position to infer and absolutely justify. This observation remains: no-matter-what can be something. We experience

this idea daily. It is the characteristic feature of our world – a
world of things.

Thing

In early twenty-first century global culture, what first comes to
mind when talking about thinghood is the material thing, physical unity, or cohesion proper to a part of space-time: a concrete
object. For example, an independent rock that one can lift, turn,
and move; a flower which grows from a bulb, blooms, and
withers; a body, with its own metabolism, which moves in space;
or a manufactured object, like a knife, with a definite function,
that one can isolate from its environment.

Other human cultures clearly put forward or had put forward
the primary meaning of what it is to be a thing through other
determinations. The ancient or classical things are substances. For
many other peoples, things are or were primarily minds and inner
things.

In our own contemporary culture, by 'thing' we primarily
understand the thing which obtains its unity in a part of matter.
For us, a thing par excellence is a collection of matter which has
some coherent qualities. A thing can then undergo spatio-temporal
displacements and transformations without its identity being altogether affected by them. A rock is, on this view, a thing because
we can lift it, remove it from a beach, or place it elsewhere. But
this rock will nonetheless remain the same rock. Insofar as this
rock can remain an identical or comparable part in space while
changing its place, it acquires the quality of a thing par excellence.

It is more problematic to consider the body of a living creature,
human being, or animal as a thing. Some think that a person must
not be reducible to a thing. A person has spatio-temporal identity,
since, while changing form (from infancy to old age), it must
nonetheless be considered as the same thing. Not only do persons
appear to have spatio-temporal identity, but also, in most cases, an
experiential and conscious identity, namely by relating – through
sensation, cognition, language, or memory – to itself as to something self-identical. Some normally think that a person is actually
a bit more than a thing.

But a human person's action leads to the production of some
things (ideas, words, movements) that we at the same time judge
to be a bit less than things: secondary, constructed effects, which

would have less objective reality than spatially identifiable and re-identifiable things.

In our contemporary prejudices and commonplaces, we primarily recognise things, and, with difficulty, during the debates and disagreements we have, we then recognise *sub-things* and *supra-things*.

Around this pseudo-concept of 'thing', we have what is greater than things, which merits respect, cannot be exchanged for other things, is valued in itself, and is incomparable. On the other hand, we have what is inferior, which is always an effect or construction by humans or other sentient beings and by their cognition of things of the least reality: not merely material things, but linguistic, computational, symbolic, intentional, chimerical, or virtual things. And our pseudo-concept of 'thing' remains that which has both spatial and temporal unity.

On the commonsensical view, spatial unity takes precedence over temporal unity. A thing is primarily what has internal spatial consistency and is independent of that which it is not, such that one can move it without affecting its form. The more a thing changes form when one changes its place, the more this thing appears to us as insubstantial, weak, vague, confused, 'pliable', confounded with its environment, or heteronomous, and becomes decidedly unthingly.

Only subsequently does the temporal unity of a thing, its capacity to seemingly remain the same as time passes, allow us to identify and re-identify it as something, a 'very much thing'. Temporal identity strengthens a thing even more. On this view, the spatial identity gives it its thingly character, while the temporal identity gives it its thingly *intensity*. Whatever quickly loses its temporal form is a 'very little thing', though nevertheless a thing, while whatever endures is nevertheless a thing in that it retains an enduring identity.

The schema inherited from ancient and classical views of substantiality still allow us to very vaguely classify things according to their spatial coherence and degree of corruptibility over time. Nonetheless, these views do not hold. We rarely have practical faith in them, insofar as we handle as many images, avatars, bundles of data, and words as we do flowers, pebbles, or knives.

In our eyes, the first problem that arises from the determination of things as spatially coherent and movable things (and not simply as substances endowed with qualities among other spatial qualities), is that we confusedly believe that spatial things are composed of smaller things. Our contemporary conception of matter thus leads us to think that things are always *in* things: elements in a thing's material, molecules in elements, atoms in molecules, hadrons and baryons in the nucleus of an atom, quarks and anti-particles in hadrons and baryons, and, perhaps, at even smaller dimensions, strings. In other words, the coherence of a spatial thing is always broken down into its component parts – if not in our eyes, at least in our at times scholarly and often vague tacit knowledge. A thing's spatial unity exists only on some spatial scale in which we handle what we describe as things par excellence (a rock, flower, knife, or body). Our consideration of spatial things is thus local, a function of the scale of our action at any given time.

Second problem: where does a 'concrete' thing begin and where does it end? I observe a stone, say, a piece of quartz. I can concretely try to draw a line or limit that follows its exact contour: where the stone ends and where the air around it begins, my hand holding it, and so on. But when I observe the stone under a microscope, this line changes: where there was some fullness, I now discover a topography. I think that the stone is imbued with holes, straits, and that the crystals, at the microscopic scale, no longer look like the stone beneath my eyes. By changing scales, the unity of the stone appears to dissolve into a multiplicity of crystals and forms that were invisible to the naked eye.

Not only are a material thing's spatial limits not the same from one scale to another, but every material thing continually loses parts from one moment to the next: the stone erodes, the flower withers, a body's cells are replaced by new cells, and so on.

On this view, a spatio-temporal thing, the ship of Theseus par excellence, is not a model of identity – we have known this for a long time.

But unlike the classical belief, an idea is scarcely any more substantial. My idea of a stone changes through my experience of stones. The idea of a stone is no less porous, malleable, and 'pliable' than any rock sample. The idea of a stone never matches its scientific concept; understood by ordinary language (that we learned to become attentive to), it is an equivocal term that does not always precisely refer to the same object: natural or man-made gemstone, reduced to the idea of a rock's fragment, equivalent to a pebble, but not quite. Scientific concepts also change from paradigm to paradigm. And even though, insofar as they do not correspond to every secondary reality, they may be the only true things in the world, they provide us with a world of very impoverished things, as the world is in general for every radical positivism.

Nevertheless, from the impossibility of reducing a thing to a spatio-temporal thing, to an ideal thing, or to a concept, we must not conclude that it is impossible to make use of the term 'thing'. Many things exist, and we cannot do without the concept of 'thing'. In the absence of things, the world becomes undifferentiated: the world is a self-saturated whole in itself which knows no differentiation.

It is very strange to claim that, in reality, only a continuous, homogeneous world exists, traversed by various intensities, but undifferentiated by themselves, and that the existence of things would only be the reflection of a division through perception, thought, and knowledge. To maintain such an assertion, one must, as certain philosophers do, proceed in one of two ways. We can push to its maximum the differentiation between the continuous world and the activity that produces differentiation, the artificial division by our actions. Or we may attempt to reduce the differentiation to its minimum, to a relational difference (between *Natura naturata* and *Natura naturans* – between the will as subject of experience and the will as object of experience). Dualists who push the differentiation between the world of continuity and the activity of the division of things to its maximum produce two distinct things pre-existing the division into things: the dividable thing and the thing that divides things. Others who instead try to minimise the differentiation to account for it within the framework of a philosophy of immanence only manage to say that the same thing, since it is different, produces differentiation – but in reality the thing is identical. Therefore, philosophers of immanence always presuppose a minimum of differences between things (between the same active and passive thing) to account for a maximum of difference (the appearance of the division of the world into things independent of each other, which are in fact only an effect of a single reality).

In both cases, one must presuppose either a minimal or a maximal difference between at least two things to account for the manifold differentiation of things according to all of their degrees.

One never accounts for the fact that there are things other than by things. A 'thing' cannot derive from anything other than another thing. No philosophical magic trick will ever give us the appearance of things from a more fundamental principle of a non-differentiation or super-difference of things. Indeed, when something is, nothing can precede a thing but another thing. If one wants to redirect the *something* of an undifferentiated totality, an immanence, an in-itself, or anything that one claims is not a product of the thingly division, this principle will retroactively and immediately be reduced to the thing's status as another thing. Nature, God, the One, the All, and Ground have never avoided, and will never avoid, the reduction to a thing's status.

In this way, one cannot do without the concept of thing, but neither can one fix it at some determination; a thing will always be a material thing, an idea, or a concept. Something is *contaminating* in the thing. When a thing is, it is seemingly impossible to limit it to particular determinations alone. It is pointless to want to impose a quarantine on it.

Instead of opposing the epidemic character of a thing, we by definition accept it. No-matter-what is something. Each barrier was erected to limit the range of 'real', concrete things to spatio-temporal objects, or to reduce them to mere well-formed ideas, concepts, or sentences. Historical attempts were made to self-saturate and define them as substances. But no limits are ever strong enough to resist the epidemic potential of a thing that no-matter-what can be, and that nothing manages to not be absolutely.

Nonetheless, human thought always conspires to resist an epidemic of things, which carries in embryonic form the menacing potential of the no-matter-what.

II. Less than a Thing, More than a Thing

1. How do we define that which is something? There are two major ways of responding to this question, each of which adds depth to the flatness of the no-matter-what.

The physicalist or materialist response considers that atoms, particles, and force fields *are* things. More precisely, the physicalist and materialist response produces more-than-things and less-than-things, vested with a variable ontological dignity. The ancients' and the moderns' atoms, our variety of particles, and the forces that govern them are more than things. They are the fundamental elements of all things, such that everything which is, ultimately, is either composed atomically or of particles. In other words, the fundamental elements of matter are all that is, but nothing is them. If there are fundamental particles, then the elements previously considered to be particles are effects or composites. Fundamental atoms, particles, or forces are more than things, for they are things without anything being them. On the physicalist or materialist view, these more-than-things are accompanied by less-than-things. For example, ideas or conscious acts are determined by the state of matter and are not autonomous things but manifestations reduced to secondary effects of material processes, either directly deducible or emergent at this or that organisational level of living matter. Generally, everything that is not material is conceived as a secondary result – deducible and reducible, or emergent and irreducible – of material composition. Everything that is not material exists, but only as a secondary thing or less-than-thing. The physicalist or materialist order thus consists in transforming the flatness of the 'no-matter-what is equally something' into a topography that ascends to more-than-things or super-things (atoms, particles, forces) and descends to less-than-things, secondary things, or infraentities (non-material effects of material processes).

2. The metaphysical or formalist response considers one, two, several, or an infinite number of *substances* to be things. The metaphysical or formalist response thus also produces more-than-things and less-than-things. The immanence of a single substance, Nature, the great All, spirit, God, Anaximander's *arche*, the Idea, the One, Being rather than beings, the duality of extension and thought, the opposition of Good and Evil, the conflict of two original substances, the infinity of monads, the innumerable multiplicity of fundamental entities – all of these are the fundamental forms of all things, which envelop, create, move, or determine them. Everything which is emanates from or belongs to this single substance, to one of two substances, or to an infinity of possible substances. Every metaphysics goes through this determination of one or several more-than-things, which are always accompanied by less-than-things – that is, by attributes, qualities, accidents, or illusory appearances. What is less than a thing is what exists only secondarily through another thing that exists by itself, is therefore substantial, and is more than a thing. A substance is a thing which is itself, not in another thing. What is not substantial exists not *by itself*, but *by that which exists by itself*. Substance has a primary,

fundamental existence, and anything that depends on it only exists secondarily. Thus, the metaphysical or formalist order consists in substantially transforming the flatness of the 'no-matter-what is equally something' into a relief that ascends to things in themselves and descends to secondary things, attributes, qualities, accidents, or even illusions depending upon essential reality.

3. The physical or metaphysical placing into relief of the flat world through the hierarchisation of particular or substantial more-than-things and less-than-things which are effects, illusions, or secondary entities, corresponds to the objectivisation of the world in the cosmos or universe.

The cosmos is the world hierarchised metaphysically by an order of substances and attributes, or substantial reality and secondary illusions of appearance. The universe is the world hierarchised physically by an order of atoms, particles, and non-material effects of material processes (thought, symbolic functioning, emotions, ideas, words, and so on).

The modern history of metaphysics is profoundly marked by a desubstantialisation and by the loss of a cosmos. The modern history of science points to the growing difficulty of representing a universe.

4. The difficulty of arranging more-than-things and less-than-things, and of placing into relief the flatness of the 'no-matter-what is equally something', unquestionably increases. Again, substances and attributes, necessary things and contingent realities, inter-comprehend each other [s'entre-comprennent], whereas particles and forces, structures, degrees of organisation, scales and laws inter-define each other [s'entre-définissent].

It becomes difficult to prevent this or that from being a thing and from being *as much as* – neither more nor less than – what appeared illusory or accidental. In every epistemic domain, it becomes difficult to prevent what was secondary from being something just as much as what was primary. The physical or metaphysical rejection of 'no-matter-what' – for there is only a science of what matters – appears through a series of resistances which shape the very texture of the modern history of ideas. But what is neither more nor less than a thing appears much flatter than what was more-than-a-thing and what was less-than-a-thing.

5. A more-than-thing is what is in itself. A less-than-thing is what is in and by another thing.

However, a thing which is neither more-than-thing nor less-than-thing is also neither in itself nor in another thing. A thing is neither the attribute of a substance nor the substance itself.

Substance

The mechanism of a thing excluding itself from the system of things because of its autonomous, necessary, or mere existence in a substratum in and by itself, corresponds very precisely to what we call *substance*. Though the dominant model of things in the history of ancient and classical Western philosophy, this idea has disappeared almost entirely from modern thought.

Today we think that our greatest difficulty is *representing* what a substance could be and what humans formerly understood by this term. The same representation is behind the seemingly conflicting plurality of definitions and complex discussions, from Aristotle to Thomas Aquinas and Descartes to Locke, who all define the concept of substance. But we hardly have a *substantial* world any more. Aristotelian substance, 'what is neither claimed of a subject nor in a subject', the primary meaning of being, substratum of qualities, quantities, and other categories; Thomist substance, an essence which exists in itself; Cartesian substance, this thing 'which exists in such a way that it only requires itself to exist'; simple, monadic Leibnizian substance, 'which enters into composites: simple, that is, without parts'; Kantian substance, this 'substratum which remains while everything else changes' – the ancient, medieval, and classical ways of thinking about substance implicitly show us what is distinct about our time: an absence of substantiality in our conception of things and of the world. The various lines drawn from one thesis to another represent the outline of substance, the key term of what we have lost (and therefore, negatively, of what we have gained): existence in itself; simples in composites; ground of all things; mode of being of what is in the things without anything being in it, without anything being affirmed of it; self-sufficiency; permanence; existential necessity; and so on. The signs of what we have grown estranged from – the idea of substance – together and separately mark the concept of a thing in itself, which is distinguished from things insofar as these things can be in them and by them, without this thing in itself ever being by another thing or in another thing except itself. In the history of philosophy, a substance is the more-than-thing par excellence. It appears that substance has always been constructed in this way by thought: a thing on which things can be predicated, but which would never be predicated on anything. Substance receives things in it, but it is not received by any thing.

Spinoza's substance is in all likelihood the purest model of this 'more-than-thing'. One finds in the axioms of his *Ethics*, even more than in Descartes, the most obvious classical model of the more-than-thing.

The modes, 'the affections of substance, namely, what is in another thing', are posited in such a way that a mode is not in itself, but contained in something other than itself. On the other hand, substance is 'that which is in itself, and which is conceived by itself, that is, that of which the concept has no need of the concept of another thing in order to be formed'.

Substance alone is in itself. Thus, modes are in a substance but not in themselves. The substance in which modes are is in itself. But everything that is in the substance is a mode of the substance – to be in a substance is to be a mode, and thus to not be in itself. How can substance be *in itself* without being *in it*?

In one sense, there is necessarily substance insofar as modes are in it as in another thing. In another sense, there is necessarily substance insofar as it is in itself. Every substance is understood perniciously in two senses: the *itself* and the *it*. We will see later that this concerns a 'formal' sense (the 'itself') and an 'objective' sense (the 'it'). Substantiality confounds these two senses.

No substance can ever be in itself in the same way as that which is in it is in it – since that which is in it is not in itself, and therefore is in it *as in another thing*. On the one side, there exists a substance that one is in as in another thing ('it'). On the other side, there exists a substance that one is not in as in another thing ('itself'). Substance is thus itself *and* substance is it.

Substance is what makes a thing more than a thing. Substance is always what makes a thing *two* things.

The idea of substance assumes that a thing may not be double or split. But by trying to constitute a thing as *one*, it always produces *two* things: one *it*-thing and one *itself*-thing. The problem is then how to explain that the two are the same, but the gap between the two can never be entirely bridged.

We can therefore present this first response: what is substantial, what is 'more-than-a-thing', is always two things: itself and it.

Since we do not want to produce two things but *one* thing, we will attempt to incorporate the dyadic or Janus-faced character of a thing into the definition of a thing: something else is in a thing, and a thing is in something-other-than-itself.

We must make a distinction *within each thing* and not distinguish *between things* – namely, between things that are more than other things and less than other things; between substantial things and non-substantial things (on the formalist and metaphysical view), but also between material things and non-material things (on the materialist and physicalist view).

The Vacuity of Distinguishing Material Things from Non-Material Things

Establishing differences between things in order to determine *formal* categories of things in general can be extremely tricky – for example, categories of 'thing in itself' and 'thing for itself' that allow distinctions between human beings and rocks. Obviously, human beings are not like rocks, but is the difference so great that they have *absolutely* nothing in common with each other as things? Some may think that a human being is *for itself* and that a rock is only *in itself*. But a human being must also be *a thing* for itself and a rock *a thing* in itself. In-itself and for-itself always appear as two modalities of the same thing. A human being and a rock are both things, but they are not identically determined things.

The main objection to making 'no-matter-what' something is that doing so ignores either the formal, substantial, or, above all, material definition of objects. One response to our view may be: 'Yes, of course, but nevertheless material, concrete objects exist.' But there is an important difference between the perceptual and tactile chair and the mental ideas from which the idea of a chair derives. Some may argue that an object is first and foremost a *material* object. Everything else is supposed to be like material objects – nonetheless, they are *sub-things*: ideas, movements, words, vague collective concepts, and so on.

The problem is that it is impossible for us to establish a definitive difference between material things and non-material things. Every thing, in fact, has something material. If I say that a unicorn doesn't exist materially, I clearly understand that the linguistic expression 'a unicorn' exists materially – it is a sound or assemblage of signs. Then I can say that *that which* this expression *designates* doesn't exist materially – I can differentiate between sense and reference à la Frege, or between signified and signifier à la Saussure, or between sign, interpretant, and object à la Peirce. However, representations of unicorns surely exist – drawn representations, cinematographic representations, and so on.

Asking if a thing is or is not 'material' is a vacuous question, since, for every thing, one will find something material and something non-material. The problem is not, in fact, the possibility of designating material things – what we can hold in our hands, what is concrete, what is not fictional, and so on. Rather, the problem is finding what is material in a thing and what is not.

The unicorn has something material, and something that is not.

One can hardly devise criteria to separate material things from other things, where the chair, rock, or my body would derive from a primary category, and where ideas, unicorns, or the concept of chair would derive from a secondary category. How can one capture each one of these things *as a whole*? How can one claim that something is material or not? You say that the chair is material? Very well. But if you posit such a claim, your interlocutor can very well act the fool, like a vaudevillian reciting the early pages of the *Phenomenology of Spirit* about the This and the Thing, and ask you: 'The chair, but which chair?' You point to *this* chair, repeating: 'This chair is material.' But if your adversary doesn't turn to the chair, instead focusing on your mouth, and responds to you, 'Hey! But it's a word, it's an idea that you just expressed', then you will undoubtedly grow impatient. So you grab the arm of the one acting the fool, making them touch the chair: 'This chair, here, is material.' However, the fool may reply to you: 'That? But that's an action!' Your face turns red: 'No, what my action points to is material!' The idiot may continue their critical vendetta: 'That's a sentence.'

In other words, if you name something material, someone can systematically choose to contemplate your act of naming and not what the act of naming names. They will then aim at a nonmaterial way in which you point to a material thing through an act of presentation, idea, or concept. Directionality is required to make something material appear. One can *always* choose to look at the direction and not at what the direction is directed at. If you are challenged to point to a material thing, you are trapped, since someone can always capture a thing by the way in which you name or represent it, rather than what you name or represent. They will, in this way, perceive the non-materiality of the material thing, its representation, its presentation, or its means of naming.

Inversely, if someone begs you to unearth a thing that would absolutely *not* be material, game over. The moment you express this non-material thing, your opponent can choose to perceive the thing at its material end. If you express an immaterial thing, you must still express it through reference, the sonority of words, and so on. In this way, there is always the chance to establish a genealogy of things, to historicise them, or naturalise them. Every idea that is given as absolute and absolutely immaterial derives from something material, which it gradually points back to, by making it relative: the soul, a divinity, desire, and so on. Each genealogical work (of naturalisation, from Hume to evolutionary psychology, and of historicisation, from Marx to Bourdieusian sociology) consists in dismissing the way in which this thing is material or natural. For example, if someone designates God, you *can* choose to not follow the direction of their designation and to look instead at the person designating: why does, and how can, this person believe that God is characterised in this way? You can give a psychological, psychoanalytical, Marxist, evolutionary, or any other kind of interpretation of the person. The person seeks to show you something transcendent through their speech, but you grasp their speech as an immanent act. The person names an immaterial thing, but you only ever grasp the materiality of its naming.

You can never *absolutely* name a material thing or a non-material thing. One can freely and repeatedly approach your material thing by its immaterial side, or your immaterial thing by its material side. But this is not a foolish game; it clearly shows how one cannot categorise a thing as material or just as an idea.

Therefore, materiality is not a good principle by which to divide things. Rather, materiality is a principle of division within each thing – between a thing's material properties and its non-material properties. By reintroducing a hierarchy between things by classifying them into material things and non-material things, one fails to perceive that this distinction is in fact made on the inside of each thing. Every thing has some material properties and some non-material properties. The common-sense criterion of materiality between things is inoperative and never yields things that are more than things simply because they are more *material* than others.

However, if there really are no material things and no non-material things, if there are only things which are material in one sense and non-material in another, then what are things in general opposed to? What is their opposite? If there is first something, certainly there is something rather than 'another thing'. But what is something other than something? Could it be *nothing*?

Nothing

What does one mean by supposing that something *is, tout court*? One implies that there is this something rather than another thing, rather than a non-something; there is something *rather than* nothing. But nothing is not the opposite of something; nothing is the absence of something, the empty place left by something. Nothing is what remains when one has removed something. However, if there is something, then there is also the opposite of something: what surrounds it, its negative. In other words, nothing is the negative form of something without this something. Nothing is therefore not the opposite of something, but rather the opposite of something *added to* the absence of this something.

Nothing is the addition of the *opposite* and *absence* of something.

While thinking this through, the meaning shifts and one confuses the absence of the thing, which is caused by a change in the presence of the thing, and the opposite of the thing, which is the very condition of the thing. The opposite of a thing is inseparable from the thing – the thing is never given without its negative, without its opposite. The absence of a thing is secondary, since it involves removing the thing from its form and its surrounding through thought, after the presence of the thing has been guaranteed. Now, if I confuse the negative of the thing – that which is not a thing – and the absence of the thing, I obtain a *nothing* which confusedly makes me imagine that this nothing is *absolute*. The absence of the thing has become its opposite, making me think that the fact that the thing is not there is the opposite of the thing itself. If I imagine the cosmos, the physical universe, and I absent it by imagining that it will one day disappear or that it once did not exist, then I may confusedly imagine that this absence of a physical universe is the opposite of the universe, namely, the background on which the universe would exist. I begin to believe, without ever managing to express it clearly (which is for me the proof of a mystery, of an aura of inaccessible, terrifying, and ineffable truth), that something exists as an alternative between nothing (the absence of the universe) and the existence of the universe. I believe that the universe emerged from nothing, its absolute non-existence, and that it will eventually disappear into the depths of this nothingness. In so doing, I have identified the absence of the universe – the form of the universe deprived of the thing that the universe is, like a mould deprived of its model – with the opposite of the universe – the negative of the universe, everything except the universe, that in which the universe is, whatever it may be. I thus thought that the absence of the universe was the non-universe, the opposite, and the reverse of the universe.

Nothing is more false.

The opposite of the universe is what the universe *already* is in, such that I consider it as something; it is its form, its negative. The absence of the universe, on the other hand, is not its form, but the form devoid of its thing, an objectless mould. Therefore, I have confounded form and absence, like someone who removes the mould of the sculpture of a woman's body and confuses the impression with the very absence of the woman, or the carefully handled hollow of the mould with the disappearance of the model. They would thus think, in one way or another, that what was completely around the woman's body to mould it was the absence of the woman's body. Now, specifically, what was around the woman's body was a mould. The absence of the woman's body is not the mould itself, but rather the *withdrawal* of the body from the mould. In fact, the mould remains the same as the body – either present or absent – and it points to an unaltered form. The clay-like mould is not the absence of the woman's body, but its negative. When the casting took place, this negative existed at the same time as its positive and it subsisted when the body came out of its coating. Therefore, absence is not an *object*, but an *event*; it is not the form of the mould, but *the event* of having withdrawn the body from the mould.

The mould is the form and negative of the body, embodied in a material object. Absence is the event of the withdrawal of the thing from its form, its negative, which persists in an objective form (as a sign, an imprint, a fragrance, a memory, an image, and so on).

The absolute nothing is born from the confusion between the opposite and absence. If I decide that absence, the withdrawal of the thing, is the opposite of the thing, then I identify the withdrawn mould with the very absence of the body, and I identify the negative, the contemporary form of its object, with absence, the event necessarily following the presence of the object in question. A dreadful vision results: I think that the absence of the thing is the form of the thing, its opposite, its very condition. For this reason, I believe that the world exists on the *grounds* of its nonexistence, that the mould of the world is the world's primitive absence. I think that my existence is opposed to my nonexistence. I think that something exists *rather than* nothing. I imagine that a thing exists *rather than* a thing's absence. I collapse trying to understand how nothing was, and how something emerged *in its place*.

In truth, if something exists, then the negative of this thing exists simultaneously: every thing's form is something-other-than-a-thing. If a physical universe exists, then it necessarily has the form of something other than that of the physical universe. The *opposite* of something is not its *absence*, its emptiness; its absence is an operation (which, perhaps, will some day have taken place) through which its form subsists without the thing itself. The absence of the universe would be the removal from the mould of the object 'universe'. Emptiness is the withdrawal of the thing, and, like absence, emptiness never preexists the thing.

In this way, the negative of a thing is inseparable from the thing. The negative of a thing is simultaneous with the thing, whereas the absence or emptiness of a thing can only follow it. But what, then, pre-exists something? Nothing other than *another thing*. If there wasn't what one calls 'nothing' prior to matter, to something, then this 'nothing' must be another thing. The Kantian argument, according to which the existence of nothing would invalidate the very possibility that there is nothing, is insufficient; if there is nothing, then there cannot be any possibility of invalidating possibilities. Therefore, the concept of 'nothing' on its own is not self-refuting, and the concept of thing is 'contaminating'. When something exists, everything which preceded this thing is reified, since a thing is a mode of division. Thus, by separating the thing from a before and an after, this division determines before and after, attributes them an end or beginning which precludes under-standing them other than as things. Every before-thing is already something, since something ends every before-thing.

First lesson: nothing pre-exists something except another thing. Second lesson: the negative of a thing can neither precede the thing nor follow the thing, but is inseparable from its existence. Third lesson: the absence of a thing can only follow the thing.

If one again asks why there is something, then we can risk giving the following responses: there was not something 'rather than' nothing, for, if there was nothing *before* something, it's because this nothing was already something, something other than what there was afterwards. There is something 'as much as' nothing, since there is necessarily something *at the same time as* something other than something, and since the negative of something always coexists with the thing in question. There is something 'rather than' the nothing that some day perhaps will be, but if some day there is nothing *after* something, this nothing will only ever be the absence of what was.

In other words, there was not something rather than nothing, since the nothing that could have been before something can only ever be a thing (insofar as the thing is retroactively contaminating), even if one wants to call it 'nothing'. There is something as much as nothing, since there is necessarily something *and* a non-something (that one can call 'nothing'). Some day perhaps there will be nothing rather than something, but this will necessarily be the nothing *of* something, of what was and is no more, the absence of what was withdrawn, even if no memory of it subsists.

The absolute nothingness that one would like to oppose to being is only the confusion, an untenable argument, between what there was before something, the opposite of something, and the absence of something. One would like to make the before-thing the nothing, the non-thing, and the thing's emptiness. But the before-thing can only be a thing as well (another thing). The non-thing is the form of things (something-other-than-a-thing). The thing's emptiness is a potential after-thing (an absence). No non-thing precedes a thing nor follows it; the negative of a thing is always contemporaneous with this thing. Before the thing, there is always already some other thing, and after the thing, there can only ever be a thing's absence, and not a nothingness.

There is no single concept of these three relations to something. Therefore, there is no nothing except from one of these three angles: a nothing which is in fact something; a nothing which is in fact the opposite of something (its form); or a nothing which is in fact an absence of something (an emptiness or an exile). Each way leads to something, with none of them leading to a nothing.

III. Something

1. Consider no-matter-what, therefore something.

For instance, a clementine. This clementine is *something*. But is the clementine, in general, something? If I am a nominalist, I will consider that only this or that clementine exists as a primary and real thing, and that the concept of a clementine is always a less-than-thing, a secondary thing, derived from actually existing things. If I am a Platonist, I will think that a clementine really exists as an idea or form, of which clementines are particular, secondary, and approximate expressions. A clementine will be a more-than-thing and clementines some less-than-things.

But let us consider for a moment *equally* as things this clementine here (that I can see, touch, taste) *and* a clementine in general *and* every clementine. Let us say that *a* clementine is neither more nor less something than *this* clementine. A clementine is a different thing, which either derives from this clementine by abstraction or precedes it, allows it, and completely goes beyond it, but a clementine is a thing *as well*. Let us try to situate ourselves on the plane where a clementine in general and this clementine here are equal and equally something. They are certainly not really equal, neither absolutely nor particularly, neither ideally nor even existentially. Some will think that only this clementine really exists; others that only a clementine in general exists absolutely. But how are they equal, other than in that they are *something*, anything (existent, nonexistent, real, abstract, constructed, true, or false)?

On this plane of equality not only are this clementine and the concept of clementine comparable, but a material part of a clementine and a whole clementine are just as comparable. Let us consider a segment of this clementine, a tenth of it. A tenth of a clementine is objectively less than a whole clementine – ten-tenths of a clementine. However, a tenth of a clementine, a segment of a clementine, is not only less than the thing of which it is the part. It is also *something*. Let us consider equally part and whole, the slice which has been removed from a clementine and the orange peel which happens to be removable from a clementine.

Let us consider a pip, a slice, and a clementine equally. Let us consider this set and each possible element of this set on the same plane.

If each part is as much something as what it is part of, the qualities of an orange must be equal to what they are qualities of. The orange colour of this clementine is not something less than the clementine which has this colour. The weight, size, density, luminosity, and sound of this clementine when I let it fall from a tree are always something, like the clementine.

But if the sound emitted by a falling clementine is something, then each event in which this clementine is must not be something less: its falling, growth, picking, shipment, throwing, gathering, coating, and so on. The life of this clementine is something in the same way as each moment of its life and each one of these events, in the same way as the object itself.

2. In this way, the equal possibility of being a thing for its parts, qualities, events, and number, unfolds from an arbitrary thing. Unity is neither something more (because more abstract) than this particular clementine, nor something less than a clementine (because unity is conceptual and arithmetical and a clementine is some concrete, physical entity).

3. On this view, two is not something more than one, nor three more than two, nor a thousand more than three. If counting is allowed through the accumulation of an additional unity, if it is constituted by *more* and by *less*, then it is always possible to encounter the plane on which three unities forming *one* three are not more than two unities forming *one* two.

4. One will claim that these somethings are divided by the concept that one makes of them, by perception, language, action, or thought. However, the problem is not to know *who* makes something and *how*, but rather to determine *what can be something*.

5. No-matter-what can be something. No thing exists which is *more* than another thing. No thing exists which is *less* than another thing. Everything which is something is equally something.

6. Something is first and foremost what appears to us, for the time being, as a 'plane', a flatness where no-matter-what is equal. The no-matter-what is that which is equal, since it is that which is equally something.

But if we know *that which is* a thing, we do not exactly know *that which* a thing *is*.

7. What do we mean by claiming that a clementine is something, that a segment, pip, orange colour, weight, unity, its falling, two, three, the word 'clementine', or its idea are something, just as me, you, an animal, or the Earth are something? We have assumed that a clementine is not *another thing*, that it is only *something*. More precisely, we have assumed that a clementine is not no-matter-what. A clementine is *this* clementine. But this clementine is not *that* clementine. Therefore, it is a matter of something, it is a matter of no-matter-what. The word 'clementine' is neither the word 'Australia' nor an animal nor the end of a storm. When this clementine is something, it is not that clementine or something else. No-matter-what, we have said, is this *or* that *or* its opposite *or* something else. No-matter-what is something, anything.

A clementine is not this *or* that *or* its opposite *or* anything else. It *matters* that a clementine be something, that is, that it can be this or that, but that it absolutely cannot be this or that or anything else. If a clementine is no-matter-what, then it is not a matter of a clementine.

8. To be something is therefore primarily to not be no-matter-what. That which a thing is, at least, is 'not no-matter-what'.

9. One can only define a thing by these two limits: *that which is something*, and *that which something is*. No-matter-what is that which 'enters' into something, and 'not no-matter-what' is that into which something 'enters'. No-matter-what is something, and something is not no-matter-what.

Therefore, every thing is a milieu, a weak connection between 'no-matter-what' and 'not no-matter-what'.

10. From this we can infer that no-matter-what, through the milieu of something, is not no-matter-what. Something is in fact that which 'detaches' no-matter-what from no-matter-what; no-matter-what is a thing, and a thing is that which is not no-matter-what.

11. A thing is never defined *as a whole*. One cannot claim that a thing equals *this* or *that*. One can only say that a thing is this or that, but that is insufficient. One must clarify *that which is* this thing. If unilaterally defining the thing is forever insufficient, it is because a thing has being bilaterally: being which enters into the

thing, and being into which the thing enters; that which is the thing, and that which the thing is.

In this way, 'something other than something' is in 'something', and 'something' is in 'something other than something'. A thing is never *in itself*, for two distinct reasons: first, because a thing cannot be its content (that which is in the thing); second, because a thing cannot be its container (that in which the thing is). A thing is equivalent to neither that which is the thing nor to that which the thing is. A thing is emptied of its content and exiled by its container.

12. Something is not *in itself*, for that which is in the thing is not the thing, and that in which the thing is is not the thing.

13. We have only defined *negatively* ('not no-matter-what') that which something is. How do we *positively* think of that which something is? If a thing, anything, is not no-matter-what, then what is a thing? What is it that makes it a *thing*?

14. That which is *one* is generally defined as being a *thing*. Unity, logical unity or counted unity, appears as the decisive property allowing us to distinguish *one thing*.

But to say that a thing 'is that which is one' is also to limit considerably the import of the thing.

We will not claim that a thing cannot be one, but rather that it is not because a thing is *one* that a thing is defined as a *thing*.

15. Is a human being a certain 'something', a thing, as a result of its organic unity, its logical unity, or its arithmetical unity?

Unquestionably, a coherence exists – a series of relations that connect this human being's bodily limbs, tissues, and functions to a biological and physical interdependence identifying this material thing as an organism. But a finger, a hand, and each cell of this body are neither something more nor something less than this organism. In other words, if it is certainly the *organic* unity of this body that makes it an *organic* thing, it is not this *organic* unity that makes it a thing *tout court*.

So, a minimal logical unity exists that guarantees the consistency of this non-contradictory body. If this being is something, it is primarily because what composes it is not logically contradictory. Nevertheless, we have admitted that 'two equals three', a squared circle, and some white which is not white, although not concepts or logically viable entities, are not *no-matter-what*, and are therefore equally something.

Thus, we will limit ourselves to counted unity. Perhaps, quite simply, if a human being is *one* human being, then a human being is a thing, just as a hand is a thing since it is *one* hand, and two hands are something since they form *one* set of two hands, just as a hot-cold thing is something if it is the impossible unity of hot and cold?

But a human being is *one* human being only insofar as it counts among human beings. Unity is primarily the possibility of being counted, of entering into the count. To be one is to be capable of being one of two, three, ten, and so on. To be one is to be capable of acting as a unity in the counting of that which one is, since one is one *something*.

Now, something is not primarily defined as 'something' because it is in another thing, entering into another thing or a series of other things. To be a thing, not merely this or that thing, a human or a hand, is to not be a thing among other things; it is not to count for a thing among other things. Among other things, a thing is always a determined thing, a thing which matters and which is countable. And this is not what makes it a thing, but rather what makes it *such a* thing.

A human being is a *human being* since it can count for *one* human being among two, three, or four human beings. A hand is a hand since it can count as *one* hand among two, three, or a thousand hands. But a human being is not a *thing* because it is one, that is, because it is potentially among two, three, or a thousand human beings. A human being is a thing since it is *alone*, that is, *solitary*.

A human being is a thing, just as a hand is a thing and a chair is a thing, insofar as it is a *solitary* thing and not insofar as it is *one* thing. Since a human being is embedded in the sequence, series, and set of real, imaginary, potential (it doesn't matter) human beings, it is *one*, it counts as one – among two, three, or more. But since a human being is in something other than humanity, it is *solitary*.

Since a human being is among other material things, a human being is *one* material thing. Since a human being is among other social individuals, a human being is counted for *one* social individual. A human being is always its unity and its counted unity.

But since a human being is not in something, whether in nature, society, the physical world, a house, or a family, a human being is in nothing which is something like a human being. Rather, a human being is in it alone.

Insofar as this or that is *solitary*, this or that is *something*.

16. A thing in another thing counts as *one*, but it is not *solitary*, because it is *one* thing in *another* thing: one hand in one body, one individual in one society, and so on.

Embedded in some something, a thing is *some* thing, but it is not one *thing*.

In 'something other than a thing', only this or that which can be solitary can be something.

A thing is a *thing* only embedded in its relation to that which is not *another* thing.

17. To be incapable of entering into a count is to be solitary.

18. Solitude makes the thing.

19. The unity of a thing is its possibility of being among other things. The thinghood of a thing is its possibility of being a solitary thing.

One is a thing only insofar as it is solitary. By being *one*, one is one *such*.

20. It is precisely because I am not *one* that I am *thing*, and that I can therefore be a thing, that is, potentially count as one.

Solitude

The world is the place of the formal equality of things and the place of their solitude. The world is where one is solitary, and one is solitary only in the world. One is solitary in the world like a rock, dust on the rock, the word 'rock', the idea that I have of the rock, a molecule of this rock, its shape, its grey colour, or its weight are solitary in the world. Each conscious, less conscious, unconscious, physical, symbolic thing, product of cognitive or linguistic activity, or segment of matter is solitary insofar as it is a thing – that is to say, as the thing exists and subsists beneath all that can comprehend it.

To be solitary in the world is therefore what is most common among things; the only common place of things, in fact, is their solitude in the world.

To be in the world is to be outside itself in something-other-than-a-thing. Every thing enters, as an object, into a manifold of 'big things' ['*grosses choses*']: relations, domains, definitions, determinations, sets, and so on. Every thing always belongs to these big things with other objects. But insofar as every thing enters into things, it also enters into something-other-than-a-thing, into that which is not a thing, which we shall call the world. The world is not a reality that pre-exists things, of which one could say that the world is this or that. The world is nothing other than what every thing enters into equally. The world is what enters into nothing.

One doesn't go outside the world because one only comes inside the world. Each thing enters into the world itself only insofar as the world enters into nothing.

The world is the common place of things. But this common place cannot be shared; two things do not enter into the world together. What one enters *together* is necessarily *another* thing: one enters together into a pair, an ideal, a bedroom, a political party, a family, a community, the composition of an atomic nucleus, a sports competition, an ecosystem, and so on. Yet each one of these complex things is in the world in the same way as what enters into the world. A sheet of paper and a fraction of this sheet of paper are equally things in that they equally enter into the world; the existence of one does not preclude the existence of the other, even if one, specifically, objectively comprehends the other.

Now, to enter equally into the world (whereas one enters unequally into things) is to enter into the world separately.

Two beings who love each other, or think they love each other, can think that they are alone together in the world; nothing is more false. They are together in their love, and each of them is alone in the world. For the fact that each of them is alone in the world is precisely what allows them to be together in something: specifically, in the idea of their love, in an isolated, withdrawn place, in a bedroom. On the other hand, their love, since it is something, is alone in the world.

From two things, one thing. Either the lovers consider their relationship as one thing ('us two'), in which case this thing – composed of at least two objects (each one of the lovers), but in fact many more (the idea they have of their love, others' perceptions of their love, and so on) – is a thing in the same way as each one of the two lovers (one of the lovers can contemplate, talk about, observe, affect, and modify their love, and is therefore a thing). Or the two lovers consider each other as two things ('you and me', rather than 'you-and-me'). In the second case, the two beings are distinct: a form exists around the first lover, and another form exists around the second lover. The first lover is a part of the world around the second, while the second lover is a part of the world around the first. In the first case, the two lovers make only one. A single form exists around the couple. One cannot win on all fronts. If the lovers are differentiated, each one of them has a distinct form, an inverse, a world which surrounds them, on the grounds of which their personhood has a unity. But if the lovers are entangled in the idea of their relationship, only the couple is distinct and has a surrounding, a world which gives it its unity. Differentiated, each one of the lovers is a thing which has a form. Entangled, they are only one thing which only has a single form.

In the case of their entanglement, the lovers are together in the envelopment of their love, of their relationship, separating them from the world, like a layer giving them a unique form. They are together in this love, and this love is in the world as a unique thing. In the case of their distinction, each lover is in the world, and the other lover is thus entangled along with everything else in 'everything which is not the first lover'. To be in the world is not to be in things, and therefore to lose the distinction of things which are all entangled in 'everything which is not me', being loved, being hated, and being indifferent.

Two things, or several things, cannot enter into the world together since they could only enter into the world all in one piece, as a 'set', and in this way would lose their distinction. If two things are in the world, then only their duality is in the world, and the two things are together in this duality, which is a 'big thing'.

I can only consider that *this* or *that* is a thing provided that I situate it in the world, that is, outside things. But what this thing is in relation to other things, namely, what it is as an object, I can only discover or construct in its relations with other things, by isolating or limiting a thing within this or that more important thing: in the physical universe, in history, in language, and so on.

Like any other thing, I enter as a thing alone into the world. Solitude is by definition the only relation to the world. Solitude is a way of being independent of unity and of isolation. Isolation is a distancing, a separation by a distance, by a wall, which has attained a certain intensity deemed significant vis-à-vis similar things. Unity consists in being one object among other objects, and therefore in counting as one among similar ones. Solitude is the result of being a thing in the world, namely, of being the only thing within the opposite of a thing, within what is not something.

The human experience of solitude is simply the *human* relation to the world, a relation different from the relation of a rock or an idea to the world. But the human experience of solitude is a meta-relation, a relational relation [*un rapport de rapport*]; the relation itself is shared, beyond humanity or life or materiality, by everything which is something. Solitude is what defines the thing in general.

In other words, things communicate only by their solitude – it is because every thing is equally alone in the world that things can be together in each other.

If things were not solitary, then they would never be together.

Solitude is equal and not shared. This coat's blue colour is something (whether it is something for me, for someone else, for the coat itself, it doesn't matter) as much as the blue of the sky and the sky are something. The coat's blue colour as a thing is alone in the world, that is to say, on the background of everything which is not this coat's blue, including the blue of the sky and the sky. But these three things are not alone together. Each one is exclusively solitary. When the coat's blue is something, the blue of the sky cannot be something, no more than the sky, this table, or the idea of war. When the sky is something, since it is something, nothing else is something. In other words, in order for the sky to be something, it is necessary that nothing else can be something. Only one thing exists at a time. The existence of a thing as a thing destroys the possibility of the existence of another thing: only this thing exists, since this thing is in everything except this thing, in that which is not a thing, which we call the world.

Each thing is alone insofar as it is *exclusively* a thing. Two things cannot be at the same time – otherwise, it is a matter of what we will call two 'objects', namely, things which are together, which count together in another thing.

To consider a manifold of objects is the ordinary act of knowledge, of action, and of perception. But in order for there to be a

manifold of given objects, some of them in and through others, it
is necessary that each one can be a thing, and therefore, implicitly, that each one be given, constructed, known, recognised, or
perceived as a thing, that is, as a solitary thing and as exclusively
a thing.

For there to be objective systems of knowledge, thought, action,
memory, will, intention, perception, proprioception, desire, or any
other active relation to objects, it is necessary that these objects
also be solitary things; their manifold is impossible without the
exclusive solitude of each one. If each thing were not exclusively
alone, then there would either be a manifold of nothing, or a
compact manifold of everything. In order for manifolds – given
or constructed by objects (material objects, historical objects,
linguistic objects, ideal objects) – to exist, it is necessary that these
objects be distinct enough to be together. Solitude in the world is
the condition of distinction for belonging to an aggregate.

And if each thing is in the world, then no thing is in itself.

IV. Nothing is in Itself

1. Spatial representational models are often employed to
describe the possibility or impossibility of something, anything,
being in itself. According to the idea of spatial location, something
is within something else like I am within this room, that is, within
either an intuitive or complex topologically determined space.
On this view, the possibility or impossibility of a thing in itself
depends on a given space.

2. Some claim that a thing is within another thing not only in a
spatial sense, but also in a mathematical sense of set membership.
Something would then be in another thing like two is in three,
since an element belongs to some collection of elements. On this
view, the possibility or impossibility of a thing in itself depends on
given axioms.

3. Some also claim that a thing is in another thing not only
in a mathematical or set-theoretical sense, but also in a very
particular logical sense concerning predication and attribution.
Something would then be in another thing like a sky which is
blue is in blueness. Everything which is linguistically attributed to

something comprehends in this way what the thing is attributed to. On this view, the possibility of a thing in itself depends on a given logical model.

4. However, here we understand the fact of 'being in' more broadly than in the context of spatial, mathematical, or logical models. If 'being in' were limited to these models, then it could always be objected that something can or cannot be in itself merely as a result of some topologically defined space, some mathematics, or some logic.

Yet, what is important is not only the 'in' in 'being in', which may refer to a spatial, logical, or mathematical model, but also the 'being'. For us, 'being in' means precisely what 'being' may mean. If 'being' is equivalent to 'being in', it is not insofar as 'in' adds nothing to the meaning of being, but insofar as being directly means 'in'.

5. To be in something and to be something are equivalent.

6. It is not necessary to define 'being in' according to a spatial model of that within which things are, but to understand the 'in' as being.

7. Being only is by two limits: that which is something and that which something is. No thing is *as a whole* another thing.

8. Every thing is defined by *that which is in the thing* and *that in which the thing is*.

9. Every thing is penetrated by that which is the thing, and penetrates that which the thing is.

10. Being is therefore the difference between two limits of every thing: that which is the thing and that which the thing is.

11. Being is 'in' because it is the difference between 'in the thing' and 'the thing in'.

12. The possibility or impossibility of being *in itself* does not derive from a spatial, mathematical, or logical model, but from the model of 'something'. If something is defined by the difference

between 'in the something' and 'the something in', by the difference between that which is something and that which something is, then how could something be *in itself*?

13. Our model of something does not entail that something cannot be in itself – because 'something cannot be in itself' is, rather, the very *meaning* of this model.

14. If something were in itself, then there would not be something.

15. That something may be in itself is not impossible, but simply the possibility that this something is impossible.

16. A thing is almost like a bag. There is what one places in the bag and what remains outside the bag. The question is: assuming that one can fill a bag with anything, can one place the bag in itself? If I grab the outside of the bottom of the bag, desperately trying to put it into its upper compartment, my exercise will more or less quickly reach its limit. At best, I will succeed in turning the bag inside out, such that what was its inside becomes its outside, and vice versa. In this case, I have inverted content and container without successfully making them one and the same.
    So a thing is not exactly like a bag, for a thing is not a thin skin or layer. Rather, a thing is equivalent to an immaterial bag without layers. A thing is nothing other than the *difference* between that which is this thing and that which this thing is – between content and container.

17. A thing in itself is both that which is in the thing and that in which the thing is. It is therefore two selves simultaneously – the self which is and the self which the thing is.

18. A thing *in itself* would confound content and container, that which is in the thing and that in which the thing is.
    To be in itself is to not make any difference between that which is and that which this is. Now, a thing is reduced precisely to the difference between that which is the thing and that which the thing is: its *self*.

Self

Everything *has* a self because nothing *is* in itself. The self is not the quality of what relates to itself (which is conscious, for example), or which thinks it does so. Nonetheless, for a 'conscious' being to relate to itself, it is necessary that this very relation be something other than the self to which it relates.

A cloud, like a record, a musical tune, a dust particle, a word, the echo of this word, or an infinitesimal part of this echo – all these things have a self insofar as they are something, they are not in themselves, and they are therefore not 'themselves'. The self is what is forbidden to each thing in order for it to be what it is. The self is what we are not, what we cannot be, and that something else is, which is us.

The self is my being which escapes my comprehension. No thing can comprehend itself. A conscious being can merely comprehend its situation, that is, represent what comprehends it.

Consciousness is far from being the faculty of comprehending oneself (which always leads to a downward spiral of discourses about the self, continually chasing away what one recaptures, the commonplace of impotent modern consciousness from Monsieur Teste to Ulrich, 'the Man without qualities'). Consciousness is the possibility of comprehending the world, that is, of doing the same to what comprehends us. We are only conscious insofar as we can turn to everything that comprehends us, to everything in which we are: physical matter, nature, culture, society, political structures, family, history, functions. But we ourselves do not comprehend ourselves, and we cannot comprehend ourselves. I do not comprehend myself, society does not comprehend itself, nature does not comprehend itself: each thing is exiled from what it comprehends, and situates what the thing is outside what the thing comprehends.

The self is not something. The self is a process through which being and comprehension are mutually excluded, a process whereby what is a thing is not confounded with what a thing is.

Therefore, there is no self-consciousness. There is only consciousness of the world. The self is the shadow of a doubt of everything that casts some light. The self is what prevents every relation of self to self, and allows a relation to the world, to something other than itself. The self is only closed to itself as a thing is in the world. What is in itself goes outside the world, or, more precisely, is defined as 'compact', that is, as only being possible on the condition of its failure.

The rock's self is the process that precludes the rock being composed of itself, and that makes the rock be in something other than itself: a desert, the Earth, a topological model, a cognitive space, a postcard.

The rock's self has nothing different from the human self, myself, yourself, a cat's self, or an adjective's self. Our self does not make us singular, but binds us to our common condition as things.

The impossibility of being myself is equivalent to the impossibility of a rat being a rat itself, a drop of rain a drop of rain itself, the entire solar system the entire solar system itself – in other words, the impossibility of being a *compact* thing.

V. Compactness

1. Being in itself is the expression of the desire to represent a being as a whole.

2. The possibility of something in itself exists, provided that one specify that this possibility is the possibility *that there cannot be this something*. If something is in itself, it is because there is confusion between 'that which is' and 'that which it is', between 'that which is in this thing' and 'that in which this thing is': 'self'. We are left with two possibilities. Either a minimal difference exists between the self 'which is in' and the self 'in which it is', in which case there is not one self but two selves. Or no difference exists between the self which is in and the self in which it is, in which case there cannot be something, since something is defined simply as the difference of the 'in' between *that which is in* and *that in which it is*.

In the first case, two selves exist. In the second case, no selves exist. Something 'in itself' either comprehends *two things*, or comprehends *no thing*.

3. Being in itself is being itself. Something which is itself parts from one of its two limits. Either there is no something to be itself, or there is no itself to be something (there are *two* of them).

In other words, being in itself is only the possibility of its double failure.

4. The possibility of the failure of its own conditions of possibilities is what we call *compact*.

5. Compactness is not impossibility, but the possibility of making itself impossible.

6. Something is not in itself, because if there were something in-itself, there would not be something to be in itself.

7. Being something is being *in* something; and *that which* something is is *that in which* something is.

If something were in something, one would confound that which is something and that which something is (since something *would be* something). Therefore, a thing cannot be a thing. For this reason, being *one* thing among other things is not what makes a thing a *thing*. What makes a thing a thing is not being counted among other things, but being a *solitary* thing in 'something other than a thing'.

8. Something is not *in* something.

9. What is something? That is to say: *where* is something? Outside.

10. To come inside a thing is to situate oneself outside it.

11. Nothing is enclosed within. Everything opens to the outside.

12. All possibilities open up in the world, including the possibility of impossibility.

Impossible

Inasmuch as no-matter-what is something, when *everything* is outside, possibility is not the opposite of impossibility. Possibility includes impossibility, since impossibility is possible in the sense that it is *something* (even if it is a word, a contradiction, a mistaken idea and nothing more). Impossibility is not opposed as a whole to possibility, but marks one possibility among others. Impossibility is not imprisoned in solitary confinement, deprived of being in the world, outside, free yet condemned to appear in the world like everything else.

The problem is not that there is nothing impossible, but that there are impossibilities which are possible.

However, by collapsing impossibility into possibility, an oft-dismissed problem must be confronted: on what does our designation of what we deny the possibility of depend? By claiming that nothing is in itself, we assume that being itself is a possibility which is prevented, inoperative, nonexistent, harmful, and so on. In short, we cannot put forward an open view of possibility, where no-matter-what is something, where no-matter-what is possible, without making use of a *negative* tool through which we deny some possibility – for example, the possibility that everything is not possible, that we deny here. Why do we rule out what we deny? First and foremost, *where* do we dismiss what we deny, if everything can be in the world? *Where* do we establish the possibility of being in itself, or the possibility that there are impossible things? If we accept these two possibilities in the world (the possibility of being in itself and the possibility of impossibility) by claiming that they are possibilities even if they are false or bad, then by assuming the contradiction we include them (since they would be in the world in the same way as the impossibility of being in itself, or as the impossibility of impossibility) and can no longer deny them. If we think that they are 'false', 'ugly', or 'bad' possibilities, then we appeal to values, to the *importance* of things, which are not requirements of *no-matter-what*.

Nevertheless, if we formally exclude these possibilities from the world by claiming that they are not in the world, that they do not exist, that they are not possible (and not only that they are false), then our claim that 'no-matter-what is in the world' and 'no-matter-what is something' falls flat. In other words, by guaranteeing that *everything* is possible, that possibility has no limit, and that no-matter-what can be something (including something unreal, false, contradictory, impossible, unthinkable, unimaginable), we seem to make the same mistake as whoever is open to making everything possible, including the necessity of its own loss of possibility. For, if everything is possible, then what is the status of impossibility? If impossibility is possible, then everything is not possible and impossibility is not possible. But if impossibility is impossible, then everything is not possible and something is impossible. In the first case, what it includes escapes from possibility. In the second case, what it precludes escapes from possibility.

The second problem is that by thinking that everything is

possible, that everything can equally be something, one surrenders, through the denial of all *negativity*, every place in which what is unwanted is ruled out. Every theory constructs its prison, a place outside the world where it dispenses with what is false, impossible, non-being, powerless, or evil. We might call this the non-place or penal colony where every theory denies what is outside the world.

On the other hand, if we claim that the world is unlimited and that nothing is outside the world, then we no longer have at our disposal this tool that every theory forges in order to reduce and limit the world. We no longer have anywhere – outside the world – to deny what is not, what is impossible, what prevents the world's functioning, what we must abandon so that there is something, so that this open world is possible.

In this way, the self is precisely what we must abandon here, so that there is something and a world. Nothing is in itself. Everything is outside itself. No-matter-what is something, is in something other than itself. A difference is maintained between that which is in the thing and that in which the thing is.

But is being in itself simply *forbidden* (which would only be a rule of operation), or, rather, is it absolutely *impossible*? What is the precise status of our denial of being in itself? The argument that being in itself is impermissible is too weak. It is still possible, but it *is not necessary* that it is possible (because it is bad or because it prevents the possibility of another thing). In this case, the denial of being in itself is too relative. To guarantee the possibility of something, one denies being in itself. Being in itself in fact would be possible if we gave up this something. This is still an option. Yet, we don't want to *forbid* the in-itself; it would not be prohibited from being in itself, simply because we necessarily prevent this possibility. This possibility, we think, forbids itself by itself, and not by some choice or theoretical 'will' on our part.

By considering the in-itself to be impossible or *absolutely* impossible, we deny the in-itself on account of the tools given to us, or on account of the disarmed state in which we are willingly situated. Since there would no longer be anything outside the world, where what we deny is thrown, we must make do in our world with what must be denied for this world to be possible.

I cannot consider the in-itself as absolutely impossible, and I cannot forbid its possibility either. Is this to say that our world, open to no-matter-what, is quite simply unjustifiable?

There remains a way of thinking of what does not fully enter into, without going outside of, the world.

We define this way of thinking as *compact thinking*.

Being itself is neither forbidden nor impossible. Try being oneself. Being itself is a possibility. We argue and talk about it, though it may be a non-being or a contradiction. Therefore, being itself is compact.

Whatever short-circuits the senses of being and of comprehension is compact. What self-comprehends itself, or rather what seeks to self-comprehend itself, is compact. Self-comprehending itself is not impossible, but self-comprehending itself is only possible on one condition: that the thing comprehend itself and that nothing be this thing.

Compactness is a self-ball [*boule de soi*]. Compactness is a theory that self-comprehends itself, a first principle, an absolute, an absolutely higher and solitary being, or a substance.

Now, compactness is not impossible. Compactness is really a possibility of the world. We will identify a number of compact points in our thinking. But what is compact is possible if and only if nothing is the compact thing. If a being is posited as being in itself, then this being is possible, but if and only if nothing is this being.

Everything which is compact is self-identical. There is no difference or distinction in compactness. Everything which is compact self-identifies.

Compactness is the opposite of the world. Everything enters into the world, and the world enters into nothing. On the other hand, compactness enters into the world (it is something), but nothing enters into it. Compactness is a self-ball, but contains no thing.

Being in itself is therefore possible, but nothing is in itself. More precisely, being in itself is possible if and only if nothing is in itself.

What is compact – what situates itself outside the world but enters into itself – doubly fails: first, because compactness is in the world, and second, because nothing is compact.

Being compact is to want to go outside the world or to not be in something other than in itself. Yet, what is in itself is in the world, and therefore in something other than itself. It is precisely in this sense that *impossibility is in possibility* – in other words, that going outside possibility enters into possibility itself. But nothing is in impossibility. Impossibility is an empty possibility.

Impossibility is therefore conceivable. However, I can consider it only as empty.

Accordingly, two problems arise. First, how can I claim that *a thing* is compact if nothing is compact, or if compactness is empty? Second, have I not brushed aside the problem of impossibility, by claiming that compactness was possible if and only if nothing is compact (which would mean that in reality the impossibility is that something is compact, simply shifting the emphasis of the problem)?

Our first response is that if compactness is the possibility of a thing to fill the world with *emptiness*, then no thing can embody compactness and be compact in the strict sense. The tool that we just forged to neutralise some possibilities without excluding them from the world already appears broken and counterproductive. Compactness exists – allowing us to consider what we deny, without situating it outside the world – only if nothing can be compact. This hardly settles the matter. But we understand that everything that we described as compact is in reality only the reflection of the same operation: being itself, impossibility, the absolute, substantiality, and self-consciousness are many seemingly different illustrations of the same capacity. In other words, being itself or being impossible is not strictly compact, but *aims at* compactness. Individuated illustrations set in motion the common operation of compactness. In this way, processes that lead to compactness begin with the assumption that being itself is impossible or absolute. Mechanisms of thought lead to self-identity. When something becomes compact, it loses its specificity, draws closer to being in itself and the absolute, and aims at compactness – at that which, being in the world, comprehends nothing.

In the strict sense, nothing *is* compact. Only things can become compact, by initiating certain thought processes (self-reflexivity, the search for substantiality, the absolute, wisdom, self-consciousness, and so on) that situate them outside the world, empty them of something that is not them, until they lose their matter and individuality. But everything that *becomes* compact fails. To successfully be compact is to lose oneself. Compactness exists, but nothing is compact.

What becomes compact contributes to its own loss. What becomes compact is neither forbidden (for example, through spiritual discipline) nor impossible (since one can do the impossible). But what becomes compact is, in the strict sense, empty.

Our second response is that by proposing this model of compactness – rather than the ideas of prohibition, contradiction, self-refutation, impossibility, impotence, non-being, or the variable importance of the ugly, false, bad, or useless – one does not simply brush aside the problem of impossibility. One neutralises it. What is compact is impossible, but if and only if nothing is compact. One might think that *something is compact* is therefore impossible. But this is not the case, for compactness operates at every scale. *That something is compact* is therefore equally compact. For the fact that something is compact is not impossible; it is a possibility if and only if nothing is *something*, in other words, that no thing is.

One might think that we continue to brush aside the problem; what is implicitly impossible is that no thing is. But once more, it is only compact, not impossible; that no thing is is compact, for nothing *in itself* is required.

Accordingly, compactness brushes aside impossibility ad infinitum. Compactness doesn't exclude impossibility from the world, but neutralises it. Impossibility is always possible, but it is compact, that is, its condition is always at the same time its failure.

Compactness is the presence in the world of impossibility, its mode of possibility: failure. Nothing is impossible, but some thing (*compactness*) is possible if and only if it fails – and fails in the world.

VI. Something-Other-than-a-Thing

1. The sole *condition* of a thing is to be in something-other-than-itself, and thus in something-other-than-something.

2. What is a condition? A condition determines something; it *forms* something: that in which something is.

An event does not take place without the condition of an event. The condition of an event is precisely its place. The condition of my saying 'yes' rests on your accompanying me. If you accompany me, this event, my saying 'yes', takes place; in other words, I would say 'yes' only 'within the context' of your accompanying me.

The condition of someone is their situation. My social condition is what socially determines me, my place, and my function. My domestic situation is the way in which my family circle models me.

Being conditioned is being reduced to what one is in.

Yet every thing has a condition, since no thing is in itself. Nothing is absolutely authentic or free (otherwise nothing itself would be compact); more or less, everything is either more or less conditioned.

Nonetheless, no thing is reduced to its condition either, since that which is in something is not reduced to that in which the thing is.

The condition of a thing is not being in itself. If a thing were in itself, then no thing would be.

Every thing is conditionally, but no thing is reduced to this condition.

3. The formal condition of a thing is *everything except itself*.

To determine the condition of this or that thing is to determine *what* it is *in* in some way or another.

To determine the condition of every thing is to determine what something, anything, is in.

In this sense, something is in 'what is not something'.

4. If I determine or define 'what is not something', then 'what is not something' must be 'something', given the open-ended definition of something, which admits of no limit.

5. If I consider what 'what is not something' may be, I arrive at an impasse. What is not something cannot be *defined* by what this something is, because this something is *undefined* by what this something is: everything except something.

6. Let us consider *what* may be 'what is not something'. Any thing may be 'what is not something'. Only 'what is not something' cannot be 'what is not something'.

I can only define 'what is not something' unilaterally: what is not a thing is what every thing may be. What is not in a thing is what *every thing* can be in.

7. When it is only possible to define something by limiting what is defined, we may call this a 'unilateral definition' ['*définition sans retour*']. In this way, 'what is not something' is reduced to every thing's possibility of being 'what is not something', what is nothing.

Nevertheless, this 'unilateral definition' teaches us a great deal;

what is in 'what is not something' is something. Therefore, a thing is in all that contradicts it. A thing is in its opposite.

8. The condition of a thing is its negative.

9. A thing, anything, ends where what is not a thing begins.

10. A thing is what is finite and defined. What is not a thing is infinite and undefined. A thing is what ends. What is not a thing is what *begins*.

11. There is no 'bilateral' [*aller-retour*] definition of 'what is not something', since 'what is not something' is endless. Nonetheless, it is possible to consider, talk about, and conceive of 'what is not something'. 'What is not something' begins. 'What is not something' is what begins *where every thing ends*. 'What is not something' is nothing other than every thing's finitude conceived as a beginning.

12. A thing begins with no-matter-what and ends with its negative.
No-matter-what is what ends as a thing, and what does not begin. I cannot define *what is* no-matter-what, since no-matter-what is precisely what no thing is. 'No-matter-what' is defined by one of its limits: that which it is. It is a definition with return and without departure.

13. A thing is defined by its two limits. I can define *that which is* something ('no-matter-what') and *that which* something *is* ('something other than something'). I can define that through which a thing begins and that through which it ends. But I cannot define a thing as a whole, unless I make it compact. There is no unilateral definition of a thing; there is only a departing definition *and* a returning definition.

14. 'What is not something' is what begins with the end of every thing, but does not end: I cannot define or end *what* 'what is not something' *is*. 'What is not something' is defined by only one limit: *what is 'what is not something'*. It is a definition with departure and without return.

15. How do we designate what is not something? We have called what something is not 'no-matter-what'. In so doing, we do not define, but we *name* what is accessible only through a single limit.

16. We name 'something other than a thing' either 'the world' or 'all'.

17. They are two different configurations of 'something other than a thing'. Since 'something other than a thing' is the *condition* of every thing, and that in which every thing is, one can name this 'the world'. Since 'something other than a thing' is the *negative* of every thing and is not a thing, one can name this 'all'.

18. 'All' is the negative of something, what is not something.

19. 'The world' is the condition of something, what something is in.

20. 'All' and 'the world' are synonymous. They correspond to the two configurations of 'what is not something'. In one configuration, 'what is not something' *ends* every thing ('what is not something' is 'the world'). In the other configuration, 'what is not something' *does not end* ('what is not something' is 'all'). Since 'what is not something' is the end of each thing and since it does not have an end, 'the world' and 'all' have two configurations, but they designate one and the same form.

Going Outside the World is a Way of Entering Inside it

Let us imagine a vicious circle, or, more literally, a snake chasing its tail, desperately trying to consume itself and to pass wholly into itself – the mythical Ouroboros, the Serpent King, the symbol of continuity, and the gnostic and Hermetic dream of the absolute. The snake begins by swallowing itself, devouring the tip of its tail and the rest of its body. In the end, the snake is caught in a trap, this mortal coil, and chokes.

If the snake could devour itself, then it would be both *all* and *nothing*. If the snake were eaten, it would not be anything any more. But if the snake swallowed itself, it would embody all, since it would comprehend itself in itself and not be in anything else. The *absolute* is in itself, alone, and independent of the rest of the world. The absolute is both the fantasy of self-fertilisation and of the alchemical concept of *en to pan* ('all is one').

Our snake representing the ideal return of eternal subsistence materialises both the hope and the failure of a complete self-adequation to itself, apart from the world. If the Ouroboros could make what is in it correspond to what it is in, then it would become a solitary container and content. What is in the snake is its tail, the bottom half of its body. What the snake is in is the top half of its body, its mouth. Its body is divided in two, eaten and eating. It devours, as form, something, as object, which is only itself.

But the gnostic Serpent King can never be self-saturated to nothingness and the absolute. Why? Because it inevitably ends by creating a loop, an increasingly limited channel of being, an increasingly tightened slipknot, which, while continually shrinking, does not vanish into thin air, allowing nothingness to subsist. The snake becomes *compact*, an indistinct mass of what is devoured and what devours – it does not remain in itself, but only forms a rather pathetic mass. We name this obstacle 'compactness' – the way something aims to be in itself in order to be all or nothing, and appears as a solid and empty thing that fails in the world. To be compact is to want to be in itself and to *fail at doing so*. To be compact is to seek an exit from the world and to *fail at doing so*. Something always resists: if not the life of the pagans' snake, at least its existence, and if not its existence, at least the fact that it existed or was possible – and, in the end, one cannot take away, and the Serpent King cannot destroy, the Serpent King's *chance*. The Serpent King does not fade from the world; it does not go outside the world by entering into itself.

A thing cannot make itself disappear from the world. To be in itself would be to not be in the world, and therefore to not be something.

Why does one withdraw into oneself when one is timid and when one plays the snake that bites its tail? Why does one retreat into the circle of self-consciousness? Because one hopes not to remain outside. One would like not to embody something. The only imaginable escape outside the world is in itself, but this escape has no *exit*.

To want to be in itself is *like another* way of being in the world. One is neither less in the world nor more in the world when hiding away in a serpentine, compact ball of timidity. In the last analysis, one is equally in the world. We cannot say that those who want to be in themselves are *less* in the world, nor that they are *more* in the world. We are neither prohibiting a thing from being in itself nor explaining that being in itself is useless. We must simply demonstrate that a thing is *neither more nor less* than a way of being in the world. We must tell this tale to every timid person and to the alchemical serpent.

Our argument does not consist in demonstrating that it is *impossible* to be in itself, nor that it is *useless*, *bad*, or *false* to be in itself. To try to be in itself is to attempt to remain outside the world. And indeed, to try to be in itself is only an entryway into this world. What interests us is precisely this *inevitable* relation of every thing to the world – whether or not the thing accepts or denies this relation.

All highways, back alleys, and exit ramps lead a thing to the world.

To not want to be in the world is one way of arriving at the world. To go outside the world is one *way* of entering into the world.

Things are in the world.

Notes

1. Émile Durkheim, *The Elementary Forms of Religious Life*, p. 300. [Translators' note: Durkheim's definition was added to the English translation at the request of the author.]
2. Aristotle, *Metaphysics*, IV, 1005b19–20, p. 1588.
3. Edmund Husserl, *Ideas Pertaining to a Pure Phenomenology and to a Phenomenological Philosophy: First Book*, p. 109.

Part II

Thing and World

World

The world is not the a priori container that pre-exists the things it contains, nor the a posteriori mental construction of the fictional set of all things. The world is strictly *contemporaneous* with things, or, more precisely, with each thing. If things exist, then a world exists.

Now, things exist, and therefore a world exists.

Some represent the world as the physical universe, the primary, material world. Others reflexively represent a secondary representation or a mental construction to totalise and unify the set of existent things.

But these representations only apply to *determinate* worlds: the world of matter (which for the materialist is the only world, the limit-world) and the world of mind (the world constructed by intentionality, the lifeworld). These worlds are not the world of things. They are the world of *material* things, the world of *mental* things, the Husserlian *Lebenswelt* or lifeworld, or the world of thought, language, or conscious life.

Every determinate world is in fact a *universe*, a 'big thing' – a set (as large as it may be) of composite things. Each determinate world embodies a thing. A determinate world is a thing that other things are, and that is thus something: nothing other than a stable *milieu* between the things that compose it and the thing that it composes. Every determinate world is the world that we represent as a physical, expanding, finite or infinite universe, and

75

is itself a cosmological object that has particular qualities (speed of expansion, cosmological constant, structure formation, and so on). It is the world that we also represent as a mere mentally constructed *universal* concept, which unifies our experiences and itself has a unity – the unity of a product of our understanding or of our mental functioning, a transcendental condition, or a result of evolutionary processes. It is the 'always already there' world of our sensible intuition, that we live on the horizon of and that we constitute as such. It is the world, in one way or another, which attributes certain determinations and is attributed other determinations.

Now, the world is what something (and not merely each object) is and what it is not.

We do not claim that the world, as we understand it, 'exists'. The materialist will ask us to show them the world, to give a form to the world, that is, to materialise the world as a *thing*. The metaphysician will call for the extension and comprehension of it, its determinations, and modes of accessibility. The phenomenologist will await the experiential description of it, and will continuously refer us to what the world is for and by us.

On the contrary, we hold that the world is not, and that this is the condition of its definition. More precisely, we claim that the world is *what is not something*. Something never is '*tout court*', any more than something is *not* '*tout court*'. Something is or is not *something*. The world is precisely what is not something. The world has no other determination; it is neither material nor spiritual, neither logical nor symbolic, neither metaphysical nor sensible. The world is not something, full stop.

But then one may object: this world is a pure non-being, a ghost, a ridiculous and indefensible mental construction, a mere fantasy!

Certainly not, for every thing obtains being bilaterally: if the world is not something, this does not mean that nothing is the world – quite the contrary. Each thing *is* the world.

Nevertheless, I cannot turn round the proposition and conclude that the world *is* 'what each thing is', since the world is *not* something. Since the world is not a thing, every thing, anything, can be the world, that is, be *in* the world.

On this view, the world is a universal impasse: each world, each thing enters into the world, and the world enters into nothing.

For this reason, the world, only a beginning and never an end, comprehends all and is comprehended by nothing. Being exists in only one sense.

Everything takes part in the world and the world takes part in nothing. When one characterises one side of the world (and not simply its reverse side), one determines it, and makes it some 'big thing'. It then becomes the world of coexistent objects that excludes other objects (that do not correspond to its determination, such as non-material objects for a material world, objects external to consciousness for a world of consciousness, and so on). This world is itself something (a god, cosmos, physical universe, the course of history, organic totality, social or cultural construction, mental perspective, and so on).

But even if everything is in the world, the world is never in anything: neither in itself, nor in something other than the world, nor in me.

I. Something-Other-than-a-Thing: The World

1. The world is the form of things.

2. If the form of a thing is its condition, this form is always simultaneously its negative, since the form of a thing is not a thing.

3. Form is what determines each thing and is simultaneously its surrounding, its reverse side, and its negative.

4. The world does not *have* any form, since it *is* the form of each thing.

5. The world is not *something*, therefore it is not.
Far from being inexpressible, unthinkable, or nonexistent, since the world is not, the world can only be caught by the tail; it remains faceless.

6. The world is an impasse: each thing enters into it, and nothing goes outside it.

7. The world does not have any particular quality.

II. Where is a Thing? In the World

1. Where is a thing? What is a thing? These two questions amount to the same thing.

2. A thing can be in an infinite number of other things. What a thing *is* changes according to that in which one considers it to be located. A thing is nothing in itself, always in another thing, the thing that it is in.

3. A thing is *in this way* in this thing, and *in another way* in that other thing.
I am in a city. I am in a society. I am in a culture. I am in atoms and molecules. I am in the perceptual field of someone who looks at me and who judges me. I am in my flesh. I am in evolution. I am in history. I am in a square metre. I am in unity. I am in baggy clothing.
But I am not in myself.

4. Each thing is in other things which are in other things. The membership relations between some things and other things are knowable. They are the subject of intuitive and common-sense propositions, and they are the subject of well-formed scientific propositions. They are objective.

5. If a thing is in another thing, then it is an *object*. An object is a thing with form that is another thing. An object is a thing limited by other things and conditioned by one or several things.

6. To consider, handle, and know some things in other things consists in proving that they are *objective*.

7. Every thing has two configurations. The first is that a thing is an *object* insofar as it is comprehended in other things. The second is that a thing is a *thing* insofar as it is comprehended in something-other-than-a-thing.

8. A thing is in a form even if it is embedded in a complex and infinite number of objective relations.

9. By keeping a dog in my basement, I do not remove the dog from the world.

10. A thing can be contained in another thing, but this situation doesn't separate the thing from the world. A thing is objectively this or that in this or that objective condition. In other words, a thing is inside some other thing, some other event, or some other situation. But a thing formally remains a thing insofar as it is alone in its condition and its negation.

11. An object has determinate conditions. A thing has a de-determinate, formal condition.

12. A thing can be in other things – be an object – since a thing always remains in something other than a thing.

13. If there were nothing *except* objects, then there would be no objects.

14. A thing can be in another thing since these two things – comprehending and comprehended – are equally but separately in the world.

15. Objects are *unequal*. A thing that comprehends another thing is objectively more than the thing it comprehends. A thing comprehended by another thing is objectively less than the thing that comprehends it.
Things are *equal*. Each thing is equally in something-other-than-a-thing.

16. The condition of the inequality of objects is the equality of things.

17. If each thing were not alone in the world, then things could never be in each other.
For the branch to be in the tree, to be a part of the tree, this branch must be in the world *neither more nor less* than the tree. As a 'thing', the branch is in the world – that is, in everything except itself, in everything that surrounds it, in everything that begins infinitely where the branch ends. As an 'object', the branch is in the tree.

18. Every thing is alone in the world. The world is that in which something is alone. And I am alone in the world like any other thing.

Without Me

If there were nothing to think about the world, nothing to be conscious of it, nothing even to perceive or sense it, would there only be one world?

It is a great logical mistake to make the existence of this something depend on its relation to something. Insofar as nothing is in itself, it is impossible to relate to something without this something existing outside itself. More precisely, it is impossible to be in relation to something that always arises from this relation. If I try to relate to something that only exists through this relation, it would be impossible for me to relate to it. I cannot relate to my relation to things, unless I relate to this relation as if it were *something*. This is possible, to the extent that the relation derives both from me and from *something other* than me.

I cannot relate to what depends only on me, or to what is only through me. What depends only on me or what is only through me would be something insufficiently distinct from me for me to enter in relation with it.

In other words, given the constraints on my relating to the world, I can most certainly not think that the being of the world to which I relate depends on the relation that I maintain with it. On the contrary, given the constraints on my relating to the world, I can only conclude that the world is something other than a thing that I am.

The *thought* world is what depends on my thinking about the world. The *known* world is what depends on my knowledge of the world. The *sensed* world is what depends on my sensation.

The world *tout court*, the being of the world, can under no circumstances depend on my relation to it. As a general rule, the fact that I see something presupposes that something outside my sight exists, and the fact that I remember presupposes that something outside my memory exists.

If there were nothing to think about the world, no thought world would be, no world that is thought about by me would be, but the world that I think about would inevitably be. If there were nothing to sense the world, no sensed world would be, but the world that this sensation relates to would certainly be.

The relation, any relation, to a thing or to the world is never the condition of possibility of the thing, but the very proof that it is not the condition of possibility of the thing. The relation is certainly the condition of *givenness* of what the relation places in relation, which means that I cannot represent what the form of the thing would be without the form in which this thing is *given* to me (I cannot visually represent what something I see would be like if there were nothing to see it). At the same time, nothing else can be given to me except what I do not already have (I cannot see something other than the thing insofar as this something-other-than-a-thing is *outside* my sight).

What I relate to always exists outside my relation to it. But what relates to me only exists for me. In other words, what I see is independent of my sight of it, but what is seen is completely dependent on my sight of it. Every relation is directional. In the direction from me to my object, the object must exist outside me and outside the relation that leads to it, otherwise the relation would relate to the relation, which would relate to the relation, and so on, such that the relation would be in itself (yet, nothing is in itself). In the direction from the object to me – that is, not the object aimed at, but the object's effect on me (through the light of an image, the perceived frequency of a sound, and so on) – by definition, this object exists only for me insofar as I perceive it.

If there were nothing to sense the world, many things in the world would be, but the world would be for none of these things. In this way, a world would be, but a world for nothing and for no one; the world would be neither perceived nor sensed, neither known nor thought.

By relating to things, I have access to the things just as they are outside me, but in a movement of departure and return through which things cannot return to me (in perception, representation, knowledge, thought) except *for* me (otherwise I would have no representation or perception of things, since things would not return to me, to myself). Every relation to the world and to things is carried out in two senses. By relating to things, I have access to what is outside me, and I cannot do otherwise. But these things must also relate to me, and I must always receive them just as they are through and for the relation that connects me to them.

By confusing the two senses of every relation to things and to the world in perception, knowledge, and thought, the two directions – from me to things and from things to me – are made incomprehensible. Either I believe that I relate to an external world, without understanding how this world can relate to me except for and through my relation to this world; or I believe that what I am related to depends on the relation itself, without understanding that I must necessarily relate to something that in no way depends on the relation that I maintain with it in order to make this very relation possible.

I can therefore imagine what the world would be without me: a departure without return, a letter without addressee, a message in a bottle without anyone to discover it, and so on. The world without me is precisely what I relate to, but without the world being able to relate to me. The world without me is what I see, hear, sense, think of, aim at, like a lost child I would welcome back; but the world without me is a world that would never return to me.

The world without me is what I always have at my fingertips, in my eyes, throughout my entire life, nothing more, nothing less, with the exception that the world would not find me if I were not to exist and will no longer find me when I exist no more.

We must not think that the world deprived of my existence, or of the existence of all human or sentient beings, would lack us or would lack itself by our ceasing to exist. Rather, I or we would lack the world. A world without sentient beings to sense it would not deprive a sensibility of its existence (which is *absurd*); this world would simply be deprived of sensibility.

III. Where is the World?

1. Each thing is in the world precisely because the world is in no thing.

2. The world is the common place where each thing is alone. It is a common place and not a particular place.

3. If the world were somewhere, this somewhere would only need to disappear in order for the world to be no more. The world is nothing other than what things have in common, but nonetheless things do not share several parts of the world.

4. If the world is somewhere, then it is not the world.

5. To identify the world with a thing, and therefore with a

'place', is not impossible, even if the world were always the 'reverse side' that does not take place.

But this is only possible on two conditions: either there is no longer a world, or this is no longer the world. In the first case, the condition for there to be something disappears; in the second case, it is necessary to find another world in the very big thing that the world has become, a meta-world.

6. We should neither codify nor prevent the identification of the world with a thing, since human thought forms bigger and more comprehensive things so as to objectively order things in the world. But since the identification of the world with something, or some, or any entity, leads to compactness, the identification does not hold unless strengthened by the use of force: social pressure, rhetorical persuasion, physical force.

7. The compact world is not contradictory; it neutralises itself. It forms its own contradiction. Compactness is a possibility that ultimately prevents or delays itself.

8. Many methods of delaying compactness exist.

9. What is not compact makes itself an exception.

10. No-matter-what is something *apart from* everything. All things take place *with the exception of* the world, which is the place.

Exception

The world is an exception. But is there any contradiction in claiming that *no-matter-what is something* and that *the world is that which is not something*? Would this not situate the world outside the world?

The world is certainly not outside the world (unlike all mystical, critical, or theoretical transcendentalisms); that the world is not in the world (unlike in philosophies of immanence) does not mean that the world is outside. In short, the world is *not*; the world is not in something. The world is neither in the world – is not a thing that we can find around us, in our material environment, or in our mental products – nor in something – the world has no face and no form; it is not a thing, a god, an ordered universe, a sphere, or a continuum, which could take form, any form.

By definition, therefore, the world is not compact. The world does not short-circuit the sense of being and of comprehension. The world comprehends each thing, but the world is not in itself nor outside itself, nor in something else. If the world did have any one of these three properties – being in itself, outside itself, or in something else – then the world could become compact: the self-saturated world (substantial world); the world that exists outside the world or outside our access to it (transcendental world); the world that has the form of a thing, which is an object-world among other object-worlds (many worlds).

The world, everything's place, is an *impasse*; being enters the world and being does not go outside the world. But the world is not a *short-circuit*. Why, then, is the world not something, when we claimed that *no-matter-what* is something? Precisely because the world is not equivalent to no-matter-what; even though no-matter-what is the world (is *in* the world), the converse is not valid.

The world is thus the *exception* to no-matter-what; in order for no-matter-what to be something, it is necessary that *what things are* is not a thing.

The world that goes outside itself excepts itself. But it enters into nothing else.

Nonetheless, precisely because the world is not something, it is possible to make something of the world. One of the primary human activities consists in representing the world, presenting the world as if it were something. This activity is neither false nor improved on by understanding the impossibility of the world being something. On the contrary, one pursues many things only because one knows that one cannot capture them. One of the strongest human tendencies is the desire to represent the world; every human being vaguely knows or senses that when the world appears to them in the form of *something*, it is because this some-thing is not truly the world. But it is precisely this consciousness of the world that contributes to the desire to represent and to try to understand the world. I want to capture the world, but I only obtain a very big thing. But I always see glistening in the things their inverse, their negative, and their world.

Thus, human beings produce more and more comprehensive *big things*: cosmological theories, arguments about the formation of matter, history, sociology, evolution, religious representations, metaphysics, and so on. Through the arts – representational forms – or through the sciences – representational rules – human cultures accumulate representations of the world in the form of big things enmeshed in each other. In Book II, we try to understand the *objective* comprehension of things.

Now, *formally* comprehending the world allows us to *objectively* comprehend more and more things. An objective progression of the human comprehension of things exists only at the cost of an equal and formal comprehension of the world, which does not progress and cannot progress.

In other words, the fact that the world is not something makes the local progress in the knowledge of objects possible, while ultimately precluding it. Since the world is not something, a faint colour of failure always stains all human, artistic, scientific, religious, and metaphysical pictures of the world, including the one in this book. But they are great pictures, allowing the meticulous exploration of objects, the plurality of shades, the precision of lines, and so on.

If the world were something, we would never know any objects. Since the world is not something, it drives us to represent the world as a thing, and to fail at completing our picture of the world.

Thus, the world cannot be something, but we can make something of it if and only if the world is not this thing that we have made of it.

We must clarify our position. No-matter-what can be something *with the exception of* the world that things are and which is nothing. Playing with this exception is the very thread by which the most beautiful and important human materials are sewn, in which we adorn our whole environment: representations of the world as if the world were a big thing, a thing *apart from* things and *mattering* among these things through the actions and knowledge of our species, which crafts very big things.

What a Big Thing is

'Big things' exist apart from the existence of human beings, and even apart from the existence of sentient or living beings – though sensibility, cognition, thought, and the human species (like other species) have made an especial contribution to the inflation of things.

A 'big thing' is a thing that not only contains matter, like every thing – that is, strictly and formally 'that which is in the thing' – but that also contains several things in this thing in a differentiated way. A 'big thing' is thus not a thing whose size is more important (in any literal or metaphorical sense), but a thing whose composition is *differentiated* and swollen with other things. A thing is both a thing insofar as this thing has *indistinct* matter and a 'big thing' insofar as this matter is composed of *several distinct things*. The sponge that a primate can crudely assemble from dry leaves in order to rinse and clean off the soil covering a sweet potato is both a thing, insofar as this sponge has matter (everything that is a part of this sponge), and a 'big thing', insofar as it is a thing composed of other things: fifteen or sixteen leaves, stems, twigs, and the intention of washing the sweet potato.

Insofar as this sponge is the assemblage, the totality of material elements and of intentions, and perhaps the totality of signs or of a cultural inheritance (if an elder taught the primate how to make a sponge), the thing that the sponge is is a big thing – in other words, a meta-thing, a thing of things. The sponge is in fact a thing which exists in the world, but which is always the totality of other things which also exist in the world. In this way, the sponge and its components do not exist on the same plane (the sponge is not an element of the sponge, but only the sum of various elements that make up the sponge), though they all equally exist in the world. Formally, the sponge and the leaves that compose it are equal. The sponge exists just as much as the leaves. Objectively, however, the sponge and its leaves are unequal. The sponge only exists through the leaves that compose it. The sponge is both more than the leaves, since it contains the leaves among other things (including the intention of cleaning the sweet potato), but the sponge can only exist through the leaves and its other elements, as a greater and secondary thing, a 'thing of things', pregnant with other things – in other words, the sponge exists only as their sum, their organisation, and their synthesis.

On this view, the 'big thing' is a kind of world-substitute for the things that compose this big thing. The sponge is the 'microcosm' of the components of the sponge, like the flower is the microcosm of the petal, or the word the microcosm of letters. But unlike the world, every big thing allows things which are in the world to exist elsewhere: the leaf can enter into something other than the sponge, and the leaf can also leave the sponge for good. A 'big thing' is a totality of several things that enter together into a larger thing.

A totality of several things can both enter into another thing and go outside the big thing. But nothing goes outside the world and nothing is in the world except as solitary.

A 'big thing' is a world-*ersatz* wherein things remain together. In this house, I am with other friends, a tiled floor, and a stove. I am with these things in the house, like I am with other natural beings in nature and with other social beings in society; together we enter as several into these spatial, symbolic, theoretical 'big things'. In the world, we are always alone; in a big thing, we are always several.

The minimal big thing is the thing whose matter is differentiated such that this thing is not simply composed of 'that which is in this thing', but of at least two things: *this* and *that*. Since the sponge is composed of leaves and of the intention of washing sweet potatoes, the sponge is not only a thing, but a 'big thing'. Now, the thing always maintains the natural difference (being a thing or not being a thing; nothing is *more* or *less* a thing) as much as the 'big thing' gives rise to every difference of degree or intensity. A 'big thing' is either bigger or smaller. A big thing composed of two things is modest in comparison with a thing composed of twelve, a hundred, a thousand, or an infinite number of things. Any 'big thing' can tend towards the 'biggest possible thing', a thing composed of an infinite number of things or consisting of all things. But the world only ever consists of one thing at a time. The world comprehends each thing alone. Therefore, the 'biggest possible thing' must be extravagant without ever being the world; a 'big thing' is always composed of at least two things simultaneously.

If there is composition, or at least two elements, there is a 'big thing'. If there is only a unique thing at one time, there is a world.

A 'big thing' is never equivalent to the world. All sentient, cognitive, and human activities tend to identify 'big things' with the world itself. Human beings produce tools, thought-systems, works, sets of sensory or mental representations, and social organisations. All of these form many big things, very big things, organised sets of things entering conjointly into a unity and acting as world-substitutes.

But every animal, every sentient and active being on the evolutionary scale, mundanely constructs things, produces cries, signs, and codes, so as to compose and decompose big things. Either by dividing things into elements or by assembling elements into things through analysis or synthesis, every cognitive activity consists in more or less transforming or arranging things into big things. In this way, a thing may be saturated with other things that this thing includes, or may enter into the composition of a more important thing. Thus, action, social interaction, metabolism, or thought yield *things of things*.

A male bird assembles its nest with twigs, spreads berry-juice on other twigs to seduce a female, and sings its song; a great primate breaks branches to scavenge ants from a hollow trunk, and communicates through 'pant-hoot', a series of cries, panting expressions, and poundings on tree trunks; a mosquito yearning for blood places things into things, and decomposes a thing into other things; and so on. Human activity prolongs the composition and decomposition of things through language, the social division of labour, or symbolic thought, so as to produce, in political, religious, metaphysical, artistic, scientific, or everyday representations, the biggest possible things. 'Big things' are our world-substitutes, as if we could inhabit our own representations and live in a big thing composed of things together, rather than in a world of things which are alone only in a world.

A 'big thing' is not a mental or biological construction. Big things exist in any case. Even if nothing living inhabited the earth, basalt would be composed of cooled magma, of different proportions of plagioclase, pyroxene, olivine, and magnetite. Basalt would also be a big thing even if no person were there to decompose it through analysis and reconstruct it through synthesis. Things are objectively composed of things, and compose other, bigger things.

But the actions of living and human things lead to inflating things, including the idea of the world. Living and human things compose and decompose things – tools, theories, images, sounds, systems of social organisation – as if they could inflate, comprise more and more things, including acting as world-substitutes.

The world would be completely compact if it were a 'big thing'. But the world acts as an idea or example to the inflation of things, and makes human activity possible. Otherwise human beings would no longer make anything without reason, without any other possibility except the indefinite inflation of our material and mental productions, and without the disavowed hope of obtaining a big thing like the world – conscious of its impossibility, but nevertheless increasing its chance through the very possibility of impossibility. Human beings would not waste their time decomposing things into smaller things and assembling all existent things into bigger things, as if these things could some day attain the size of the world.

'Big things' organise the operation of things, the way in which things enter together, and not separately or alone, into something common. From dust particles to universal history, from partons (quarks and gluons) into hadrons and leptons (electrons, muons, tauons, and neutrinos) into mesons and baryons, into protons and neutrons, into atomic nuclei, into atoms, into molecules or metals or ionic composites, into cells, into tissues, into organs, into organisms, into the biosphere, into the planetary body, into the planetary system, into the stellar system, into the galaxy, into galaxy clouds, into clusters, into superclusters, into the universe ... Things are in things which are in things. Every thing is a plenitude of other things, elements, relations, and structures existing at different organisational levels, and following heterogeneous laws. In this way, things are *together* in matter. They are also in symbolic systems, in power relations, and in individual lives, enmeshed in each other, not simply as things but as *objects*, since a thing, insofar as it enters among other things into a 'big thing', is an object. This is what makes the composite texture of objects, totalities enmeshed in each other.

Objects exist in this way. The human species magnifies and inflates objects by making use of big things as so many world-substitutes for and through the human species, often in competition with each other, sometimes thought of as if they were logically many worlds. By continually treating 'big things' as the world, we allow what we attribute to things and to the world to circulate, and thus consider the world as one *object* among others, an idea which makes the meaning that we attribute to the world compact.

Many Worlds

Cosmology treats the material world as a *thing*. Several metaphysical and logical theories consider the world instead as an *object* in their representations of a plurality of worlds, presented as 'possible worlds', which involve a great variety of modalities. In David Lewis's modal realism, these 'possible worlds' can be actual. To logically represent the world as an object is to take the world (which is only 'our' world, what 'we' are in in the last instance) to be one object among other (possible, actual, real) objects, one world among a plurality of other worlds.

On the cosmological view, to make a thing of the world is to legitimately try to establish the world in the world. Moreover, it is to take apart the world as world (that in which something is), so as to consider its qualities and particular properties as a thing, as a *big thing*. In so doing, the world that one studies is no longer the world, of course, but instead 'the biggest of given things', which is the definition of the universe.

On the logical, possible worlds view, making an object of the world is a very different act. One relativises the world as a thing by attributing this world to a plurality of other things, on a modal plane (like that of possibility), which are other, although different, worlds equal in 'worldhood'.

Yet, if a basic human drive is to make a thing, a big thing, of the world, then the desire to relativise the world as one object among other objects is a source of confusion and error. We gain nothing from it (either in possibility or in reality), and we lose the meaning of the world.

Our psychological attraction to the idea of many worlds resembles the enchantment of a child who enters into a carnival attraction's house of mirrors for the first time and discovers herself multiplied, having the impression of being one among other selves, though these selves are nothing but reflections.

To discover one's image seemingly reproduced ad infinitum, through a vertiginous series of different perspectives, provokes the profound pleasure of recognising identity (it is myself who is reproduced ad infinitum) and of discovering simultaneous variation (in a blink of the eye, through an observation which quickly disappears in the reflections and gives the impression of the infinite, I see myself from the front, back, three-quarters, unlimited perspectives).

To represent many possible worlds is to let the world glisten in an infinite series of possibilities and reflections, by adding a minor variation to each image obtained. 'Another world' is the 'same' world, but in which an actual given object and event are replaced by another object or another event: a world in which Napoleon had won the Battle of Waterloo, since these are the kind of 'historical' examples favoured by possible worlds theorists (which classically represent the intersections between possible and actual 'great' historical events assumed to determine the course of future phenomena); a world in which yellow bears exist (evolutionary or natural variation, rather than historical variation); a world in which lead is lighter than air (variation of physical laws); a world in which I did not write this sentence (reflexive variation of the very conditions of the act of variation), and so on.

It is important to mention that one never represents one or more worlds absolutely different from the world that we identify as our own (which is reduced to the actual world of what 'actually' happened and 'really' happens). Instead, we represent worlds which reflect our own through a process of subtraction [*suppression*] and variation.

The first necessary operation required to obtain apparent possible worlds consists in subtracting possibility from the world and transforming it into a strictly actual world (an operation as groundless as that of reducing the world to a world of strictly material objects, for in reality there is no distinction between actual events and non-actual events, but a distinction, for each event, between something actual and something non-actual). Yet, Germany's victory during World War II is *something* which exists in the world, which is not nothing; it is a non-real past event that one can represent and describe in many ways – as a fiction, as a playful or serious hypothesis, and so on. This event, insofar as it was not *really* something, is no less really *something*; in this sense, this event belongs to the world (according to modalities which historical knowledge, for example, is concerned with determining).

However, if one subtracts and excludes this event from the world on the pretence that this event is not real, attested for, proved, or accomplished, then one reduces the world without obtaining anything in the world, and one reduces this form of every thing to a single form of real things (a category determined by inevitably fuzzy limits). One redeploys another world around an event excluded from this world, antecedent and subsequent to its temporal limits.

After the *subtractive* operation, the second operation consists in *variation*. This is the pleasurable exercise of redrawing around a thing a spatio-temporal environment which reflects what is henceforth 'our' world (and not the world), as if this world were partially the same and partially different. Of course, the limits to this thing always entail a problem. Where would a 'German victory' during World War II begin and where would it end? Where would a 'I turned left rather than right' begin and where would it end?

The pleasure of believing that one can go outside the world, a basic human drive, joins with that of discerning our world from other angles, in a changing and changeable perspective.

To think about oneself as one possibility among others is to doubly put oneself at ease. On the one hand, I am not alone. Other selves of mine exist in other worlds, or perhaps correct the mistakes that I have committed in this world, by no doubt committing other mistakes that I have avoided – I am but an intermediary being somewhere in the middle of all my possibilities, worse than some possibilities and better than other possibilities. On the other hand, I can imagine represented in a whole range of worlds the accumulation of things and events, though what is represented in the world is the same for all.

If I choose the fictional angle rather than the historical perspective, I can eclipse the German defeat in 1945 with a Nazi victory. But these two correlated events exist in fact together in a single world. They are two sides of the same coin. I can consider each side separately by dividing the coin widthwise, so as to establish heads and tails in two different worlds; I have granted a new *verso* to the *recto*, a new *recto* to the *verso*, and so on.

Possibility is the *verso* of actuality for every event. If I separate and arrange them into as many worlds as possibilities, then I brush the problem aside and transform *verso* into *recto*, and henceforth seek the new reverse side.

There is not a 'world' where I was never born. The possibility that I was never born appeared with the coming of my birth, consigned to it, like *verso* to *recto*. That this cat is white when it is black is the reverse side, since being black this cat is not white. All that things are not is the negative and form of what they are.

Yet, that which a thing is and that which it is not are equally in the world, although differently.

By subtracting the opposite of what things are, what happens, and what was from the world, we attempt to make not simply a *form*, but a *limit* of the world: the limit between actuality and possibility.

The concept of 'world' then acts as a principle of discrimination between several modalities, whereas the world is in fact what 'de-modalises' things and forms them as things, whether they be possible, necessary, contingent, true, or false.

By projecting, through variation, around each 'possibility' expelled from the world, the illusion of many worlds is created. This illusion ultimately reassures us, since we are always in a world (which is not something) and contained in things (which are not worlds) – as if we were capable of being in worlds which were simultaneously identical and different objects.

The world is not something.

IV. Something-Other-than-a-Thing: All

1. We call *all* what begins without ending.

2. The whole is the negative of something.

3. All is not the place of the whole of existent things. All is not where all things are *together*.

4. When things are together, they are objects.

5. What forms all is not all things together, but each thing separately.

6. All is not that in which this *and* that *and* something else *and* so on are, but that in which this is *and* that in which that is *and* that in which something else is, and so on.

7. To have all, it is enough to have something.

It is enough to grasp what begins where a thing ends. In the twilight of everything which ends, one sees born what *only* begins.

8. All things which are have nothing else in common except *all*.

9. All is what remains equidistant from each object when objects accumulate.

Many

We can understand the accumulation of things in two distinct ways: on the one hand, as the *formal* accumulation of things, and, on the other hand, as their *objective* accumulation.

Formally, more and more things quite simply are, since what begins to be possible never stops being possible. More and more things can only be insofar as nothing stops being possible, nothing ever stops being something, though new things ceaselessly begin to be. Things always begin to be and always end in the world.

Things do not go outside the world or stop beginning to be in the world.

Formally, things accumulate since more and more things are between things. However, there are never more things in the world (since only one thing is in the world at one time).

Objectively, however, things as objects accumulate, and *always* accumulate *more* in a different way. In human cultures, and especially in our own era, which may some day end and which has nothing necessarily, memory (including history), technology, progress, the division of labour, epistemic domains, and the desubstantialisation of things have made us especially subject to the accumulation of things *through* the accumulation of objects. Objects accumulate in at least five ways.

First, objects accumulate without us. But they also increasingly accumulate with us, primarily because we remember them. We collect them, write histories about them, refuse to forget them, and even rediscover them (archeology) – Nietzsche's 'disadvantages of history for life'.

Second, objects increasingly accumulate because we create new objects: technologies, the partitioning of time through the structure of fashions and of seasons, the division of human actions and needs into many functions correlating to functional objects. In other words, we continually multiply the number of objects that are useful for us. Technological objects become outdated, though we retain the memory of their earlier versions as novelty items: the telegraph after the telephone, the wire telephone after the cellular phone, the Minitel after mobile Internet access, the cathode ray tube after the LCD screen, the Walkman after the iPod, and so on. Things are invented and piled up on the cadavers of other things preserved in the hype of fashion, museification, and nostalgia – for example, the return to vinyl (reacting against compact discs or corrupt mp3 files) or to classic automobiles (reacting against hybrid electric vehicles). In this way, the restoration of the old must add to the continuous accumulation of the new. Restoration reacts against accumulation, but, far from neutralising or slowing down this accumulation, intensifies it.

Third, objects accumulate because the idea of progress guides us, according to which accumulating things allows us to go beyond things. The idea of scientific, artistic, or social progress leads us to believe that one assimilates and realises things by amassing them. We believe that a path or a passage leads us over a mountain peak of things, whose size we increase as we climb it. We hope that a passage exists beyond the mountain of our objects. But it recedes as we approach it, since we accumulate at least as many layers of waste at our feet as we cross the distance to the desired goal.

Fourth, objects accumulate through division and not merely through addition or multiplication. We divide our actions and knowledge with a precision resulting from the idea of progress mentioned above. Our division also causes a division of our practical and theoretical objects, increasingly demarcated, specific, and smaller. On every scale, these practical and theoretical objects renew formally identical and objectively different problems.

Lastly, objects increasingly accumulate because our representations have considerably desubstantialised our objects in relation to other human cultures. We implicitly believe in the equality of part and whole. We consider properties as much as substance, attributes in the same way as their support. In this way, no thing is absolutely *less* or absolutely *more* for us – the still discouraging and incomplete picture of a 'flat world', where everything would be equally something, neither more nor less than another thing. In this way, all things comparable to each other appear to us as objects. Through our representations, we multiply the objectivisation of everything and anything. Taboos, sanctity, everything that, by definition, ought not to be something (said, thought, imagined, conceivable, comparable, exchangeable, reifiable) makes these objects objects of contempt.

Objectively, therefore, more and more objects are for and through us. We live among them. We make do with objects. We perceive objects. We think about objects. The world does not become a desert. No, the world satiates itself because the 'dustbin of history' is nonexistent. The old remains, and the new does not stop coming.

This objective accumulation is our condition. We experience existential suffocation from it, but it also forms an opening allowing us to take in the world amidst objects. The hyperbolic accumulation of objects may lead us to consider the formal equality of each thing underpinning and allowing this accumulation: that each thing only enters alone into the world; that objects enmeshed in each other certainly make big things, but never a world; that the world is only made of something, anything; that we can obtain the world from each thing, under layers of objects.

V. The Accumulation of Objects

1. Objects are in things.

2. Objects accumulate because nothing ever ceases to be possible, and since new objects become possible.

3. Existence disappears, but possibilities always accumulate. Even if everything disappeared, the extinction of everything would always be something *more* added to the past possibilities of what has been and is no more.

4. The possibility of things can only grow. Every diminishing of being and of existence is an event which adds to the possibility of a weakened existence.
Formally, a diminishing of existence is an augmentation of possibility.

5. The existence, utility, or beauty of things is perhaps in the process of diminishing, whereas the possibility of things is always in the process of accumulation.

6. Where does the accumulation of objects take place? In a bigger thing. Things do not accumulate in the world, since always only one thing is in the world at a time.

7. The accumulation of objects denotes the hierarchy between things. What is in what? What is part of what set? How much what is in such a series? What is smaller than what? What depends on *this*? What determines *that*?

8. The formal condition of the accumulation of objects is its opposite: the equality between all things.

9. *All* is never at the end of the list of things.

10. *All* is not the result of the accumulation of things. *All* is the condition of this accumulation.

11. When I have three things rather than two, I am not at all closer to the sum of everything, but I am no further from it either.

12. All is very precisely what is neither further from nor closer to few or to many.

13. Things between things always yield things: more important things, less important things, smaller things, or bigger things.

14. The list of things is not groundless as long as one doesn't expect a *sum* from this list.

15. If we know that the list of things always yields something *more*, then the accumulation of things is neither fallacious nor illusory.

16. From every element of the list, it is possible to obtain all; it is enough to consider an object as a thing.

17. In the strict sense, things do not accumulate. They *are*. No thing is in another thing; no thing adds to another thing.

18. To add is to be one among others.
The accumulation of objects is the set of operations through which new things add to objects: division, multiplication, addition, invention, creation, communication, propagation, emergence, dissemination, and so on.

19. No thing disappears absolutely.
Objects disappear as much as they accumulate. If things appear, they never disappear.

20. An object disappears when it has no more limits.

21. An object which has been *is no more*. A thing which has been *is*.

22. Everything becomes plenitudinous, everything expands, and everything augments, except the world. Several objects form an additional big thing. A thing becomes a supplementary object by entering into another thing, but the plurality of things will never augment the whole.

All is that through which *one* is never less than *several*.

One, Several, Whole, Equal

Many things never yield a whole, only a new thing. But if plurality ends in unity and never in totality, why do we even need the idea of totality? Could one not do without it, and consider that plurality produces unity and that unities compose pluralities?

In one thing, one obtains several things. We could always make one thing of several things. Let us take an example. One thing, A, would be composed of several things, a, b, c. Several things, A, B, C, would compose one thing, A', and so on. A plurality would make a unity, and every unity would be the sum of a plurality. a, b, and c are in A. Even more things are in A'. In fact, a bigger thing has a plurality of things that compose this higher-order thing. This big thing, A', is always itself a part of a plurality composing another thing – but A' is *absolutely* greater than A and a, which are parts of A'. From A', one obtains A or a.

How does this entail compactness?

One could argue that nothing is *absolutely* greater (since every thing would obtain its place in a plurality), but being greater, on the other hand, appears to be *absolute*. Indeed, it would be impossible to think that a could include A'. A' includes A, B, C, a, b, and c. a is in A and thus in A'. But A' cannot be in a. Suppose that a, which is less than A and therefore less than A', could be both more than A' and include A' among other things. This supposes that a relates to A' in the same way that A' relates to a (includes it), and therefore short-circuits our system. If no thing is absolutely greater in this model, being greater and being smaller are nonetheless made *absolute* in the comprehension of things.

If one thinks that plurality composes a unity and that every unity is composed of a plurality, then one accounts for both an upward infinity (what is ultimately composed) and a downward infinity (what composes ultimately). In addition, one establishes a strict and compact scale between the two, according to which all things accumulate vertically, without ever obtaining horizontal equality or having any common plane. What enters into the composition of a thing is absolutely less than this thing, and one cannot account for the equality between the elements and the composition by conceptually maintaining a relation between unity and plurality. Every unity in a plurality that composes a greater unity is absolutely smaller than the unity of a plurality that it is a part of. If I am a member of a people and these people are a great individual, then I am *absolutely* less than this great individual. I am a little individual, since I am, as a unity, a part of the plurality of these people. For this reason, a proton would be *absolutely* smaller than an atom. The detail of a landscape painting would be *absolutely* less than the landscape painting, that is, than the unity of a plurality to which the detail belongs.

If unity is in a plurality, or if plurality is in a unity, then being greater and being smaller become compact, since they would be in themselves.

It is at this stage that the concept of *totality* intervenes. In order for a greater thing to be in some sense equal to a smaller thing (which composes this greater thing), they must both relate to an entity that considers them as equal – namely, an entity which would not be an ontologically greater thing, but, rather, be ontologically different from a thing.

All – far from being an absolute concept – is quite precisely what allows things to remain equal in some sense. All is what makes the smaller thing count just as much as the greater thing. Totality is certainly not the greatest thing, which would comprehend several things and realise the greater unity of these several things. No, *all is simply what each thing is in equally*.

If there were not a whole, then there could not be several things that accumulate between things. If things were not equal in a sense, then what is smaller would systematically dissolve into what is greater. How can a part outlast the greater unity of its organism? Why is there always *a*, when *a* is in *A*, and when *A* is in *A'*? If we have *A'*, then we already have *A* and *a*. Why do *a* and *A* subsist, when they remain entirely in *A'*? Because they do not exist *except* in *A'*. For a part to outlast a greater unity that comprehends this part among other parts in a plurality, the part and the greater unity must be equal in relation to something *else* – the whole.

If some things compose other things, it is because all things are situated equally and separately in another thing – otherwise the smaller unities would systematically dissolve into greater unities, and so forth. Nothing would subsist in what is composed of what composes. If there were only unity and plurality, then there would be neither unity nor plurality, since everything would tend towards diminishing into some never-ending compact unity always comprehended in a plurality – continually vanishing into some systematically greater unity.

How can there be *several* things? Several things must have something in common and must be in the same something, in order to remain in each other. Plurality never yields a whole; only a whole can allow a plurality, since a whole makes things *equally* alone so that they can be together.

Equal

No thing enters other than alone into the world. To be in the world is to be in the company of nothing and to be only one. In this way, the world is precisely what is not shared.

Atoms are several in a molecule, individuals are more than one in a society, fingers are multiple in a hand, units are repeated in the number four, phonemes are various in a language, lovers are together in a couple, seconds are sixty in a minute, and so on. In short, things are always several in a thing, a big thing that they compose. Things that enter into another thing, which in one way or another comprehends them, we call 'objects'. A thing in another thing is an object. A thing in the world – that is, in something-other-than-a-thing – is a thing.

Every object is accompanied, for in order to enter into a thing, to make another thing, one single thing is insufficient. One thing always makes the world. Two objects together always make one other thing. Every collection of objects is one thing: not a whole, but a *big thing*. Society, history, nature, the physical universe, language, a body, a table, and a word are all big things insofar as they are things themselves, composed of things: a society composed of individuals, social structures, values, and domains; a history of moments, epistemes, events, periods, and agents; nature of living beings, genes, vital forces, proteins; a language of morphemes, syntactic rules, usages; a body of tissues, limbs, functions; a table of weight, a plane, wood; a word of letters, a definition, an etymology, and so on.

Big things are both more than each element that, on one plane or another (whether material, symbolic, intentional, temporal, spatial, or logical), enters into their composition, and as much as each one of their elements. The number six comprehends the number two, which the number six is a multiple of (what the number six is in is *more* than the number two, since the number six comprehends both two and something other than two). But the number six, like the number two, is also something. Six is more than two, but two has something more than the number six, which is the absence of what six has more of. Every big thing composed of things that enter into this big thing itself has something more than each one of its elements, and also something less in relation to each one of these same elements. What two has more of, in its relation to six, is the absence of four additional units: to be nothing but two. What the finger has more of, in comparison with the hand to which it belongs, is to not have other fingers. What the individual has, and the society to which it more or less belongs lacks, is to not comprehend all the other individuals and to be only one of them. Yet every society admits being *less* than an individual, every sum admits not being a part, every hand admits not being a finger. What comprehends other things can never be what this thing comprehends.

To comprehend a reality or a set of things is always to be excluded from it. For, if to be is to enter into what one is, to comprehend is to go outside what one is.

To constitute a physical universe or space-time continuum is to comprehend all that takes place in space-time, everything that is in space-time; it is also to exclude space-time from spatio-temporal comprehension. To comprehend all social phenomena or events in society is to exclude society from the social domain and limit oneself to the impasses of sociological reflexivity. To comprehend all historical events, or to claim that all is historical, is to exclude history from historicity.

What precludes a big thing from being among its objects – what separates *being* and *comprehension* – is, however, the very possibility that a big thing only be one thing, that is, be equal to the things which compose this big thing as objects. If a big thing is capable of what the objects composing this big thing are capable of, that is, belonging to this big thing, then the big thing would be absolutely greater than the objects which are in and through this big thing. If nature were natural in the same way as natural beings are in nature, then nature would be absolutely more than natural beings. Yet if nature were absolutely more than what composes it, then nature would no longer need the things which compose it in order to be; nature could just as easily replace natural beings, history historical facts, and so on. If the number six were absolutely greater than the number two, then the number six would efface the existence of the two, go beyond the two, and diminish the two by realising the two; this is the dream of *Aufhebung*.

But the two *subsists* beneath the six, the individual *subsists* beneath society, the finger *subsists* beneath the hand, and so on. Why? Because what enters into a thing always has a quality that escapes the thing that this thing enters into; what this big thing comprehends is not this big thing; what enters into this big thing is in this big thing, which is not in this big thing. What a historical event has more of than all of history is the possibility of being historical, namely, its unity, its individuality, the property of being a solitary event and not being another event, its capacity to enter into history, to be a member of this set that is not a member of itself.

In other words, what an object has more of than the big thing into which this object enters, that this thing composes among other things, is a point of equality between part and whole, between object and big thing, a point where both are equally determinate unities which enter into the world.

Objectively, things are together and unequal. *Formally*, things are alone and equal.

The equality between part and whole is formal. This equality must not be confounded with objective inequality. Objectively, in the domain of objects, an object is less than the big thing in which this object is comprehended (this may be an injustice or normal). Objectively, two is less than six; a hand is less than an entire body; a brick is less than a brick building. Objectively, a minute is less than an hour. But formally, a minute is equivalent to an hour due to the fact that an hour and a minute are each *alone*. The unity of a minute excludes other minutes (which are comprehended in an hour), but the unity of an hour excludes the exclusion of these other minutes, and therefore the possibility of being in an hour. What a minute has that an hour will never have is the possibility of being in an hour, of belonging to an hour, of being a minute of an hour – and not the possibility of comprehending the other possible minutes of this hour. An hour will never be a member of an hour (but only a member of every time interval greater than the hour).

This formal equality is the equality of things between a minute and an hour, between a finger and a hand, between a letter and a word, between a component and a composite. The possibility of being equally a thing alone, for a big thing as for an object, guarantees their equality, the common plane which forever maintains their existential possibility.

That the part is formally equivalent to the whole, insofar as the whole is a thing, guarantees the subsistence of both part and whole. If what comprehends several objects were absolutely greater than each one of these objects, then these objects would not subsist as such. Take an example. I try to count, but since each natural successor number is absolutely greater than its predecessor, the greater natural number effaces the smaller natural number's existence. I count: one, two, three, and so on. But, when I reach three, I no longer absolutely need two insofar as it is two, since two is comprehended objectively *as well as* formally (that is, *absolutely*) in three, in such a way that two effaces itself in the three, which effaces itself in the four, and so on. In other words, if big things were objectively and formally (that is, absolutely) greater than the objects which compose these big things, we would never be able to explore the world except in the sense of a departure without return. By observing the fingers of a hand, I could no longer return to the fingers from the hand (the fingers would be absolutely comprehended in the hand, which would no longer allow itself to be divided into fingers and palm), which would efface itself in the body, and so on. By looking at an organism part by part, I cannot obtain the meaning of the parts from the whole. There would only be a possible synthesis, and never an analysis. I could count from one to a very large number, but I could not return to a smaller number from this large number. Soon, the whole world would appear to me as a *big compact thing*, a being comprehending each thing absolutely, in such a way that I could never pick out from this world things that compose this world, and from these things I have little by little returned to this world.

If no formal equality existed between a big thing and objects, it would never be possible to climb up the chain of being of things of the world, to go from smallest to greatest, from simple to complex, from minimum to maximum, from parts to whole. Moreover, it would be literally impossible to descend this chain, to obtain individuated existences, comprehended and realised in the totality.

The world would only have one sense, the one that ascends from *being* to *comprehension*. The world would have lost its dyadic sense, which allows us to also descend from *comprehension* to *being*.

Part III

Being and Comprehending

I. Being is Being Comprehended

1. Can one be without being *something*?

Either one is something (a thing is another thing: a lamp is a source of light), or one is something other than something (a thing is the world: a lamp is (in) the world, a light is (in) the world).

Either one is a thing, or one is the world.

Being nothing is still being *something* (since nothing is something, even if it is only a word, a false concept, or the union between a before-thing, the negative contemporaneous with a thing, and the absence following the thing).

Therefore, being is not one member of a pair such as being and nothingness, being and non-being, being and becoming, being and beings. Being is not opposed as a whole to another thing.

2. Being has no opposite, but it has an opposite sense: comprehending.

Being this or being that is belonging to this or that, being *in* this or that. We say that this or that 'comprehends' that which is this or that.

The sense of 'being' is the opposite sense of 'comprehending'. The sense of 'comprehending' is the opposite sense of 'being'. Being can only be explained through comprehending, and vice versa.

3. Being is *being comprehended*. Comprehending is *being been* [*être été*]. The active sense of one is the passive sense of the other.

4. Being is a sense attributed to the relation between two things or between a thing and that which is not a thing.

5. Being is not primary, which means both that no being is *in itself* and that no being is *before* things. Being is secondary and the handmaiden of things, which means that being is the sense attributed to one thing in relation to another thing.

If being is secondary and things are primary, how can one claim or know that *there is* something? To *have* something, must something not *be*?

6. To be something, the thing must be in something-other-than-itself; this is its only condition.

7. To be something, it is not first necessary that something be, but rather that *both* something *and* something-other-than-something be, so that one may *be* the other.

8. If there is *only* something, then there is not something.

9. Something *is*, if something has something other than itself to be, if something is not compact.

10. Thing and world are in this way *primary*. Being and comprehension make a thing be the world and the world comprehend a thing. Being and comprehension are *secondary*.

11. Comprehending something is 'being been' by this thing.

If I comprehend this, it is because this is in me. If that comprehends me, it is because I am in that.

12. Comprehending something is not the same as being this something. The whole comprehends the part, but the whole cannot be this part. If the whole were this part, it would then be necessary that the whole be in the part – in which case, this thing would be compact.

13. It is possible to be something if and only if this something does not comprehend this something.

One does not comprehend what one is. One is not what one comprehends.

14. Comprehending is having something inside itself. Comprehending is also comprehending an element by being a set; comprehending one quality by being a substrata of qualities; comprehending someone by appreciating or paying attention to this someone; assimilating a way of thinking or an idea; having a part when one is a composite; or comprehending a temporal, historical, or evolutionary moment in a longer timespan.

15. Being is belonging to something. Being is also having a quality; being an organism; being in a situation, that is, being situated in some thing, and, more precisely, in a series of objects in each other, like Russian dolls but impossible to completely hierarchise; being a body; being a history; being a social function; being a community; being a language; being a consciousness; or being a sexual organism.

But being is also being what is not something, namely, being the world.

Being the world and being *in* the world are equivalent.

16. Being is entering.

17. Being is not a mystery.

18. Being is a sense attributed to the relation between something and what contains this something, or between something and what this something contains. Insofar as no thing is as a whole, each thing enters and is entered. The direction from the entering to the entered, we call 'being'. The direction from the entered to the entering, we call comprehension.

19. A thing is not a unit that one could arrange on a (material or thought) plane, so as to say: this thing *is* this or this thing *is* that, by identifying this thing with a name, idea, or something else as a whole. A thing always marks the difference between two senses or directions of being: that which enters into and that which goes out.

20. Being makes the difference between that which enters into a thing, and that into which the thing enters.

But what is the thing *really*? Does the thing have any consistency, like a thin layer of being separating what is in this layer and what this layer is in? Things really manifest a solidity or a matter, since I can touch them or hold them in my hand. Things have a *matter*, which is everything which enters into these things. But things *are* not their matter, since things are not *in* their matter.

21. One never grasps something as a whole. One divides something and one can obtain it through one side of being or through another: through *that which is the thing* or through *that which the thing is*. But one will never reconcile the thing as a whole, as a very compact unit in my hand. For, if one made being a thing as a whole, without distinguishing *that which is the thing* and *that which the thing is*, one would situate the thing outside the world, and there would not be anything to be this thing.

22. The thing is primary, but it is dyadic. Being is simple, but it is secondary.

Being is Secondary

In French, '*comprendre*' has the linguistic advantage of being easily grasped by its active and passive facets: to comprehend, and to be comprehended. The verb '*être*' has a similar structure, which makes it something passive and something active. But the French language tends to confound the two sides of a thing into a misleading unity, a kind of mysterious compactness of 'being' – confusing *that which is something* and *that which something is*, as if they were the same thing.

In this way, being is often defined as 'being is that which is'. But in this definition, *that which is* and *that which this is* are confounded. What being is is that which is. It is as if one could claim that what a bag is in is what is in the bag. Being appears to be conceived as the non-distinction between being which is and being which 'is been'. Like all verbs, in fact, 'to be' has two facets that must not be confused: 'to eat' has the property of eating and the property of being eaten; likewise, 'to be' has the property of being and the property of 'being been'. Being is always both sides of the coin: that which is, and that which this is. The best way of untangling this knot in being is to understand 'to be' like the verb 'to comprehend', but conversely. *Being is being in, being comprehended*. What does it mean that I am this or that I am that? It means simply that I am *in* this or *in* that, that that comprehends me. Being is always being something. Therefore, being is being a part of this something. In the sense of 'being comprehended', the verb 'to be' formally has but a single reference: the world. I am (in) the world and every thing is (in) the world.

In its other sense, the verb 'to be' (in a 'passive' sense, if you will) corresponds to the fact of comprehending. 'Being been' is comprehending. When I say that 'the wall is white', I am aware that I am claiming something about the wall. But in fact, I am primarily expressing my judgement about whiteness. I am saying that the wall is comprehended in whiteness, is among white things. I am not expressing a quality of the wall, being white. If that were the case, the wall would comprehend, among other qualities, the fact of being white, as if this quality were hung to the coat rack of the thing. No, rather, I am expressing a quality of whiteness. This whiteness can comprehend the wall. The wall can count within the set of what is white. In the sentence 'the wall is white', the *thing* is not primarily the wall, but whiteness. Otherwise, I ought to say that whiteness is the wall – that is, that the wall comprehends the whiteness in the things which compose this wall. Likewise, I often say 'I am a person'. I think that I am expressing one of my determinations, namely, personhood. No, I am expressing one determination of the set of humanity which is able to contain and comprehend me. If I want to assert the fact that humanity counts among the things that compose me, I ought to say that a person is me – some personhood is in me.

What does this rhetorical inversion mean? Nothing, except that in a predicative expression the *thing* must be sought on the side of the predicate rather than on the side of the subject. This is, of course, an anti-substantialist method. Why is there no substance? Because in a sentence which talks about 'being', the subject is a component of the thing situated on the side of the predicate. The subject is always the part, and the predicate is the whole, the set. When I say that x is y, I mean that x belongs to y, that x is a part of y, that x composes y, and that x takes part in y's matter – that is, x is comprehended by y. Since x is y, y comprehends x, y is external to x, and y is 'outside' x.

The first major consequence of interpreting 'being' as the inverse of 'comprehending' derives from the product of an 'antisymmetric' relation. It may seem that being is the sign of a symmetric identity relation: if a is b, then b is a. No! Being is antisymmetry par excellence: if a is b, then b cannot be a. Being means nothing other than this unidirectionality [*ce sens unique*].

If I am comprehended in something, then what I am in cannot be in me. If I am x, then x is not me.

The second consequence of interpreting 'being' as the inverse of 'comprehending' is that this antisymmetric relation reverses the linguistic categories of classical, substantialist philosophies. Being some thing does not mean comprehending this thing as some quality, determination, or predicate. No, being some thing is being in or counting as a part of this thing. Here, we do not consider a substance that could *be* its attributes and that could be predicated on nothing. We consider a thing which can be in another thing and in which another thing can be, provided that *that in which this thing is* and *that which is in this thing* are never confounded.

Our concept of being has three dimensions.

First, we think that being is no big deal (the deal is the thing, things, and the world), since being is the *handmaiden of things*. For us, being is nothing other than the antisymmetric relation par excellence, which allows us to avoid the unit of identity [*bloc d'identité*], compactness, and the 'mystery' of a Being of beings.

Second, we think that this antisymmetric relation is the inverse of what comprehending means: being is being in, being comprehended – and this is certainly not comprehending. Therefore, being is completely without comprehending.

Third, being as 'being comprehended' presupposes a distinction between *that which is something* and *that which something is*. The sense of 'being' as the opposite sense of 'comprehending' is a theory of things: something is saturated with something-other-than-itself, and saturates something-other-than-itself. Being corresponds to one of these two senses. Being is the handmaiden of things since it is on both sides of the coin: being comprehending and being comprehended. Being is betrayed by confusing the two sides of being, making being into a solid, compact being – by which you would be something in the same way that something is you.

A thing is never a unity, but always has two faces. How are things split? Can we simply divide a thing in two and claim that here is 'that which is the thing' and there is 'that which the thing is'? How are the two sides distinguished?

By conceiving of a difference between that which is *in* the thing and that *in which* this thing is.

In

To say that *being* means *being in*, or rather *entering*, is not a spatial metaphor.

The 'in' merely has a local meaning in ordinary language: a moment of time is *in* another, a predicate is *in* a subject, a smaller number is *in* a larger number, and so on. What is necessary to the definition of 'in', which is an intersection between inclusion, membership, measurement, counting, and localisation?

Being is not only *being in*, but *entering*, which means, if not a movement, at least a *direction* [*sens*]; being is an oriented relation, one of two possible directions of the relation between two things, or between a thing and something-other-than-a-thing.

Being is entering into the membership of something which comprehends us.

In other words, being implies being in a relation with something. This something is in a relation with a thing that one is not oneself in a relation with. Being *in* something is entering into the membership of a thing that comprehends us, that is, includes us *among other things*. Being in a room is being in a spatial relation with a thing (the room) that has a relation to us. This thing (the room) also maintains a relation with other things, though we do not ourselves have this relation. What does it mean for the room to comprehend us or to be greater than us, other than that there are things in the room which are not in us? A bouquet of flowers, a rug, a washbasin, and a certain density of air are in the room but are not in me. The spatial relation between the room and me is such that the room extends beyond me, for this room has the same relation to me (capacity) as to some things that I do not relate to (I do not contain them, therefore the room is greater than me).

Being is being comprehended in any modality. Being is being in a relation to a thing that maintains this same relation to some things. What is being red, for this peony? Here we do not seek to define the 'red' of 'being red', but the 'being' of 'being red'. Being red is being in a relation with a thing (redness, a colour, a quality, a part of the electromagnetic spectrum, and so on) that maintains an identical relation to other things (a table, flag, or dress) that the peony does not itself relate to.

Therefore, comprehending is maintaining an *unequal* relation. Entering into a relation with a thing and at least one other thing, without these two things being able to have the same relation between each other, is like loving two people equally who do not love each other. When I comprehend the behaviour of two different people, I relate myself to each one of them in a way that they do not relate to each other or to me.

Being and comprehension are the two modes of inequality in the relations between things. Comprehending is relating identically to things that have this relation neither to themselves nor to me. Being is being comprehended. What I am is what comprehends me.

Being is often structured according to *genera* and *species* precisely for this reason. Being a dog is relating to the idea, concept, definition, or qualities characterising a dog. In this way, the concept or idea of dog relates to this dog in the same way that this concept or idea also relates to other individual canines or dogs. No individual canine can relate to other dogs in the same way that the concept of dog relates to all dogs.

In this sense, *being in* or *entering* is not a spatial metaphor; instead, it is the idea of an unequal and oriented relation: being is one direction and comprehending is another. Being is entering into; comprehending is going outside. Comprehending objectively is having the same relation to several things which cannot share this relation among themselves (and is also not being able to maintain this same relation to itself). Comprehending is having an effect of identity from a plurality of things, an effect of identity that these things cannot have on each other, and that one cannot have on oneself. Comprehending is an effect of being greater, offset by the impossibility of being what one comprehends.

From an objective standpoint, being is having a relation to a thing, one solitary thing, which has this same relation to other things. Being is an effect of being smaller, offset by the chance, by comprehending less than what one is, of being something more.

Thus, one never comprehends what one is, and one never is what one comprehends.

But this dynamic of the two senses of being and of comprehension is neither strictly spatial nor mathematical, neither set-theoretical nor numerical; it concerns sense and inequality. Being is one sense of things; comprehension is the inverse sense of them. It is a matter of the two possible senses of the directed relation between things or between one thing and something-other-than-a-thing. The spatial sense of being (entering) and the set-theoretical sense of comprehending (including) are in fact *determinations* of the sense of being and of comprehending (and not the inverse).

Entering *locally* (in the sense of entering into a place, of passing from an external space to an internal space) is the primary sense of being determined by space. Comprehending *mathematically* (in the sense of being a collection of elements belonging to a set) is the primary sense of comprehending determined by the count and the axioms of set theory: maintaining an identity relation with different things that do not maintain this relation among themselves.

Being defined as being *in*, by the fact of entering, is not a spatial metaphor, but a generic meaning with a spatialised definition that appears as a determinate and limited sense.

Between

Since being is a certain sense of the relation between things, every thing is enmeshed in a dyadic relation with being: that which is this thing (that which enters into this thing); and that which this thing is (that into which this thing on its own enters).

Formally, 'that which is a thing' corresponds to its matter, and 'that which a thing is' to its form, that is, to the world. From the formal point of view, all things have the same form, since they all enter alone into the world.

Objectively, 'that which is a thing' are objects – things which are in this thing and which compose this thing; 'that which the thing is' can be the big thing into which this thing enters among other objects.

On the one hand, there is that which is this chair, that which is the idea of justice, that which is a person, that which is red, and that which is a supercluster. On the other hand, there is that which this chair is, that which justice is, that which a person is, that which redness is, and that which a supercluster is. The concepts of logical extension and comprehension only incompletely account for the two sides of the sense of being. First, since it is not merely a logical problem of the concept (of its extension and comprehension), but also a problem of the very being of things. Second, since they do not demonstrate how that which is a thing and that which this thing is correspond merely to the displacement of the thing in question; in that which is the thing, the thing is the result of being's relation, and in that which the thing is, the thing marks the starting point of this relation. Every thing exists *between* the fact of being and the fact of 'being been'.

I can ask *what this thing is* as a chair, and I can ask *what is* a chair, but I cannot ask what is a chair's being as a whole. By asking what this thing is as a chair, I leave open, by the other side, a part of the being of the chair: the 'being been' of the chair.

No problem or solution contains the being of a thing; by focusing on that which the chair is, this thing opens up the problem of that which is this chair, and by focusing on that which is the chair, this thing opens up the problem of that which this chair is. The being of a thing is never a whole, since a thing makes sense only between *that which is it* and *that which it is*. 'Chair' simultaneously names the conjunction and disjunction of that which is, of that which *enters* into a chair, and of that which a chair is, of that into which it *enters*. An empiricist will still infer *that which the chair is* from *that which is the chair*. An idealist, conversely, will infer *that which is* this or that thing from *that which this or that thing is*. For both the empiricist and idealist, the leap from one sense of being to the other is possible; either I can determine that which it is to be this chair from everything which is a chair, or I am allowed to determine that which comes under the definition of a chair from the idea of chair.

Now, both the empiricist and idealist explode the chair's connection: the irreducibility of that which is 'this' to that which 'this' is, is precisely 'this'. We could produce the concept of chair from the plurality of objects on which one can sit without knowing a priori what this chair is as a chair, what this chair is as the idea of chair. But doing so would only generalise all that is a chair, and no existent 'chair' thing would be. On the contrary, only absolutely singular entities in themselves would be, from which thought, knowledge, or language produces the general idea, the 'chair' effect. However, between the two, nothing would be. If I could determine from the idea of a chair what corresponds to this idea and recognise this or that singular, sensory thing as belonging to some 'chair' species, no chair would be. Rather, only the distorted sensory effects of an ideal chair would be.

For the empiricist and idealist, what always explodes is the chair. The chair makes sense, like every thing, only *between* what is a chair and what a chair is.

Yet, what a chair is depends on what this chair is in. On the one hand, what the chair is in is this room, this space. On the other, what this chair is in is my perception, memory, language, culture, a set of furniture. The chair is, formally, in the world.

In the world, the chair is nothing more and nothing less than a thing. In a determinate space, in a symbolic, historical, or cultural domain, in and for a determinate subject, the chair is a determinate object, uniquely determined.

The 'chair' thing changes according to what this chair is in. In this way, no thing is a substance, an identity in itself. Rather, each thing is something changing, with a form that varies with the variations of its matter, *that which this thing is* transforming *that which is this thing*, and vice versa.

Nonetheless, things are not transient realities. When a thing begins being possible, it never stops being possible. Our thought, knowledge, and perception do not stop going from one thing to another by identifying a thing with the next thing, insofar as they are generic actions of a sentient being who strives to produce changing things. I identify this chair, here and now, with the chair which was here a few minutes or seconds ago. I momentarily substantialise the chair by identifying several things with one and the same object, by transforming the passing time into a context within which what I have identified as being the same chair changes slightly with the passage of time.

In reality, the chair of a second ago is something other than the chair now before my eyes. In reality, the chair that persists and remains identical over the course of these few seconds is always something else, a third comparable entity. However, one may ask, by placing the permanent chair and the chair at each moment of time on the same plane, what connection subsists between the chair of a second ago and the present chair? For, if there is so little between this chair and that chair, each of which exists neither more nor less than the chair that becomes, one could just as well think that it was a rhinoceros that became the present chair and that the chair of a few seconds ago became a table, and so on. Formally, and formally alone, the chair that endures and each chair that is at each moment are equal – and equal to the rhinoceros or table. However, the *objective* connection between the chair before and the chair after is the chair that becomes. The chair before and the chair after, not as *things* alone, but as *objects*, belong to a 'big thing', in this case *the chair that becomes*. On the other hand, the rhinoceros and the chair before do not together belong to a 'big thing', which would be the becoming-rhinoceros of the chair. But if something like a becoming-rhinoceros of the chair existed, then this connection would certainly exist. Poetically, we can always imagine this.

In other words, objectively, the same chair at different

moments belongs to a 'big thing', the continuously becoming chair. But, formally, the chair at each moment is something as well as, neither more nor less than, this continuously becoming chair.

II. That which is a Thing, That which a Thing is

1. We can easily understand how and why 'that which is a thing' is equivalent to all that this thing comprehends. That which is this thing is not reducible to its material components. In an artisanal object, the surface and idea of this object are as much its components as are its concrete elements. What composes a thing is not only material; what composes the non-material components of the thing – for example, the idea of it or its Aristotelian formal cause – can always matter. The idea of the artisanal object, insofar as the artisan expresses it, consists of representations which will always consist, ultimately, in cognitive phenomena, neuronal, chemical, and electrical events.

2. What is an idea or thought may always be reduced to a material phenomenon. When we talk about what things are, we must, in the last instance, come upon *matter* while breaking these things up into component parts.

3. In the final analysis, matter is in things, but things are not in matter.

A compact materialist (and reductionist) will maintain that not only does matter compose things (and therefore representations and conscious phenomena as well), but also that things are of matter and are *in* matter.

If we wish to understand how things are composed of matter and comprehend matter, we must admit that things are not material.

No thing is of matter. No thing is *in* matter.

Things do not take place in matter.

4. That which a thing is is always formally this thing, and never materially this thing.

5. How do we understand what a thing is? First, negatively: a thing is all that is not this thing. A thing is in all that is not in this thing.

More broadly, each thing is the world, that is, everything except something.

6. No object is permanently this or that. An object can eternally be an object (like certain truths), but an object will always be an object in such an object. An object's identity is not transient; it does not depend so much on the passage of time, but rather on what the object is in or what one makes this object be in. Rather, an object's identity is *objective*. Objective does not mean 'outside every perspective', but 'in an object'.

7. Being a chair, being granite, being beautiful, being three, being false, being Italian, being a believer, being a woman, being red, being painful, being nitrogen, and being a foot will appear as identities. These identities are hardly comparable, except through a linguistic effect. Despite their objective differences, they are nonetheless, in more or less intense degrees, identities which depend on the membership of that which is of this or that object, objective situation, or objective event.

There is no natural difference between value identities, essential identities, and mathematical, logical, or physical identities: they are all *objective* identities. That which an object is (that is, a thing in another thing) is that to which it belongs. There is no support or receptacle of these objective identities. A thing is not a coat rack on which one could hang qualities, attributes, or value judgements.

8. An object can be in another thing, but an object cannot be *any arbitrary way* in another thing.

One is not a relativist if one claims that there is no thing in itself and that every thing is that in which this thing is. A relativist thinks that that which a thing is depends on the *point of view* that one adopts towards it. Whatever point of view one adopts towards a thing, this thing cannot be no-matter-what. No thing is *no-matter-what*.

A thing cannot be no-matter-what, since things are finite. A thing is always finite whenever what composes this thing ends.

What composes a thing prevents this thing from being no-matter-what. By ending this thing, what composes a thing forces this thing to begin (yet, no-matter-what is what does not begin, since nothing returns into no-matter-what).

9. *That which is a thing* cannot determine *that which this thing is*; what composes a thing never allows us to necessarily determine what this thing is. As a result, if that which is a thing yielded *that which the thing is*, the thing would be compact; *that which is the thing* would be *that which the thing is*, and there would be no more thing.

10. A thing is precisely the difference between *that which is the thing* and *that which the thing is*. A star is the difference between what composes a star and what a star is. Nothing more, nothing less.

11. Reductionism reduces what things are to what composes these things. Physicalist or materialist reductionism reduces things to the matter that composes them. Evolutionary or naturalist reductionism reduces a living organism to the evolutionary processes of which the living organism is a result.

Other types of reductionism capture the chain of being from the other direction, and reduce a thing to what it is, that is, to what it is in. Social reductionism reduces a social element to its function in the social whole. Historical reductionism reduces a historical event to the history within which it obtains its place.

Reductionism consists in refusing to consider the irreducibility of that which is a thing to that which it is.

The cost of reductionism is the conception of a compact point.

12. That which is a thing does not determine that which this thing is; but that which is a thing prevents this thing from being *no-matter-what*. A composite thing thus and not otherwise cannot be all and its opposite. And one cannot determine what this thing is from what composes this thing.

13. How can one know what the thing is? By comprehending the thing, by going outside it, and by observing what it is in. One can then know that a thing is in this or that other thing.

14. Trying to capture a thing as a whole is to close it off on one side and to let it flow out on the other side.

Comprehending something is comprehending this something as a passage: comprehending what enters into this something and what this something enters into; comprehending how what is the thing yields what the thing is, without ever being able to determine the thing.

One never accounts for something. One never accounts for an event. One accounts for *that which had entered into* this event, and one accounts for *that into which* this event *had entered*. Between the two, there is no causal relation, no rule or law, but rather a thing: namely, an event.

15. A thing is precisely the connection or relation between what composes this thing and what this thing composes.

16. Determining the passage from the matter of things to their form, from what composes to what is composed, from what takes place to the place, from what enters into what happens to what happens, accounting for this passage in terms of causality, emergence, or any other expression is to eliminate things.

Searching for rules, laws, or conditions of passage and becoming between things is to not understand that they are things that act as a passage or intermediary between that which is and that which it is – and that things never have any other identity.

Searching for what accumulates to form an event and wanting to understand how the composition of this event gave rise to this event, to what it meant, is to fail to understand that an event is nothing other than what connects what formed to what it gave form to.

Determinism replaces things with causes. What binds what produces to what this thing produces is not an event, but a causal relation. In other words, a determinist believes that things as a whole exist that follow from each other through causes and effects (relations), whereas things are merely the relations that bind what enters into these things to what they are in.

17. That which a thing is is not the *result* of that which is in the thing. Rather, that which a thing is is what begins wherever what composes this thing ends.

18. That which a thing is cannot be no-matter-what because its beginning is determined by the end of what composes the thing.

But that which a thing is cannot be strictly determined, for that which a thing is, formally, does not have an end (only a beginning).

19. A thing is not only in the world, in something-other-than-a-thing. A thing is also an object in other things. What a thing is *objectively* is all that there is between the end of this thing and the end of the thing in which it is.

20. The sense of being is to go from *comprehended* to *comprehending*, from matter to thing, from thing to form. The sense of being is the inverse of the sense of comprehending.

21. Compactness short-circuits the very *meaning* of things.

On Meaning

Meaning is not signification. Signifying is equivalent to being a sign, to entering into a meta-relation. C. S. Peirce defines a thing as equivalent to a sign. A thing enters into a relation with its object through a series of other signs that Peirce called 'interpretants'.

Signification is always the use of some things in relation to other things, in relations that entail other relations. Near the scene of a crime, a metallic blue paint mark on a gate and tyre tracks of a car are signs for the detective that the murderer's car was metallic blue. The thing 'blue mark' and the thing 'the murderer's car was blue' are combined as signs through a series of other signs (the signs 'the mark is visible at door-level', 'paint may peel off painted objects', 'metallic blue is a common car colour', and so on). Likewise, if the sign 'flight' relates to an object, such as a bird or a plane, then it is because two things, the sign and its object, are triangulated by some other signs: 'soar', 'bird', 'air', 'travel', and so on. If in place of these signs one established the signs, 'jewellery', 'money', 'bank', 'burglar', and so on, then the sign 'flight' would relate to an object, namely, the act of departing uncaptured from the scene of the robbery.

Therefore, a sign is a relation between a thing equivalent to a sign of another thing and this other thing, but through other relations and signs, which entail other series of relations. In this way, every singular relation of signification is always directly enmeshed in an infinite network of significations. A signifying relation can only fall within a complex set of pre-existing signifying relations.

Nonetheless, signs are not the only things that have meaning. Meaning cannot be reduced to a signifying operation. There is signification only when there is an operation upon the things and the relations between things, an operation turning some things towards other things or placing some things in other things. Signification is the hierarchical order of things in each other, in which a relation between two things always relates to other relations, themselves related to others, and so on. Therefore, signification exists only if a (cognitive, symbolic, social, linguistic, or thought) activity relates some things to other things and relates some relations to other relations. If no thinking, talking, or 'cognitive' animals existed, then nothing in this world would have signification. Things would be in each other, but no relation between them would be directed at and related to the others. The imprint of a rock fallen from a cliff would be in the snow, but the imprint of the rock in the snow could never signify the fall of this rock; nothing would turn the mark towards what it is the mark of. The rock fell in the snow, but the mark left in the snow leads nothing – neither the eye, nor the brain, nor the subject – to the rock which rolled there.

However, even if nothing signified anything, if everything took place without a consequence ever pointing at its cause, without an arrow ever directing anyone in the direction of its tip, things would still have meaning. Nobody would be there to ascribe signification to this meaning, but something would circulate between things.

The meaning of things extends beyond signification as much as signification extends beyond the meaning of things. Meaning and signification only sometimes intersect in cognitive, linguistic, and thought operations, through which the meaning of things encounters the signification that we give to them. Meaning is primarily a directed sense, such that if there is a meaning, a sense to something, then it is always because there is another meaning, a possible opposite sense. The meaning of a relation is the division of this relation between two possible relations: the relation of the first relation to the second, and the relation of the second relation to the first.

The unique relation that connects a son to his father has two senses: the sense from the father to the son and the sense from the son to the father.

Every meaning is an orientation of the relation between two things. But when signification is triadic – that is, between a relation and a series of other relations, of other signs – *strict* meaning is only the order of circulation from one thing to another thing.

More precisely, the meaning of a thing is not the relation of this thing to another thing, distinct from this other thing, through other relations, but rather the relation that connects one thing to *that which is in this thing* and to *that in which this thing is*. In other words, meaning concerns relations between things which are not on the same plane, whereas signification arranges things on the same plane.

Every thing has two senses: what is in the thing or what enters into the thing, and what the thing enters into or what the thing is.

We may reasonably wonder what is the meaning of life, the meaning of existence, the meaning of history, or the meaning of the world, without even establishing the problem of the signification of the terms 'life', 'existence', 'history', or 'world'. What logicians and semioticians do not always understand is that *meaning* is not a qualifying statement about the *signification* of a thing. If I search for a meaning to my life, I do not ask for an explanation of how 'my life' is the sign and what this sign signifies. If I find a meaning to my life, I do not simply need to find what object 'my life' is in relation to, through other signs, or to clarify my confusion on this subject through an analytic or semantic explanation. If I give meaning to my life, I find out in what my life has value as something and know in what my life is comprehended, what goes beyond my life, and that my life is: an Idea, an ideal, a familial line, a community, the progress of humanity, the solitude of the world, the thought of death, nature and evolution, a genetic strategy, a work, a God, a nothing.

Finding the meaning of something is not to attribute this meaning to this thing, but rather to discover where and how one can or is willing to fix what something is in what it is. Meaning is in things. I find meaning in things, but the problem is that a thing has as many possible meanings as there exist things that this thing can be in. Finding a meaning to something is therefore essentially to subtract a certain number of meanings by considering them inessential, secondary, or in the background, so as to discover (or to fail to ever discover, if the search for meaning is ungrounded) the thing's ultimate meaning.

The ultimate meaning of each thing is *to be in the world*. But this meaning does not have sufficient signification to satisfy every individual or collective search for meaning: knowing that I am in the world as much as a stone is in the world, that my life has no more and no less meaning than the stone's existence, is not psychologically a sufficiently distinguishing meaning to guarantee to everyone that what it is has a *proper* meaning. Everyone searches for an identity, for a single meaning, and a *common* sense to things. Therefore, everyone fixes the meaning of things, of their life, of the life of another, or of their acts at a specific sign.

Each thing has as many meanings as things in which the thing is. If I am a being embedded in the evolution of the species, then my meaning is natural evolution. If I am a being which believes in the idea of world, then my meaning is to be in the world. If I am athletic on the field, my meaning is to contribute to my team's victory (and once this victory is acquired, once this meaning is past, to feel the absence of this meaning, and to be projected into a momentary emptiness). If I believe in salvation, my meaning is to be saved, and so on.

Meaning is never given, but obtained through the elimination and relativisation of other possible meanings.

Every thing has two senses, and each one of these two senses is stratified according to the containing or contained thing that one fixes this thing at.

Thus, there is given meaning and received meaning: I give meaning to what I comprehend, and I receive meaning through what comprehends me. Comprehending is giving meaning. Being is receiving meaning.

My life gives meaning to everything that my life comprehends; the meaning that my life gives is stratified according to the objects that my life fixes on, and so on. I give meaning to what I see, to what I perceive, to the past that I contain, to my memory, to my body parts, to everything that constitutes me, and, ultimately, I am the meaning of everything that belongs to me and belonged to me, since the tip of an arrow points to the meaning of everything that it carries behind it.

My life happens to know how and what to direct this meaning at. Therefore, everything inside me leads me to orient myself towards what I give meaning to. I therefore search for what I am inside, what gives meaning to me, what comprehends me. To decide on or seek the meaning of my life is thus, in one way or another, to fix or refuse to fix what I consider that I am in. If I consider for a moment that I am strictly an individual, then I give an individualist meaning to my life. If I think that I am part of a (political, moral, or religious) idea which goes beyond me, then this idea gives meaning to my life. If I think that I am a natural being, then nature is the meaning of my life, and so on.

Therefore, every object is caught in a network of significations which gives it value as a sign relative to other signs, for us or for other living beings. We add signs to signs, we connect and direct the connections between things by making them *significant* – which they are not without us. But every thing is already caught in a *meaning*, the meaning that the thing gives and the meaning that the thing receives. Things, caught between what enters into them and what they enter into, have meaning even without us. What we do, as thinking and speaking beings, is select or decide on one meaning rather than another meaning for things, for ourselves, and for others.

We give significations to things and we decide on their meaning. Signification is a circulation of things in networks, in meta-relations. Signification is created through our use of things. Meaning is the circulation of being in things. Meaning exists without us, but we act upon meaning by fixing or determining it, by considering the received meaning and the given meaning of each thing.

Meaning and *signification* intersect. Significations concern signs, rules, and uses; meaning concerns being and comprehending, choice. Through signification, things are between each other; through meaning, things are in each other. Signification is a continuously woven fabric; meaning is an overlapping of Russian dolls. The *signification* of a thing places that thing into a partial and external relation with other things and other relations. The *meaning* of a thing concerns what is completely in the thing and what the thing is completely in.

There is a logic only of significations. There are only choices (from all the objective meanings of things) of meaning.

Everything signifies, and everything can be a sign of another thing. But the being and comprehending of things concerns meaning rather than signification. Comprehending, giving meaning, is not primarily a signifying operation: one comprehends the meaning of a thing; one discusses significations of a thing.

The meaning of a thing is always one of the two possible meanings of this thing. A meaning exists if and only if two meanings exist: the meaning that a thing gives and the meaning that it receives – that is, what a thing comprehends and what a thing is.

When one confounds *meaning* and *signification*, the possible meanings of a thing become its significations, and the thing becomes a thought about the thing, in such a way that the object becomes the relation to the object. Then, as is often the case in semiotics, the meaning of things is unfortunately modelled on their use as signs.

III. The Two Senses

1. Being is *one* sense.

2. Being is an intransitive sense.

3. The intransitivity of being is nothing other than the unfolding and deployment of things.

4. *My sight of the chair* is not *my sight of the chair*, and *one chair* is not *one chair* either, since being does not identify a 'chair' unit with a 'chair' unit. We cannot know whether being continues to be the same being or another being. If they are the same, how do we differentiate them? If they are different, how do we identify them?

5. *Being* is not an equality between two object-units, but rather the inequality between what comprehends and what is comprehended.

6. Compactness is the total equality between things: one thing which is what it is, arranged alongside another thing which is what it is. Now, objectively, things are unequal: some things are other things, which are then comprehended by other things.

7. Objectively, nothing is equal, since there is no objective plane of equality of things. We cannot compare two things, arrange them side by side, and consider them as objectively *equal* from any point of view.

8. One is excluded from what one comprehends.

9. Human beings who comprehend their childhood prove they are outside childhood and can no longer live in it.

10. Nostalgia is the comprehension of what one has been.

11. Whoever claims to comprehend themselves simply does not know what they are.

12. All enthusiasm results from the incomprehension of what we are at any arbitrary moment.

13. The logic of conscious life rests on the oscillation between *being* and *comprehending*.
Consciousness is the assimilation [*digestion*] and subtraction [*suppression*] of being as comprehension.

14. Comprehending is not primarily a mental act, but can become a mental activity that does what the world, what surrounds us, does to us.

15. Being self-conscious is the primary drive of the will to be compact.

16. Self-consciousness, comprehending what I am, exists when one takes oneself as an object. But I am not, or am no more than, what I comprehend.

17. Every human self-consciousness is tragic since it leads to compactness and self-defeat.

Tragedy

Tragedy is not exactly human. Rather, tragedy is human consciousness' responsibility for the structure of the world: that what is does not comprehend itself.

In this way, tragedy is the consciousness of the inverse relation between *being* and *comprehending*: I will never comprehend what I am and I will never be what I comprehend. This relation exists for every thing. For example, the area of sand that comprehends many sand grains is not one of the sand grains which make up the area of sand; the beach does not exist on the same plane as the particles that compose the beach. This gap becomes tragic when it is assumed by consciousness – that is, by a cognitive activity capable of reciprocating or of making something of what makes something of it. This gap is the source of the human feeling of inadequacy between the structure of the world and the structure of every consciousness. Every consciousness considers as a thing what makes consciousness a thing (consciousness of the milieu, of the environment, of the physical universe, of familial, social, cultural, and linguistic determinations, and so on). But every consciousness also has access to the fact that comprehending (that is, making a thing) and being (that is, being a thing) are two opposite directions of the same relation. Every human action – interests in the animal kingdom, culture, science, an art, a social function, a community, contemplation, the body, love, friendship, action, and so on – discovers tragedy, which is not simply a tone, an accent, a certain colour of human narratives, a vague feeling, or a cultural construction, but the conscious way of assuming and confronting the inverse senses of *being* and *comprehending*. If I comprehend my object, I separate myself from this object, and I am not this object.

Though I may think that I comprehend myself, it is not myself that I comprehend, otherwise I would add myself to myself, I would comprehend myself comprehending myself, I would be an I-squared or a meta-I, so to speak. If I am this or that, then I do not comprehend this or that. Sometimes, with the passage of time, I fall from being to comprehending. How did I not see that I was this way! Nostalgia then is the relation splitting the time when I did not know that I was, and when I made something without knowing what I made. Not only mental comprehension, but every comprehension (for example, the act of holding a thing in one's hand, enveloping this thing, and taking this thing in itself, or our relation to a part of ourselves) is a separation; this is the necessity of abandoning being. What I comprehend, I cannot be, am not, and am no more. On this view, there is no difference between being *no more* and *not* being. I have not assimilated or gone beyond what I comprehend; I am separated from this; I am not this.

This is the tragedy of the passage of time and ages of life. This is the tragedy of impotent consciousness. And this is the structural tragedy that every dialectic – whether Platonist, Hegelian, Marxist, or negative – seeks to squander, arrange, or stage: that non-comprehension is a price to pay for being, that non-being is a price to pay for comprehending, and that no consciousness is to be gained from being.

I cannot thoroughly comprehend what I am: as long as I am what

I am, and as I am what I am, this escapes me. Who comprehends this? Another person? Society? A community? A god? Space-time? The world? Everything that I am not comprehends me. Only I cannot comprehend what I am. Every being is a beautiful idiot; everything except beautiful idiots comprehends what the beautiful idiots are. Beautiful idiots exist as such without ever being able to glimpse through the false mirror what others and what the world comprehends of them. These beautiful idiots will only ever have a completely indirect idea of a beautiful idiot, exiled as beautiful idiots are from themselves.

Every tragic feeling has its roots in the relationship of consciousness to *being* and to *comprehension*, which never face each other, but remain two sides of the same coin.

Tragedy is structurally in the world; in fact it marks the conjunction of the two opposite senses of things, in the flat world as in the dramatised world of interests. The 'flat world' is the *flatly* tragic world; what is something does not comprehend this something; what comprehends something is not this something. The *dramatic* world is the world in which tragedy is brought out through action, thought, language, the consciousness of living beings, human beings: henceforth, tragedy concerns interests, aimed-at ends, wanted or desired things.

Humanity *dramatises* especially what is structurally tragic about the world by combining its interests with things that humanity is and that humanity comprehends, on the grounds of a non-human, long-tragic, and disinterested world.

On Interests

Before me is a picture, a painting, framed and at the centre of a museum. I try looking at this landscape, this scene, this composition. But as soon as I look carefully at the painting – if I no longer consider the room of the museum that the work belongs to – I am no longer very certain of truly seeing it. I am seized by doubt. I plunge into the painting. I examine a mass of significant or seemingly insignificant details – distant characters, scattered objects, movements, layers, shades, and so on. By examining the varnish, I perceive coloured matter and its tiny waves on the surface of the canvas. I follow the brushstrokes. I approach an area where there is a subtle overlapping of an almost transparent sienna and Bismarck red, and so on. I see the object closer and closer, but in so doing I have lost sight of the object as such.

I wanted the thing, but only ever had *that which enters into the thing*. This is comparable to watching the sleeping beloved, like Proust's narrator, contemplating her closer in order to penetrate her mystery, until discovering what she is in herself. In her skin, through her breath, beneath her closed eyes, her expanding and contracting chest, her freckles, her curled lip, her untied hair. I want the lover herself, and yet I have only found what was in her, what was the awaited person. Her? I have lost her. Dissolved as a thing, she has slipped through my fingers. I have lost her appearance, her profile, and her unity.

Now I attempt to obtain what she is, this thing. Here I am in search of the meaning of the painting, like the meaning of what the person I love is. How do we proceed? By thinking of the painting in some context and history, I can survey its effects, its consequences, and its posterity. But I also have the opportunity to situate the painting within my singular history, to obtain control over its accidental relationship with what I have experienced up to now. It is possible for me to place the painting in many contexts, with many conditions, and always seek the *meaning* of the painting. What the painting is is what it dwells in, where it is situated. If the painting remains in its historical context or in art history or in the perception that I have of it or on the market, and so on, the painting always has *one* distinct *meaning*. Its matter (what is the painting) will be the same. But *what the painting is* will depend on what the painting is temporarily located in. Nothing is in the painting but its 'material matter' (pigments, a quantity of iron oxide and manganese oxide, degrees of calcination, transparency, the dryness of oil, and so on) and the artist's intentions, what they included, what they omitted, what they left a place for despite themselves. In the same way, what my lover thinks of herself, her way of standing, her way of considering her body, and her presence as much as her skeletal frame, her muscles, or her skin, and so on, are in my lover. An *analysis* can teach me all that. But the meaning of the painting will depend on what the work is placed in. In the same way, the meaning of the beloved, what the beloved is (a beautiful woman, a small animal, a faithful companion, an unfathomable and desired being, the mother of my children, an artist, someone that others consider in this or that way, a French woman of an arbitrary age, someone of this or that social class, and so on) depends on what I consider my lover in.

That which is its meaning will remain the same, but *that which its meaning is* will depend on that in which it is.

As soon as I look carefully at this thing, the painting or the lover, I realise that I always apprehend this thing as split; either I grasp what is the painting, what is the lover, or I grasp what this painting is, what my lover is. I no longer see the thing, but I only see either that which is the thing or that which the thing is. However, one may say, this is obviously a thing. In fact, this thing is a thing even when I am not especially interested in it – that is to say, when this thing is in the world. Thus, it is one thing among other things, encompassed in a thing much larger than this thing (a room or the biosphere, for example). But if I no longer apprehend the thing as a component of a more important thing, or if I relate to the thing as such, then I no longer obtain its unity. I grasp the painting and approach the lover only if I consider them as something other than themselves – outside the painting, outside the beloved person. As soon as I entered into the painting, as soon as I come to the lover, I lose them.

I do not obtain the thing in the thing. Seeing the thing is not to see a thing *which is a thing*, a solid, compact unit, a self-ball. No, seeing the thing is precisely to continually differentiate what composes the thing from what the thing composes: being grasped by and analysing the painting, desiring the beloved and examining her in detail.

Ultimately, the painting is in the world in the same way that the lover is in the world – even though the lover may be conscious, unlike the canvas. The ultimate meaning is this: the fact of being things equal to each other, each equal to an empire or to half of an acari, nothing more and nothing less.

Is this ultimate meaning interesting? No. It hardly teaches us anything. For a fingernail clipping, an intoxicating perfume, an irrational number, a useless gesture, two unrelated events, an imaginary fact, a nonexistent Siamese cat, and so on, are in the world and are also the world. We grasp nothing interesting from the painting that we appreciate or from the being that we love passionately by comprehending that these things are in the world. We reasonably have the impression of better apprehending and of doing justice to their meaning if we relate them to our expression, life, desires, or recent history, and so on. Within these limits, the meaning of the painting and the meaning of the lover turn out to be clearly more *interesting*. They reflect my different interests. In passing, they account for the choice of this rather than that for and by me. In the last analysis, if there were total *un-interest* in this painting being in the world, or in this beloved being in the world, neither would be whatsoever, neither the one nor the other would remain within the different limits that make me interested in them.

At the foundation of this *interest* in a thing, and of its meaning, which derives from a complex system of limits, a total *un-interest* resides: here is a thing, and this thing is in the world.

What a thing is is without interest, in both senses of the term: it is uninteresting and uninterested (without an interest to stand for). But the interest of this un-interest is that it allows the objective interest that can be attributed to it by limits.

One must remember that every meaning, every significant transmission, every capture of an object arises within the context of a destructive un-interest. The latter meaning neutralises everything that matters to me most in life, what I love. But it is also the meaning through which things can exist – things which count or do not count for me, but without which I would have nothing to love, desire, appreciate, or value.

The grounds and condition for the interest in things that matter to me is always the common place (the world) of their un-interest, of disinterestedness. One day or another I need to understand that things that I have a taste for exist and that the taste that I have for them simply does not exist.

It is possible to make this formal model vary, to increase its objective limits. A thing is then no longer in the world, but rather, for example, in the society where I live; and a thing is no longer composed of things, but rather of present-day social things. By affecting what a thing is in (history, the economy, life, a region, a group, and so on) – by circling it with a limit in order to make us interested in it, so that it matters to me in one way or another – one also changes the definition of what composes this thing. In other words, if one operates on the form of the thing, and ascribes limits to it in order to take some interest in it, then one transforms the very matter of this thing through this operation.

The question becomes: what is *primary* – the matter that constitutes the thing or the form that the thing constitutes? By affecting one, I indeed affect the other, delimiting the thing so as to make one interested in it, so that it matters.

Primary

Asking what is *primary* really makes no sense insofar as there are always *two* senses.

In the sense that matter is what is in the things, what is the things, matter is primary, since matter enters into things and constitutes them.

'Matter' is the name given to what makes things, to what constitutes them, in such a way that, in the final analysis, everything that is something proves to be material. Ideas, intentions, symbols, words, or qualities constitute things, but these ideas, these intentions, these symbols, these words, or these qualities are themselves constituted by other things (among which are still more ideas, intentions, and so on), in such a way that, from analysis to analysis, the only residue that remains in the decomposition of all these things will be what is not itself composed and only composes: matter. In the end, there is no mind, no 'spirit', no occult force, and no pure will that composes things. If there were spirit or such forces, then they would not be primordial, but themselves composed in some way of matter, which is the only buffer of all that is.

In the strict sense, matter is what is primary for being: that which is and that nothing is. In a broader sense, matter is the *region* of primary, primordial, or particular things. Fundamental physics studies the laws and modalities of matter. Matter is the region that comes closest to the *primary* for being – step by step, symbols, intentions, and instruments are themselves used to model and discover that these particles and forces reduce to more fundamental particles and forces. It is worth mentioning that this region evolves over the course of scientific discoveries, which bring about a reorganisation of the very knowledge of this region. As the region of what composes things, matter is a zone with frontiers that are renegotiated with increases in our knowledge, an increase that consists in our capacity to increasingly make secondary and composite things from what was simple and primary. For example, the atom (from Democritus to Perrin) is no longer a *given*, but rather a *result*, so that we know how an atom composes and makes itself. Today we believe that these particles are fundamental, but we hope one day to know how these particles compose and make each other.

It is an obvious fact that there is an infinite (but not indefinite) progress in the scientific investigation of the 'matter' region. Of course, fundamental physics does not aim to discover the simple and primary absolute, but to transform – and to describe how to effect the transformation – the fundamental into a composite, matter into an object. The aim of a science of matter, and of its multiple subdivisions, is not to study matter in itself, but rather to understand how matter can take on the appearance of objects, how what appeared as a buffer to the *fundamental* is always a result. Therefore, there is something in what we believed was nothing knowable.

A science of matter is a science of the way in which the matter of objects proves to be a complex of objects. This very matter must in turn become a complex of smaller, more fundamental objects.

In this way, a science of matter is the art of transforming the former into the latter.

But matter is always primary for being. In the direction of being, from that which is to that which it is, matter is really primary since nothing comes before it. In the opposite direction of comprehending, matter is secondary since form is primary in comprehending.

In the direction of the comprehension of things, that is, in the direction from that which the things are to that which is these things, matter reaches the end of its course, as closure or as impasse and not as foundation. The world – that is, the form of things – is an impasse when one ascends from matter, which is primary, to the world. But in the direction of comprehension, the world is primary (the world is what comprehends each thing) and matter is its impasse: matter comprehends nothing.

Being a materialist *absolutely* is to reduce the meaning of things to a unique and primary meaning, from matter to the world or form of things. A materialist thinks that one can make do with a departure without return – that I ascend the chain of a thing's being from matter to what this matter composes, without ever comprehending, that is, without ever taking this path in the other direction. I will never draw any comprehension from a thing's being. As a materialist I can well understand how matter, what is primary, composes and decomposes between matter in the non-relativist sense – 'cold matter', characterised by a very slow speed of thermal motion – and relativist matter – or 'matter' *tout court* in cosmological models, included in the categories of radiation. As a materialist I can well understand how a thermal equilibrium initially emerges in an environment of high density and temperature;

how matter and radiation separate; how matter, initially ionised, opaque to electromagnetic radiation, proceeds to a recombination stage; how structures and particles appear; how nucleosynthesis progresses; how galaxies form; how our solar system and our planet arose; how the atmosphere forms; how photosynthesis appears and emerges from living organisms; how evolution functions; through what processes of mutation and selection organisms develop; what the evolutionary advantages are of this or that aspect of cognition, and so on.

In this way a meaning of things, the direction of being, is wound up, like we wind up a watch. But then one only covers the distance in a (materialist) sense without admitting that the path of things functions only insofar as one can both ascend this path, in the direction of being, and descend, in the direction of comprehending. *Comprehension* is not comprehension in the strictly epistemic sense of the term. Comprehension is more broadly the sense from that which a thing is (that which contains a thing) to that which is a thing (that which a thing contains).

Therefore, what is primary is the world, the form of each thing, this impasse that every thing is, and which is nothing.

By departing from matter, we arrive at the world, account for the world, scientifically characterise the world, and follow the order of being. But by departing from the world, we never depart; matter remains a weak point of departure that is never accounted for. By departing from matter, like every materialist, one never comprehends matter; it is the open door to misunderstandings like a 'bigger soul', a transcendental meaning attributed to matter by the somewhat confused inquiry into a 'meaning' of the whole, which abandons the materialist ascent. In truth, materialism never requires a meaning: it *is* itself a meaning. But materialism is only one of them. What materialism needs is *another* meaning.

Insofar as materialism must be retained as such as a sense of things, the sense of being of things, every materialism requires another sense, the sense of comprehension. This sense does not depart from matter, from what is primary, but rather is the sense that arrives at matter.

By comprehending things – and this is partially what we accomplish in this book, by departing again from the world as from a primary sense – we obtain matter in the last sense, as the ultimate sense of things.

Matter is what arrives secondarily when one comprehends things. Matter is where one ends at and what ends at nothing else. For an absolute materialist, matter has no sense, since matter is primary. The materialist is therefore condemned to seek a 'sense of the world'. For us, the world has no sense (the world is nothing; it is not something), but matter is the ultimate sense of the world. From the world, we can only depart to rejoin what is each thing, what enters into things, matter – which is the only sense that we can attribute to the world by following the descending course from comprehending towards being.

Matter has no sense when one envisions it as primary, but if one considers matter as secondary, matter *is* an ultimate sense.

The only sense of the world is comprehending matter, obtaining something *that may be* the world.

IV. In Things: Matter

1. It is fruitless to define *that which is* the matter of things. Matter is what is ultimately in things.

Matter is what is, but that nothing is. Matter is the buffer inside things.

2. The physical sciences, fundamental physics, must establish a minimal determinate picture of what matter is. They present the primary image, the 'first light', to each era, of what the matter of things is.

Matter is never defined scientifically. What is defined is *that which* matter *is* minimally: atoms, elementary particles, forces, and fields. Physical science determines the primary objects of matter. These objects are then comprehended in the things that they compose, and so on.

Due to changes in observational techniques and theoretical modelling, the primary objects of matter later become secondary and composed by more primary components.

3. Matter is not itself material.

Matter is not composed of components of matter. Matter is what composes the primary components, without being itself composed.

Nothing is less material than matter.

4. The problem with materialist reductionism is that it puts forward a schema according to which things *are* material. In other words, it composes things with matter, and composes this matter with the things that matter composes. The shift in language is decisive: if atoms, particles, and forces composed matter, then the universe would become compact.

5. *Not* being a materialist, on the other hand, is absolutely to think that things exist that have a composition that cannot be reduced to matter, and to think that entities, spirits, ghosts, ideas, concepts, representations, energies, forces, fields, movements, spirituality, souls, and so on that are not composed – step by step, through symbolic objects, thought processes, or language – by *matter* also exist.

The argument is not that everything is composed by the primary material objects attributed to everything by the contemporary physical sciences, but rather that *several* sources of being and existence do not exist, such that there would primarily be bodies and minds, matter and something mysterious, opaque to scientific knowledge. Everything which is a thing is composed, step by step, and can thus be reduced to matter.

Nonetheless, matter is not itself material. But anyone who is *not* a materialist absolutely must consider this difference on the same plane, and claim that there exist things that derive from matter and other things that derive from something other than matter, a vital energy principle, a modern 'Psi', Prana, or Qi. These energies always short-circuit the relationship between matter, thing, and form, leading to a compact point that becomes their representation of the absolute.

6. A rock is not material, but everything that is a rock is indeed material.

On the Composition of a Thing

What is a thing's matter? What is its form? Consider a wooden cube, a child's toy. First, one may think that its matter is the wood and that its form is the cube. This means that the wood composes the cube and that the conjunction between the wood and the cube (the cubic form) yields this object that the wooden cube is.

But such a conception raises a major problem discussed by

Aristotle. Does the wood compose the object and does the object compose a cube, or do the wood and the cube together compose the wooden cube? Does matter *fill* the geometric form, or do matter and geometric form *together* constitute the object?

One can rephrase the question in this way, assuming that my body is a certain spatial, geometric figure: are my skin, blood, bones, and all of my body's material components in this geometric figure? In other words, do they fill this geometric figure? Or do all these material components, as well as the geometric figure, *together* constitute my body?

Put another way, must we think that:

(1) Matter → Geometric Figure = Object

or:

(2) Matter → Object → Geometric Figure

or, lastly:

(3) (Matter + Geometric Figure) → Object?

(1) Is the geometric figure of a thing the container of this object's matter? If matter is in a geometric form that yields the object, then, in one way or another, the geometric form is in fact a *part* of the object's matter, since the geometric form is a part of all that constitutes the thing. Yet matter *is* what constitutes things. If 'matter in the geometric figure' is the object, then form is conceived as a kind of secondary matter or meta-matter of the object.

(2) Or it may be that matter is in the object and the object is in its geometric form. In other words, the wood is in the thing, which is in a cube. But in this case the cube is not a form, but rather a limit. The cube would constitute an impalpable layer around the object made of wood – *however, a cube is not enclosed in the cube.* My body is not surrounded by an infinitesimally thin layer which would constitute its geometric form.

(3) The only solution that avoids the difficulties of (1) and (2) is to consider that 'geometric' form, a body's figure, is not its form but rather a part of its matter. Its *form* is something else. Considered in this way, the geometric figure of the cube is not the form of the cube insofar as it is a thing. The geometric figure of the cube is something that constitutes it in the same way as the wood. The cube's wood and geometric figure are equally *components* of the matter of this object, the wooden cube: they both enter into the wooden cube.

We understand 'matter' not simply as the cube's wood but *everything that enters* into the thing, everything that makes the thing, everything that composes the thing: all its elements. Yet the cube's figure is as much an element of the wooden cube as the wood is an element of the wooden cube. We must not confound what we call form with *geometric form*, which is an objective form that belongs to the matter of things – geometric form is always some spatial limit of form.

'Geometric' form must consist of 'matter' – some material, like African Blackwood, Carrara marble, and so on – to compose a thing. Formally, geometric form is as much matter as the afore-mentioned matter.

The halting point of what one calls 'matter' is relative and slightly *unstable*. One may fix the matter of things at physical matter (concrete materials, rock, their molecular, atomic structure, and so on). Such an operation is undeniably beneficial to knowl-edge. But it is only ever *an end*. One cannot altogether exclude the remainder of what composes things, which we generally consider as non-material – for instance, geometric forms – from the matter of things. One can *fix* matter at an observable, concrete, 'material matter', but this decision may always be questioned. For what we call 'geometric' or mathematical forms will continue operating, entering into the composition of things, and taking part in the composition of atoms through combinations of quarks, the spin of electrons, and so on. We can objectively *fix* matter at a part of formal matter by limiting it to objective matter – for example, observable, concrete, or extended matter. But this fixing remains delayed. It is always possible to question this by correctly consid-ering that a thing's matter is formally similar to *everything* that composes a thing, including non-material things such as a geomet-ric figure or form.

By fixing the limits to this matter and form, by thinking that a thing is composed of atoms, for example, and that a thing has a 'geometric' form, one substitutes a certain limit (a geometric, spatial pattern) in place of the form (the world). And we pass from the formal to the objective.

Limit

Every limit is a triadic relation between two limited objects and a limiting object.

A limit is an object that seeks to disappear between two other objects. It is the companion who says to the two others: 'pretend as if I was not there, forget me!' The line that separates two spaces is always itself a space. What distinguishes two objects is always – in a smaller size – an object of the same nature as the objects that it allows us to distinguish.

Every limit aims at being *nothing*, an invisible net, an inconsistent barrier, but it must still remain something to limit what it limits. In this way, a limit is a thing that must be as small as possible but still sufficient to exist between the things that it must at once distinguish and leave almost alone together. Nothing is ever alone together, but a limit stages two things *as if* they were almost alone together: *alone*, since separated; *together*, since united by what limits them and brings them into contact.

The relation between a thing and its form is dyadic. First, a thing is alone in its form (something-other-than-a-thing). Second, nothing is between a thing and the form. A form is a thing's negative, reverse side, and condition. My hand's form is everything except my hand, my hand's world. But my hand's limit is necessarily the limit between my hand and another thing: my arm, the air of the room where I am, and so on. A limit is between my hand and another thing. A limit may be a rather important thing. Indeed, several kilometers are between my hand and the Eiffel Tower. On my scale, the limit between my hand and the Eiffel Tower seems to be a rather consistent spatial expanse. But a limit may be a much smaller thing – for instance, my arm between my hand and my shoulder. A limit can be a thing that may ultimately appear as *nothing* – for instance, one may claim that nothing is between my hand and the air of the room where I am seated, but there must be a limit, a very thin layer of what is neither my hand nor the surrounding air. Something must be between my hand and the surrounding air in order to separate my hand from the surrounding air. What? The outline of my hand, its limit.

The limit is the non-excluded third. I must conceptually distinguish a hand's thin layer from my hand, in order to limit it and separate it from the air. I cannot say that *only* my hand and the air around my hand exist. The dyadic relation only exists between a thing and something-other-than-a-thing – between my hand and everything except my hand (the world around my hand). Another thing always exists between two things.

If I draw a black circle on a white sheet of paper, by drawing this black circle I create a between-the-circle-and-the-background, which is the circle's limit. If I can separate the circle from the rest of the sheet of paper (for example, by cutting it out with a utility knife), I demonstrate that I can enlarge what separates the circle from the background of the sheet of paper. If there were theoretically nothing miniscule between the black circle and the white sheet of paper, I could never cut out the circle: to cut it out or to separate it is always to increase the distance between the circle and the white background of the sheet of paper. Therefore, there was already something between the circle and the white background, which I have opened and increased by cutting out the circle in question.

Likewise, if I can remove my hand from the surrounding air, move it, and vacuum-seal it (at my own risk), I can increase or change the between-thing that separates my hand from the surrounding air. If there were nothing between my hand and what I consider to be the surrounding air, I could never remove my hand from this surrounding air, as I could never remove the circle from the white sheet of paper. What I can remove from a thing is what is separated from this thing by a limit.

What I cannot remove is what is not *limited* but *formed*. I cannot remove my hand or the circle from the world, since nothing even miniscule separates the circle or my hand from the world, and nothing separates a thing from its form. But a limit distinguishes one thing from another thing.

Like the threshold of human rites of passage, a spatial, symbolic, or material limit is a thing comparable to things between which it is placed, but considered for a time as different. The limit between two spatial things is a spatial thing; the limit between two symbolic things is a symbolic thing. But in this way the spatial limit is neglected as being almost-not-a-spatial-thing (one counts it as nothing) and the symbolic limit is taken for almost-not-a-symbolic-thing (that is nothing, that is only a *passage*, and not a *state*). However, the distinguishing feature of every limit is that one can consider it as a thing, until the question of the limit arises between the limit and the limited things. Adolescence could be a *limen*, a mere threshold between childhood and adulthood. But since adolescence, this pure moment of passage, is also an enduring state, an age like childhood and adulthood, the question of the threshold between childhood and adolescence, between adolescence and adulthood, and so on, is again raised.

If a line separates the circle from the white background, what is it that separates the black circle from this line? What is it that separates the line from the white background? Some smaller, different limit which we may also consider as a thing, and which will eliminate the problem.

Therefore, a limit always corresponds to some transitional point between-two-objects. It is an object between two objects that we momentarily take as not counting as a thing. When the limit is transferred to the counting [*reversée au compte*] of things, the problem of the limit changes scale and continues between the limit as something and the limited objects.

Every limit is homogeneous to limited objects, but, in some circumstance, every limit is temporarily judged heterogeneous. A limit is the transient state of an object between-two-objects, concealing itself.

A limit is a process that leads to the infinite. Form is a fixed relation between a thing and something-other-than-a-thing, a non-homogeneous relation between thing and non-thing, leading to a single state. A limit concerns a state of objects among states of objects. A limit is like a player temporarily chosen as referee, even though she is in fact a player like the other players, no less legitimate a player than them. A limit is a negotiation between things. Form is the outside of things.

A limit is between things and always a thing. Form is outside things and not a thing.

All limits are transient. Form is atemporal.

Many limits and possible relations exist between things. But there is only ever one form, the same for each thing, completely around things.

Hand Prints

That things have limits means that things are contained in something-other-than-themselves, which, in order to be other things, are no less things. A limit is a *thin layer* that surrounds a thing and that is of the same nature as a thing. By tracing the limit of a thing, one creates a membrane around the thing, separating it from the rest of the world.

To establish a limit on a thing is to isolate it from the world. On the other hand, to give form to something is to establish it in the world. Form is infinite, whereas a limit is finite.

The early prehistoric human beings who made hand prints in caves perhaps intuitively grasped the difference between limit and form; placing their hands against the cave wall, they began to paint negatives of their hands. They perhaps understood that if by covering their hands with pigment they did not paint what constituted their hands, they ought to cover with pigment what their hands constituted – that is, the negative of their hands. By applying paint around the hand to draw its form, was there any reason for them to stop spreading the paint? The question must not lure one into the traps of some kind of fictional Paleolithic psychology. The question concerns rediscovering the primitive meaning of negativity and form. By beginning with their hands, the human beings who used them like stencils discovered an *infinite* possibility. When should they stop? Did the form of their hands have some limit? Yes and no. The form did not have a limit, since they could conceivably colour the entire world apart from their hands, cover up the whole of its negative, which begins without ever ending: form has no limit. Why should the form of a hand take up two centimeters of thickness, rather than three centimeters, a thousand, or a million kilometres? Form is not a thing; it ends only by the beginning, and not by the end.

At the same time, Paleolithic human beings, with whom some may sometimes identify, could have discovered that this impossibility of determining any end to the form of their hands, which were nothing other than the very world, is accompanied by material problems. Indeed, the cave wall only extended a few metres. The rock itself, after all, was not infinite, no more than the earth – even if Paleolithic human beings didn't know it. Painting the entire world as the negative of our hands was inconceivable – how can one cover in black the sky and the stars, sounds and smells, ideas, and so on. The negative of our hands appeared as an unlimited form. But the negative of this hand was also strictly limited by non-inferential material conditions which *were necessary*. Painting the negative of the hand was not absolutely limited by the cave wall's length, since, during the birth of the symbolic, one could have imagined painting the ground and mountain, and invented a means of making the sky entirely black – but objectively, even so, this operation seemed relatively difficult and *limited*.

On the contrary, what characterises form is that it is not a thing. A limit is what separates a thing from its form, like a quarantine line around a thing, isolating a thing from that which is not a thing – its form. A thing may be extremely limited, but it is still no less formed by its limits.

Since form delimits a thing, form cannot be delimited on its own. *What stops is unstoppable: form.* However, we determine a *limit* when we *stop what stops.* Unlike form, there is something contingent in a limit, which makes us continually question it. Look closely at the book that you are reading. This book is limited by the room in which it is, provided that it is in a room, just as it is limited by its time – it is enclosed in a place, in a time, in the consciousness that you have of it, in its economic value, and so on. If I put this book in a bag and close it, this bag captures it. This is yet another limit. But limits change and depend on a point of view, on interests attributed to a thing, on a scale of perspective. Does the bag or the house in which the bag is limit the book? If I come closer to the limit, I perceive an increasingly fine membrane around the thing, like a thin transparent layer. I begin to believe that this is the thing's absolute limit, an immaterial line surrounding it, completing the total circumference of its geometric figure.

However, no thing is wholly in a spatio-temporal, geometric thin layer. What dimension could this thin layer that separates the object from the world entirely around it have? Does it have an infinitesimal dimension? Even if the limit were limited only at the limit, one could certainly not avoid the fact that this limit's limit would naturally be arbitrary. Indeed, one can limit a thing's limit, but it is *we* who limit it. Just because *we* limit it does not mean that this limit cannot be limited in an infinite number of other ways, with an infinite number of layers. A thing does not have *one* limit, but can have as many limits as one wants it to have or as one discovers it to have. What one does not choose is its form. One cannot limit a form.

Now, to be able to limit a thing, one must still limit it within the context of its form. A limit is a stopping point on the form of a thing. A limit is *another thing* that comes in *between thing and world*.

Form is always fixed with some thing, and, at the same time, fixes it elsewhere, for a reason. Limits can be established only *relatively* and in an *interested* way – unlike the form of a thing, which is without interest and not itself something.

V. Outside Things: Form

1. That which a thing is is its form. Matter is a thing as much as a thing is a form.

2. The form of each thing is the world.

The form of an object depends on what an object is in.

A thing can be the form of an object. Since my finger is in my body, my finger has this body as a form. Since my finger is in the air, my finger has this air as a form.

But my finger as a thing, and not as an object, has the world as a form, that is, everything except itself: everything that ends where the world begins, its surrounding.

3. The formalist separates form from things and makes form the most important thing.

The curse of the formalist is being condemned to subtract forms from things. If one considers form as an object, one attributes unity to this object. The problem then arises as to whether there is one Form (the Form of forms) or several forms, if each thing has its form, or if several things can have the same form.

4. The distinguishing feature of form is to begin without ending. The distinguishing feature of matter is to end without beginning. Since form does not end (since form is not a thing, and since form is not itself in a thing), every form is the same form.

By beginning, as many forms exist as there are things. But by ending, or rather by the fact of not ending, only a single form exists.

More precisely, form is what connects the infinite plurality of things to an identical formal infinity; each thing has its form, which is the same form for each thing. By ending, each thing begins a form different from others, which ends in the same way, or rather which in the same way does not end.

To obtain a very approximate representation of the way in which form connects together the singularity of each thing and a common place, one could imagine a space containing three forms of geometric objects: a square, a circle, and a triangle. By observing each one of these objects as if it were surrounded by a stencil negatively defining its form, it is possible to imagine covering up the triangle with an infinite space pierced solely by a triangular cut, the square with an infinite space pierced solely by a square zone, and the circle with a similarly infinite space from which one could remove a corresponding circular section. Let us consider each one of these stencils with infinite extension. They are only bordered by the *inside*, an empty triangular, square, or circular *inside*. Their beginning is therefore always of a different form. But their infinity (the external edge that they will never join), the space that they define entirely around this emptiness, is certainly the same. Their external infinity, on the *outside*, is always identical.

They begin differently and (do not) end identically.

Such are the forms, and such is form. *Some* forms exist by the beginning and *one* form exists by the end, which never ends.

5. If one makes an object of a form, one must *end* this form. We can call this the Platonist impasse: form-objects – if there are many, and if one must count one of them for each thing – would lose their form and become doubles, duplicates of objects. If these form-objects are confounded into a single (Plotinian) form, operating through emanation up to singular beings, they lose their objectivity. In the last analysis, a great compact, single form remains, as if there were no more *limits*.

6. A limit is a contained container.

7. Every object has a limit.

8. Every object is embedded in a membership relation with one or several things.

9. There are no solitary objects.

10. To identify what an object is is to understand that in which an object is what it is. It is to cut it off from the background of a big thing.

11. Perceptions, actions, and ideas are ways of dividing objects.

12. Dividing objects is, in one way or another, to define limits.

Considering a branch is to actively limit the branch by separating it from the tree. Sleeping is to limit one's time of sleep within one's time of awakening. Seeing is to limit objects in a field of vision. Speaking a language is to divide nouns, actions, tenses.

13. Dividing objects is to give up on certain things mattering.

Perception, action, and thought do not divide up things ad infinitum. They only retain some distinguished things from the division-into-things. In this way, these distinguished things reach their limit.

14. Dividing objects is to only consider a finite number of things.

But it is always possible to reduce an object to, and to dissolve an object in, an infinite number of things.

15. An object is a thing that matters within another thing.

This table is an artefact that is important for those who touch it, see it, make use of it, or name it, within the network of industrial and artisanal human productions.

This horse is a living object, an organism that matters within its species, within evolution, and for other species.

This word is a symbolic object that matters within a certain language.

16. To consider, handle, or contemplate an object, or to make it function is to temporarily prevent this object from being reduced to an infinite number of things. It is to attribute unity to an object by making the object be in another thing: a consciousness, a series of events or reactions, a moment, a membership structure, a goal, a value, a domain, or a group.

17. A thing has no unity. A thing has finitude and solitude.

Attributing unity to a thing, or making an object of a thing, is to make of it *one* among *others*.

A cloud is a thing since a cloud is solitary, finite, and in the world – that is, a cloud is.

The same cloud is also an object because there are other clouds, it is a cloud in the sky – that is, in another thing, embedded, for instance, in meteorological relationships of atmospheric pressure and depression, condensation and movement.

18. A thing has a form. If this form itself takes a form and becomes a limit, then this thing is an object.

Listen to a sound, the noise of a stone falling on the ground. This noise has a form; it begins, endures, and ends. Everything that is not this noise, before, during, and after it, forms this noise. The form of the noise, what begins where the noise is not or is no more, in space, in time, and in my perception, is infinite. The noise is in this form, it is solitary in this form, nothing else can be with or in the company of this noise.

But if I define the form of this noise, or if I consider the noise in time, by dividing the form from the beginning to the end of this sound, its appearance and dissipation on a spectrum of sonic frequencies, I attribute a form to its form: time. The form of the noise is then a thing on its own; it is definite and finite.

The noise, limited more or less strictly in time, becomes a temporal object, an event whose duration is determinable.

19. To know is to divide objects. An epistemic model is a system of limits.

To act is to divide objects. To make something is to attribute unity to something by moving it, transforming it, fusing it together, or allowing it to interact with another thing.

20. Objects never have a world.

21. Objects are together, in each other.

22. I cannot make another thing of a thing. But I can affect the composition of an object, what is an object, and make another object of an object.

23. I cannot act on a thing. I cannot know a thing. I can only be or comprehend a thing.

24. To be a thing is to be in this thing. To comprehend a thing is to have this thing inside and to be its world.

25. When I comprehend a thing, being a thing myself, I limit this thing, and I make an object of this thing.

26. To comprehend something is to make of this something one object among others.

27. The relation between form and thing is formal. The relation between things is objective. Things are objects when they are between things.

28. There is no relation between form and objects.

Forms

Every metaphysics accounts for its forms, but unfortunately treats them as objects. The Platonist grappling with the third man of the *Parmenides* and the infinite multiplication of his Ideas; the Aristotelian of the sublunary world who finds *ousia* as much as things; the nominalist who denies some things their existence; the Lockean or Humean empiricist who constructs them one by one; the Cartesian who postulates two of them; the Spinozist who has but one of them; the Leibnizian who wants an infinite number of them; the Kantian who organises their grammar, a priori forms of sensibility, ideas, schemata, and categories; the Hegelian who dialectalises them; the Wittgensteinian who shows them by saying them; the phenomenologist who obtains them through eidetic reduction; Whitehead, who finds four notions, four series of Categories, eight Categories of existence, twenty-seven Categories of Explanation, nine Categorical Obligations, and so on.

The eternal problem of a speculative metaphysics is accounting for its forms as objects. Whether I obtain one form or two, several, or an infinite number of forms, as long as there are things, the vacuity of the concept of 'form' derives from attempts to conceptualise it, to construct something-other-than-a-thing, the opposite and condition of the thing, making it quite clearly one thing among others, and therefore an object, a *countable* object.

In a compact version of formal universalism, if I claim that there is only one form, I cannot really account for the plurality of objects. If there is only one form, and all of the things have the same form, then things are not different and no objects exist.

If I claim that as many forms exist as there are things, I redouble the objects, and I cannot account for what they have in common as *things*; form becomes the phantom of an object, its projected shadow, and nothing more, in an abstract, ideal, and spectral world.

If I claim that several forms exist, but not as many as objects in each other exist, I begin to construct a hierarchy, tables of categories, or other old-fashioned spells of scholastic metaphysics. I give the illusion of a proper order to forms (to essences, to Ideas, to forms of sensibility, to concepts of the understanding, it doesn't matter). Forms would be a plurality ordered into a reduced model of the chaotic world of objects. In this case, forms embody precisely what we no longer want: more-than-things, martinets of the world of objects, less singular than the more general and organised things in an army corps.

What remains?

What good is it to reformulate a metaphysics, one may object, if one wants neither a compact mysticism of Form or a single Idea – that what remains to us is to contemplate the ground beneath our feet in the disorderly world of objects – nor a spectral metaphysics that redoubles the world of objects in a world of useless and always secondary corresponding forms, nor an order of forms, a grammar, or hierarchical formal categories for knowing the given world of objects . . . ?

We do not think that some single Form exists outside objects embedded in each other. No Solitary being, absolute Spirit, single and formal reality, coronation of the heaven of Ideas, or Divine Being will save us from the multiplicity of objects around and in us. Neither do we think that a form exists for each object, a *Doppelgänger* of every thing, an original ideal or a faded photocopy, with reduced intensity, of objects that inter-comprehend each other, always, everywhere, and increasingly. Finally, we do not think that a government of forms exists – a reduced number of representatives of the many-coloured people of objects, who govern by formal laws, rational and excessively ordered categories.

Nonetheless, we do not think that *only* objects exist – that is, things between things, things in things, and nothing else.

Forms exist. But we must above all not treat them as objects, count them, list them, categorise them, or classify them in light of some epistemology. No differentiated forms exist. Forms exist only insofar as only one of them exists. That only one of them exists does not mean that it is an absolute, a higher form, or an object of contemplation, since form is the form of each different thing.

We want neither an order of differentiated forms, the root of every metaphysics as epistemology, nor a single Form, the root of every metaphysics as wisdom and as contemplation.

A form always has *two* senses. Just as a thing has a sense of being (that which the thing is) and a sense of comprehension (that which the thing comprehends), so too a form has two senses: its beginning and its end, what the form ends and how this form ends.

Every thing ends something (its matter, what the thing comprehends, what is in the thing) and is ended by another thing (by its form). A form has an endless end. A form has a positive sense and a negative sense. By conceiving of form, and not only objects, we can imagine what begins without ending.

Form is in contact with a thing in one sense (at its beginning). But form has nothing to do with a thing and escapes from it in another sense (a form does not end).

Metaphysics-as-epistemology (Aristotelianism, empiricism, Cartesianism, Kantianism, phenomenology) isolates forms at their beginning, where things end, in order to put forward an objective order of them. Metaphysics-as-wisdom-and-as-action (Plotinising Platonism, Augustinianism, Schopenhauerian theory of will, Nietzschean vision of power) isolates the form that leads to its end, where there are no more individuations and no more things – which are only constructions or reconstructions.

Of course, forms are different in their beginning, since they begin where every thing ends; things are different where they end, which is where their form begins. The form of a cat is not the form of a dog; a cat and a dog are different, since their forms, that is, everything that is not a cat and everything that is not a dog, begin differently.

But every form ends in the same way by not ending in the same way. Since a form is not a thing, it does not end and has no ultimate determination; it is everything that is not a cat and everything that is not a dog. Is what is not a dog similar to what is not a cat? In other words, is the form of a cat the form of a dog? What is not a dog begins where a dog ends (its profile, its determination, everything that constitutes a dog), but never ends, infinitely comprehending everything, anything, that is not a dog. What is not a cat begins differently, by beginning where a cat ends, but continues in the same way by not ending in the same way.

Since the formal is in contact with each thing, as many forms as things exist at the beginning, but only one and the same form exists at the end, which does not end and is not something. Since forms tend to not end, to not be something, and to be nothing, forms are the soundest intuition that we have of the world. They are what every different thing aims at. Forms are the many-coloured reverse sides of every different thing, which fuse increasingly, ad infinitum, in the colourless unity of the formal.

The formal is what forms of things tend towards. The formal is not a supreme value, an object of contemplation, an ethical regulative ideal, Spirit acting through the negativity of all things, a mental construction, and so on. The formal simply indicates the *vanishing point* of the form of things.

Objects, things in each other, are all in different places that tend to become a common place.

The subject matter of this first book – the formal, that which comprehends everything – is at the same time that which is *nothing*, in the same way that the primary matter of things comprehends *nothing*. Singularly, what makes the world is made of nothing. What comprehends everything is comprehended by nothing. Between the two, in the two senses of *being* and *comprehending*, things inter-comprehend each other, and, so to speak, 'inter-be' each other; then the realm of objects arises – things among things, between that which comprehends all and which is nothing, and that which is nothing but comprehends all.

Since matter constitutes things by *no-matter-what* (since nothing is no-matter-what), forms comprehend things and are confounded in a single form which is not something, which is not differentiated, which is nothing. Matter dissolves into no-matter-what. Forms gather into a formal system that all is and is ultimately nothing – this was the subject matter of this first book.

Between *no-matter-what*, which makes the matter of things and that nothing is, and *totality*, which is the vanishing point of the form of these things, which is nothing, things are and comprehend each other. Filled and filling, things function, in each other, by each other, between matter and form, between anything and everything, between what nothing is and what is nothing, between what everything comprehends and what comprehends everything, in the realm of objects, different and differentiated.

We have little more to say about the formal world in which each thing is solitary, about the bilateral relation between thing and world, the two senses (*being* and *comprehending*), the ascent and descent, developed at length above.

The formal system is poor and flat. We have proceeded by conceiving this formal system; embedded between no-matter-what and all, we have obtained some weak but certain truths, both minimal and complex, difficult to explain and deploy, like Japanese paper flowers coursing in a river. But this trickle of water is quite meagre. It is an arid, abstract, deserted system, like the system of form, and it is always the same. The formal system was rigorously expressed and described through a series of finite propositions. Now we must rigorously attribute a discursive order to them, with everything there, at once, simply, with neither hierarchy nor priority.

What could be more different than the objective system, the realm of objects, of things between things? The formal system is poor, although necessary, while the objective system is rich in content, in significations, in relations, in novelties, in accumulation, in choices, in disciplines, divided and multiplied in every direction, ad infinitum.

After the solitude of things and the minutia of the few, the intoxicating variety of objects and the vertigo of the many are disclosed to us. Until now, we have only provided a philosophical glimpse into other human actions, scientific disciplines, uses, practices, and methods.

After the necessary traversal of the desert of the world, the swarming universe at last opens up to us.

Book II

Objectively

Chapter I

Universe

1. The Formal and the Universal: The Biggest Possible Thing

Objects in each other form big things. The biggest possible thing is what we call the *universe*. While the world is the reverse side or the form of each thing, the universe is a big thing, the identity of which is variable. The universe is always defined with a superlative: 'the biggest thing'. Thus, we cannot conceive of a more important thing at the present moment, and we do not know if we will find a means to augment it further in the future.

The maximal comprehension of objects is what we call the *universal*. To be universal, or to make a universal judgement, is to claim to comprehend the biggest possible object. Yet the universal must be distinguished from the *formal*. We call the formal the comprehension of each possible thing.

Many difficulties result from the confusion between *universal* and *formal*. While the search for the universal presupposes an objective knowledge, a knowledge of the state of objects in each other in the universe, the formal always implies a consciousness of each thing being equally in the world.

Universality – the universality of the laws of nature or the presumed universality of cultural phenomena – resembles a maximal comprehension of differences. It is always a continual process of the cumulative assimilation of differences. For example, when one establishes that some human groups consider non-human animals to have minds similar to theirs, while others take them to be without internal states or in some way different from humans, the universal operation consists in adding up the differences of opinion while returning to what remains in common. Universally, one may claim, humanity relates to and always maintains a comparative relation to non-human living things, expressible through identification and differentiation.

One may draw a *positive* lesson from knowledge of the universal as an assimilation of differences, producing an identity likely to be differentiated in turn: humanity must pay attention to its relations with other animals, since it is through these relations that humanity defines itself. One will infer from this the idea that it is necessary that one not cut humanity off from its animal environment, and that it is therefore necessary to protect other animal species, but without artificially isolating them from our everyday lives.

The formal knowledge that one can acquire from the observation of cultural differences is quite different. Formally, one may identify the 'price to pay' for each position. By considering humanity as similar to other animals, one formally distinguishes humanity from other animals (since other species do not consider themselves similar to humanity). But to distinguish humanity from other species is to make humanity formally similar to other species (for example, by allowing humanity to disrespect animal life, one makes possible an appeal to the predation that makes humanity animal-like). Formally, one may therefore say that a determinate position is 'equal' to another position, insofar as what escapes one is what belongs to the other, and vice versa.

Therefore, one cannot derive an objective lesson from formal knowledge, nor can one determine, in virtue of this formal knowledge, what is best or more just. The universal permits the assimilation of differences, reducing them to a positive and new identity; the formal permits only the reduction of these differences to a plane of equality, which flattens them. The universal permits the determination of particular positions as *differently the same*; the formal permits their determination as *identically different*. The universal thus reduces objects to a universe that comprehends all objects, while the formal reduces things to a world that comprehends each object.

For example, it is an objective possibility that *universal* human rights exist. By considering humans as objects comprehended in one and the same humanity, while accounting for these human objects' communal and social membership in determinate groups, each with their own customs, laws, and values, it is possible to arrange something like a human universe. In this universe, human objects are included in larger objects, their cultures, themselves comprehended in the universe of natural or biological humanity.

Therefore, the rights of all humans comprehend the rights of humans of this society, this class, or this caste.

On the other hand, it is less clear whether or not *formal* human rights exist. Formally, like each society and all of humanity, each human is a thing which is in the world. If humanity comprehends each culture, each culture also comprehends humanity, since each culture defines humanity in its own way.

The formal is not a relative realm, some paradise of the relativist. Far from it, since all things are in the same world. Rather, the formal is the possibility, the ultimate foundation, and, at the same time, the bad conscience of the universal. If one acquires the rights of all humans, then one must lose in particularity what one gains in universality.

While the universal is cumulative, the formal is the presentation of the loss that accompanies every gain. Formally, one can affirm nothing other than this: 'Choose this universalising option, but know well what you lose by choosing this option'. The universal requires decision, whereas the formal allows nothing other than consciousness to bring objective inflation [*progrès*] to the flatness of equality.

But no universal would be without the formal. If there were no *things*, equal and equally in the world, there could not be unequal objects in each other to form a universe, a 'biggest possible thing'.

For example, only hypothetical universal laws of nature exist, since it is possible to differentiate scales in nature. One can open up the limits of the universe to the infinitely large, which comprehends increasingly more, and the infinitely small, which is comprehended increasingly more, from particle to particle, from composite to simple. However, it is well known that the universality of the laws of nature was increasingly threatened by this expanded opening of scales and the growing difficulty of relating the laws of the very large to the laws of the very small.

What holds the universe together is the possibility that the smallest things, like quarks, may be equally in the world, neither more nor less than a nebula – that is, that a plane of equality is maintained between what is comprehended on a microcosmic scale and what comprehends a mass of objects on a macrocosmic scale. However, no law of the relation between a quark and a nebula exists, since this relation is strictly formal, not relating two objects to each other, but relating two different things to the same world.

The universality of laws, values, and rights concerns the accumulation and order from the comprehended to the comprehending; a physical, social, or symbolic object which comprehends other objects relates the differences of what it comprehends to the identity of its comprehension. It is always possible to establish an order of objects in objects, which leads to a universe – namely, to 'the biggest possible thing' – manifesting the maximal comprehension of differences. From individuals to communities, from communities to societies, from societies to humanity, from humanity to nature, to God, or to an idea, from protons and electrons to atoms, from atoms to molecules, from molecules to bodies, from bodies to stellar systems, from stellar systems to galaxies – this objective order is processual, since it always depends on the capacity to arrange from the comprehended to the comprehending, by relating differences to a thing's identity, itself different from other possible things, and assimilated into a bigger thing. The universal is processual and antagonistic, for it is negotiated at each scale. But the universal is *possible* and corresponds to the capacity to organise worldly things into universal objects.

Nonetheless, what permits the universal is also what precludes it; the formal is both the condition of universality and the dissolution of the universe. At each stage of universalisation, formalisation makes possible the problem of one object's comprehension by another. For example, a social class is comprehended in a society, can comprehend this society, contain it entirely, and determine it. In this way, the order from the comprehended to the comprehending is formally short-circuited. Human nature comprehends different cultures, but each culture comprehends human nature and fashions it in turn. Formal equality may thus potentially block the order of universality at each stage.

The relativist's mistake consists in confounding the universal and the formal, by attributing a universal character to the formal: each thing could *objectively* comprehend what comprehends it, thus each culture could comprehend its nature in the same way that nature comprehends each culture. But two very distinct orders of things exist: an *objective* order and a *formal* order. Humanity *objectively* comprehends different human cultures, while a human culture can *formally* comprehend humanity. The relativist aims at compactness by supposing that what is particular does to what is universal exactly what the universal does to the particular. For the relativist, a universal right is immediately a particular right like any other, since the relativist considers that a particular community can prescribe a universal right as *one* right in the same way that a universal right can be prescribed to a particular community as a *universal* right. The relativist strikes back.

Some universals exist for the relativist, since they need a *plane* to 'place on the same plane' things that they make equal. This plane of equality, this plate on which the relativist places what they make relative, is the formal world, the flat world where each thing is equal to another. But the relativist makes this world (where each thing is *solitary*) a universe where things are *together* equal to, and comparable with, each other. Thus, the relativist universalises the formal.

Now, the formal and the universal are not identical. The universal is an objective order, which the formal permits, grounds, prevents, checks, and controls. The formal is situated either beneath or above the universal, but never beside it or on the same level as it. The relativist combines the formal and the universal into one and the same order. They conflate the universal and the formal to produce the relative.

In fact, things can be in each other, comprehended and comprehending, like objects, since each thing is equally in the world. The formal may short-circuit the objective order, since what comprehends – what is largest, what assimilates differences into an identity – is formally equal to what is comprehended – to what is different or smaller.

The formal traps the universal by making it possible and then sabotaging it. The universal is possible *between* the formal as condition and the formal as failure; it is only ever possible in this case.

While the relativist makes the formal universal, the absolutist makes the universal formal. In absolutist thought, the universe becomes the world, and objects become things. Consequently, the accumulation of objects produces a formal, absolute order, the order of the world; what comprehends something is never comprehended by what it comprehends. In this becoming-world universe, universal rights are absolute, since they can never be short-circuited. If there were a dialectic between what is lost and what is gained, it would always be on the side of the gain. In the universe absolutised into a world, nothing comprehends the biggest possible thing, the physical universe (absolute materialism), human society (holist sociology), or a god, allowing the establishment of laws, values, and rights that comprehend and assimilate differences between things into identities that cannot be differentiated, related to other possible identities.

The relativist grasps the formal system according to which each thing is equally in the world, neither more nor less than another, in order to universalise it; each object is equivalent to another object, and nothing comprehends something without being objectively comprehended in turn by what it comprehends. The absolutist grasps the universal system according to which an object comprehends other objects, but they assimilate differences into the maximal object, the universe, in order to formalise it; an object that comprehends other objects is formally superior to these other objects, thus determining them and prescribing its identity absolutely on their differences.

For the relativist, a universal human right is a particular right, neither more nor less than another. For the absolutist, a universal human right assimilates particular rights, comprehends them, and protects them without losing them.

But both the relativist and the absolutist confound the universal and the formal. For anyone who knows how to distinguish them, a universal human right is not objectively a right like any other, but it can only be chosen with full knowledge of the cause, knowing that they lose in particularity *as much* as they gain in universality.

The universal exists and is not a particular claim to the non-particular, but the universal can only be known and defended on the condition of knowing that it doesn't formally yield more than what it causes us to lose. Therefore, the universal is the object of a real choice, since it never offers the guarantee of an absolute profit, but the prospect of a calculated loss.

2. Universe, Universal Parts, Universal Scales

The universe is the biggest possible thing, but it is only ever a thing. The universe carries the contradictions of every thing that is supposed to comprehend without being comprehended. But since every thing is in two directions, the universe is never a world.

One can attempt to know the universe, the object of scientific knowledge, in three ways: as a unity, through parts, or through scales. First, the universe as a unity or whole is a cosmological object. Marc Lachièze-Rey defines the universe in his introductory text on cosmology:

The study of the universe or cosmos, cosmology, is the most global and all embracing study possible [. . .] The notion of the cosmos involves more than the collection of the diverse heavenly bodies under the umbrella of a single name. It implies the existence of global and universal properties and relations.[1]

Lachièze-Rey emphasises 'the uniqueness of the universe as a cosmological object. There is only one universe, and we are part of it'[2] as a whole. Therefore, cosmology consists in the study of everything that, materially, is a sufficiently big object, the formation, properties, and structure of which cannot be comprehended except in relation to the whole universe:

> We have known since the beginning of the twentieth century that matter exists in the form of galaxies [. . .] Galaxies are the main objects of study in cosmology. They are the largest objects whose nature we understand. Most importantly, we believe that their properties are explained more by cosmic processes than by local conditions. Unlike planets and stars which live in a local environment and have no direct relationship with the rest of the universe, galaxies must be seen in the cosmological setting.[3]

These differences, which are subtle and continually on the brink of revision, are the only ones between our knowledge of objects, which derives from the comprehension of the whole universe, and our knowledge of objects considered possible locally, independent of the biggest possible thing, which comprehends these objects.

Second, through parts the universe is knowable locally or regionally. In this case, our galactic, solar, and terrestrial environments mark the specific centres of our attempts to acquire knowledge of the universe. The atmospheric and earth sciences are local sciences par excellence. They presuppose the universe to be a maximal container object, but almost entirely neglect and ignore this assumption in their research. A local science is a science that must presuppose the existence of a universal, global object, without this being relevant to the study of its objects. In this way, debates about the cosmological constant or cosmic background radiation do not, or almost do not, concern – until further notice – the establishment of our knowledge regarding the earth's crust, continental drift, or the history of the earth's inner core.

Third, the universe can become the object of objective knowledge through scales – that is, the laws of the universe derive from the order of magnitude of a chosen frame of reference. In this case, knowledge is not exactly local, but 'scalar' (in the geographic sense, rather than in the mathematical sense). It does not concern a part cut off from the universe, but *the whole* universe at another scale. One then considers the smallest objects, comprehended in more important objects, not locally, but in their totality. Whereas a local objective knowledge divides some objects in the midst of other objects, a 'scalar' objective knowledge considers all objects comprehended together at some scale, by setting aside comprehending objects.

In a scalar objective knowledge – of elementary particles, for example – one allows the emergence of laws and the assimilation of differences under certain identities, which are distinct from or contradictory to the laws of another scale. In this case, for example, at the quantum scale, the universe is considered neither as one, nor through parts, but through *levels*. What is true on some level is not true on another level.

Each of these ways of knowing the universe is objective and not formal, since each presupposes an order of objects: some things are comprehended in others, which are in turn comprehended in new ones. The rigour of this order makes possible the search for laws, whether of the whole universe, of a universal part, or of a universal level.

The formalisation of objective parts of knowledge can always cause problems. The major impasse of contemporary cosmology, and of all cosmology since Antiquity, is the search for a form of the universe (expansion, stability, future retraction) – that is, the transformation of the universal container into content. Yet cosmology only functions if it understands the universe only in one sense ('the biggest possible thing', what contains all objects) without having the opposite sense – that is, the form of this big thing, or its limits and its characteristics insofar as it is comprehended and not merely comprehending. To consider the universe as a thing can only be a formal act of non-objective comprehension.

The problem of local knowledge derives from the ambiguity of its relation to the universe as an insignificant condition. All local knowledge presupposes the existence of the universe as its ground, while setting aside this distant environment in order to determine the knowledge of a determinate place (like the planet earth). The risk lies in gradually transforming this place into an island

and conceiving a part of the universe as a self-sufficient object. Since humanity lives on earth, knowledge of the earth provokes humanity to more or less consciously identify the universe with the planet. In doing so, humanity limits its own horizon.

Every scalar knowledge of an atomic or subatomic universal level may lead to the illusory existence of basic, ultimate components of matter, objects smaller than everything, primary objects, or universal elements of all objects and all scales.

3. Science of the Smallest, Science of the Biggest

Matter is not the object of particle physics. The smallest possible things are its objects. The universe, the unitary cosmological object, is the biggest possible thing. The objects of a fundamental knowledge of the properties of matter are the smallest things, that is, the things tending to appear as *being* without *comprehending*, composing without being composed.

Therefore, matter is to particles what form is to the universe. The universe is not the form of things; it is the world which is the form of things. Particles are not worldly matter. Particles are things which are worldly matter. The universe is the thing which approaches the biggest. Particles are things which approach the smallest. They are stages along the path formed by the problem of the 'structure of structures' of all material things. Frank Close writes,

> [i]t is possible that in discovering the existence of quarks we have found the ultimate seeds of nuclear matter. However, it may be that there is a layer of reality beyond quarks, entities which cluster to build up quarks as composite structures, and which we are currently unaware of through lack of powerful enough microscopes to resolve them.[4]

Through modelling and observation, physics transforms basic and primary objects, such as quarks, into composite and secondary objects. This decomposition of physical objects from level to level is not the limit, but the function of physics.

'Scientific' objective knowledge exists only between the smallest and the biggest, neither beneath nor beyond. Beneath the smallest and beyond the biggest, it is not an objective problem, but a problem of things and world, and therefore of formal knowledge.

The smallest and the biggest only exist through objects in each other, that is, what is comparable and what inter-comprehends. According to Brian Greene,[5] the contemporary desire to replace the functions of particles with 'strings' betrays attempts to proceed from 'perfect points' to primordial lines, that is, from 'zero-dimensional' primary objects to 'one-dimensional' primary objects. The 'Theory of Strings' as a hypothetical framework for resolving problems of quantum gravity corresponds to the objective reorganisation of the dimension of the universe's primordial objects and their identity, rather than to problematising the very form of the universe as a totality of objects at different levels. That the primary objects are 'vibrating strings', having tension, with a frequency, allowing one to consider the actual particles as secondary effects, deducible and predictable, merely continues the processes transforming simples into composites, primary things into secondary things, particles into effects, for our knowledge. Likewise, the existence of many other dimensions, more or less enveloping each other, expands the universe and continues its processes of objective unfolding for knowledge.

The superlative of the biggest – the universe – and of the smallest – the particle – derives from the projection ad infinitum of comparison between objects: an object such that no other object is bigger or smaller ad infinitum.

This superlativisation, which marks the conception of a universe or of elementary particles (or of 'strings'), allows for the bidirectional opening of a domain of objects accessible to objective knowledge. A science is nothing other than the (global, local, or scalar) effectuation of processes that open the universe to the biggest and to the smallest.

Therefore, particle science discovers neither objects nor particles which absolutely pre-exist particle science's examination of them. It does not invent or project these objects in nature. A science divides these objects in the universe step by step.

A science is the establishment of properties specific to the way in which a higher-level object comprehends lower-level objects: for instance, how protons, neutrons, and electrons make up the atom, how atoms make up the molecule, and, possibly, how the graviton may be the effect of a string with wave amplitude zero, generated by a closed string, and so on. In a scalar knowledge like that of contemporary physics, these properties only make sense step by step, from one level of comprehension to a higher or lower level.

In this way, an atom may be inside a molecule, a proton inside the nucleus of an atom, and quarks inside a proton, even though quarks do not exist *as such* in a molecule; it is necessary to pass through the atomic division for quarks to be.

Imagine a straight line. On this straight line, we divide a line segment AB. Then we point to the middle of this line segment, called C. The location of point C already existed on the straight line, but point C could only be determined, *as the midpoint between A and B*, once A and B were established on the straight line. In the same way, the midpoint D between C and B did not exist *as such* on the line segment AB; its properties only appear once the line segment BC was divided within the line segment AB.

Since every science of the universe is an objective *division*, the same goes for our knowledge of a universal level. Protons are not a projection of some scientific paradigm onto the atom, but an objective discovery. Nonetheless, protons could only have been discovered after the atom had been discovered. Levels immediately beneath or above some level merely pre-exist our knowledge of a universal level. An infinite stratified scale of the material universe does not exist, concealed from view, from the smallest to the biggest, as if one could examine it like one ascends and descends a staircase.

A single homogeneous level follows at every ascended or descended step. By placing our feet on this level, we make on this same level a new possible stepping stone to a lower or higher level.

Knowledge does not create its objects. Knowledge creates the *stratification* of its objects. By comprehending a material object, we make of its undifferentiated matter a set of objects that may conceal an undifferentiated matter.

Knowledge of the smallest and of the biggest opens up the universal domain, divisible into local knowledges that are often centred on humanity's place in it, and presupposes a step-by-step division that makes skipping any stage impossible. Knowledge is precisely the structuring of the universe into stages. For each known thing, it is possible to obtain both a smaller set of things that each known thing comprehends and a bigger thing that comprehends each known thing. But the passage to a higher or lower stage presupposes either comprehending objective differences within an identity, or discovering distinct differences in an identity; the specificity of each level makes up the *objective* stuff of knowledge. Before something smaller or bigger can be sought, one must guarantee the step-by-step continuity that presupposes the establishment of consistencies and laws.

Trinh Xuan Thuan, a defender of strong anthropism, conceives of this universal process in relation to the human being that observes it. He writes in *The Secret Melody* that

> [t]he Big Bang universe is the latest in a long line of successive universes that began with the magical universe, and passed through the mythical, mathematical, and geocentric universes. It will, undoubtedly, not be the last universe. It would be surprising if we were to have the final word, and were the chosen ones finally to reveal the secret melody. There will be, in the future, a whole series of universes, which will come progressively closer to the true Universe (with a capital 'U' to distinguish it from the universes created by the human mind).[6]

The problem with such a position is that it implies that a Universe (with a capital U) exists behind the universes that humanity creates or discovers through an infinite progress, by trial and error – what we have called the 'world', that is, the form of each thing and the whole. But the universe, the biggest possible thing at any given moment, does not progress and does not lead to the world or to the whole, insofar as the universe is not any closer to the 'whole' than the smallest thing is. The world – the universe with a capital U for Trinh Xuan Thuan – is formal, while the universe is objective. The latter does not reduce to the former, and therefore there is no *formal* progress in the human discovery of an increasingly comprehensive material universe. Only accumulation is effectuated through the step-by-step division and stratification of universal levels. When Roger Penrose entitled his book on the contemporary status of physics *The Road to Reality*,[7] he committed the same faux pas, as if the road to the knowledge of universal levels, to the smallest and to the biggest, aimed at reality when it in fact divides and opens up reality. He ought to have titled his book 'The Road *of* Reality'.

The meaning of a science of the cosmological, local, or scalar universe (knowing that cosmology has become scalar) is to open up the universe step by step through the smallest and through the biggest by discovering properties and their changes (determination, overdetermination, underdetermination, emergence) among objects, from the comprehended to the comprehending and from the comprehending to the comprehended. What interests science is the bidirectional opening of the universe, the ascent from the infinitely small to the infinitely large and the descent in the other direction, knowing that this opening is not the examination of an a priori open domain and that it is not the invention of this domain either. This opening is the discovery of the outer edges that, once mapped, allow new edges to appear and that always exist step by step.

The world of this universe, its whole and its place, like the things that ultimately compose it, is the object not of a universal knowledge, but of a strictly formal knowledge.

World and things can be known only through form. The universe can be known only through bigger or smaller objects and events.

Notes

1. Marc Lachièze-Rey, *Cosmology*, p. 1.
2. Ibid., p. 2.
3. Ibid., p. 10.
4. Frank Close, 'The quark structure of matter', in *The New Physics*, p. 396.
5. 'According to string theory, if we could examine these particles with even greater precision – a precision many orders of magnitude beyond our present technological capacity – we would find that each is not pointlike, but instead consists of a tiny one-dimensional loop', Brian Greene, *The Elegant Universe*, p. 14.
6. Trinh Xuan Thuan, *The Secret Melody*, p. 261.
7. Roger Penrose, *The Road to Reality*.

Chapter II

Objects and Events

1. Absence and Presence

Small or large *existent* objects are not enough to make a universe. They must be *present*.

One may claim that objects exist in a dead or absent universe. The fact that objects once *were* but are no more would produce an absence of objects. Objects would exist, but they would be absent. But the universe *is not* merely existent; it is *present*. Being (and comprehension) is not enough to account for the fact that things are *there*.

Objects can be by always being absent, which means that a universe where objects *are* could very well turn out to be a dead universe where objects *would be*, but would be *dead* or *absent*.

The universe as we know it is not a dead or absent universe, because objects are, but are not limited to being – they are present.

In an undead, eternal world, objects could just as easily not be *here and now*, but *eternally*. In a certain Einsteinian interpretation of time, causal connections alone would exist objectively, and past, future, and present would always be signs of the subjective insufficiency of our specific relation to these causal connections. In this *eternal* world, objects would not have to be present, and events would be reducible to objects. They would not happen, but they would be.

But the fact that things are present for me, or for us, is enough to assume that presence is in the universe. Since I am a part of the universe, the fact that presence is *for me* sufficiently demonstrates that presence is *for the universe*.

What is presence? Far from being either an intuitable or indexicable mysterious concept, presence is a relation that connects a thing to what a thing is in. More precisely, the connection between a thing's two senses, being and comprehension, constitutes its presence. Presence is a thing's being and comprehension, which in turn become *something*.

Let us get around the problem of this proposition by defining absence. If only one presence exists, two types of absence exist. Every absence is an operation on the presence of a thing. Let there be an object A comprehended in an object B – for example, my heart in my body. Suppose that an absenting operation is carried out. Suppose that either B comprehends A and A is not in B, or A is in B and B does not comprehend A. In the first case, my heart is removed from my body. I claim that my body comprehends my heart (no body without a heart), and that my heart is not in my body. My body lacks my heart. In the second case, my heart is in my body (a heart can only develop within an organism), but my body does not comprehend my heart (it is empty). My heart lacks my body. Thus, I consider either an absence of my heart for my body, or an absence of my body for my heart. But absence is unilateral; it is the absence of something *for* another thing.

Absence is either comprehension without being, or being without comprehension. In the first case, absence resembles *emptiness*: something comprehends another thing that is not there. In the second case, absence resembles *exile*: something is in another thing, but this other thing doesn't comprehend this something.

The two faces of absence, emptiness and exile, are the two possible operations on presence (either removing being from comprehension or comprehension from being). Being present, on the other hand, is being in what comprehends me and being comprehended by what I am.

I am present in this room when I am in the room and when the room comprehends me. I am absent from this room when this room comprehends me in some way (the room comprehends my memory, the fact that I was there, my footprints, the possibility that I could be there, for my thought or for that of another), though I am not inside the room. And I lack this room if I am in this space – for example, by imagining that I remain there – when the room doesn't comprehend me or is not around me.

An object is present in another object when the *being* and *comprehension* of two objects are conjoined. Therefore, the presence of the first object in the second object is the dyadic meaning of the relationship that binds them together (being and comprehending) as a single thing.

Presence exists between two objects.

Every presence is bilateral: the first object is in the second object and the second object comprehends the first object. Absence is the operation through which one object does not correspond to the other object, either through emptiness or through exile.

Either an object's presence always exists for another object, or a thing's presence always exists for the world. Either an object is present in another object (and in the universe), or a thing is present in the world.

An object or a thing can *be* without being *present*. If not *present*, it is *absent*, since being is never strong enough to demonstrate or guarantee the presence of what is. Comprehension can be emptied of being, or being can be exiled from comprehension.

The presence of objects is their bilateral relation; their absence is a unilateral relation. If a person disappears from my life, then either I comprehend this person, and this person exists for me although I do not exist for this person (since the person is dead), or this person can comprehend me, although I pay no attention to her existence. By absence, I mean in every case a unilateral relation.

On the other hand, presence is a bilateral relation between two objects.

What we call presence in the world is nothing other than a relation that connects me to the world, through which I am in the world, and through which the world comprehends me and counts me among the number of objects in it.

Far from being inexplicable, the presence of things is simply their bilateral relation – the fact that they exist for each other. The presence of things is disclosed not merely in our sensible intuition of things, but also in thought and in language. By making the presence between things and world compact, one reduces presence to an inexpressible mystery, inaccessible to thinking, or considers it possible to restrict access to presence through rational reduction. In truth, the presence of things allows one to experience *as well as* claim that presence exists, if one defines it through the conjunction of being and comprehension.

Since 'being' and 'comprehending' are two terms that cannot be defined separately, presence is always primary and absence must be an operation through which one artificially splits a thing in two. By accumulating the memory of my lover, which is with me, and the fact that my lover is currently elsewhere, I create the chimera of an absence, an emptiness, or a being that I comprehend within me, but which is not with me. In reality, my lover is not absent, since I must relate to her memory or to the projection that I make of her actual, distant being: her memory or image is present for me. Strictly speaking, of course, my lover is neither her memory nor her image. But since I can identify my lover with what she is in my memory or in my imagination, I can lack her, I can artificially comprehend her, contain her inside me without her being there inside me. This is what we call emptiness.

If I have the impression of always being in my country, while my country does not comprehend me, while it is not around me, I can remain in something without this thing accommodating me. This is what we call exile.

While presence is real, absences are only subjective operations on reality. Absences exist no less than presence, although differently.

2. Presence and Event

Objects and events exist in the universe. Objects are things in other things. Events are presences of things or presences of objects.

A primary event is a thing's presence in the world. While this chair is an object, like this colour green is an object, *the fact that this chair exists* is an event, and *the fact that this green exists* is also an event. *The fact that this chair is green* is a secondary event, since it is not an event of a thing, but of an object. The existence of this chair in the world makes this chair a thing. The existence of this chair among green objects makes this chair an object (a green object). On the other hand, the fact that this green chair exists in the world is again a primary event, an event of a thing, because this green chair is 'something'.

An event always concerns a thing's or an object's mode of presence. An event is in fact an object that hinges not around a thing, but a thing's *presence*. Whether things appear, disappear, change, or whether they are so or otherwise, events exist.

Some ways of thinking conceive of worlds of events, rather than worlds of objects – for example, ways of thinking about relation, flux, becoming, or states of things. They make a derivate event of an object, an artificial division from the primacy of what happens, of the more or less intense presence of things.

But, in truth, objects and events are equal. Mutually indifferent to each other, they equally relate to things. Things exist. Things placed in relation to each other are objects, and the relations of things to other things are events. In the strict sense, objects and events are equal and belong to the same system – the objective system of accumulation and of the universe. However, objects and events are equivalent to things without belonging to the same system. Things are formal; they are solitary and in the world.

Thus, we rule out any consideration of objects and events as secondary in relation to things. Instead, by triangulating their relations, things exist formally and objects and events exist objectively. Objects are things in other things. Events are the ways in which things belong to other things.

Every ontology that privileges events over objects and things, or objects rather than things and events, or things to the detriment of objects and events, is groundless and systematically leads to compactness.

3. The Universe of Events and the Universe of Objects

Let's consider an event such as a murder. Suppose a person kills another person. In a policed society a murder may be an exceptional event, or during wartime a common event. But the properties of an event are not affected by one claiming that an event is an exception or a rule. We must not conflate an event with an exception.[1]

Someone killing someone else presupposes the mobilisation of a certain number of objects: physical objects, such as the murderer's body and the victim's body, the weapon used, the scene of the crime, clothing, or other accessories; non-physical objects, such as representations of the crime, the murderer's and the victim's intentions, actions, memories; and symbolic objects, such as traces or clues.

An event cannot emerge as such from this set of objects; a set of objects forms a bigger thing, and that is all. The interaction between all these objects always produces another thing: the murder. For it is necessary to distinguish the murder as an *object* – since the murder is something comprehended in another thing, in a temporal series, in the investigation, or in the investigators' representation – from the murder as an *event*, which consists in a person killing another person.

What is the difference? The murder as an object is an outcome, a *deed* [*fait*]. The murder as an event is a *doing* [*un faire*]. Every event can become an object once it is done; once accomplished and determined, an event can be represented in the form of a brief narrative or picture ('the murder of somebody by somebody else'), and so on. Like many novelists, one may attempt to exhaust the various aspects of an event in the form of objects; an object lacks what makes an event: the fact of taking place.

Whereas an object is present (or absent), an event self-presents (or self-absents): a knife is here or there, but a knife does not happen or take place. What happens is *that someone took a knife* or *that someone dropped a knife*. The taking of the knife is an object insofar as it is or is not present (is there or is there not someone in the process of taking a knife?), but its presence and the way in which it is present are an event. In this way, the red armchair is certainly an object, although the fact that the armchair is red (that it is red for only a minute, that it has always been red, that it is increasingly more or increasingly less red) is an event.

Imagine a universe that would only comprehend objects. In this universe, the deed exists, the murderer killed their victim; the murderer, the victim, the motive, the weapon, the armchair bathed in blood, and so on, also exist. Everything exists in the form of objects, which are present, like wax figurines of a macabre tale. Even the moment when the murderer strikes their victim and the moment when the victim collapses exist. It is not that nothing moves, that nothing comes to life in this world of objects; it is that everything is equally present. In a world of objects, everything is certainly in the world, but nothing is *either more or less* in the world. What has been and what will be are equal, and equally objects.

Yet, even in the eyes of a god, the universe is never a series of objects, such that all is a deed, is accomplished, and that nothing becomes. A universe of objects is a universe of presentless presence. In, prior to, and subsequent to this universe, one obtains objects that are before or after other objects, in a fixed, eternal causal series, but never past, future, or present.

The universe of objects lacks events.

But now imagine a universe constituted only by events – for example, the Nietzschean ocean of pure power,[2] the world of Wittgenstein's *Tractatus*,[3] where everything happens; or, in a very different way, the purely qualitative world of Bergsonian duration, Whitehead's process universe,[4] or the Deleuzian plane of immanence.

In this universe, a doing exists: the murderer kills the victim. But prior to the doing, something like 'a murderer', 'a victim', or 'a weapon' did not exist. The murderer was born, grew up, and one day encountered her victim. We separate these many events by producing substances or objects, identities such as the identity of the 'murderer', which blocks the path of all that took place in the stable and objective person. In this universe, a person tightens their arm, but neither the person nor arm exist, since people and arms are effects of a series of events. The brief tightening of the arm, all that happens and takes place exists. But nothing resembling an object – what can be present or absent – exists. Only modes of absence and presence, ways of being present and becoming present, exist, but nothing exists to be these modes. Action is primary and exclusive, rather than the acted or the acting. In this universe, a murdererless and victimless murder that one commits exists; merely the murderer's action and the victim's death exist.

An evential universe is a universe that dissolves the consistency of objects into objective modes of presence, gradually reduced to being mere changing effects of presence. Some present ultimately exists in this universe, but nothing exists to be present.

In the universe of objects, a murder, a murderer, and a victim exist, but the murderer doesn't kill the victim. Presence exists, but no present and no action exist. In the universe of events, the murderer kills the victim, but neither murderer nor victim exist. The pure present exists, but nothing present and no objects exist.

Some may leap between ontologies of objects and ontologies of events, abandoning the encounter between them through some dialectical conjuring trick. But objects and events are not solitary; they both relate to things.

Things, when they are in each other, and not merely alone in the world, form a universe through their inter-comprehension [entre-compréhension]. However, since everything always has two senses, it is possible to take things in either sense. One may consider a thing which is in another thing that comprehends this thing, and the thing is an object; or one may consider the being of the primary thing in the secondary thing and its comprehension by this secondary thing, by making this relation the thing itself, which is an event.

An object is a thing in another thing. An event is the inclusion of this thing in another thing. An object is either present or absent from what the thing is in. An event is the presence or absence of a thing in what comprehends the thing.

In this way, the murderer, weapon, victim, and armchair are each things in the world, and are in the universe of objects *and* events.[5] Objects and events never communicate between each other, but only through things; the armchair in the room and the fact that the armchair became red are only related to the fact that the armchair is 'something'. Several objects never yield an event and an event is never composed of objects; objects are among objects and events are among events, but events and objects only communicate through things. Given all the objects of a murder, I can never derive an event from the murder, the fact that the murder *happened*. I can never decompose the event, in which one person kills another, into fixed objects, but only into earlier events in some causal chain. Things connect the chains of events to the pictures of objects. Each object is a thing and each event is also a thing. Given that the armchair is red, I can infer that the armchair is some *thing*, that the redness is equally some *thing*, as is the red armchair. So, given the object that the red chair in this room is, I can obtain these same *things*.

Objects and events objectivise things differently. The distinguishing feature of objects corresponds to what escapes events, and vice versa.

Yet, the passage from *presence* to the *present* is what objects always lack and events exclusively carry.

Notes

1. For example, Anatole France deliberately conflates event and exception when he asks: 'But what is an event? Is it a fact of any sort? No! it is a noteable fact. Now, how is an historian to discriminate whether a fact is noteable or no? He decides this arbitrarily, according to his character and idiosyncrasy, at his own taste and fancy, – in a word, as an artist', *The Garden of Epicurus*, p. 123.
2. In paragraph 385 of *The Will to Power*, Nietzsche presents his world as an ocean of power [translated in English by Walter Kaufmann and R. J. Hollingdale, paragraph 1067, pp. 549–50]. The Nietzschean world is certainly not a world of objects, but a determinate event, which becomes intensified in various ways in objects, sometimes enclosing itself, and produces effects of subjectivity. For Nietzsche, the world is a singular self-sustaining event which appears in the form of distinct objects through intensive variation.

3. The *Tractatus Logico-Philosophicus* (1922) is the most beautiful modern example of the construction of a world where objects exist (since something must happen in events), but where objects are relegated to a secondary level of the world. The states of evential things separate the objects which enter into them from the world that they constitute, as a necessary stage of the structure of all that is. This is the modern symptom of the knotted alliance between world and events, where things are confounded with objects.

4. For Alfred North Whitehead, the Category of the Ultimate marks the eventialisation of his metaphysics, particularly in *Process and Reality* (1929). Whereas we distinguish *that which is the thing* and *that which the thing is*, Whitehead prefers to articulate the disjunction of plurality and the conjunction of its unity, in such a way that for him the *passage* from plurality to unity becomes primary, 'Ultimate'.

5. In *Dire le monde*, Francis Wolff makes an important distinction between the concepts of 'thing' (which we call 'object') and 'event' in defence of an original contemporary Aristotelianism. The world of things is the world of 'what is' and the world of events the world of 'why', since for Wolff every world is realised in and through linguistic categories. Even if we try, unlike him, to conceive of a world which is not constituted by the possibility of talking about it, we fully endorse his distinction between a world seen as a set of events and a world seen as a set of things (that we call 'objects'): 'It is only if the world is made of events linked together that the world may be structured according to the ordered relation proper to *why*. On the other hand, it is only if the world is made of things strictly speaking that the world can be structured according to the identity relation proper to *what is*. Just as, with the world of things, one can only really and completely say what they are by naming them by their proper name, one can also only, with the world of events, really completely say why they happen by resorting to impersonal verbs.' Wolff, *Dire le monde*, p. 101 [translation is our own].

Chapter III

Time

1. Presentism and Eternalism

The problem of defining time concerns the status attributed to the present.

Since at least Saint Augustine,[1] understanding time from the present only leads to confusion. The past is not, since it is no longer present; the future is not, since it is not yet present; and the present is only insofar as it slips by and is already no more, since its being is to become. Augustinian confusion essentially comes from the desire to define the present as presence (to the mind), and presence as being or as existence. The present is what is present, and what is present is what is.

On the other hand, understanding time without invoking the present, by restricting oneself to the order of events before and after, allows the creation of a series organising what is prior and what is subsequent, but which does not exist – for example, as we see in McTaggart's analysis of the connection between past, present, and future in 'The Unreality of Time'.[2]

Two possibilities emerge. Either the past, present, and future are equally real, in which case the present is no longer really present (since it is no longer a distinguished presence, but only one presence among others); or the present is really present, in which case the past and future are no longer really real. One never carries the theoretical day on all fronts.

Trenton Merricks writes:

> *Eternalism* says that all times are equally real. Objects existing at past times and objects existing in future times are just as real as objects existing at the present [. . .] With all this in mind, let's say that the eternalist believes in a *subjective present*.[3]

On the other hand:

> *Presentism* says that only the present time is real. Every object that exists, exists at the present time. Objects that exist only at other times – like objects that exist only in fiction or objects that exist only in other 'possible worlds' – simply do not exist at all [. . .] With all this in mind, let's say that the presentist believes in an *objective present*.[4]

If I identify the present with presence, and presence with being, then I cannot really understand how a past (which is not present and therefore is not) or a future (which is not present and therefore is not either) exist. Only the present exists. Before and after do not exist except in the subjective projection that I can make of them, through memory retention or imaginative expectations, for example. We are thus led back, like Augustine, to a phenomenology of subjective time.

But understanding time without invoking the present, by restricting myself to the order of events – to the 'before' and 'after' – I can most certainly conceive of a series organising what is prior and what is subsequent. The order of events is thus present, and *eternally* present. 'Now' is always an effect of my limited position in space-time, an indexical effect, with a significance derived from the circumstances and subject of its enunciation. We are thus led back to the shores of subjective time.

In both cases, time – that is, the assembling of the present with a future and a past – is split in two. One part is always dismissed by attributing subjectivity to it: either time is the retention of the past and the protension towards the future, or it is the perception of a present within the eternal order of past, present, and future events.

However, by understanding time as retaining its concept and maintaining both its idea and those of all of its own possible modes (past, present, future), we must neither reduce time to an illusion veiling a higher reality (eternity) nor imagine the existence of a single part of this time (the present) to the detriment of all others. How may one conceive time *alone* and time *completely*?

In the absence of a complete time, things are not organised into objects and events. If there were no present, but only an order of deeds, everything would merely be objects. If no past or future existed apart from the present, everything would merely be momentary events, and there would be no objects (we would never see a chair, but simply that a chair is there right now).

Since the formal system of things does not work without an objective system of objects and events, time must be both the present and some order of past events. Yet, in the twentieth century, a third position conceived of time midway between *presentism* and *eternalism*. Today, this is what we call 'Growing Block-Universe Theory' (GBUT). Taking up Merricks's terms, one could claim that this third position – which is non-dialectical but attempts to accommodate the two positions – considers the past like the eternalist (the past is as present as the present, the past really exists), but the present like the presentist (the present has an exceptional, privileged status: the present exists eminently; the present is the latest moment in time).

2. Growth of Presence (Growing Block-Universe Theory)

Growing Block-Universe Theory (GBUT) is prima facie close to our position. Since objects accumulate, the universe continually grows in presence. The universe is unlike the formal and flat world, in which nothing is ever richer or poorer, has any intensity, or is ever present or absent. Therefore, the objective universe continually and forever grows; it is enriched with presence and comes into existence; nothing ever really disappears in it. This representation of the universe emerges in some GBUTist accounts, particularly in Michael Tooley's,[5] in which a dynamic conception of the universe does not reduce the temporal modes of past, present, and future to subjective operations (the Kantian a priori condition of the inner sense of time; the Husserlian operations of protension and retention through consciousness).

In 1923, C. D. Broad presented the first coherent formulation of GBUT, though it did not yet bear this awkward name. Broad addressed a series of epistemological problems and responses to McTaggart. Broad presented an original description of the universe inspired by Albert Einstein's then recent work, which soon led to general relativity. The past and present really exist, but the future does not exist. The universe continually grows in presence, like a perpetually expanding block: 'when an event becomes, it *comes into existence*; and it was not anything at all until it had become'.[6] The present is thus this coming into existence. The universe can only expand with presence; everything happens and nothing ever disappears:

There is no such thing as *ceasing* to exist; what has become exists henceforth for ever. When we say that something has ceased to *exist* we only mean that it has ceased to be *present*.[7]

Broad is thus asking us to imagine the present, coming into presence, as a fixed light beam that could make things enter into existence. Things can go outside presence, the light beam, but not outside the domain of existence. Having been, things will never return to nothingness, but merely to absence. In order to philosophically respond to the emerging conception of relativist space-time, Broad describes a universe that could have its own memory, but also an active frame transmuting nothing into something:

> [W]e imagine the characteristic of presentness as moving, somewhat like the spot of light from a policeman's bull's-eye traversing the fronts of the houses in a street. What is illuminated is the present, what has been illuminated is the past, and what has not yet been illuminated is the future.[8]

Broad draws from this model McTaggart's claim that 'futurity' cannot be a predicate applied to an event: 'the first thing that we have to say about McTaggart's argument is that no event ever does have the characteristic of "futurity"'.[9] Broad's position is the following: that the future does not exist, and that no event becomes before being present. His heirs willingly forget that he derives this concept of time from Bergson and Whitehead, and limit their genealogy of the philosophy of time to McTaggart (for example, in L. Nathan Oaklander's anthology[10]): something radically novel is in the universe. Eventiality goes beyond the domain of possibility, which chases after actuality without managing to contain or avoid it. For this reason, the sum total of everything that is present ceaselessly grows: 'the process of becoming which continually augments the sum total of existence and thereby the sum total of positive and negative facts'[11] (that is, what had been and what had not been, which can only appear when what had been *had been*). Indeed, at each moment something novel is present, becomes, and adds to the past, which does not cease being and continues existing objectively.

But like eternalism and presentism, Broad's position has a disadvantage in that it considers the presence of the past in the same way as the presence of the present, thus generating two categories of presents. Its Achilles heel is that it considers the present as a *fixed* beam of passage to presence and existence. For this reason, the present moment remains, for Broad's position, always *equally* present, whether it is past or not. Like David Braddon-Mitchell's criticism of Peter Forrest, one cannot know if 'now' is really now, or if 'now' is the now of yesterday. An objective order is distinguished from the past, but no distinction is made between the 'now' of now (a meta-now, so to speak), the 'now' of yesterday, the 'now' of 1644, the 'now' of the accretion of the earth, and so on.

Craig Bourne notices this scission between the objective privilege of presentness and the indexicality of 'this present moment'. If the scission always objectively exists in the universe, the sensation of presentness that I had yesterday remains this indexical sensation that indicates 'this present moment'. However, this scission no longer corresponds to the objective present, which would no longer be the 'today' of yesterday, but the 'today' of today.

> So here I am, a no-futurist, convinced that my present time is the *present* [Bourne italicises the objective present, while leaving the indexical present unitalicised]. But wasn't I just as convinced yesterday [. . .]? So there am I as I was yesterday [. . .] believing that I am *present*, and thinking pretty much the same things then about my previous selves as I think today. Yet I know now that my earlier self is mistaken; so how do I know that I now am not?[12]

GBUT produces two presents instead of one: the present that each moment has been and that each moment always is; and the present of these presents, the objective and punctual present. But from the present of my present moment, I will never obtain the objective present; nothing assures me that I am not already in the past, thinking that I am still 'now'. Nothing guarantees me that my present, which I live and experience as actual, is not an already dead present; nothing guarantees me that I am not *deceived* by time. And in such cases the venom of hyperbolic doubt always regains its effectiveness.

Therefore, we think that such analytic divisions of time are condemned to value only a certain aspect of time so as to better conceal another aspect of time. And we think that neither presentism, nor eternalism, nor GBUT completely disproves the concept of time in its entirety. At the very most, these positions revitalise doubts about the reality of this or that aspect of time.

Why? Because they all divide time into temporal extensions, considering past, present, and future as temporal parts of a whole – some real, others illusory. Since these philosophies of time lead to impasses, we ought to consider past, present, and future not as extensive parts, but perhaps as *intensive* variations.

3. Present, Past, Future: Intensive Variations of Presence

Unfortunately, identifying the present with presence means the present becomes an absolute and undermines past and future, which are reduced to non-being. If the present is *all that is present*, only a negative possibility of being in the past and being in the future remains.

The confusion undoubtedly arises from what one attributes to the idea of presence, a discrete rather than continuous property: either one is present or not present; one is not *more* or *less* present. According to Aristotle's conception in the *Physics*, time is number of movement, 'not fast or slow – any more than any number with which we count is fast or slow'.[13] Time is not subject to variable intensities, but only to extensive divisions: long or short, many or few. Without refuting Aristotle's claim that time has objective homogeneity, we will circumvent it by discovering what it prevents us from perceiving: that presence is subject to variable intensities, such that time is an extension, but presence is an *intensity*.

Time shows us that presence does not fall into the category of what is or is not absolutely. To modalise presence through categories of action, potentiality, or virtuality changes nothing. To divide presence into distinct modes of presence allows us to consider the passage from one mode to another (for example, from potentiality to actuality), like a leap from the future to the present. But that never solves the problem of intensive variation from the present to the past. The past cannot be called either 'virtual' or 'potential', since it has been. How shall we understand its real presence, in actuality, without conflating it with the present, like GBUTists do? Our solution is to understand the presence of the past as an *intensive variation* of presence: what is past is really present, as the present is present, but the past is *less* present than the present is present.

I snap my fingers. Now my snapping has ended. Let us imagine that my snapping, become past, continues to pass. Since some new present becomes every past time, it increasingly slips into the past and moves away from presence. I snap my fingers again. What distinguishes my first snapping from the second? If both were from then on equally nonexistent, if they each collapsed into non-being, then neither would be; nothing differentiates them in pure negativity. However, I can surely consider them as *two* objects, when I subjectively and retroactively refer to their occurring. In other words, I can rely on an *order* of the past; everything that passes is not equally past, but passes according to an order, which makes one slice in the expanding universe earlier than another. If all pasts were equally non-present, then everything that is no longer would be the same age, and neither geological strata, nor fossils, nor the history of the universe would exist.

The past is not an *absolute* non-presence, but a *relative* non-presence. The past is what is less present than the present. It follows that the present is always *the maximum of presence*.

What we call present is *the greatest presence*: what cannot be more present. Presence is the being and comprehension of things in each other, when one thing is in another. The present is *the maximal state of the being and comprehension of things*.

Consequently, the past corresponds to the overtaken [*dépassé*] present, to the present that is not what is *more* present any more; the past is, it exists objectively, but is a lesser presence. Insofar as it is a process, the past is all that weakens in presence. The more the past passes, the less present it is. But we know, and not only because we have faculties of memory, that the past is not purely absent: it is a state of increasingly weaker presence. My childhood is present in me and in the rest of the world, in the traces that I have left of it, in objects, photographs, imprints, and changes that I have caused; the past is not an absolute non-being, but a fading presence, which withers and passes. Already less present today than yesterday, the past tends towards absence. If, one day, the earth dissolves in the burning sun, ending life, my childhood and the moment of this childhood will tend towards total absence without entirely being reduced to it. My childhood existence takes part and counts as an infinitesimal part of terrestrial life and presence in a solar system on the verge of destruction.

If the present is the greatest presence, then it is also the weakest absence. In the present, a part of absence (even reduced to its minimum) exists, since the present is never an *absolute* presence, a compact presence. If the past is the minimisation of presence, then the future is the maximisation of absence. The future is not a non-existence, but an absence that could not be greater – which does not mean that this absence is absolute, but simply that nothing is ever more absent than the future.

The continuous intensive variation of presence is what we call time. The present is its peak, its unfolding is the past (the order of relative weakening of presence), and its foundation is the future (maximal absence, with a present, increasingly present, that endlessly moves away).

The future is indeed the greatest possible absence of determination. It is what the present can dissolve. On our view, counter-intuitively, my future was closer to me at my birth, at the moment when, even defined by my familial history and my social situation, I could become all or nothing: dying young, being famous, anonymous, good or evil. This future will in reality be further from me at the moment of my death; I will die, determined and completed by a past. The past, to the extent that it extends, therefore separates the future from the present, which is increasingly loaded with determinations – whereas the future remains the maximal indetermination.

4. The Present Moves Away from the Future

No event has ever existed in the future. A blink of the eye had not been present before being present. Thus, a determinate event never begins being future (since the future is indetermination) before being present and then past. An event is first present when it appears, and then is increasingly past. An event always remains at the same distance from the future, which is the maximal state of indetermination, the gauge, so to speak, by which events organise themselves. The distance between a given event – for example, a blink of the eye – and the future is a degree of determination, this event's coefficient of presence. This coefficient derives from what preceded the event. I blink my eyes again; the coefficient of presence of my second blink is greater than that of the first blink, because the second blink came after the first, and the second has more past than the first. The second is more determined, and therefore more distant from the future, from the maximal absence of determination. And the distance that separates it from the future when I begin to blink remains, and will remain the same as this blink sinks into the past.

The future makes possible two separate temporal locations: *that which the present is* continually moves away from the future, since the present is increasingly present; but *that which is present*, that is, this or that present moment – for example, my first blink of the eye – when it appears, forever remains at a determined distance from the future. In this way, my present is increasingly further from the future, since it is increasingly more determined. On the other hand, the moment of my birth, which sinks into the past as my life advances, had a future when I was born and has since retained this future, in spite of what followed. Otherwise my birth would no longer exist; only my childhood, completed in my life, death, posterity, and so on would exist, until the present moment. In other words, all pasts would be drawn into the present. But each moment of the past retains its chance of remaining individuated, that is, of not being absolutely governed by the following moment. What makes every moment of the past retain an individuated form, which history or memory can voluntarily revive, is not the relation between the past and present moment, which engulfs and buries it. On the contrary, it is the relation between each past moment and what was its future, *and which remains what was its future.*

Recalling my birth, before I became what I am, is to extract this event from the order of the past, from the progressive weakening of its presence in relation to the present, and to consider it in relation to the future. In relation to the future, my birth has remained what it was – an event whose consequences and continuation are indeterminate.

Every determination of the future – through a psychological projection, a prophecy, a science fiction narrative, the determination of probabilities or of laws of nature (on the grounds of radical contingency, as Quentin Meillassoux claims[14]) – is therefore a transformation of the future into an ersatz past, a determined order of (particularly causal) events. Due to this ersatz past projection, the future is wrongly placed after the present, which is supposed to come after the past – an unending source of confusion for common sense.

Rather, one ought to think about every present event as being at the top of an infinite stack of sheets of paper. The future is the foundation, the ground on which the stack of paper rests. The present is the sheet at the top. Each time a new sheet covers up the previous sheet, any particular sheet in the middle of the pile, a 'past sheet', moves further from the top, which becomes situated higher and higher. But the distance that separates our 'past sheet' from the foundation – from the ground, however far that may be, perhaps even infinitely far (if one assumes that time has no beginning, that no pure future or pure primordial absence has ever been) – never changes.

The key to our model of the temporal order is therefore the following: every event is doubly temporally localisable – in relation to the present (the top of the stack) and in relation to the future (the bottom of the stack, what the stack rests on). The same event, for example the accretion of the planet earth, sees the present move away from it, but, once past, remains at the same distance from the future that it had and that it retains. This permanent relation to a fixed future safeguards its possibility of always being the moment that it had been, of not completely fading into a continually renewed present. If our stack had no bottom, then every event would only be localisable in relation to the changing present; every past event would only exist in relation to this present, which alone would really be. Within this present, absorbing the totality of what had been, we would no longer be capable of regaining the more or less past. We would only ever discover an instantaneous eternal: a bottomless stack of paper whose most recent sheet would always subsist, the others already disappearing into non-being.

A stable ground, which is the future, and a moving top, which is the present, are therefore necessary for the intensive order of presence in the universe.

The problem of presentism is that it does not allow one to conceive of the reality of the past. For the presentist, a past moment exists only insofar as it is comprehended in the present; a past moment is a recollection, a trace, an actual consequence; it is an illusion that it is *past*. The problem of eternalism is that it does not allow one to think about the reality of the present. For the eternalist, a present moment exists only insofar as it is in a successive order similar to that of the past; it is only an illusion that it is *present*. The problem of GBUT is that it attributes an equal and non-variable reality to the present of now and to the present of yesterday, so that the set of all that is past grows and the present remains a permanent and absolute form.

The only means of avoiding presentism and eternalism, without falling back into GBUT's rut, is to conceive of the past as an objective (and non-subjective), intensive classificatory order of presence, and to conceive of the present as a maximal intensity, continually changing. If the *now of now* is not the *now of yesterday*, then the present moment is increasingly present; what is present in 2011 is objectively more present than the present moment was present in 1644, for example. The present that I live through when writing these lines is objectively more present than the present that an individual from 1644, at the moment of the fall of the Ming Dynasty, could endure. And one identifies the present of now insofar as nothing more present than the present of now exists. If you read these words, the moment of your reading them is objectively more present than the moment of my writing them, which is from then on a past moment. But at the moment when I wrote these lines, what I imagined could be the moment of your reading them is only a current projection of my imagination, which does not really go beyond the limits of what is more present: the present. This moment that I project does not exist in the future, but in the present. And this present from 2011 is more than the present which was last year, which is more than the present which was in 1644, and so on.

One can therefore *order* presents – and the past is nothing other than one present in this classificatory order of presents. Time is a classificatory order of the present, past, and future into intensities of presence. Time is the order of presences in the universe.

The universe, the biggest possible thing, is increasingly loaded with presences and determinations. Time is the index of this accumulation. And, paradoxically, since new things, supplementary presences, always exist, the future, the maximal indetermination, moves away from the present.

For this reason, the objective universe has a history, a certain order of presence of events which have been. A local part of this history, limited for the time being to just one planet of a stellar system, away from the centre of a medium-sized galaxy, matters to humanity: the history of something new, that we call *life*.

Notes

1. Augustine, *Confessions*, Book XI, 20.
2. J. M. E. McTaggart, 'The Unreality of Time'.
3. Trenton Merricks, 'Goodbye Growing Block', p. 103.

4. Ibid., p. 103.
5. Michael Tooley, *Time, Tense and Causation*.
6. Charlie Dunbar Broad, *Scientific Thought*, p. 68.
7. Ibid., p. 69.
8. Ibid., p. 59.
9. Ibid., p. 81.
10. L. Nathan Oaklander (ed.), *The Philosophy of Time*.
11. Broad, *Scientific Thought*, p. 83.
12. Craig Bourne, 'When Am I? A Tense Time for Some Tense Theorists?', p. 362.
13. Aristotle, *Physics*, IV, 220b. Translated in English by R. P. Hardie and R. K. Gaye, in Jonathan Barnes (ed.), *The Complete Works of Aristotle*, p. 373.
14. In *After Finitude*, what Quentin Meillassoux calls 'hyper-chaos' represents the power of time, unthinkable by physics, to destroy or to create laws, without cause or reason. Yet, if time cannot be subject to laws of nature, it is because it is never entirely resolved in presence: the future, the maximum of absence, cannot be reduced to an ersatz past, that is, to an order of (particularly causal) presences, modelled on what has already taken place.

Chapter IV

Living Things

1. An Intensified Universe

A living thing is an event that intensifies something novel in the universe. The emergence and development of living organisms is not a rupture that *introduces* something novel into the universe, nor is it the mere continuation of physico-chemical novelties which occurred when there were no existent living things anywhere in the universe. Even though living things are local events, which are mere fractions of the objective universe, living things are also events that considerably intensify the universe. Living things augment the universe more than formally (by simply adding new things). Living things *give value to* the universe (by adding things which are more than what they are).

The emergence of living things does not mark the passage to another universe, nor the perpetuation of the same universe. It consists neither in an irreducible rupture with the physical universe, a qualitative leap, nor in a pure and simple continuation, whereby living things could have been potentially comprehended in the antecedent properties of matter. The emergence of living objects is the intensification of certain structures of the material universe, that is, the local growth of certain mechanisms and properties, including the phenomenon of self-transmission. This intensification does not mean that living things were potentially contained in inanimate things, but only that what we call 'living things' corresponds to a certain degree of intensity in the relation between the being and comprehension of objects of the universe. Intensity is not *formal* – since formally everything is equal – but *objective*. Therefore, life cannot be derived from the flat world of things, which is altogether extensive and without intensity. Objectively, on the other hand, in the universe, which is constituted by objects that more or less comprehend each other, everything is subject to variable intensities. In the universe, thoroughly objective (non-formalisable, non-derivative) conditions allow objects to self-intensify. This process of self-intensification, which includes reproduction, the maintenance of metabolism, the consumption and expending of energy, and intergenerational information transmission, constitutes a local *living* universe.

The universe of living things is not an empire within an empire, but an objectively intensified place of the universe which, like the universe (the biggest possible thing), is stratified into levels of comprehension, through the embedding of levels of objects in higher levels, themselves comprehended in even higher levels. The universe of living things reproduces the structure of the universe, the structure of comprehended and comprehending objects, but it also intensifies it by including a novel intermediary *cellular* level between the molecular level and the bodily level.

Neil Campbell writes in the introduction to his textbook, *Biology*, that:

> Biological organisation is based on a hierarchy of structural levels, each level building on the levels below it. Starting at the lowest level, atoms, the chemical building blocks of all matter, are ordered into complex biological molecules. Many of the molecules of life are arranged into minute structures called organelles, which are in turn the components of cells. Cells are subunits of organisms, and organisms are the units of life. Some organisms, such as amoebas, consist of single cells, but others are multicellular aggregates of many specialised types of cells [. . .] Multicellular organisms exhibit three major structural levels above the cell: Similar cells are grouped into tissues; specific arrangements of different tissues form organs; and organs are grouped into organ systems.[1]

Living things can be apprehended, like every objective reality, through a system of being and comprehension in *levels*: an object comprehends other objects, and it is itself comprehended among other objects by a more important object. The objective order derives from the *differences* between levels (whereas the formal order derives from their equality, which short-circuits the objective order). 'Properties' or 'characteristics' are what allow one to differentiate the levels, to separate what is comprehended and what comprehends into distinct, hierarchical planes. Therefore, a living organism comprehends organs, which comprehend tissues, which comprehend specialised cells. The cell is the primary object of the local universe of living things. It is the object that all living things comprehend, but it comprehends nothing living. The cell is therefore the *lower* limit of life.

But, Campbell writes:

> In the hierarchy of biological organisation, there are tiers beyond the individual organism. A population is a localised group of organisms belonging to the same species; populations of different species living in the same area make up a biological community; and community interactions that include nonliving features of the environment, such as soil and water form an ecosystem. [A group of different ecosystems, spread across a vast geographical expanse, makes up a biome; the latter introduces uniform climactic conditions that determine a dominant type of vegetation. Finally, the biosphere comprehends all environments where life is, in water as well as in parts of the soil and air surrounding the planet.][2]

In this way, living organisms are comprehended in a population, comprehended in a biological community, comprehended in an ecosystem, comprehended in a biome, comprehended in a biosphere. The biosphere is, for the time being, the *upper* limit of the local universe of living things. Because it is a local universe, it is a limited part of the universe (the biggest possible thing), which is structured into levels like a universe. Everything between a cell and the biosphere is living. Campbell concludes: 'Investigating biological organisation at its many levels is fundamental to the study of human life [. . .], beginning with the chemistry of life and ending with the study of ecosystems and the biosphere, the sum of all Earth's ecosystems.'[3]

Living things are thus places of the universe, structured like a universe. They are something novel, since they have not always existed. They correspond neither to appearances, on the grounds of nothingness or of something absolutely nonexistent before, nor to actualisations of potentiality or of something latent in the matter of the physical universe. A living thing is the objective intensification of what we have formally defined as a 'self', that is, of a thing's difference between *that which is in the thing* and *that in which this thing is*. The physico-chemical intensification of this relation – under objective, non-formal conditions, impossible to anticipate, derive, or formalise – is the key to the emergence of what are described as 'properties of living things'. Campbell writes:

> With each step upward in the hierarchy of biological order, novel properties emerge that were not present at the simpler levels of organisation. These *emergent properties* result from interactions between components. A molecule such as a protein has attributes not exhibited by any of its component atoms, and a cell is certainly much more than a bag of molecules. If the intricate organisation of the human brain is disrupted by a head injury, that organ will cease to function properly, even though all its parts may still be present. And an organism is a living whole greater than the sum of its parts.[4]

This trivial thesis has a formal meaning that we must clarify: an organism, like every thing, cannot be reduced to what composes it. On this view, no differences exist between protozoa, crystal, or dust particles. *That which something is* is not *that which is this thing*. In contrast to what some biologists may think, the irreducibility of what forms a thing to the sum of all its components in no way accounts for the emergence of living things – in particular, since it accounts for *everything*, that is, the functioning between things and world, in general. It is certainly a condition of the novelty of living things – but it is also a condition of our galaxy's formation.

Therefore, the emergence of living things cannot restrict an organism (a macrolevel of the universe) by reducing it to what composes it (a microlevel of the universe). Instead, the emergence of living things is the *intensification* of this irreducibility. The property of irreducibility of a thing to what is in this thing, is this thing, and composes this thing accounts for the stratification of the entire material universe into levels. The emergence of living things is conceivable from the fact that this irreducibility has a particular *intensity*.

When Campbell, who expresses the most widespread opinion in contemporary biology, dismisses 'vitalism' by summoning emergence as the irreducibility of certain structural properties of a macrolevel to a microlevel of material organisation, he is undoubtedly correct, but he does not see how his argument is weakened as soon as one understands that no thing has properties that are reducible to the properties of what composes it.

This theme of emergence [seems to support the theory called *vitalism*, according to which life results from a supernatural phenomenon that goes beyond the laws of physics and chemistry. But in reality it] accents the importance of structural arrangement and applies to inanimate material as well as to life. [In the inanimate world, a change in the structure of a substance also attributes emergent properties to an emergent substance.] Diamonds and graphite are both made of carbon, but they have different properties because their carbon atoms are arranged differently. [Vital phenomena are not explained by a mysterious 'vital force', but by physical principles applied to living beings.] The emergent properties of life are not supernatural, but simply reflect a hierarchy of structural organisation without counterpart among inanimate objects.[5]

Emergence is not connected to living things, but rather to the irreducibility of a material level of organisation to a microlevel. Moreover, it is connected to the irreducibility – otherwise a thing becomes compact – of *that which is a thing* to *that which this thing is*. But the radical difference of living things, their novelty, their events, does not therefore derive from emergent properties, from a structural organisation 'without counterpart' among inanimate objects, since Campbell just showed that diamonds and graphite have different properties that emerge from different arrangements of carbon atoms. One cannot maintain both that the emergence of living things is no different from the emergence of novel properties in the material world, from one level of organisation to another, and that the emergence of living things is due to a novel structural organisation of living matter 'without counterpart' in the inanimate universe. The emergence of living things is connected to a structural organisation of matter *comparable to* that of inanimate things, since there is nothing in living things that is not also in inanimate things (including structures) – with the exception that the organisation of living things is *intensified*.

2. Life and Self

How does one define the intensified form of matter that we call living things – all levels of living things, from cells to the biosphere?

Several modern definitions of living things employ a set of concepts whose only commonality appears to be the 'self': reproduction, nutrition (and other metabolic functions), growth and development, energy transformation, adaptation to environmental constraints, transmission of genetic information, the capacity to fulfil these functions in an autonomous manner (a requirement which poses problems, and risks limiting the definition to auto-trophs, but aims at avoiding the struggle against viruses or parasi-toids), and so on. What cuts across all definitions of living things, from Antiquity to their renewal in the evolutionist undertaking, is a definition of *selfhood*.

Formally, we have seen that 'everything has a self', in the sense that every thing, anything, is the difference between *that which is the thing* and *that which the thing is*. For every thing, the self is nothing other than the difference between what this thing compre-hends and what comprehends this thing. Now, however one looks at the problem, it seems that a living thing is a thing that *intensifies* its self, the difference between that which is in the thing and that in which the thing is. On this view, reproduction is an object's possi-bility of beginning in another object. If reproduction is asexual, the self repeats and undergoes a change. If reproduction is sexual, the self becomes another through another. Whereas every temporally existent, non-living object loses its novelty as it endures, a living object retains something of its novelty as it endures: the possibil-ity of reproducing. This possibility does not consist in beginning exactly as it was, but rather in beginning something different from its identical possibility (although affected by mutations).

The novelty of the event of an organism is thus retained as an object inside this same object. This object, which can expand and grow, is living insofar as it temporally intensifies and supports its self. Metabolism, in the end, refers to the set of functions that organise the relation between what is in the organism (the living object) and what the organism is in (its environment). What is living is what supports, accentuates, and maintains this difference, until constituting the self not as the formal difference between what is comprehended and what comprehends, but as an objective limit between inside and outside.

A stone's self marks the difference between what composes the stone and what this stone is in. An organism's self is the greater or lesser intensification, through physico-chemical processes, of the relation between what composes the organism and what this organism is in. Energy transfers between what is embedded in the environment and what is inside the organism maintaining this organism correspond to a self-activation particular to living things.

Every living organism uses energy as a means of self-preservation, through the degradation of organic matter, photosynthesis, nutrition, and the ingestion and digestion of vegetable or animal organisms. What maintains *itself* and supports *itself* lives.

The cell was discovered in the seventeenth century, but only considered as a primary component of living things by Matthias Jakob Schleiden and Theodor Schwann in the nineteenth century. The cell is the primary object of living things and the object par excellence which functions as an intensification of self-difference, that is, as an intensification, through energy exchange, of the difference between what is in the cell and what the cell is in.

At each level of living things, all the objective definitions that we can give to living things are traversed by formal self-determinations: homeostasis, the internal regulation that maintains an internal milieu within vital limits, despite the fluctuations and influence of the external environment (for temperature in particular); self-regulation; the adaptive characteristics of living things (the taking into account of *that in which it is* for the evolution of *that which it comprehends*).

3. Intensification of the Self

The possibility of living things cannot be derived from the flat world of things, since no *formal* definition of life exists. It was not possible that living things were before living things were, since a living thing is an *objective* novelty and not a formal property. Nonetheless, living things correspond to an intensification of something formal: the self. The conditions of this intensification are objective, local, and connected to the terrestrial environment. But what is intensified in life is nothing other than what all things already had: a self, that is, an extensive difference between that which was in them and that which they were.

The emergence of living things is neither an appearance nor the actualisation of an inherent material potential. Rather, it is the passage, in a universe subject to variable – greater or lesser – intensities, against the background of an equal world, of self-intensities through self-reproduction, self-preservation, self-maintenance, and self-evolution. These self-supporting objects are organisms. Comprehended and comprehending, they have stratified the local living universe as a universe, between the cell and biosphere, into differentiated organisms.

Living things are therefore this local universe where living objects comprehend each other: 'Life does not exist in a vacuum', writes Campbell:

> Each organism interacts continuously with its environment, which includes other organisms as well as nonliving factors. The roots of a tree, for example, absorb water and minerals from the soil, and the leaves take in carbon dioxide from the air. Solar energy absorbed by chlorophyll, the green pigment of leaves, drives photosynthesis, which converts water and carbon dioxide to sugar and oxygen. The tree releases oxygen to the air, and its roots change the soil by breaking up rocks into smaller particles, secreting acid, and absorbing minerals. Both organism and environment are affected by the interaction between them. The tree also interacts with other life, including the microorganisms associated with its roots and animals that eat its leaves and fruit.[6]

The local living universe – this comprehension of living objects by each other in different levels – does not expand the universe with objects any more than a small inanimate section of another galaxy of a comparable size does. Living things do not extend the universe. Rather, living things locally give a novel intensity to the universe. Living things do not inflate the quantity of possible objects, from the standpoint of the entire cosmos, but produce more intense objects, and give value to the universe.

A eukaryotic cell marks an accentuated difference between *that which is in it* and *that in which it is*, a certain energy resistance of this difference. A block of quartz in no way precludes the distinction between what composes it and what it is in; this difference *exists* (since the block of quartz can be 'something'), but it does not *resist*, in the sense that no energy is expended in maintaining this difference.

What is living expends energy to maintain the difference between what it comprehends and what comprehends it, spatio-temporally. The set of synthetic and degradation reactions which make up the metabolism of a cell – energy extraction through cellular respiration in carbohydrates, and the formation of the cellular metabolic network, accelerated through enzymatic processes and anabolic or catabolic pathways – marks the physico-chemical intensification of the self, both through the integration of what exists on the outside into what is on the inside, and through the resistance of what is on the inside to what is on the outside. What is living comprehends what comprehends living things to continue being.

Since every definition of living things is objective though with formal determinations, a 'self' ultimately belongs to the objective knowledge that grasps living things. Since the synthesis of new Darwinism and the assimilation of molecular biology, biology defines living things, not philosophy. But the biological definition is the common limit between the objective and formal systems. The biological definition is objective because it depends on the knowledge of all living things, and on taking into account, or not, limit cases (like the thorny problem of viruses). Moreover, it is objective because living things are not formalisable, but only possible from objective conditions, which one cannot derive a priori. An example of these objective conditions would be the well-known role of water, its cohesion and high surface pressure – which makes possible its passage through plant veins – its adhesion, its high specific heat, its efficacy as a solvent, its expansion during its transformation from a liquid to a solid state, and its de facto influence on the emergence of living things. These biological characteristics cannot be derived from the form of things; they are the results of an objective knowledge.

But the definition of living things is also formal, for no biological definition of living things can overlook a formal self-determination, this concept, or the relation between *that which is in a thing* and *that in which the thing is*, unless it transforms the emergence of living things and the intensive passage from an inanimate physical matter to a locally living universe into a mystery.

4. Neither Vitalism, nor Biologism

In his article 'Hérédité et évolution (l'inné et l'acquis en biologie)', André Pichot critically examines some of the major arguments concerning living things: the historical reversal between Jean-Baptiste Lamarck and Charles Darwin; the crucial role of August Weismann. Pichot reconsiders the modern invention of the non-vitalist *characteristic property* of living things. He unearths something essentially repressed in the contemporary concepts of living things that derive from Weismann's work. Biology, which cannot do without something *formal* to define living things, assumed that it could rid itself of all forms of vitalism by espousing a physicalism, which established in an encoded genetic memory (what became known as the karyotype) everything that, in the formation of living things, escaped the mechanical laws of matter.

According to Pichot, Claude Bernard understood that, by defining living things through homeostasis, through self-preservation in some changing environment, he could not simultaneously account for the dynamics and *evolution* of living things:

> Unfortunately, in this thesis, the living being must be constant; it passes its time restoring itself and re-establishing its homeostasis. Essentially, the constancy of the internal environment is a static, fixist conception (even if this constancy on its own results from a dynamics). This is why it cannot account for development and growth. Furthermore, by restricting life to the preservation of chemical composition, it renders insoluble the problem of the form of living beings. In order to compensate for this lack of dynamism and form, Claude Bernard had to resort to a morphogenetic force, which he describes as 'metaphysical'. This force allows him to account for both the form of living beings and their development. For him, this force was superimposed on the controlled set of physical laws responsible for homeostasis, and modelled 'living matter' during embryological development. Claude Bernard consistently attributes this 'force' to heredity, by making of it a kind of impulse continuing the life of future generations.[7]

For Pichot, Bernard deserves credit for accepting the necessity of a *form*, even if this form must be metaphysical, as a substitute for the laws of physics. It is a problem of defining living things not merely as living things function, but as living things form, develop, change form, and survive from generation to generation.

> Unlike those who today claim to be his followers (and who hide this aspect of his thinking), Claude Bernard understood that, in his conception, the actual set of physical laws does not entirely account for living beings, but only for their functioning as a controlled automaton. We must still account for the construction of the automaton. This is the problem which the late seventeenth-century mechanists solved through preformation. But in Claude Bernard's time, embryology had long since abandoned preformation for epigenesis; hence this 'metaphysical morphogenetic force' particular to living beings. Nevertheless, such a force was also difficult to accept in the latter half of the nineteenth century, for it was too vitalistic.[8]

Pichot appropriately remarks that the desire to break with vitalism, that is, with a reduction of the definition of living things to formal things, leads, in Weismann and in Darwinism, to the rejection of *every* possible formal thing in the determination of living things. In this way, an apparently objective definition of living things was advanced, eliminating all form in favour of objective and physical content, from Weismann's *germen* to James D. Watson and Francis Crick's double helix. The support of living things, which distinguishes living things from non-living things, is no longer a 'formation' or 'preformation', but rather an 'information' tied to a physical support. By rejecting vitalism, or the compact formalisation of living things, the nineteenth century was able to rid itself of every possible formal thing in living things. In the twentieth century, this would lead to an altogether objective concept of living things:

> The Bernardian model is a model of the controlled animal-machine and, since the seventeenth century, the animal-machine called preformation. It therefore had to reconcile preformation (intrinsic to the animal-machine) with epigenesis (imposed by embryological descriptions). Weismann undertook this reconciliation a few years after Claude Bernard's death. Weismannian heredity is indeed a programme *avant la lettre*. Now, a programme is nothing other than an 'encoded' preformation. Instead of the germ containing, in miniature, a preformed being, it contains the instructions controlling its formation. 'Codification' allows epigenetic construction. If it is not preformed, it is at least 'pre-written' (the etymological sense of 'pro-gramme'). God would guarantee preformation, whereas the chance and necessity of Darwinian evolution will guarantee programming.[9]

Pichot's heretical conception appropriately allows us to understand that modern (Weismannian) biology and contemporary biology (the neo-Darwinian synthesis between molecular and evolutionary biology), powerful as they may be, have not succeeded in objectively dismissing vitalist forms or completely doing without something formal in their definitions of living things. Weismannian heredity and the genetic programme, as *information*, are, after all, forms that are not admitted: internal 'encoded' (and not analogical) forms that control a living organism's formation.

Instead of a metaphysical intergenerational morphogenetic force, Weismannian heredity (the germplasm) is a physical structure controlling the formation of living beings. Heredity compensates for the insufficiency of the set of physical laws by superimposing on it a control structure (this set is therefore no longer free, as in the case of the formation of a crystal; something is added to it, a physical control structure instead of a vital force).[10]

While evolutionism seems to introduce a *historical* dimension into living things by distinctly giving them self-control structures determined by generational inheritances, in the end, it has only given *memory* in physical form to living things:

> The explanation of a living being is thus limited to the inside of a single generation, and even to the inside of a single being [. . .] Therefore, the explanation is wholly physicalist, in accordance with the claims of biology at the end of the nineteenth century, and no longer accepts a vital force, in accordance with the claims of modern science.[11]

For Pichot, modern biology derived from the desire to no longer define the formation of living things by an intensive 'vital force'. Instead, it would define them by a physical apparatus, a memory, treated as 'information' – for example, in the work of John Maynard Smith and Eörs Szathmáry.[12] Pichot claims:

> Biology desires to be physicalist, but it cannot eliminate its historical dimension, which physics does not know how to approach. Biology therefore places the historical dimension in the present in virtue of a memory, ignoring any consideration of anything except the current (atemporal) set of physical laws.[13]

The attempt to define living things by their genetic apparatus marks the *objective* and operative part of the modern determination of living things through the current set of physical laws. But it does not eliminate the *formal* part of their determination. By attributing a strictly physical appearance (the genetic apparatus) to the characteristic property of living things, one thinks that the definition of a living thing can do without a 'self', its preservation and its support – which is central to all conceptions of what lives, and which resurfaces today in evolutionary theory and its tropism towards a certain finalism, and in the temptation to project the self-form beneath the organism onto the gene (the evolution of life in Richard Dawkins) and beyond the organism onto the species (evolution in Stephen Jay Gould). The self-form thrown out of the door of modern biology necessarily comes back in through the windows of contemporary biology.

Between ancient vitalism and contemporary biologism, there is formal continuity and objective rupture:

> In the eighteenth century, G. E. Stahl claimed that it was the soul that guided the set of physical laws towards the construction of the body and prevented it from corruption. The vitalists claimed that the soul was a vital principle, natural, of course, but rather mysterious. In the nineteenth century, Bernard gave this role to a 'metaphysical morphogenetic force'. Today, one claims that it is genetic information. On the surface, progress has been made. But it is not necessary to consider too closely the physical aspect of the explanation, for we rather quickly realise that it is no less 'magical' than the explanations implemented in the past.[14]

How do we avoid this magical aspect colouring the determination of 'living things' and their formation? Or how do we accept it without making it irrational or compact? The problem of vitalism is to formalise the characteristic property of living things that becomes a principle whose possibility can be located in the formal world, in the very becoming of the inanimate universe, before the novel event of living things. Conversely, the problem of the synthesis between molecular biology and evolutionism, which dominates contemporary biological thinking, is thinking that we can give living things an altogether objective definition.

Ancient *vitalism* makes a form of life, and ultimately finds living things everywhere, but fails to distinguish non-living things from living things. Contemporary *biologism* refuses to find the formal in life, and merely sees living things in their objective determinations and physical properties, but fails to distinguish living things from non-living things.

The objective intensification of something formal is specific to living things. By merely retaining and formalising intensity, one makes of it a vitalist principle. By merely retaining the objective, one makes of it a series of emergent properties of the physico-chemical universe, embodied today in the transmission of genetic information. Nothing, however, is more abstract than the concept of 'information' through which contemporary biology attempts to objectively articulate materialism and the definition of living things. That living things are *informed* and *informing*, in the last analysis, merely perpetuates the idea according to which the *formal* is included in every definition of living things. Contemporary biology unwillingly rediscovers it in 'information', since no objective definition of what lives can entirely do without form – whether Aristotelian form, the form of the soul, Bernard's 'metaphysical morphogenetic force' (and producer of form), or information.

5. Variable Intensities of the Self

The problems raised by the neo-Darwinian synthesis, which are generally attached to the problem of finalism, are first expressed in the determination of what living things formally have. Before knowing if evolution has meaning – an *end* [*fin*] – if it has not assimilated something from the theologies and teleologies that it dismisses, it is necessary to know if living things have a *form*, and if so what it could be.

In order to avoid either vital or biological compactness, we must consider living things as objective events of the intensification of something formal. A living thing's information is nothing other than a self redoubled by the possibility of reproducing and transmitting its possibility.

Evolutionism is consequently a way of thinking about the time of living things as a set of variable self-intensities: a karyotype's possible self, a phenotype's present self, a species' macroself, and so on. Everything is interpreted, for an evolutionist, as a time of living things through variable self-intensities. What is retained? What is lost? An organism's self is enmeshed between a 'selfish gene's' self (using Dawkins's expression[15]) and a species' self. An organism's self is always a self-*moment*.

Contemporary taxonomy, the classification of living things assimilating the supplementary dimension of evolutionary time, consists in distinguishing kingdoms, species, genera, and so forth, not as closed categories, but as effects of identity within the continuous differentiation of living things. Monera (in particular, bacteria) are still defined as the class of all prokaryotes, but Protista are no longer recognised today except as the class including cellular eukaryotes as well as pluricellular eukaryotes 'neighbouring' unicellular eukaryotes. The distinction is no longer very clear-cut. Lastly, the three kingdoms of living things are primarily distinguished by their nutritional mode, their means of finding energy outside themselves in order to differentiate themselves. Mycota are the decomposers that degrade the complex molecules of dead organisms and debris (like dead leaves and faeces). Vegetables function through photosynthesis. Animals feed through the ingestion and digestion of vegetable or animal organisms.

Animals are therefore living objects that obtain their energy through the consumption of living things. The problem becomes knowing how to divide them up and individuate them among the events and intensities of life.

Notes

1. Neil A. Campbell and Jane B. Reece, *Biology*, p. 2.
2. Ibid., p. 3. [The additions in brackets are found in the second French translation of the sixth English edition. See Campbell and Reece, *Biologie*, p. 3.]
3. Ibid., p. 3.
4. Ibid., p. 4.
5. Ibid., p. 4 [See note 2; Campbell and Reece, *Biologie*, p. 5]
6. Ibid., p. 8.
7. André Pichot, 'Hérédité et évolution (l'inné et l'acquis en biologie)', p. 21.
8. Ibid., p. 21
9. Ibid., pp. 21–2.
10. Ibid., p. 22.
11. Ibid., p. 22
12. In *The Origins of Life*, Maynard Smith and Szathmáry define this 'informational' character of life as one of the three major evolutionary transitions.
13. Pichot, 'Hérédité et évolution', p. 23.
14. Ibid., p. 25.
15. Richard Dawkins, *The Selfish Gene*.

Chapter V

Animals

1. Divisions into Species

Animals are living beings defined *among* other living beings and *by* a specific animal: the human animal. Animality is defined through a division of living things into kingdoms, themselves divided into branches, classes, orders, families, genera, and species. Species are the fundamental classes of the division of living things. The divisions into species make animal species *events* rather than *objects*.

In the history of Western knowledge, species were once a principle of dividing several things into objects, which were dependent upon the living object's ancestral relations and resemblances. Georges Cuvier's fixist conception of species 'includes the individuals which descend from one another, or from common parents, and those which resemble them as strongly as they resemble one another.'[1] Augustin Pyramus de Candolle soon after recast Cuvier's fixist classificatory system. But the introduction of an evolutionary concept of living things, in which form passes through genetic information and its transmission through self-levels, affected the definition of species considerably. Ernst Mayr's and Theodosius Dobzhansky's important work contributed to the establishment of the twentieth-century neo-Darwinian synthesis. In 1942, Mayr famously defined a concept of biological species that broke with idealism and 'typological thought': 'species are groups of actually or potentially interbreeding natural populations which are reproductively isolated from other such groups'.[2] Mayr's use of the term 'potentially' reintroduces into the definition something it aimed to avoid (an abstraction). The import of Mayr's work lies in the following: a species is a division of living things that does not account for the existence of extraordinary types, dear to the taxonomists and amateurs of cabinets of curiosities – thus, no criteria of resemblance, morphology, or external form permits us to define a single type or idea of species among the diversity of individuals. For the neo-Darwinians, genetic information – a population's gene *pool*, and its allelic diversity, which reproduction mixes over several generations – is the only specifically concrete reality. No ultimate comparative criteria between organisms exists from the standpoint of their appearance or external form. One can only compare the existence of the organisms' information with their characteristics. Genetic combinations in the species and the absence of genetic combinations between species become the sole criteria. Since the living chain is unbroken, the *species* concept admits of the phenomenon of *speciation*. Reproductive isolation, the geographical grouping together of a population into an ecological niche, isolated from other populations' ecological niches, allows us to consider speciation. Speciation is the phenomenon by which genetic population mixing results in the separation of genetic inheritance, differentiating to the point of no longer being able to combine and mix.

In 1982, Mayr explicitly added this ecological criterion or reproductive isolation factor to his definition, by specifying that groups of interbreeding populations must 'occup[y] a specific niche in nature'[3] to become a species. In 1989, Alan R. Templeton[4] advanced another definition based on inclusion and demographic exchangeability. Numerous other variations on Mayr's model fuelled scientific discussion. Most importantly, a species is not understood as an *object* (of classification), but rather as an *event*. A species is some intensive degree of *speciation*. In this way, living things are not divided into objects, kingdoms, and species (for example, animal species) as in the age of evolutionary theory, but rather into speciation events and speciation processes.

This upheaval involved a return to the nominalist temptation of the individual's compactness. Nominalism reduces a species to a secondary effect, a cognitive or linguistic construction. Several philosophers emphasise species as linguistic constructions by drawing on Wittgenstein's concept of 'family resemblance'.[5] For example, Massimo Pigliucci considers a species as a language game involving fertility, semblance, and descent.[6] Jody Hey emphasises cognitive constructions.[7] Hey holds that the conceptualisation of 'species' is connected to two mechanisms: the first founded on the brain's internal rules of recognition; the second connected to a 'prototype-effect' making our cognitive images coincide with various natural forms. We will return later to the compactness of every existential critique of objective classification. We will restrict ourselves here to asking the cognitive scientist how she can distinguish the two cognitive mechanisms from humanity's distinct conceptualisation into 'species', if not as two different *species* of cognitive functioning. We will ask the Wittgensteinian how she can reduce the concept of species to linguistic operations on 'family resemblances', if we do not understand that the 'family resemblance' between objects connects a metaphor to a meaning that is precisely the result of (at least partially genetic) relations, reproduction, and a *specific* characteristic. By reducing the classification of species to a secondary effect, one fails to account for the distinctions that one must make use of precisely to be able to dissolve it: distinctions between different *species* of cognitive functioning and between different *species* of language games.

By making the idea of species compact, one reduces a species to an effect on individual objects that would have nothing specific about them on their own. Objects are in fact never alone. Things are alone. Objects exist only together. Therefore, pure individuality cannot be grounds for dividing them; objective classes are real, and different objective species are in living things. But we must understand that the present-day objective conditions of defining living things lead us to consider living things as a set of events, and not as a set of objects.

The phylogenetic classification of living things[8] accounts for a species' evolutionary history by replacing the traditional classification, which isolated taxa into several objects. Phylogenetic classification divides living things into groups or 'clades'. Each clade includes an ancestor and all of the ancestor's descendents, which must have at least one derivative characteristic common to the whole group. The principle of division stems from this characteristic, which is *derived* from morphological and genetic characteristics, and which transforms a set of taxa into some instantiated 'thing'. A monophyletic group is isolated on the phylogenetic tree when a new characteristic, deriving from mutations, is shared by this group. For example, the presence of four feet among tetrapods is derived from the presence of four pairs of fins among fish.

This process assumes that ancestral states are always simpler than evolutionarily derivative states. On the other hand, it presupposes the sometimes problematic recognition of homologies, identities between different organisms. For example, a crocodile's gizzard is homologous to a rooster's gizzard. Division is possible only if one thinks that different things can remain together in the same thing (an evolutionary species) through an objective, collective distribution [*partage*] of 'something', a distinguishing feature in these different things.

Living things are, then, represented as a tree of complex groupings, with clades as its branches. Each clade is divided according to its own derivative characteristic. Each node between one branch and another branch represents a group's ancestor. This cladic representation is the very image of *speciation*, the division of living things into arborescent events.

This privilege afforded to speciation raises some problems when biology attempts to redivide these events into macroobjects. The theory of punctuated equilibria[9] supposes that selection – not between individuals but between species – is a macro-level selection mechanism, solely responsible for macro-evolution, for example. The theory makes a species a super-object, evolution's object par excellence. But the theory represents a higher-order individual of a species *in the image of an individual*. Its evolutionary 'Leviathan' demonstrates all of the drawbacks of the representation of supraindividual organisms as individual kinds.

Louis Thaler skilfully criticises this conception by contrasting it with scalar differences. Like all objective things, living things exist on several levels. In the classical sense of the term, a population is a monospecific collection, and a community is a plurispecific collection. The transition from individual selection to species selection does not involve access to *another* selection, but merely to a change of view about the diversity of living things: 'as in every scalar change, what one gains in depth, one loses in detail: the species genotype is "comprehensive", and neglects intraspecific variations in favour of interspecific variations'.[10] From individual selection to species selection, which is the key to speciation, there is no transition to a metaorganism, only a scalar change in the perception of genetic diversity. The emphasis is thus on interspecific differences, rather than on intraspecific differences.

Species selection differs from individual selection not as a metaorganism differs from an organism, but through the particular interaction between differences and identities. When confronted with natural diversity, we cannot say that a species is a mere linguistic or cognitive effect. Nor can we say that it is an evolutionary reality distinct from the individuals that compose it.

Species are objectively intensive events of living things, rendered temporarily extensive through our division of living things.

Animal *species* thus exist in the same way as animal *speciation*, which is currently conceived and provisionally fixed as a classificatory system. But, if one defines species merely as living things, animal species will always be events: transformations, becomings, processes, continuations, phenomena of reproductive isolation, mutations, hybridisations, and so on. No animal species could be an object in the strict sense, other than as a long-term impediment to these events. Animal species, like all other species, are primarily events, fixed into objects through a provisional systematic division.

But by defining animals *merely* through the speciation of living things that constitutes them as a kingdom, one considers animals via a pure systematics, grounded on their morphology and genome. This fails to account for the fact that animals are part of living things, defined both by what constitutes them and by what they constitute.

Guillaume Lecointre, co-author of *The Tree of Life*, distinguishes between biodiversity and systematics. Biodiversity derives from what living beings 'do'. Systematics looks at what living beings 'have'. What they 'do', their role within an environment, would for us correspond to *what they are*, what they enter into. On the other hand, what they 'have' would correspond to their genetic inheritance, to what enters into them, to *what is them*. The specific modern division of living things therefore tends to specify taxa by articulating *what is an animal* and *what this animal is* – what enters into it (as an environment) and what it enters into (its environment).

What is an animal derives from the evolutionary processes of living things. *What* an animal *is* derives from the relationship that animals have with their environment in general. But a particular animal species has gradually organised what animals are around its own environment, transforming this environment into *society*. We will now focus on this environment of intensification and transformation of what animals are, to understand the exceptional division between a certain species and all others.

2. The Society of Species

The relationships between humanity and other animal species are of an incredible variety. They differ culturally and have evolved considerably. We will not present a detailed picture, but simply explore a change in the relation between one part of animality and their totality. This change concerns both the mode of presence of other animal species near the human species and the feeling that accompanies this mode of presence.

In Antiquity, Pliny the Elder described the relation between humanity and other animals by the carefully chosen term *societas*. The term may appear paradoxical if one politicises it by making it the distinguishing feature of humanity, but it nevertheless quite correctly expresses the relation between humans organised into cities – unlike other animals, Aristotle would say – and those who socialise with other animal species.

Pliny's work is remarkable in that it is both an attempt to classify zoological and geographical data of animals (into objective species rather than into evential speciations) and their reproductive and parental behaviour, and an attempt to define what connects humans and other animals. More than Aristotle, Pliny articulates the order of species and the singularity of animals as living beings defined by the relation between a certain species and other species. The idea that animality is defined not only by the classifications of (evential) living things, but also by the relationship between its whole and one of its parts, traverses every way of thinking about animals, in particular the ethical animal. To the extent that the ethical animal makes humanity responsible for the suffering inflicted on other species and attempts to construct a trans-species justice, the ethical animal defines animality by the moral relation between the totality of species and one species in particular.

As in Aristotle, the observation of the specific diversity of animals provokes in Pliny a feeling described by Liliane Bodson in *L'Animal dans l'Antiquité*: 'The abundance and ingenuity that nature manifests through animals touches Pliny, and inspires astonishment mixed with wonder and admiration – in Latin, it's all the same.'[11] But Pliny does not stop at the 'wonder' for the specific diversity of the animal world. He is, above all, interested in the connections between specific diversity and the capacities of a particular species, the human species:

> There are a thousand other facts of this kind [of intelligence]; and the same Nature has also bestowed upon many animals as well, the faculty of observing the heavens, and of presaging the winds, rains, and tempests, each in its own peculiar way. It would be an endless labour to

enumerate them all; just as it would be to point out the relation of each to [the *societas* of human beings].[12]

Societas is not really the oft-dreaded sign of 'speciesism', the formal and objective privilege attributed to one species, in relation to which all other species are thought, judged, and evaluated.[13] Rather, *societas* gives concrete expression to a common bond between the specific capacities of different animals and what one species in particular, the human species, can make use of. *Societas* denotes both the human species' inclusion in the same community, and the possibility of exchanges between humanity and other animals – provided that humans, through attention, care, and an equitable attitude (that other animals do not have, as other animals have no justice), return what they take from the different animal species which serve them through the fulfilment of some function or another.

Bodson analyses the use of this decisive term *societas* with much care, and emphasises the various meanings that it can take on:

The word *societas* is full of particularly stoic connotations. Cicero employs it precisely when explaining how the public fights for the cause of elephants massacred in 55 BCE, during the games staged by Pompey. By this, he conveys the perception of a 'community' between the human species and Pachydermata. For Mary Beagon, who explicitly refers merely to a single passage of *The Natural History* reproduced above, the term *societas* in Pliny the Elder means nothing other than an 'affinity between animals and man', founded on simple analogies and resemblances of a physical and instinctive order, outside all reference to the *ratio* that, according to the Stoics, differentiates humanity from animality. However, she fails to ask how we know that the appearance of *societas* in Pliny's account entails an express reference to stoic thought and terminology. The encyclopedist is known for her philosophical eclecticism, wherein stoic ideas are well represented. But this simple acknowledgement does not suffice to resolve the case of *societas*. Pliny employs the word twenty-eight times in *The Natural History*, with nine occurrences in books VIII through XI, in addition to related terms (like *socius*). Among the attestations from the books on zoology, at least three can at once be approached from book VLII, 102, for they concern the relation between humanity and animality. Whether it is a question of the collaboration between fishermen and dolphins, Thracian bird-catchers and diurnal raptors, or apiculturists and bees, none of them is reduced to an expression of instincts or to a simple analogy. They do not a priori entail an allusion to stoic thought. Pliny introduces the term *societas*, which consists in a complex relationship founded on interspecific exchange in the broadest sense of the term: the actions of animals in favour of humanity; humanity's appreciation of the service received, and, in return, an equitable attitude towards the animal that provides it.[14]

Bodson explains that Pliny's *societas* means both the animal community, shared by the human species and other animal species (expressed through compassion), and collaborative possibility, possible interspecific exchange, and social relations between the human species and other animal species. Animals can fulfil functions for human beings, and human beings return to animals what animals give to human beings through an 'equitable' attitude, that is, both a care and concern transcending the specific differences that the other animal species occasionally manifest, and that humanity can generalise.

Human and non-human animal *societas* is thus neither an exploitative relationship, even if it can become an unequal one, nor a trans-species communion between humans and non-humans, even if it can be expressed through compassion (as in the case of the elephant massacre mentioned by Cicero). Rather, *societas* is the twofold articulation of a shared sense of belonging to the same thing (the animal community or the community of sentient beings) and the recognition of specific differences, differences between species (that are in fact differentiations), separating distinct faculties and competences. Exchanges are therefore possible between species through a particular species, the human species. The human species exchanges its capacity to transcend the limits between species for the functionalisation of certain animals. What humanity must give in exchange for the use that it makes of other animals is not competences that would be useful in helping other species. Instead, it is precisely its capacity to take aim at the differences and identities between species, that is, to consider other animal species as *other* than humanity in one sense, but *identical* to it in another. No animal other than the human animal has ever surrounded itself so much with other animal species. It is not simply a question of an instinctive domination, but of a capacity to form a *societas* with these species. This *societas* assumes both the difference between species (which 'anti-speciesists' deny) and the identity between animal species (which the modern age tended to assert in theory and deny in practice).

The meaning of this human *societas* between a particular, human species and other animal species is one of a mutual and functional co-presence. One does not live between species equally, as between citizens, for species are differentiated by their biological apparatus, their competences, and their interests. But by recognising a community beyond differentiated species, one establishes the possibility of trade, of exchanges with animals, that is, of giving them functions, since one cares about their suffering, needs, and interests, without confusing them with our own.

3. Separation of Animals

On the whole, one could say that this mutual and functional co-presence has held sway for a long time among most Western people. They established a *societas* with other species, and therefore systems of discerning identities with and differences from the human species, by attributing functions to other animals (domestication, food, labour, company, protection, symbolic functions, and so on). At the same time, they recognised the interests and needs specific to other species, by ritualising exchanges between humanity and all other animal species.

But from the end of the Middle Ages, somewhere between the Renaissance and the Enlightenment, this mutual and functional co-presence between the human species and other animal species was gradually replaced by a very different relationship. Although, theoretically, humanity identified with other animals, by acquiring its sense of belonging as a species to the animal kingdom, beyond the religious and philosophical doctrines that separated human from beast through a series of 'characteristic properties' (soul, spirit, consciousness, *logos*, free will, and so on), practically, humanity separated itself from other animals, putting an end to the *societas* that connected humanity to other animals. Becoming predominantly urban in the twentieth century, humanity restricted its everyday acquaintance with other animals to companion species, nature reserves, zoos, and symbolic functions (animals in children's stories, metaphors by which we still identify people and groups with animals that we hardly ever spend much time with: rats, foxes, bears, lynx, tigers, and so on).

Little by little, Pliny's *societas*, the mutual and functional co-presence between species, gave way to a culpable absence through theoretical identification and practical estrangement. The relation between humanity and animality is no longer one of mutuality and functionality, but of culpability. Animals became absent beings onto which humanity projected all of its faults, as if animality were the internalised outside [*l'extériorité intériorisée*] through which humanity could expound its errors, all that was evil about humanity. Humanity increasingly identified with animals, but at the same time stopped spending time with them. This great distance gave birth to a bad conscience which, for us, increasingly formed an image of animals as expiatory figures of Human Evil. Indeed, animals are both in us (humanity is nothing but an animal species) and outside us (humanity separates itself from animality). For us, animals have become the ideal support for all that we are guilty of. The evil that human beings do to themselves is always equivocal, for its meaning can only be decided in a closed channel between humans. The evil that we do to other animal species is both an evil that we do to ourselves (since our species is also an animal species) and an evil that we do to something other than us (since they are species other than our own). Our way of thinking reduces, and our way of life increases, the gap between species, no longer filled by a *societas*, or mutual co-presence.

4. The Rift of Compassion

Vegetarianism was the primary way of showing resistance to the mutual and functional co-presence between the human species and other animal species. By claiming that it is not necessary for humanity to kill and eat other animals, vegetarianism touched upon what defines animality: the animal kingdom is determined by the ingestion and digestion of vegetables and animals. Vegetarianism holds that humanity must respect the life of other animals and deny something about its own animality (the fact that it eats other animals). It combines humanity's claim to go outside the diet of human animality (the predation and ingestion of other animals) and affirmation of an animal community (by respecting other animal beings and other human beings). Yet, in most cultures, the human ingestion of animals of other species is not, strictly speaking, animal- or beast-like. It is a highly culturalised act. The human species carries out an act shared with many carnivorous animal species and ritualises it. Humanity herds livestock together,

transforms an animal's death into a ceremony, and makes predation functional. Some animal species have a nutritional value for
humanity, which does not mean that humanity merely slaughters
them, but rather that it transforms the relations between humans
and other animals that other animals also have with each other
(predation, the hunt, the fact of being carnivorous). Humanity has
long lived in the presence of animals that it killed. The *societas*
between human and other animal species was realised through the
use of animals as food.

Vegetarianism arose from the reduction of differences between
species. The horror of eating oneself, which led to treating eating
another animal being as if it were the same as eating a fellow
human, gave way to the refusal to maintain a nutritional exchange
with other species.

Above, we have seen how our way of thinking about living
things leads to an elimination of species in favour of speciations,
differential events, which lead modern sceptics to 'speciesism'
– which, in a way, is a pejorative name for Pliny's *societas*.
'Speciesism' is the bad conscience of modern human beings, who
identify with other animals through their way of thinking but
separate themselves from them through their way of life, bring-
ing an end to the *societas* that connected them to other species.
Richard Ryder's use of the term 'speciesism' in his eponymous
article[15] is partly at the root of modern animal ethics movements.
The fact that the idea was forged through analogy with 'racism'
shows that humanity, in its relations with other animal species,
projected the guilt of having allowed unjust discrimination within
its own species. Racism derives from the projection of differences
between animal species onto the human species. 'Speciesism' is
the mirror image, reversed by the bad conscience of this projection, and the possible projection of a discrimination internal to
the human species outside the human species, in its relations with
other animals.

Jean-Baptiste Jeangène Vilmer argues in *Éthique animale*[16]
that ancient vegetarianism made claims similar to those of anti-
speciesism, but for entirely different reasons: Pythagoras justi-
fied it out of concern for metempsychosis; Empedocles out of
care for everything that lives and that is one; Plutarch through
the moral will to distinguish trivialities and what is not necessary (killing animals) from human necessities. The refusal to eat
meat, to kill animals for food, always passes through a morality

of human health, often through the conception of a corporeal equilibrium, as in Hippocratic dietetics or Montesquiou's belief that the ingestion of meat 'fattens and thickens the souls'.[17] But the primary concern remains the bodies and souls of humans themselves.

Though these positions remained more or less the same, the reasons for these positions changed in the seventeenth and eighteenth centuries, especially in England. Like Michel de Montaigne in the sixteenth century, the specific difference between human and other animal species was supplanted by differences of degree, of intensity. We see that the severing of the *societas* between human and other animals, through urbanisation and the mechanisation and industrialisation of breeding and slaughtering, gave birth in human thought to the idea of a culpable absence. The more animals are theoretically closer to us but practically distanced from our lives, the more they are absent, and the more the *mechanical* estrangement from what is *vitally* close to us is expressed through guilt.

After contemplating all sentient creatures, the jurist Sir Matthew Hale, in 1676, claimed that there was 'a certain degree of justice due from man to the creatures, as from man to man'.[18] Hale thus shows that species-difference gives way to a scale of degrees, and that the demand for justice must follow. For Thomas Tryon, guilt becomes clear. This well-known theorist, whose works convinced Benjamin Franklin to give up meat consumption, bases his vegetarianism on religious arguments: 'It is not said, That the Lord made all Creatures for Man to Eat, as I have heard many affirm, but he made them for his *own Glory* and eternal Honour, and for the manifestation of his Wonders.'[19] Tryon claims that Beasts do not only share flesh and blood with Man, but also a number of passions, such as love, hate, and anger, which do not make them mere carnal, edible beings, but living creatures like us, though deprived of a soul.

Vegetarianism, which was a private asceticism in the Ancient world, becomes a religious conflict where the very meaning of Man is at stake. However, the decisive argument which will structure human guilt towards animals is only disclosed in the work of the doctor, Humphrey Primatt (who will inspire Henry Stephens Salt, the first great militant of 'animal liberation'). By a historical analogy, Primatt compares humanity's treatment of other animal species (more precisely, birds, flies, and worms) to the white man's treatment of black slaves; the guilt that burdens human beings who enslaved their fellow creatures extends beyond the limit of the species, which is no longer really a limit.

In his dissertation on duty and mercy and the sin of cruelty towards 'brute' animals, Primatt strongly condemns slavery. If it had pleased God, he says, to cover some men with white skin and others with black skin, and that there is neither merit nor demerit in this 'complexion', white men have no right, by virtue of their colour, to reduce black men to slavery and tyranny. For, considered abstractly, skin colour is 'neither a subject for pride, nor an object of contempt'.[20] Yet Primatt writes in 1776 that God's love and mercy are present in all his works, from the most rational being to the least sentient creature, from the most beautiful thing to the most ugly vermin, and that our own love and mercy cannot confine itself to our circle of friends and neighbours any more than to the broader sphere of 'human nature', or to creatures with whom we share our form and capacities, but, to be just, they must also be extended to all animals. For Primatt thinks that, from the most miserable to the most complex creature, *suffering* alone is common to all that lives, whatever form this life takes.

This text, even if it is not yet decisive, is the harbinger of modern compassion [*sensibilité*]. The human species is a communal sphere of forms and capacities, embedded between micro-spheres (neighbourhoods, nations) and macro-spheres (other suffering animal species). A century and a half later, Mayr refused to assimilate external form and resemblances into his definition of species, only taking into account the information specific to all living beings, valuing speciation rather than the division into species. Primatt, for his part, refuses to define a sphere of justice through the shared inclusion in the external human form. He argues that only the compassion shared by all animals is relevant to justice.

Eighteenth-century England prepared the way for evolutionary theory and gave birth to utilitarianism. But it also gave birth to guilt as the new compassion towards other animal species, by analogy with racism. This is, of course, the century of the English Industrial Revolution; it is both *theoretically* because humanity acquired the meaning of its inclusion among other animal species, and *practically* because of human urbanisation, that the mutual and functional co-presence in Pliny's *societas* gave way to a culpable absence.

5. Speciesism and Anti-Speciesism

In the 1970s, the work which paved the way for animal ethics continued, and developed both sides of the eighteenth-century positions defended in England, except that their origins most often stemmed from increased awareness of the industrialisation of animal slaughter. Since Ruth Harrison's *Animal Machines*,[21] Brigid Brophy's 'The Rights of Animals',[22] and Peter Singer's[23] and Tom Regan's[24] work, the same more or less utilitarian line has been drawn, beyond the particularities and perspectives adopted by each:[25] the refusal of 'speciesism'. The prevalence of a species difference is denied as a foundation for values and justice. This is symptomatic of the historical weakening of the concept of species, through which everything could be explained.

Everything is connected: the passage to an evolutionary schema for analysing living things; the formal definition of living things through their information rather than through their form; the replacement of an objective division into species by an evential division into speciations; the refusal of 'speciesism', since species differences are not strong enough any more; the combination of a way of thinking about human animality with a culpable sense of estrangement from other animals; the change to an urban way of life; the industrialisation of animal slaughter for food; the severing of the *societas*, the mutual and functional (and equitable) co-presence between other animal species and the human species; the projection onto animals of human guilt; the formation of a figure of non-human animality as humanity's 'outside-inside' | '*dehors-dedans*']; and so on. All this resulted in a fault line between 'speciesists', holding on to species difference as grounds for our rights and duties, and 'anti-speciesists', counting on the weakening of the species difference in order to base rights and duties on the recognition of the suffering of all sentient beings.[26]

The problem is not so much knowing whether or not 'speciesism' is structured like racism, but, instead, why one comes to think that 'speciesism', this *natural* and *ethical* difference between the human species and other animal species, is structured like racism. The response is simple: because racism structures differences between humans and other humans like differences between humans and non-humans, one today thinks that differences between humans and non-humans could over time be revealed to be no more than the differences between humans and other humans. This is how the 'anti-speciesist' theorists often respond to their critics, as if their critics took historical responsibility for being judged by future generations, as human sensibility changes – in the same way that we view yesterday's racists today.

Perhaps they are not wrong that human sensibility changes, and that our relations with animals seem committed to a movement which brings us closer to them through our way of thinking and feeling, but which distances our mode of existence from theirs. But they are blind about what motivates the movement they are caught in, which leads to theoretical compactness. 'Anti-speciesism', which denies the species difference between human and other animal species, acts as a possible foundation for a right that produces discrimination. It leads to a compact concept of 'animal'; its condition of possibility is quite precisely its failure. Indeed, the condition of success of 'anti-speciesism' is humanity's refusal both to produce animal suffering and to behave like an animal species (and thus have specific interests). The complete assimilation of humanity into the community of all sentient and suffering beings would thus mean that humanity goes outside this community. Human beings would index all their behaviour with respect to all living and suffering beings, as if there were no species difference at the foundation of ethics [*fondement du droit*]. Human beings would be beings that deny their specific identity and exclude animal species from humanity.

Conversely, to exclude humanity from animality, to think that humanity must be conceived in opposition to animality, is to makes its species a compact species, since the condition of success of this position is its failure: to make humanity an animal species like others, which does not particularly care about other species and which produces no *society* between species, except in a marginal or parasitic form.

The speciesist who considers the human species as absolutely outside other animal species fails because she makes a human animal an animal like others, destined to realise its nature and defend its species by excluding other species from the ethical sphere [*de son droit*]. The anti-speciesist who ethically assimilates the human species into other animal species fails because she isolates humanity by assigning to humanity the task of moralising its relations with species that do not moralise their own.

Both positions dissolve the idea of species, and in particular the human species. The 'speciesist' who situates humanity absolutely outside animality, makes humanity more than a species: an idea. But the 'anti-speciesist' who wants to assimilate humanity absolutely into all living and suffering beings dissolves the very significance of the concept of species.

Yet humanity is a species that understands itself as between an animal that embodies the species and an idea that the species embodies. Species are currently defined not as *objects*, but as *events*. This shows that the human species, like every other animal species, is a temporal event, which occurs between animal and idea. The idealist turns humanity away from the animal *which is humanity* and makes humanity similar to an idea. The naturalist turns humanity away from the idea *which humanity is* and makes humanity similar to an animal. Both make this particular species of animal an equally compact animal or idea.

Notes

1. Georges Cuvier, *A Discourse on the Revolutions of the Surface of the Globe*, p. 73.
2. Ernst Mayr, *Systematics and the Origin of Species from the Viewpoint of a Zoologist*, p. 120. See also the entry for 'espèce' in Patrick Tort (ed.), *Dictionnaire du darwinisme et de l'Évolution*, pp. 1392–7.
3. Ernst Mayr, *The Growth of Biological Thought*, p. 273.
4. 'The cohesion concept species is the most inclusive population of individuals having the potential for phenotypic cohesion through intrinsic cohesion mechanisms', Alan R. Templeton, 'The Meaning of Species and Speciation', p. 12.
5. Ludwig Wittgenstein, *Philosophical Investigations*.
6. Massimo Pigliucci, 'Species as family resemblance concepts'.
7. Jody Hey, 'A Reduction of "Species" Resolves the Species Problem'.
8. Guillaume Lecointre and Hervé Le Guyader, *The Tree of Life: A Phylogenetic Classification*.
9. In 1972, Niles Eldredge and Stephen Jay Gould developed this theory. They assume that evolutionary changes affecting species unfold over relatively brief time periods, separated by long periods of stability.
10. Louis Thaler, 'L'espèce: type ou population?'
11. Liliane Bodson, 'Le Témoignage de Pline l'Ancien sur la conception romaine de l'animal', p. 341.
12. Pliny the Elder, *The Natural History*, Book VIII, Chapter XLII.

13. In *Animal Liberation*, Peter Singer, who takes up Richard D. Ryder's concept, defines it thus: 'Speciesism [. . .] is a prejudice or attitude of bias toward the interests of members of one's own species and against those of members of other species', p. 7.

14. Bodson, 'Le Témoignage de Pline l'Ancien', p. 342.

15. The term 'speciesism' first appeared in Ryder's leaflets, privately distributed among the Oxford Group of anti-speciesists. See his seminal 'Experiments on Animals', in Stanley Godlovitch, Roslind Godlovitch, and John Harris (eds), *Animals, Men and Morals*.

16. Jean-Baptiste Jeangène Vilmer, *Éthique animale*, pp. 21–5.

17. Robert de Montesquiou, *Roseaux pensants*, p. 16.

18. Matthew Hale, *Contemplations, Moral and Divine*, p. 117.

19. Thomas Tryon, *Health's Grand Preservative; or the Women's Best Doctor*, p. 13.

20. Humphrey Primatt, *A Dissertation on the Duty of Mercy and Sin of Cruelty to Brute Animals*, p. 12.

21. Ruth Harrison, *Animal Machines*.

22. Brigid Brophy, 'The Rights of Animals'.

23. Singer, *Animal Liberation*.

24. Tom Regan, 'Animal Rights, Human Wrongs'.

25. Whether 'welfarist' (*primarily* aiming at animal well-being) or 'deontologist' (*primarily* demanding animal rights).

26. On the contemporary debates about speciesism and anti-speciesism, we refer our reader to our work, *Nous, animaux et humains*.

Chapter VI

Humans

1. Divisions of Humanity

The identity of humanity is partially nomadic and extendable: 'what is humanity' is an animal species, but 'what humanity is' is variable.

The Brazilian anthropologist and metaphysician Eduardo Viveiros de Castro shows how Amerindian 'perspectivism' defines *what humanity is* as a form rather than as an object: the form of what is a subject of its cosmos. The determination of *what is humanity* thus depends on an adopted view, on an object considered as subject:

> Typically, humans see humans as humans, animals as animals and spirits (if they see them) as spirits; however animals (predators) and spirits see humans as animals (as prey) to the same extent that animals (as prey) see humans as spirits or as animals (predators). By the same token, animals and spirits see themselves as humans: they perceive themselves as (or become) anthropomorphic beings when they are in their own houses or villages, and they experience their own habits and characteristics in the form of culture.[1]

Viveiros de Castro claims that human form and culture, which can be attributed to other animal species, function as a kind of cosmological 'pronoun' or 'deictic', immanent to perspective. 'Humanity' would not be very different in this perspective from an infralinguistic 'I'. 'I' is not an objective identity, connected to the definition of one particular object. Rather, it is an identity assumed by whoever says 'I', whoever adopts this form. 'Humanity' would be a comparable form, without objective definition, but assumed by all animal organisms that have a view of the surrounding world. 'Humanity' means, then, the position of whoever has a world when she considers herself in this world. In the world *for us*, one animal species among others, we are 'humans', but in the world of jaguars, another animal species, a jaguar is 'human' for itself.

But it seems that this formalisation of humanity, which appears among some human peoples, does not, or does not exactly, correspond to our way of defining humanity.

A number of Western peoples have indeed enclosed the form of humanity within itself by substantialising this form and conceiving of a form in itself, before desubstantialising and objectivising it. The substantialisation of humanity's form consists not in making form an identity taken on by every animal world view, but rather in the characteristic property of a single species' world view. But this operation implies cutting out the characteristic property attributed to animal species. By substantialising *what humanity is*, one removes humanity's form not merely from all animal species that can take on this form, as some assume, but also from our own particular animal species. Humanity becomes a form in itself, a *substance* that the 'human' animal species cannot take on (as substantial humanity would then be in itself). In this way, humanity can only be *given* to the human species – generally by a divine being.

The determination of this form in itself – the soul, spirit, mind, consciousness, *logos*, or breath of intelligence – varies among different peoples: it is 'what humanity is'. This quality corresponds to enclosing what humanity is within itself, and forms a sphere of humanity in itself that our own animal species cannot embody or enter into, any more than any other animal species. The explanation consists merely in assuming that this 'humanity in itself' was given to one species among others, and that this species happens to be our own.

As this gift became problematic, since species were scientifically considered as events, it was necessary to explain how and why one species rather than another was given humanity in itself. The characteristic property of *gifted* humanity – present in numerous Ancient and Christian myths – thus occasionally gave way to a characteristic property of *developed* humanity. This is the idea that one particular animal species could have developed some objective quality in order to distinguish itself from other species. This was the modern step towards a determination of *what humanity is*:

neither formal nor substantial, but objective. Humanity derives from some intensified objective quality. It was therefore not determined by form, but by content (technology, tool use, language, laughter, culture, the division of labour, and so on).

But the evolutionary event of the human species will never connect this objective quality to the human species. An insurmountable gap remains between the evolution of the 'human' animal species and the objective quality given to it that distinguishes it from other species. The human species always distinguishes itself from other species through an evolutionary mechanism that other species also share.

An insurmountable gulf separates *what is humanity*, one particular animal species, from *what humanity is*, its idea. Formal determination produces a form that could equally be taken on by any species, and not only the one that produces this formal determination. Substantial determination yields a substance that is taken on by no species, but must be, incomprehensibly, given to a species through divine election. Objective determination yields objective qualities that are derived from the evolution of one species among others and encloses *what humanity is* within *what is humanity*, until the snake bites its tail.

The crises of humanity's determination derive from the attribution of an exclusive quality, whatever it may be, to humanity.

2. Properties Given to Humanity

The extension of humanity's form is like an open space on a Cartesian plane, with a 'vertical' axis from beast to god and a 'horizontal' axis from animals (a set of self-differentiating and self-evolving species) to machines (artefacts imitating human cognitive functions).

The Enlightenment privileged the y-coordinate, extending the form of humanity, as Pascal writes, between 'beast' and 'angel'.[2] The modern age privileged the x-coordinate, considering what humanity is as an evential form extending between the animal species to which it belongs and the artefacts that it can produce in its image.

How did the coordinates shift? Through the episodic history of 'the property of man'.

In the Promethean myth, humanity attributes to itself what makes its humanity. Humanity is therefore compact: what humanity attributes to itself is what allows humanity to differentiate itself from other animal species. We can call this human, Promethean, or divine compactness: an absolute being attributes to what is humanity what humanity is. Humanity's given form is substantial – for example, 'spirit' in most cosmogonies. In the ancient Greek world, the form of humanity as substantial spirit led in particular to the concept of *logos*. Rational speech allows one to define humanity without directly making humanity enter into its composition and definition; human beings are those who have access to *logos*; in other words, the access to *logos* is open to humanity. 'Man is the only animal who has the gift of speech',[3] writes Aristotle, after having defined the *zoon politikon*, the species which, among other species (especially bees and other gregarious animals), is the human species.

> And whereas mere voice is but an indication of pleasure or pain, and is therefore found in other animals (for their nature attains to the perception of pleasure and pain and the intimation of them to one another, and no further), the power of speech is intended to set forth the expedient and inexpedient, and therefore likewise the just and the unjust. And it is a characteristic of man that he alone has any sense of good and evil, of just and unjust, and other like notions, and the association of living beings who have this sense makes a family and a state.[4]

Logos is therefore the access given to what is humanity (an animal species), to reason, the distinction between justice and injustice.

Logos is both the mode of human access and what it gives access to: speech and reason as distinctions of substantial values (just and unjust, good and evil). *Logos* is a sphere of 'what it gives access to' and of 'what allows access to it', in such a way that nothing else allows us access to reason except reason, and that the reason we access is our capacity to have access to it.

The history of Western philosophy will regularly revisit this nagging problem of the compactness of *logos*. In this way, the Cartesian soul corresponds to an attempt to differentiate between what gives access and what it is given access to, exclusive to humanity. The soul is the possibility of accessing reason. The property of humanity is precisely this possibility of accessing what differentiates it from other animals. The substantiality of the property of humanity may be understood in two ways: what makes the difference between human and animal is the faculty of accessing this difference; and this difference is ultimately the capacity to be rational, to self-differentiate from animality.

Descartes especially articulates the difference between beasts and God (infinite will and finite human understanding in dyadic relation to the divine infinite and the finitude of beasts) and the difference between animals and machines. But he identifies animals and machines as much as possible in order to differentiate humanity between the two.

In fact, a machine imitating an animal may be conflated with the animal imitated, whereas a machine imitating a human can always be distinguished from the human that it imitates:

> I made special efforts to show that if any such machines had the organs and outward shape of a monkey or of some other animal that lacks reason, we should have no means of knowing that they did not possess entirely the same nature as these animals; whereas if any such machines bore a resemblance to our bodies and imitated our actions as closely as possible for all practical purposes, we should still have two very certain means of recognising that they were not real men.[5]

The two means that Descartes refers to are speech and reason. Speech expresses thought and reason allows us to act freely at any moment of life – reason is not a programme. 'Now in just these two ways we can also know the difference between man and beast.'[6]

The same thing distinguishes human from machine and human from animal. The Cartesian *criteria* are compact, since they present the same argument against the reduction of human to animal and against the reduction of human to machine. Humanity's property is not relative to what it allows us to distinguish humanity from. Rather, humanity's property is valued *in itself*. 'The soul' distinguishes humanity as a substance, and distinguishes humanity from animal and machine. The soul's substantial property, expressed in the Aristotelian *logos* through access to the distinction between justice and injustice 'and other like notions', is also expressed for Descartes in free will, the possibility to decide on truth and goodness. Moreover, freedom remains a residue of humanity's substantial property to the extent that humanity's property desubstantialises itself. Freedom remains Jean-Jacques Rousseau's determining criterion, and appears again in Jean-Paul Sartre's 'humanist' definition, which resists humanity's loss of substance.

Every substantial determination of what humanity is fixes on a *given* feature, an external, transcendental instance that places the determination onto humanity (Descartes' God, for example) or a primitive gift to humanity (Sartre's 'for itself' or Rousseau's 'perfectability', for example). But it is unknown how this gift was given. All properties given to humanity self-compact, since what differentiates humanity is what gives humanity access to what differentiates it (spirit, soul, *logos*, free will). What differentiates humanity? Its capacity to have access to humanity. Compactness is the price to pay for a substantial property, an 'in itself'. Since spirit, *logos*, soul, and free will are substantial – valued by themselves – one can understand what differentiates other species from the animal species which have access to it only on the condition of arguing that it already possesses what it is allowed to acquire. The vicious circle of all properties given to humanity is this: one must possess a property in order to acquire it.

Given properties function only to the extent that one believes in them. When doubts arose about whether or not the human species was *substantially* different from other animal species, the human species lost access to this substantial difference. By losing access to this difference, one loses difference itself, the possibility of having access to difference.

Substantial *given* properties were succeeded by *developed* properties.

3. Properties Developed by Humanity

The idea which guides all conceptions of a 'developed' property of humanity is that the human species, as an animal species, has something *less*, a natural lack, which forces humanity to invent and overcome itself. A natural lack in the human species thus produces a development of something other than nature: culture.

The idea according to which the nature of the human species develops its *own* nature, its own event, runs from Rousseau's concept of indefinite perfectability, in the second *Discourse*, to the Kantian claims about man as being naturally free and about reason as man's instinct. The weaknesses and impoverishment of humanity in its natural state, the human animal species' natural deficiencies, are illustrated by several examples – for example, the absence of claws, scales, or bodily protection show us what humanity has *less* of and establish something *more* that it must develop. Rousseau defines this faculty, which is again given in the human species and in every human being, but which humanity develops for itself, as:

> the faculty of self-perfection, a faculty which, with the aid of circumstances, successively develops all the others, and resides among us as much in the species as in the individual. By contrast an animal is at the end of a few months what it will be all its life; and its species is at the end of a thousand years what it was the first year of that thousand.[7]

It is clear that this developed property denies in advance making the evolutionary animal species an event, which Darwin theorised a century later. Kant, on the other hand, takes up the idea of humanity's natural impoverishment. Lacking a given nature, humanity produces its own nature, freedom: 'nature gave him neither bull's horns, lion's claws, nor the dog's teeth, but only his hands'.[8] 'Unsociable sociability'[9] is the motor driving humanity's development of its own reason, independent of instinct. Humanity draws from itself everything that goes beyond the 'mechanical' assemblage of its existence as an animal species, but it must draw this *from itself*, which is a product of an animal species. One finds remnants of such a dialectics in Karl Marx's *The Germany Ideology*:[10] humanity, which must provide for its own needs through work, is naturally condemned to remove itself from nature. Marxist anthropology, moreover, took up the classical examples of the natural qualities of animal protection and survival that were absent in humanity for the sole purpose of forcing humanity to invent these qualities.

Thus, humanity's *more* derives from a natural *less* through a developed (and not given) property. This led to various theories of 'neoteny' in the writings of Louis Bolk,[11] Arnold Gehlen,[12] Clifford Geertz,[13] and Edgar Morin.[14] In these theories, humanity is naturally constituted by a lack or incompleteness that justifies its self-development. The problem with all theories of a developed property of humanity is that they take root in a substantial and objective determination of what humanity is. What develops in humanity must always, in one way or another, be naturally *given*, that is, be substantially present in the animal species that becomes human, rather than in other species. Self-development is not substantial, but it is the result of the work of a human who, through this work, acquires objective qualities: technology, equipment, language, culture, and so on. Developed properties differ from substantial properties in that the latter provide access to humanity's difference from other animals (possession of soul, *logos*, or free will), while the former guarantee the formation of objective qualities, of non-given, distinctive capacities, that the human species develops over the course of time. Nonetheless, the *possibility* of this development must remain given and substantial. Theories of developed properties are more or less dialectically trapped between the substantiality of a property of humanity and the objectivity of a differentiation between human and other animal species.

After the appearance of evolutionary theory, theories of a developed, substantial, and objective property partially gave way to scientific theories of an objective property of humanity, enveloped in its specificity or humanity's speciation. What humanity is in particular is nothing other than the particular evolution which led to humanity's speciation.

But we still must at least distinguish between the human species as an evolutionary *event* continuing through the present, and humanity as an *object*, that is, the set of actual human qualities or fruits of evolution that must not be objectivised and delimited. The evolutionary event of the human species only makes sense in relation to consideration of the human species as object, even though the human species as object is nothing other than an instantaneous, transient evolution of humanity at any arbitrary moment.

The objective property of humanity becomes the instantaneous objectivisation of human evolution: what is humanity is a differentiated species; what humanity is is the objectivisation at any arbitrary instance of this differentiation.

4. Humanity Reduced to an Evolutionary Event

The objects which distinguished humanity from other animal species were made into events by situating humanity between animal and machine. On the one hand, twentieth-century animal ethology dissolved most of the residual objects which remained between the human species and other animal species (laughter, tools, language, culture, and so on). On the other hand, artificial intelligence research tried to replicate some of these qualities. The objective property of humanity thus became an evential property. All the objects which human and other animals can share were shared by human and other animals, but with humanity they underwent a particular differentiation. Humanity is no longer an object, but a changing, evolutionary event.

Animal ethology, the scientific study of animal behaviour, allowed the dissolution of the last objective differential residues between the human species and other animal species. This work consisted in observing the behaviours of several species, looking at behaviours comparable to those believed to be properties of humanity, and in redefining these behaviours that are shared between humans and other animals, in order to understand how humans and other animals share them and the differences separating what they had become in humans and other species. Benjamin Beck's work, *Animal Tool Behaviour*,[15] is a good example of this approach. Through empirical observations of the entire animal world, tools are redefined. Tool use becomes the use of an object of the environment, which must remain independent of its foundation, in order to alter the form, position, and condition of an inanimate object, of the user, or of another living organism. The great ape's use of a stone to catch ants and crack walnuts fall under this definition. The determination of humanity through the use of *polyliths* is ruled out, since it appears to be an *ad hoc* determination, a desire to salvage the phenomena and to attribute an increasingly restricted, complex, specialised, and specific faculty to humanity.

Dominique Lestel argues for the existence of an 'animal origin of culture'. He takes lessons from modern ethology and turns the residues of the properties of humanity into events. Everything that humanity produces, culture, is an evolutionary event that has its origin in the natural evolution of one species of living things. For Lestel, a human animal is not a special animal, but a particular animal, 'a creature different from other animals, just as the Australian bowerbird is different from other animals, but for other reasons'. Indeed, 'far from opposing nature, culture is a phenomenon which is intrinsic to living things, of which it constitutes a particular niche, [. . .] one obtains from it the beginnings of animal life'.[16]

According to Lestel, *what* humanity *is* must be understood as revolving around *what is* humanity: one particular species and nothing more, different from others as others are different from it. Humanity's difference is perhaps more *intense*, but it is not, on its own, different from other relations between animal species.

The key to this particularisation was the potential for non-human, specifically the great apes', language learning. Since Aristotle, language provided access to human specificity and was at the same time understood as this specificity itself. Language was at the core of the Cartesian criterion of the differentiation between humans, animals, and machines. From Rousseau to Marx, language was the sign of development distinct to humanity. When it was discovered that non-human apes could partially learn language, *what humanity is* was enclosed within *what is humanity*: a species different from others as others are different from it.

5. What Humanity Comes From: Talking Animal

Language was the primary objective residue of the properties of humanity. But evolutionary theory had made language relative. Humanity had long considered language as a tool, and not as something that thought could be reduced to. Language became the object of a two-part research into animal ethology. On the one hand, the study of animal communication contributed to linguistic stratification, in that certain linguistic degrees could be observed in other animal species. On the other hand, and perhaps more importantly, a series of unprecedented though more or less successful undertakings to teach languages to non-human great apes were symptomatic of changes in the relations of humanity to itself.

The study of animal communication, the controversy around Karl von Frisch's dancing bees (are the dances languages or codes?), the discovery of the existence of a genuine although primitive generative grammar in the black-capped chickadee's song, the growing knowledge of whales' acoustic signatures, Gregory Bateson's critical remarks on the dolphin's whistle[17] – all of this research contributed to introducing various degrees of mastery over different linguistic faculties, for want of languages, in non-human animal species. The twentieth-century adventure of 'talking apes' became an event determining what humanity is.

Simultaneous scientific and affective attention was given to other great primates (gorillas, orangutans, chimpanzees, and bonobos), and suddenly reinforced between the wars. It is quite fascinating to observe how, during this period, early research into artificial intelligence (AI) is contemporaneous with the desire to scientifically understand and change the animals that are evolutionarily closest to us. In the heart of the twentieth century, humanity grasped its two limits by raising certain animals to the level of humanity's cognitive faculties, and raising these same faculties to the level of artefacts. The identity of humanity is situated between the machines and animals to which humanity attempts to attribute what humanity is. Humanity is, in this way, considered from the outside. The joint research developments into animal ethology – which risked laboratory experiments of language instruction to great apes – and artificial intelligence – which risked the fantasy of Singularity – are not coincidental. They indicate the two limits of the segment on which modern humanity still seeks to define what it is as an event.

The early stages of the behavioural study of great apes were connected to the desire to test out various schema and models of the human mind and of human behaviour on animals evolutionarily close to humans. Robert Yerkes evaluated the significance of the 'trial and error' method in learning with Prince Chim and Panzee. In the Canary Islands, Wolfgang Köhler validated his Gestalt intuitions with Sultan. This occasional usefulness of non-human primate subjects in the context of psychological experiments gave way, in the life and work of Louis and Mary Leakey, to the intuition of the value of the studies of great apes for the paleontological understanding of our own evolution. 'Leakey's Angels', who were among the first to begin studying different species of great apes in their natural habitats, paved the way to the *empathetic* era of the behavioural study of these species. Jane Goodall, at Tanzania's Gombe Stream National Park, who named her chimpanzees David Greybeard, Goliath, and Flo, among others, discovered the existence of laughter, murder, tool use, cooperation, hunting, and other carnivorous behaviours among them. Dian Fossey studied mountain gorillas in Rwanda's Virunga volcanoes. Biruté Galdikas studied Bornean orangutans. These ethologists argued for a sensitive, empathetic approach towards these great apes, and contributed to the emergence of the great non-human primate as a twentieth-century 'noble savage'. Their approach was neither distrustful nor contemptuous of the beasts that we separate ourselves from, but, rather, full of wonder and kindness, understanding and guilt, that we will henceforth maintain with these animals. The approach partly explains the passage to a new phase: the astonishing desire to raise some individuals of these non-human species as human beings, under laboratory conditions, to prove how they can become like us. The projection of the evolution of the human species onto animal individuals gave birth to this fantasy: to educate simian individuals in the way in which our own species has evolved. In an unspoken manner, one projected what humanity has achieved as a species onto individuals of other species.

These projects of animal transformation, and not only of the study of their 'natural' behaviour, multiplied from the 1950s onward. Luella and Winthrop Kellogg adopted the chimpanzee Gua, and raised her alongside their son Donald. Beginning in 1967, Allen and Beatrix Gardner taught American Sign Language to Washoe, who in turn was encouraged to teach this language to Booee and Bruno. Roger Fouts, Washoe's teacher after the Gardners, took Loulis, Washoe's adopted son, into his care with Lynn Miles, who in turn took the orangutan Chantek into her care. Herbert Terrace, contesting previous experiments, took interest in Nim Chimpsky. Francine Patterson took care of her gorilla Koko. David Premack surrounded himself with Sarah and Gussie. Sue Savage-Rumbaugh became strongly attached to Kanzi the bonobo.

The distinctive feature of all these unprecedented experiments is the decision to combine modelled and quantifiable scientific experimentation with emotional adventure. Couples often 'raised' the subject-ape. It soon became clear that progress in the acquisition of linguistic structures could only be obtained if very strong affective bonds were formed between the great primate subject and human observer. A thin line separates experimentation from sentimental education.

In the early years, the recourse to American Sign Language (the adopted language of Anglo-Saxon apes in order to compensate for the absence in great apes of the larynx necessary for speech) allowed, according to Gardner,[18] Washoe's assimilation of 130 signs in four years and her assimilation of functions of agency, action, location, possession, nomination, and recurrence. Over a fifteen-year time period, some so-called 'naïve' experts, who were not involved in the experiments, verified the ape's spontaneous and appropriate use of the signs. In three years, Washoe mastered and added 132 more signs to her vocabulary. The ape signed herself, even showing herself capable of over-generalising, and when she lacked certain words for objects, Washoe made use of the sign 'more'.

Roger Fouts[19] continued experiments with the technique of *moulding*, or modelling, which consists in forming the sign directly on the hand. This system allowed for imitation, instantaneous modelling, and, in particular, Washoe's potential dissemination of signs to other chimpanzees. Fouts noted that these chimpanzees exchanged signs with each other about food and games. To avoid influencing the experiments, observers adopted scientific procedures and limited themselves to the use of seven signs, hoping to see Washoe teach the signs that she had mastered to others. Washoe's adopted son, Loulis, eventually imitated signs that she used in order to be tickled by the observers. In order to be tickled, Loulis first copied Washoe's behaviour without signing it, then made the sign for himself, and finally addressed the sign to the scientists. In the end, approximately seventy signs were communicated between the chimpanzees.

Considering that sign language limits potential learning, David Premack[20] changed methods, using plastic figurines associated with grammar (words, phrases, class concepts, copula, quantifiers, and so on) to test Sarah's access to a meta-linguistic level. Sue Savage-Rumbaugh and two other linguists[21] want to go further by creating an artificial language in the 'Lantek' project: a simple, ideographic artificial language composed of lexigrams (non-iconical symbols) classed according to an elementary grammar. The bonobo Kanzi learned to make 'sentences' through conversations on a touch screen. He assimilated relations, numbers, colours, and pairings. With access to a computer with a keyboard that functions like a typewriter and on which each key is equal to a word, he gradually expressed sentences by interacting with a scientist stationed in another room.

Of course, these experiments are open to criticism and they were rightly criticised. Not only do they reduce language to certain properties that do not exhaust language, and model learning on a strange brew of affective dependance, *behaviourist* coldness, reward, profound empathy, and anthropomorphism, but they owe their fascinating power more to their implementation, in fact, than to their results. Herbert Terrace[22] presented a radical critique of these results; whether using graphic symbols, gestures, or lexigrams, one only ever finds 96 per cent of queries and 4 per cent of indicative propositions. Later, Terrace's self-criticism led him to claim that non-human subjects never assimilated any grammar, and that symbols were only learned through a Pavlovian mechanism. But Terrace misses the essential affective dimension of these experiments, which is symptomatic of a change in human attitude, a new trans-species empathy, with regard to the animal species nearest to them.

In Aristotelian terms, to speak is to speak together, to exchange 'common notions'. There must be common interests in order to share a language. On this view, linguistic interactions with other apes are indisputably possible, but they ultimately reveal that great apes have nothing, or almost nothing, to tell us. The individuals who learned these protolanguages did so affectively, through the connections that united them to members of a species distinct from their own. In fact, one could argue that 'talking apes' made efforts to acquire the rudiments of human language because they were engaged in an affective bond with humans who claimed language as their own, and that we made scientific efforts to understand these apes because we felt committed to an affective community with these neighbouring species.

Chimpanzees, gorillas, and orangutans can learn to approach language for us. They can speak in a very restricted sense, but they have nothing to say. But any human child has something to say, in babbling, before even mastering the rudiments of language.

Therefore, what is important is not only knowing if these experiments failed or succeeded, if language or something in language is a property of human beings. What matters is understanding why such experiments were made possible, and what they reveal about a new determination of what humanity is for the human species. The idea of teaching human languages to other animal species rests on the following fantasy: an animal species can become human by progressively acquiring language; it must therefore be possible to do to a neighbouring animal species what was done to us – namely, make it acquire language.

What is the meaning of this fantasy? On the vertical axis from beast to divine, it embodies the implicit desire to remake what made us. If what makes us human – in particular, language – was given to us by a divine transcendence, then the possibility of giving this language to another species would allow us to depart from humanity as creatures in order to construct an identity of humanity as creators. In short, it makes us equivalent to the divine. On the horizontal axis from animals to artefacts, this fantasy embodies an analogous idea. If we make other species evolve into what we are, by allowing them to acquire our language, then we will become subjects of an animal evolution, which, up to then, we were the objects of. And humanity will overcome itself.

Through the ethical concern to give animals rights and the ethological fantasy of teaching them language, humanity makes other animals human in order to make itself more than human. Why? Because *what humanity is* is reduced to *what is humanity*: one particular animal species. The modern desire to make other species, and even machines, human was to rid ourselves in some way of this humanity. We even sought to give ourselves a new identity: we are no longer the species that speaks, but the species that teaches other species to speak.

The blurring, if not loss, of the formal, substantial, and objective determinations of what humanity is partly led our species to self-differentiate by identifying the human species with the animal species that it derives from and with the artefacts that the human species produces.

6. What Humanity goes Towards: Artefactual Intelligence

In the twentieth century, artificial intelligence research developed around two distinct goals. The first goal was to produce systems that could be proven to be equivalent to different human capacities. In other words, humans are not specifically different from machines. The second goal was to produce higher-order systems that would go beyond human competences: in other words, to produce an idea according to which one could *make* something *be* more than what one *is* – for example, Vernor Vinge's concept of 'Singularity'.

The earliest appearances of automata – the priest-controlled statue of Amun in Egypt, the legendary crows of Ctesibius in Alexandria, described by Vitruvius, before the Christian influence made the project of imitating humanity through artefacts difficult – are indicative of our desires to reproduce the *external* form of natural organisms. After the Middle Ages, this project reemerges. We know this through various more or less well-known anecdotes: Roger Bacon's automata, Leonardo da Vinci's lion automaton, and Salomon de Caus's and Giovan Battista Aleotti's invention of a variety of machines for the king's court. In the eighteenth century, Jacques de Vaucanson's famous automated duck realised and concluded this early stage in the history of automata. His copper duck, which presumably could drink, eat, quack, and digest, was programmed through a system of switches on its legs.

The transparency of its abdomen allowed one to observe its digestion, resulting in a kind of green purée. The now lost artefact not only imitated an organism's external form, but also its internal form.

Beginning in the nineteenth century, automatists focused on this *internal* form and on the imitation of information. The definition of living species by their morphology and visible form gradually gave way to the definition of living species by their constitutive genetic information. Shortly thereafter, art's imitation of living things became an imitation of information. The analytical engine, Charles Babbage's difference engine, proposed but never constructed, marks the passage to *informatic* automatism. Between the wars, when interests were focused on our nearest relative animal species and on the possibility of teaching them language, interests in early computing focused on the possibility of constructing machines that were closely related to our brains and of ascribing them a language. Alan Turing's[23] and John von Neumann's[24] well-known work opened up the path to the ideal of conceiving, in response to the Hilbertian problem of computability, of a computing machine that would calculate all possibilities. The construction of machines programmed, with the help of formal languages, to calculate in place of humanity was first made necessary as a result of administrative and bureaucratic needs. Herman Hollerith's punched cards were useful for the census. At Harvard, Howard Aiken's project of a giant calculator was supposed to rationalise office filing. Herbert A. Simon's early work in artificial intelligence, at the end of the 1950s, still concerned the resolution of administrative tasks that had become too important for human individuals. In 1959, John McCarthy spoke for the first time of 'artificial intelligence'.[25] Almost a decade later, Marvin Minsky, distinguishing weak and strong artificial intelligence,[26] clearly explained the project of constructing computer artefacts capable of fulfilling tasks which are currently accomplished more satisfactorily by the human brain, for they required learning, memory, critical reasoning, consciousness, and so on. Imperceptibly, the goal became to imitate the data processing produced by human intelligence, and therefore to produce machines capable of learning. For a number of decades, the ideal type of this intelligence concentrated on a chessboard model. Various steps in the research made programming easier and allowed the testing of autonomous systems, like 'Sad Sam' from 1957 (which memorised kinship relations), Frank Rosenblatt's famous 'perceptron' from 1958 (a synthetic retina associated with a simplified layer of 'neurons', electrical connections, and decisional cohesion), and SHRDLU ten years later (a 'micro-world' made up of pyramids and blocks, equipped with an animated arm intended to select and arrange various objects into boxes).

Like the 'talking ape' experiments, though AI's applications were more numerous and immediately perceived by the general public (through improvements in robotics and computer science), it is not the success or failure of these programmes which matter to us here. Their best critics were often those who were the first to work in the field. For example, Minsky showed the limits of the 'perceptron'. Many theorists commented on the foreseeable failure of passing from a closed 'micro-world' like that of SHRDLU to an open world of possible significations and events. What interests us are the extrapolations and dreams associated with these projects, and their meaning for the current determination of what humanity is as an object.

It is clear that the fantasy of artificial intelligence – which is a transformation of the old dream of automatism, its transposition from the external form to the very information of living things – is connected to the representations of evolutionary theory and to the determination of humanity as an evolutionary event. If humanity is nothing other than *what is humanity*, which evolves naturally, then the only means of claiming a human identity, of not producing compactness, is to imitate natural evolution by making it an artefact. It is the dream of arriving at a definition of humanity not from *what is humanity* (an animal species that has evolved), but from *what humanity makes* (artefacts, machines). Or better: the only way not to compact humanity, not to reduce *what humanity is* to *what is humanity* (an animal species), is to fabricate something that goes beyond humanity, and thus to humanly make more and better than what natural evolution had produced. Therefore, a present-day tension exists between a human reduced to a natural product and to this same nature.

One could follow the various threads of the modern history of humanity's own overcoming, from Friedrich Nietzsche to Michel Foucault, from Pierre Tielhard de Chardin's 'Omega Point'[27] to Vernor Vinge's 'Singularity',[28] from Frank J. Tipler's 'future God'[29] to Raymond Kurzweil's 'transhumanism'.[30] But even discussing and criticising 'transhumanism' or present-day human desires to transform humanity – for example, Francis Fukuyama's moral criticism of the 'dangers of biotechnology'[31] – is an empty gesture. It is equally trifling to support this movement, like Nick Bostrom.[32] For it is equally naïve to believe in or to fear an 'artefactualisation' of humanity or its overcoming. Present-day humanity's relations to animals and to artefacts makes us hopelessly attempt to prove what humanity is as an object. It is clear that humanity's identification with other animal species or with machines that go beyond some of its intellectual faculties has no other function than to identify humanity in its own eyes. During the Enlightenment, humanity recognised itself by self-differentiating from animals and machines, identifying itself between them. In the modern age, humanity recognised itself by differentiating animals and machines, identified as the two limits of humanity's being.

Humanity identifies with machines to self-differentiate from other animals. Humanity identifies with other animals to self-differentiate from machines. That is not all: who acts the angel acts the beast, and vice versa; however, who acts the machine no longer acts the animal, and who acts the animal no longer acts the machine.

7. Artefactuality Relieves Humanity of Animality, Animality Relieves Humanity of Artefactuality

Humans exist only *between the two*.

Humanity not only has an environment, like all other animals, it *is* an environment. What is humanity, that is, a certain animal species which evolved, like all others, determines what humanity is in an unpredictable, and sometimes errant, way. Humanity may be formal, substantial, or objective.

However, the decision to consider living things in an evolutionary representation led us to consider humanity as a specific event enclosed within itself. In this view, humanity is one particular evolved species, different from others, but, like others, a particular evolved species. Thus, humanity took itself to be less an object (a creature) *between* beast and god than an event *between* animal and machine. It is naïve to enthusiastically or fearfully believe that in doing so humanity changes and changes itself. Humanity only ever changes by being the same humanity. For a long time, at the very least in Western thought, humanity distinguished itself between beast and god as *creature* and *creator*. Then humanity distinguished and identified itself between animal and machine. Then it identified itself with animality to distinguish itself from machines, and identified itself with machines to distinguish itself from animality. Therefore, modern-day humanity does not reduce itself to animality; it only ever did so to avoid reducing itself to a machine. Nor does modern-day humanity reduce itself to a machine, other than to avoid reducing itself to animality.

When we feel that we are nothing but machines, we remember that we are animals. When we think that we are nothing but animals, we remember the artefacts that we produce in our image. We have no other identity and we cannot refer to a transcendent human identity. This would be a mistake. We only exist as humans *between*. We can cure ourselves of animality only through artificiality, and of artificiality only through animality.

Humans no longer think they are the centre of the world, but they remain a milieu. Humanity only makes sense *between*.

So, the human animal species acquired the capacity to handle objects of its environment as forms, and to grasp objects in order to make of them the form of another either present or absent thing. This twofold capacity to present and represent places the human animal species in an environment of present and represented objects, through which it continually intensifies the living universe. Amidst these presences and representations, the human animal species is itself something. It lives between the animality that constitutes it and the representations that it constitutes.

Humanity is a representation-producing animal species which more or less coexists with the representations that it produces in the form of artefacts.

Notes

1. Eduardo Viveiros de Castro, 'Cosmological Deixis and Amerindian Perspectivism', p. 470. Cited in Philippe Descola, *Beyond Nature and Culture*, p. 139. Viveiros de Castro argues that the concepts of '"human beings", "persons", and "people", seem to function pragmatically, if not syntactically, not as *nouns* but as *pronouns* indicating the position of the subject; they constitute an enunciative marker, not a name', Viveiros de Castro, *Métaphysiques cannibales*, p. 24.

2. 'Man is neither angel nor beast; and the unfortunate thing is that he who would act the angel acts the beast', Blaise Pascal, *Pensées*, ed Lafuma, p. 678.

3. Aristotle, *Politics*, I, 1253a9–10, p. 1988.

4. Aristotle, *Politics*, I, 1253a10–18, p. 1988.

5. René Descartes, *Discourse on the Method*, V, 56. Translated in English by Robert Stoothoff, in *The Philosophical Writings of Descartes, Volume 1*, pp. 139–40.

6. Ibid., p. 58. Stoothoff translation, p. 140.

7. Jean-Jacques Rousseau, *Discourse on the Origins of Inequality*, p. 26.

8. Immanuel Kant, 'Idea for a Universal History with a Cosmopolitan Purpose', p. 43.

9. Ibid., p. 44.

10. 'The first condition of all human history is, of course, the existence of living human beings. The first historical act of these individuals, through which they are distinguished from animals, is not that they think, but that they begin to produce their means of existence.' Karl Marx, *The German Ideology*, p. 31. [Translation modified.]

11. Bolk's 'fetalisation theory'. See Louis Bolk, *Das Problem der Menschwerdung*.

12. According to Gehlen, a 'biological deficiency' of humanity leads it to a 'world-openness', not shared with other animals, controlled by culture, law, customs, and discipline. See Arnold Gehlen, *Man: His Nature and Place in the World*.

13. Geertz considers a human as an 'incomplete animal'. See Clifford Geertz, *The Interpretation of Cultures*.

14. Morin describes human beings as 'unfinished from birth'. See Edgar Morin, *L'Identité humaine*, p. 274.

15. Benjamin Beck, *Animal Tool Behaviour*.

16. Dominique Lestel, *Les Origines animales de la culture*, p. 8. He also quite correctly writes: 'The distinction between human beings and animals is not superimposed on the distinction nature/culture, as we once believed. Human beings as well as animals evolve on the interface between nature and culture.' Ibid.

17. Gregory Bateson, *Steps to an Ecology of Mind*.

18. Allen Gardner, Beatrix Gardner, and Thomas Van Cantfort, *Teaching Sign Language to Chimpanzees*. This collection includes the famous eponymous article of 1969.

19. Roger Fouts and Stephen Tukel Mills, *Next of Kin*.

20. Ann Premack and David Premack, *The Mind of an Ape*.

21. Pår Segerdahl, William Fields, and Sue Savage-Rumbaugh, *Kanzi's Primal Language*.
22. Herbert Terrace, *Nim*.
23. Alan Turing, 'Computing Machinery and Intelligence'.
24. John von Neumann, *The Computer and the Brain*.
25. John McCarthy, 'Programs with Common Sense'.
26. Marvin Minsky, *Computation*.
27. Pierre Teilhard de Chardin, *Man's Place in Nature*.
28. 'Within thirty years, we will have the technological means to create superhuman intelligence. Shortly after, the human era will be ended', Vernor Vinge, 'Technological Singularity', p. 88.
29. Frank J. Tipler and John D. Barrow, *The Anthropic Cosmological Principle*.
30. Raymond Kurzweil, *The Singularity is Near*. According to Kurzweil, the Singularity will appear around 2029, when humans and machines will merge into hybrid forms of non-biological intelligence.
31. Francis Fukuyama, *Our Posthuman Future*.
32. Nick Bostrom is co-founder of the World Transhumanist Association, and author of a famous and controversial article that defends the strong probability that we are already living in a computer simulation created by future intelligence, after the coming of the Singularity, such that our present would be a kind of virtual imperfection from the future.

Chapter VII

Representations

1. Self-Representation, Selfless-Representation

What is a representation? This concept can be understood in at least two ways: on the one hand, the representation of an object by an *object*; on the other hand, the representation of an object by a *subject*. Subjective representation always appears as 'self'-representation, a representation which only is what it is through self-presence. The representation that I have of the table that I see before me only remains what it is as long as it is my representation, and not someone else's. If some other person takes my place in front of this table and obtains a visual representation of it, she will undoubtedly self-represent the same object, but she will not have the same *representation* of it, because this will be her representation, and not mine.

On the other hand, a painting that represents a landscape does not *self*-represent the landscape that it represents. The painting is not a subject. I can self-represent the painting, as the person next to me can, and we will undoubtedly have partially different representations, but we will have these various meta-representations of one and the same representation.

Self-presence thus allows us to distinguish two representations: those which define a self (sight, hearing, imagination, and so on), and those which define an object (painting, music, film, and so on) which does not have a self or has a self *no more*. Of course, one will notice that a painting needs to be painted to be able to exist as a painting, and that it was necessary that a being who *self*-represents made a representative object of it. However, once painted, the painting as an object gives a representation that does not *self*-represent what it represents. The painting does not see what it shows. One will also notice that everything that represents needs one to *self*-represent it to be capable of existing as a representation: what is a painting, if there were no eye to self-represent it? Undoubtedly, every representation aims at what one *self*-represents, but this *representatio sui* only intervenes subsequently, as a representation of a selfless-representation.

No imagination exists without someone to imagine, no sight without someone to see, and no touch without someone to touch; these representations are indissociable from selves, which they help to constitute. In the *representatio sui* view, a photograph's singularity, for example, is its capacity to exist, including when nobody exists to look at it. A random Polaroid may remain buried for years beneath piles of paper in a dusty attic, so that nobody – not even its photographer – has seen it during this time, without it ceasing or not beginning to exist. But how do we imagine a sight that nobody could see, or that we could altogether cease seeing? If a visual representation exists, then, by definition, someone, a living being or an animal, exists to imagine this image. If an auditory representation exists, then someone exists to imagine this sound.

Since a *representatio sui* presupposes a self, that is, a subject of the representation, even minimally, *representatio sui* cannot literally be shared. What someone *self*-represents cannot be *self*-represented by others, without replacing the first person's self-presence with another's self-presence. It is certainly possible to communicate an *effect* of *representatio sui*, but not to share it in its entirety.

On the other hand, a selfless-representation, a representation by an object, does not presuppose a self to self-presence, because it does not *self*-represent what it represents. A selfless-representation constitutes what is shareable, exchangeable, and communicable par excellence. Anyone who has the capacity to see can see the same film, can *self*-represent (differently) the same selfless-representation that the film is.

2. Representation of Objects and Objects of Representation

Several epistemological theories attempt to model *representatio sui* and perception. Since the nineteenth century, certain modern theories of representation conceived of some general form of representation that extends self-representation to different selfless-representations. These theories revolve around the concept of 'reference' and involve problems of intentionality. Jocelyn Benoist has shown[1] that the analytic and phenomenological schools have a common ancestor: Bernhard Bolzano. What they have in common is that they trace a new controversial dividing line between 'objective' representations and 'subjective' representations. Bolzano's *subjective* representation intersects with much of what we have described as *self*-representation, which concerns a representation's psychological dimension, its construction in a consciousness or in a perceptual system. On the other hand, an *objective* representation is not a *selfless*-representation, but a representation *in itself*, independent of any representing subject. If every subjective representation refers to an objective representation, every objective representation does not necessarily correspond to a subjective representation. Bolzano indicates at the end of paragraph 48 of his *Theory of Science* that 'there can be objective ideas that – with the exception of God – are not taken into the consciousness of a single thinking being'.[2]

But an objective representation does not at all correspond to what we have called a 'selfless-representation', an object that represents without self-representing what it represents. An objective representation embodies the ideal part, independent of the conscious support of any possible representation – the cat that I self-represent insofar as the cat is not my own representation.

Consequently, the modern problem of representation, reformulated in terms resembling though departing from Aristotelian and Scholastic thought, was that of the relation between representations of objects and objects of representation. This relation is no longer conceivable merely in terms of correspondence or adequation. Once we set aside the psychological side of the question, how can we distinguish the representation as an object (*the cat that I self-represent*) and an object of this representation (*the cat* that I self-represent)?

The conception of phenomenology as a theory of intentionality (the reduction of an object of representation to the representation of the object, the primacy of the action over the object) and the conception of the analytic paradigm first formulated by Gottlob Frege[3] (the connection between a representation of the object and an object represented by a logical function) led to debates about the ambiguous relation between representation and its object. The primary aim of these debates consisted in resolving the problem of objectless representations. How can representation exist without an object? How can representation refer to an impossible or nonexistent object? Franz Brentano,[4] Kazimierz Twardowski,[5] Alexius Meinong,[6] and Bertrand Russell[7] attempted to resolve these problems either by extending, as we do, the domain of objects beyond the law of non-contradiction, to include contradictory objects, impossible objects, non-contradictory, and non-impossible objects, or by claiming that the idea of objectless representations is meaningless. But they all accept the division between representations of objects (the representation that I have of an object) and objects of representation (what the representation is aimed at). Epistemologies take this distinction for granted. But these representations are *self*-representations (a psychological or logical subject of these representations exists), even though they are representations of objects that are independent of selves.

Benoist points out that, for Frege, sense is not subjective. Sense is objectively contained in the statement, independent of the fluctuations which may be connected to the speaker's intentions or to the 'effect' that her speech has on it. Frege's semantic objectivism clearly recalls Bolzano's. Sense is a means for an object to present itself objectively, independent of whether or not someone knows this sense of the object or expresses a statement about the object which has this determinate sense. This is Frege's theory of the 'third realm' between representations and things, a sphere of ideal objects, entirely objective but not real in the ordinary sense of the word 'reality' (they are devoid of any causal relation).

Therefore, the modern problem of representation – here essentially logical representation – confuses representation of a self which self-represents what it represents (that sees what it sees, that hears what it hears) with selfless-representation (of a picture that does not see itself, of music that does not hear itself). It also misunderstands the distinction between the subjectivity and objectivity of the representation. The major problem of selfless-representations is thus eclipsed.

We also find these confusions and distinctions in phenomenology. Though they may be fruitful, they indicate a common blind spot: the initial and terminal incapacity to distinguish my visual field from a photograph, my auditory field from a melody.

Twardowski takes up Brentano's distinction between *primary* and *secondary* objects of perception – a distinction later criticised by Edmund Husserl. Twardowski applies it to the example of a painting. The landscape as it is painted in the painting constitutes 'the primary object' of perception. The painting itself as a physical object constitutes 'the secondary object' of perception. First, the landscape as it is painted; then, the painting that depicts it.[8] The painting, a *selfless* representation, appears to a subject that self-represents it – which masks the primary fact that, unlike the observer, the painting does not self-represent what it represents.

Twardowski applies this schema to interpret our *self*-representational content. Benoist writes:

> Twardowski plays on the two meanings of the concept of image. On the one side, the cognitive 'image' that the content is represents the object of which it is the image. It may be treated strictly speaking as an image, that is, as an *image of*. On the other side, the image has in itself some consistent form. It constitutes a certain kind of object, which is immediately perceptible without reflection – in what the Brentanian school called secondary perception – always echoing, so to speak, the object's primary function, directed outside the object.[9]

An image (or sound) is here, as was often the case, used as a model of representation: every representation is both an object that represents and an object represented. The interface between identity and difference allows one to characterise *self*-representation in general. The same object is perceptible both as a passive object – an object that I self-represent – and as an active object – an object that represents. But this characterisation conflates two levels: the representation that I make of the painting and the representation that the painting gives me access to. Like phenomenological theories, Twardowski's theory directly combines the painting that represents something with the fact that I can self-represent this painting either as an object or as a representation. In other words, *self*-representation and *selfless*-representation are conflated, unfailingly connecting a representational state to a subjective state. However, paintings and images represent *without selves*. Whether someone looks at this painting or not, it represents something. Since the painting first represents *without itself*, *my self* can then self-represent it either as a representing object, or as a mere represented object.

Modern theories of representation, springing from the shared ancestry of analytic philosophy and phenomenology, have reduced the fact that an image is a landscape to the fact that we can perceive or experience it as a landscape. But a difference exists between an image that represents a landscape and a landscape that I self-represent; the former is a *selfless*-representation, while the latter is a *self*-representation. This means that one cannot think of a painting and sight in the same way – for instance, in Descartes' theory in *Optics*.[10] Sight is an image that cannot not be seen, since sight is always someone's sight. A painting is an image that can sometimes not be seen, and thus can *occasionally* be seen by someone.

Modern theories of representation do not exactly *ignore* this distinction, but it is *neglected* in favour of the relation between an object of the representation and this representation as an object, in the painting as in sight. The emphasis is placed neither on selfless-representations nor on the division between *self*- and *selfless*-representations. Rather, the problem concerns the division between the subjectivity and objectivity of *self*-representations.

Every epistemology that produces a general theory of representation tends to reduce *selfless*-representations to *self*-representations and to combine these two concepts into a single concept divided in two: a representation of the object and an object of the representation. However, some human actions can produce or form objects that are *selfless*-representations, objects that do not always but *occasionally* require a subject. In other words, it is not necessary for a subject to *self*-represent these objects in order for these objects to represent.

I can self-represent the sea. Like any sentient being with comparable sensory modes, I can imagine, see, or hear the sea. If I disappear, then my imagined, seen, or heard representation of the sea will also disappear. Nobody else but I can have my imagined, seen, or heard representation of the sea, since these representations presupposed my presence and presupposed that they were mine in order to be what they were, although anyone could imagine, see, or hear this sea in their own way. Since my representation of the sea was *representatio sui*, it was connected to me. But my only means of transmitting it as such is to express it through a *selfless*-representation: a cry, some words, a drawing, a melody, a sculpture, and so on.

I can therefore represent the sea (without *self*-representing it). I can describe it by writing some sentences on paper. I can draw or photograph it. I can record the sound that emanates from it. These representations do not need me. Once they are made, they no *longer* need me to represent this sea, since they do not *self*-represent what they represent. They are subjectless representations, representations in object-form.

3. Representation in Object-Form

We know that the early stages of humanity's production of objects involved the formation of things. For example, humanity formed objects like flint tools, *Excalibur*, hand prints, cave paintings, and other examples of *forms* defined negatively. When humanity became a producer of objects, it handled forms; to make an object, one must know how to cognise and recognise its form, distinguish it from what is not this form.

If form is the container of any thing (except itself), then humanity is capable of using some objects as forms. Ontologically, every thing has a form, but humanity has the very distinct capacity to use certain objects, or relations between certain (material or symbolic) objects and forms, such that, ontologically contained as a thing in a form, an object on its own becomes the container of another thing.

This capacity is to be understood in a very broad sense. By conceiving of a piece of clothing, for example, humans manufacture a plenitudinous object, a thing, which can become a form if it contains a body – a piece of clothing hides or emphasises a body's appearance. Since humans cognise and recognise the form of things, they can grasp objects and make use of them as forms. It clearly seems that all human art consists in this formalisation of certain things. In dance, a human body, a thing, has a form. It becomes a form, a receptacle, or a way of receiving a foreign body. Consider Loïe Fuller who veils and unveils, Ruth St Denis who, so to speak, uncorsetted her body in an Indian dance, Isadora Duncan disconnecting her shape from the surrounding air, or Martha Graham's contractions and relaxations. In sculpture, the plenitudinous object, which has a form, becomes the form of something that it may contain or that may be in it. Auguste Rodin's scandalous casting of *The Age of Bronze*, Henry Moore's *Locking Piece*, and Donald Judd's untitled boxes all appear as containers of things that are actually nonexistent.

We can therefore establish a new relation between form in its *artistic* sense and form in its *ontological* sense. In its ontological sense, discussed in Book I, form is a thing's negative and outside.

Each thing has a form. In its artistic sense, humanity is capable, through art, of manipulating certain objects as if they were them-selves forms. In this way, these objects lead a double life: they ontologically remain things, which have a form, but artistically they become forms, which can themselves have objects.

But what exactly do these object-forms, as containers, contain?

This is the crux of the problem. Object-forms can contain present things (as clothing contains a body) and actually non-existent things (a painting contains a face, a melody contains an emotion). It is therefore possible to manipulate objects in order to either present present forms (*presentation*), or present absent forms (*representation*). While all animal technologies form objects or give form to objects, some particular technologies do not merely give form to objects (when building a shelter or manufac-turing a tool, for instance), but also transform these very objects into forms (painting, sculpting, the use of an instrument, and so on). The possibility of this transformation splits human actions in two. By manipulating an object as if it were an object-form, we can attribute to it present things, which are *presented*, or nonexist-ent things, which are only *represented*.

4. Presentation and Representation

But a gap clearly exists between a piece of clothing and a Gustav Klimt painting. It is not a problem of knowing whether or not these objects are useful or purposeful, which would make them non-artistic. What we must understand is that a piece of clothing gives form to an *existent* body, while a painting gives form to a *nonexistent* body.

The difference, then, is that a representation is an object that a form will always lack – which makes it open to an original kind of interpretation: the search for what fills this emptiness. We may certainly know that Dora was the model for some Picasso canvas, that Dora is not in the canvas, and that the painting is a form, a container, whose content remains absent. We can therefore fill this absence with something else, project ourselves in it, interpret it in other ways, and so forth.

The presentation of some nonexistent thing should absolutely not be confused with figuration. For example, an Yves Klein blue monochrome and a Pierre Soulage black are also presentations of something absent, quite simply because they are the absenting of something present. Indeed, a painting – the monochrome – this three-dimensional object, this canvas mounted by a stretcher bar, is not a three-dimensional object whose sides are all equivalent, but rather a coloured surface contemplated as such. For example, to see the monochrome – which figures nothing – is to not consider the painting as an object whose front and back are equivalent, to not dwell upon the edges of the painting. Rather, to see the monochrome is to contemplate its surface, to reduce this three-dimensional thing to two dimensions: a surface of a single colour. Although a painting figures nothing and does not copy an existent object in the world, it nevertheless represents by absenting one dimension, the third dimension, in order to create a surface effect. By absenting one dimension of the object, we recognise the pictorial form of this work. It is because a spatial dimension is absented from the present object that something absent, whatever it is, is presented on the canvas.

Through a law of exchange, which is the very definition of representation, the absenting of something present entails the presentation of something absent.

Therefore, unlike a presentation, a representation consists in some relation between *absence* and *presence*: a present object (an image, sound, material, and so on) absents itself by becoming a form (an object's negative) such that something (anything) absent becomes present.

Whether it is pictorial, poetic, musical, graphic, or cinematographic, a representation has this price to pay: to make present something absent, one must make absent something present.

In photography, the fixed light on a surface, this plenitudinous and solid material thing, appears as a hole, like a void, which gives form to faces, streets, and landscapes which we know are absent. This exchange is not altogether contractual (it is not *primarily* a cultural rule). Rather, it is the possibility, which humanity inscribes in things, that this thing may not be a thing, but the form of another thing.

5. To Absent A Presence in order to Present an Absence

We must at all costs distinguish this concept of representation from the classical idea of *mimesis* – or substitutable representation (what is represented duplicates something which could be present) – and also from the modern idea of 'signification'.[11]

Unlike in *mimetic* theories, representation cannot be reduced to producing a duplicate. A work can represent something absent, which is not necessarily present 'elsewhere' and does not necessarily exist prior to the work representing it.

Unlike in *semiotic* theories, representation cannot be reduced to a triadic relation. The difference between a sign and a representation is that a sign can always vary without affecting what it signifies, whereas a representation cannot be affected without affecting what it represents. *To signify* is to attribute a sign to an object through one or several other signs. *To represent* is to attribute a presence to an absence and vice versa. In the sign, presence withdraws from the relation. In the representation, nothing other than some relation exists between presence and absence. Of course, every representation is open to interpretation, and can thus be used as a sign. But this is precisely because a representation as a signification is equivalent to a representation that is *not* a signification. This is the difference between a notice signifying a ban on smoking and a painting representing a cigarette.

The notice that signifies the ban on smoking can be affected without affecting what it signifies. We can cross out the cigarette with a red or black line, add smoke to the cigarette, break off its filter, replace it with a pipe, frame it in a circle or a square, and so on. The meaning will be the same: it is forbidden to smoke here. On the other hand, as a pictorial image or representation, if I change the painted or drawn cigarette's colour, if I modify its form, it will not at all represent the same thing.

A visual or sonorous sign is understood only within a triadic relationship, between the sign, its object, and a series of interpretants, that is, with other signs that attribute the sign to its object. By affecting a sign, I can very well not affect its object, if the series of interpretants continues to connect this sign to this object (a pipe can replace the cigarette while continuing to signify the act of smoking).

On the other hand, a pictorial, musical, poetic, narrative, architectural, or scenic representation is limited to a two-term relation between *presence* and *absence*. If I affect the present and absented object, I also affect the absent and presented, and thus represented, object.

Every representation can make us a sign, neither more nor less than a present object: a melody can signify as much as a cry; a drawing can signify as much as a trail of tracks in the snow; a dance can signify as much as a threatening gesture, and so on. Signification is a much more extensive system than representation, and goes beyond much of the latter.

A black flag can signify for a traumatised woman the death of her mother, or, on the contrary, for another, the pirate ship of his childhood, constructed with friends. Any phenomenon, when it is connected to different interpretants, can refer to a different object.

6. Neither *Mimesis* nor Signification

Let us treat the classical position of representation, *mimesis*, and the modern position, signification, on the same footing.

In *mimesis*, representation is a relation between *object* and *form*. Painting a bird implies taking a bird's form as a model, such that a painted bird is the reproduction of an unpainted bird, the model of all birds. In other words, by painting a bird, I imitate an existent bird. I can improve it by painting it in its ideal form. Or I can be faithful to it, if the bird painted on the canvas and the living bird, with flesh and feathers, have the same form, but not the same matter. One conceives this relation ontologically. Two objects share an invariable form, but on their own they embody variations of this invariable form.

In signification, a painted bird refers to an unpainted bird through one or several interpretants, signs which allow us to interpret the painting of the bird as representing a bird. This relation is no longer ontologically stable, since an invariable sign can continually change objects through a variety of cultural or individual interpretants.

Let us weigh the comparative merits of the two positions – the first abandoned and held in contempt, the other accepted today as an obvious fact. *Mimesis* allows us to consider representation – the relation through which an object is an object other than what it is – on its own. But it does not allow us to consider *all representations*. Signification allows us to consider *all representations*, and ultimately allows us to consider *all phenomena* which are potentially signifying.

Mimesis indexes a representation to its referent. A representation refers to a model. Thus, representations without referent become impossible. According to an altogether mimetic theory, for example, a piece of music will always reproduce – or will at least aim to do so – ideal harmonic relations or pre-existent mathematical forms; architecture will always materially reproduce some blueprint. It will in no way help us to claim that this or that work refers to nothing. Mimetic theorists will always have half-smiles, knowing airs. They claim that every representation aims at, reproduces, and realises an idea, a pre-existent form. It is clearly impossible to *prove* the opposite. Nevertheless, such a presupposition completely prevents one from understanding the aesthetic difference between a mere representation with referent and a vanguard representation without referent. In this way, the difference between literary naturalism and surrealism is inconceivable if all representations are equally mimetic and referential.

Signification extends the domain of representation to an extreme degree and indexes representation to interpretation. Representation makes things relational for a set of interpretative signs. Theories of signification view all representations as signifying and permitting interpretation. An extreme realist representation of a refrigerator or a photograph of a refrigerator will always be the sign of a refrigerator, through signs which allow us to interpret it as such. (Someone of the distant past, unfamiliar with perspective, the use of depth, or the use of these colours, will not perceive a refrigerator-object, *a fortiori* if she had never before seen a refrigerator.) With a knowing air, the theorist of signification will insist that all representational means which bear a resemblance to objective means (perspective, depth of field, exact proportions) are in fact constructed, interpretative means, only meaningful for an expert, that do not immediately represent real objects, but only do so through a medium, through the means of interpretants. Erwin Panofsky's work is representative of this orientation.[12]

It is clearly impossible to *prove* the opposite. Nevertheless, such a presupposition, according to which no representation is without an operation of signification, prevents us from understanding object-representations other than as signs. One of the characteristic features of the contemporary position is indeed, quite unlike *mimesis*, to demonstrate the impossibility of considering a representation as something other than a sign, that is, an interpretative medium.

However, the difference between representation and sign is conceivable, and, moreover, it *must* be conceived – unlike in the classical position of *mimesis*.

The first conclusion we can draw from this is that an object-representation is selfless. A painting, unlike sight, endures without being seen. In other words, it subsists. A melody endures without being heard, unlike an auditory perception. The difference between *self*-representation and *selfless*-representation assumes that a representation in object-form is not substantially connected to a subject's presence. An image does not assume that someone exists, right now, to see it. A text does not assume that someone exists, right now, to read it. Images and texts can wait.

Representations in object-form left alone do not require my existence in order to be the representations that they are – unlike a sign, which needs interpretants, is handled by an interpreter, to signify what it signifies. Indeed, signification depends on the triangulation that the interpretant makes of a sign. An interpretant makes a sign's object vary. A bird's feather can signify a bird, but also gentleness or writing or an Amerindian or a zoological species, depending on the interpretants mobilised (animal, touch, tool, headdress, and so on). One claims that the interpretation of a painting's signification (the great exercise of modern aesthetic criticism) varies just as much. The painting of a bird can signify the vanity of terrestrial life, the melancholy of the artist who painted it, a utopia in troubled and dark social times, the upper-class ideals of this time period, an allusion to Baudelaire's albatross or swan, or the memory of a bird whose feathers my uncle plucked in the backyard during our vacations in the countryside, and so on. A painting's signification, which implies the presence of interpretants, varies, but not the representation of what appears as a bird, which remains the same. Significations are varieties of a representation, as they were of a feather.

If one considers a painting like we considered a feather above, then one may claim that both are mediums of signification. But if one considers their *difference*, one must explain that one is the product of *art*, while the other is not. Games of signification do not allow us to establish this difference; anything signifies as much as a painting, since signification is a variety of interpretants triangulating sign and object.

Therefore, games of signification do justice to meaning, to a painting's various meanings, but not to the *art* of painting.

A painting's representation, and not its signification, does justice to the art of painting: its capacity to represent without my existence. An object-representation, unlike a sign, presupposes the capacity to exclude itself from what we perceive. To make something signify is always to include oneself in the network of relations between things, to make them vary in relation to other signs. To let something represent is always to exclude oneself from this thing and to understand that it does not require a self to be what it is.

Such a proposition does not mean that we must not interpret representations or that they do not require interpretation. Rather, it indicates that object-representations, in order to represent, do not require seeing their signification interpreted. The modern hermeneutic and semiotic tendency to make representations signify makes us miss them.

Let us reexamine our bird painting – perhaps one by John James Audubon. One may argue that we must certainly interpret it as a bird-representation in order to grasp it as a bird representation. If this is a cubist painting, perhaps by Georges Braque, we must prove ourselves capable of mobilising the necessary cultural references in order to recognise the bird, which is not a 'ready-made object', in the decomposition of forms. Of course. But the painting, to *signify* a bird, need not be painted as it is painted. A brief summary of the painting can also signify 'bird' or 'bluebird'; so, to signify a melancholic bird or the melancholia of the bird, a summary statement like 'melancholia of the bird' will signify what one interprets just as well, with less effort.

If a representation were first and foremost a signification, it could easily be translated – and we wouldn't need several arts to represent things. One would limit oneself to language or to an image alone, perhaps the simplest possible one. Detailed commentary would cloud understanding rather than allow for it. A representation, in its materiality, complexity, and details, always goes beyond its possible meaning or meanings.

A theory of signification uses representation, but does not give an account of it, since it envelops it in a general theory of the triadic relation of things through interpreting signs, such that representation, lost in signification, loses its specificity. To represent is to use this or that form of representation. To paint is not to sing; to narrate is not to photograph. Signification is always translatable. Representation is never translatable.

Indeed, a representation in object-form, unlike a signification, is not a triadic relation, which implies an interpretant; it is a selfless relation between two objects which fascinate us *precisely* because it excludes an interpreter.

In contrast, signification is an operation that includes an interpretant, making a sign and an object relational. For smoke to be
the sign of fire, one or several interpretants must recognise it as
such, through habit or experience. In the same way, for this stone
placed in the room of a museum, on its pedestal, to signify something for me about death, minerality, eternity, or anything else, it
is necessary that I be there to handle these interpretants, choose
them, for them to awaken something in me.

A painting representing a bird can awaken in me a signification
connected to death, whiteness, or lost childhood, such that I may
weep before it. But that is not all – unlike fire, a piece of wood, or
a stone, a painting does not only *signify*. It only signifies because
it represents, and, in order to represent, it does not require my
existence. While a signification includes me in the object-relations,
a representation excludes me from them. I know that if I leave the
museum, the piece of wood (like the 'beach art' dear to George
Dickie[13]) on its own no longer has meanings of lost childhood or
death – I am the sole repository of these meanings. On the other
hand, if the painting no longer has this signification, it will continue to represent what it represents. I am continually compelled
to interpret what it represents, but I interpret it because I know
that something in this painting resists me, is independent of me,
and is represented.

Twentieth-century art was in large part dominated by the
schema of contemporary art and fascinated by the pure singularity of objects. As a result, it quite favourably welcomed theories
of signification, which have become a commonplace in current
art theory. Spectators are, indeed, supposed to produce the work
as much as the artist, since they carry with them its signification.
A work is never finished or closed, but is open, since a variety of
interpretants affects its very essence and continually transforms it
beneath the changing horizon of expectations.

In so doing, one has literally rendered unthinkable the distinction between a stone placed in the museum, which can signify (by
'exemplifying', according to Nelson Goodman,[14] being valued as
a sample of some remarkable properties), and a painting, which
only signifies by representing.

7. The Art of Representation, the Meaning of Representation

We can thus imagine responding to a latent problem found in all modern theories of representation, in different forms, in Frege, Husserl, and Peirce: is representation inscribed in the object that represents, or is it nothing without an interpreting consciousness? In other words, if nobody were there to see an image as such, is it still an image? This is the initial problem that we raised by evoking the possibility of *self-* and *selfless*-representations.

Our response is the following: a representation is an object, a manufactured artefact like a form, which we can always consider as an object and not as a representation, since it concerns an object that all *art* is precisely a representation of. We will therefore hold the following theory: the *meaning* of a representation is never inscribed in the representation itself, since meaning depends on the relation of the representation as a sign to other signs, which change from one culture to another, and from one individual to another. On the other hand, the *art* of representation is imprinted in an object. A drawing can be interpreted as a non-drawing, but the way it was made is inscribed in an object: this object has the *form* of a drawing.

Art is, quite simply, the way of making a form of an object, which differs from the *meaning* of an object. Meaning is a partially transcendent relation to an object, which connects this object to other signs and objects through a process of interpretation. Art is immanent to an object, the way in which one makes a form of an object.

Our response is therefore not quite the same. It is not that we claim that the art of an object, unlike its meaning, was inscribed in it as a representational form. Rather, we define art as what is inscribed in an object which represents. It is not the product of interpretations or the meaning given to this object, but a part of the object itself. The meaning that one gives to a painting or to a piece of music is a variable relation, dependent on other (cultural) signs. But the pictorial or musical form of an object *is* in the object itself thanks to the art that made it what it is.

Arthur Danto sought to relativise the art of an object, its representational form, by more or less reducing it to its *meaning*. Someone who does not benefit from a theory of the interpretive art, he claimed, cannot recognise, in front of a painting, for example, that an abstract painting is a painting, a work of art, and therefore a representation. But Danto intentionally confounds meaning and representation, interpretation and art. When one does not benefit from a theory of art capable of elucidating a drawing's rules of representation, of course one cannot truly grasp the *meaning* of these representations, which is not inscribed in them. On the other hand, one grasps their *art*; we know very well that these are representations or pictorial representations. In this way, in front of Palaeolithic cave paintings, one cannot understand or interpret the precise meaning of these representations, their rules having escaped from us. But we have access to their art, which is inscribed in them. We have access to the fact that these are representations, that is, presentations of absent objects. We no longer know the meaning of these painted animals, but we recognise that some things – cave walls and pigments – were conceived as forms for nonexistent things. We do not exactly know what they refer to (what they represent), but we can still make out their form (the fact that they represent), their empty place and shape. The referent which filled this space in the minds of those who made them was lost.

Contemplate hand prints on a cave wall. Through these works of art we have retained the form of our representations of yesteryear – what was forgotten were their *rules*.

Notes

1. Jocelyn Benoist, *Représentations sans objet*.
2. Bernard Bolzano, *Theory of Science*, p. 79.
3. Gottlob Frege, *Écrits logiques et philosophiques (1882–1923)*.
4. Franz Brentano, *Psychology from an Empirical Standpoint*.
5. Kazimierz Twardowski, *On the Content and Object of Presentations*.
6. Alexius Meinong, 'The Theory of Objects'.
7. Bertrand Russell, 'On Denoting'.
8. Twardowski, *On the Content and Object of Presentations*, pp. 12–13.
9. Benoist, *Représentations sans objet*, p. 121.
10. René Descartes, *Optics*.
11. In particular, in C. S. Peirce's foundational work, *Écrits sur le signe*.
12. Erwin Panofsky, *Perspective as Symbolic Form*.
13. The recurring example is that of a natural object found on a beach, which can be considered as an artefact according to the circum-

stances, context, and way of considering the object in question; see especially George Dickie's *Art and the Aesthetic*.

14. Nelson Goodman, 'When Is Art?'

Chapter VIII

Arts and Rules

1. Rules

What exactly is a *rule*?

It seems that a rule is a paradox, a seemingly blatant contradiction. In order for a rule to exist, one must claim that it is impossible to do certain things that can be done. For example, it is *impossible*, in French, to combine a verb conjugated in the second person with a first person subject; it is *impossible*, in English, to write word 'bird' as 'burd'. Of course these rules, by definition, vary with use, context, register, and through all the regular and irregular articulations which a linguistic theory can shed light on.[1]

To modalise the previous propositions through alethic operators ('it is necessary to', 'it is impossible to') or deontic operators ('it is permissible to', 'it is forbidden to') masks the problem rather than solving it. This method merely avoids confronting the contradiction, immediately determined in distinct senses of modality. It is not enough to say that one *must* not do certain things that one can do; rules do not merely preclude, by way of 'necessity', certain combinations which fall within the domain of 'possibility'. Indeed, it is not merely *condemnable*, in the register of what is impermissible, to say 'skrmmneugh black stomach'. It is impossible to say this in the framework of propositions such as 'I have a stomach ache'. If it were always possible to say *no-matter-what*, it would become impossible to say *something*. Absolute irregularity would empty a language of any possibility of representing things, since language signifies only with regular use. Many poets experiment with this absolute irregularity, from Stéphane Mallarmé to Bernard Heidsieck, from Antonin Artaud's glossolalia to Velimir Khlebnikov.

A language represents reliably only through its regular use, that is, through the use of rules (which one can always break) that define the possibility and impossibility of certain possibilities. At each moment, a language – adjusted by its context or register – is constituted by an infinite sum of possible combinations of representative elements (ideograms) and non-representative elements (arbitrary signs), of which some are possible and others impossible, without which this language would cease to function.

A rule is therefore the collective and individual conception (which can transmit rules, such as moral rules) of the *dyadic* possibility and impossibility of possibilities. Some possibilities are doubled – possible *possibilia* – while other possibilities are contradictory – impossible *possibilia*.

A 'game' is an activity that consists in making use of rules. In the game of chess, as in board games, football games, the game of love, the play between lion cubs and their mothers, or the game of Russian roulette, one categorises and identifies all that one can do according to two qualities: (1) what one can do *and* can do; (2) what one can do *and* cannot do. In chess, it is possible to take the bishop and move it to the other end of the diagonal on which it is located. I *can* make this move. It is also entirely possible to take the rook and move it to the other end of its diagonal. But I *cannot* make this move. I can even add two pieces to the chessboard. But I cannot do so. I can eat the pieces or kill my opponent, but I cannot do so because rules other than those of the game of chess, strictly speaking, intervene: social rules or rules of survival.

The ability to cheat is an integral part of the idea of a game. Moreover, if it were formally or logically impossible to cheat, a game would not be a game. But a game is precisely this relation between the possibility of cheating and the impossibility of doing so (and not a mere prohibition). In order for a game to exist, it is necessary to be able to cheat. However, in order for a game to function, it is necessary to not be able to cheat. Any experienced cheater knows this. By knowingly cheating, we are conscious that we are not really playing the game any more, or, more precisely, we are conscious that we have replaced one game with another. We no longer play the game that we are playing; instead we play at trying to avoid getting caught, which is a completely different pleasure.

Therefore, every game moves between these two limits: the possibility of cheating and the impossibility of cheating. No game exists without these limits.

What would a game be if we could not cheat? We certainly have an idea of it, for example when thinking about an artistic activity.

If I begin to paint, I will begin by learning certain rules in order to represent bodies proportionately, to make good use of colour mixtures, and so on. But I quickly realise that these instructions will not teach me to *paint*. They teach me to paint *in this or that style*, in a classical, baroque, Flemish, Chinese, impressionist, or expressionist style. By learning rules, such as the rules of drawing, one does not learn to draw, but to master some language of drawing.

I can make a mistake within the framework of one of these languages. I can fail to draw in cavalier perspective. However, if I think about it, I have not really made a drawing mistake, I have made a *classical perspective* drawing mistake. So I wonder what making a mistake or error of pure drawing would mean. I draw a vague, abstract form. I reflect, and I see a drawing there of a completely different kind, whether it is beautiful or not. I doodle furiously. But what I have just drawn on the paper is no less a drawing.

I understand, in fact, that by drawing I can never be mistaken, nor cheat. If I draw, it is clear that I draw, and that's all there is to it.

Unlike chess, which is a game in which it is necessary to be able to cheat, and unlike every language, in which it is necessary to be able to be mistaken, it is formally impossible to cheat or to be mistaken when one devotes oneself to an art, which therefore proves to be a distinct human activity. I can fail to sing according to the rules of this or that kind of song, but I cannot *absolutely* sing wrongly or make a 'song mistake'. I can sing or *not* sing.

I can neither cheat nor be mistaken by using this or that art. I can only be mistaken or cheat within this or that *kind* of art.

2. Art is a Rule-Bound Representational Form

If we have defined a game as the use of rules, then we will define a language as a set of representational rules. In every language, representation is possible only through the observance of rules. But one can take language, as a body of representational rules, and use these rules as a form. We call this *ars poetica*.

Poetry is the art of considering the rules of language as a form, such that impossibility does not double possibility. Language then becomes a representational form – the opening of a container for *no-matter-what*: 'Rrummpff tillff toooo',[2] 'ptyx',[3] a squared circle,[4] and a third person verb coupled with a first person subject ('I is another'[5]) all have a right to poetic existence.

If a language (rules that represent) exists, poetry is the art of making a form of these rules (which limit and close off possibilities in order to be able to represent things).

Therefore, languages and games are not arts. A game is an activity that makes use of rules. A language consists in the representational use of rules. In contrast, an art is a completely different human activity, consisting in making use of representational forms. Formally, an art is the opening of the possibility of representing *no-matter-what*, that is, of making a thing present – anything – by absenting another thing. Each art is thus primarily a form, and not a set of rules.

But why do the human arts appear so rule-bound? How do we consider poetic versification, the rules of musical harmony or of theatrical performance? How do we describe certain 'faux rock' songs? Why do architecture manuals exist? How do we approach, for example, John Dickson Carr's statements about the four fundamental laws of the detective novel?[6]

If rule-bound representation is a property of a language, and if art is a form without rules, a possibility without impossibilities, how do we account for the overwhelming majority of human art objects which seem to fulfil implicit or explicit generic rules?

Is an art or representational form capable of becoming a game or a language? This is the task of every representational genre that regulates the artistic potential of access to the no-matter-what.

3. Rule-Bound Representational Genres

In the arts, genre is the most common thing there is. Each art, in its temporal evolution and spatial and cultural diversity, has a generic differentiation: poetic genres, narrative genres, musical genres, architectural genres, performing arts genres, graphic novel genres, detective genres (hard-boiled, suspense, procedural, historical detective), science fiction genres (hard, fantasy, dark or light, cyberpunk, dystopian, alternative history), recorded popular music genres (jazz: bop, hard bop, cool, free; folk, country, blues, surf, girl groups, psychedelic, glam, prog, metal, hard rock, hardcore, punk, new wave), and cinematic genres (musical comedy, western, war, biopic, romantic comedy). Genre exists in every art and culture: the *cihuà* of the classical Chinese novel (for example, the *Jin Ping Mei*), or the Kathakali, a south Indian dance-drama.

A genre is nothing but a taxonomic category, a classificatory tool, a minimal division, as we will see later. It is an active principle in the use of representations in every art. It does not limit itself to gathering a posteriori the diversity of what exists in order to divide this diversity into sets and subsets. But it is an active principle which closes off the possibility opened by a form, and offers in this way many representational combinations.

A representational form is infinitely extensive and open. Each art prepares the ground of possibilities that it opens through smaller territories, limited by rules, codes, and figures. These territories or regions of possibility are precisely what we call *genres*. They transform the wasteland of possibility into geography. Through technical, combinatorial rules (versification or the rules of harmony, for example), or through figures (for the western: cowboys, indians, a frontier, cattle, steeds, saloons, and so on), a genre imposes the *objective* representational possibilities and impossibilities on an art's *formal* possibility. Consequently, it becomes possible to make errors or to cheat. One can cheat with the form of the western (which Italian 'spaghetti' westerns brilliantly showed in the 1960s and 1970s), or one can make a false sonnet (with fifteen lines of verse).

Therefore, a genre does not classify; it divides possibilities into regions and defines impossibilities. Why? In order to allow combinatorial and accumulated representations. Each western presupposes the existence of other westerns, and thus allows the genre's figures to be combined in a novel manner that plays with codes. A game, as we have defined it, is a certain use of rules. Each genre permits a *game* and constitutes its art as a genuine language by representing certain things through the use of rules. One could say that the ode is a certain idiomatic tongue of *ars poetica*, just as the western is a certain idiomatic tongue of the cinematographic art (and other arts).

It seemed that all human artistic productions (African, Amerindian, Eastern, Oceanic, or Western; Ancient, Medieval, or Paleolithic), at least until the nineteenth century, belonged to *art genres*. Sculpture observed, played, and expressed using certain representational rules. Architecture, drawing, and music observed a body of rules or figures (defined by the community or human group that produced them) which included them in a genre and in an art.

One must therefore be able to say that, until what appeared to us as 'modernity', genres and arts appeared indiscernible. An artwork – pictorial, sculptural, musical, or narrative – was only a work of this or that genre.

What we do not mean to say is that, until modernity, human artworks belonged only to genres or a body of rules, and not to forms or representational possibilities. On the contrary, we mean that modernity is nothing other than the gradual disclosure that the arts are primarily forms, and not bodies of rules. Modernity showed us that we could deprive arts of their rules and figures. They appeared to us stripped bare, in the appearance of a form, of a mere possibility without impossibilities. This movement constituted the core of what was called 'the work of the avant-garde', that is, neither more nor less than the *formalisation* of the arts which were formerly organised into genres.

4. The Regulation and Deregulation of the Arts

Often, in the history of each art, a questioning of the rules and figures of some genre suddenly emerges, wherein the rules appear old-fashioned and conventional, sometimes resulting in caricature.

Singular and non-generic works emerge. They belong to their form rather than to a genre. Of course, it is always possible to launch a surprise attack on a mortified and conventional language, and to present the possibility of what this language renders impossible. Since each genre marks a regionalisation of possibility, a work can invoke the opening up and adventure of possibilities beyond the limits of the genre, in order to show the narrowness, provincialism, artificiality, or conventionalism of this genre. In order to represent through some kind of game or combination, a genre limits itself to certain figures – but these figures can at any moment be reduced to their mere possibility. Why does one always represent cowboys on saddled steeds? In Christian painting, why does one systematically represent descents from the cross, the entombment of Christ, and Madonnas? Why does one respect the sonata form? Why does one represent a childlike and asexual hero in graphic novels? They are only some possibilities among other possibilities, and can suddenly be presented as contingent and not necessary.

In cinema, the modern European art of Michelangelo Antonioni, Robert Bresson, Ingmar Bergman, and Jean-Luc Godard, through hyperbole or breaking the codes of generic representation, revealed the identity crisis of post-classical Hollywood cinema. Suddenly, genre figures, like cowboys, detectives, and musical dancers, appeared to be entirely contingent. In each art, the tension between the *generic* and the *singular* occasionally arises. The generic limits the representational possibilities through rules and figures, allowing certain combinations and games. The singular art then reopens the formal domain of representation, with neither rules nor figures. In order to function, an art intimately intertwines the generic and the singular, belonging to genre and belonging to form.

Genre is indeed as vital to artistic representation as the form of an art is: to represent generically and not formally is to agree to use figures and rules that no longer represent anything by themselves, for the sole purpose that their combination be representative.

In a western, a cowboy no longer represents anything. He is no longer, as in Raoul Walsh's or Budd Boetticher's films, the *historical* tenant farmer of the late nineteenth-century North American western territories; here he is only a symbolic figure of law and order, marginality, and respect of the community. He then becomes an inherited code, and, in the end, the mere symbolic sum of what he was up to that point in the history of cinema. Interest in the classical western no longer stems from this stereotypical figure; to transform Robert Mitchum into an Oedipus troubled by a primitive scene of 'spurs' in *Pursued* was to assume that the ordinary figure of the western hero was assimilated and deformed by giving him an anti-hero interiority.

While a generic work *plays* with the figures and codes to represent the world regionally, a singular work rejects every prerequisite in order to represent the entire world only through its (poetic, cinematographic, science-fictional) form. The old-fashioned and attacked genres then fade away. They are representational genres which pass with time, whereas forms remain: forms which are only representational possibilities. In spite of the slogans of yesteryear, like 'the death of painting' (or of tonal music), it is neither more nor less possible to produce a pictorial representation today than it was before. Aesthetic history changes nothing. A possibility remains open and always infinite. The representational rules, codes, and figures change and are no longer always possible; they emerge and fade away.

Of course, most important artworks simultaneously have a generic part and a singular part. They represent both formally and generically. But it is, in any case, impossible to understand the history of any art without grasping this relation between genre and form. An art is a representational form that, through its history and present functioning, uses rules and figures in order to close off the representational possibilities that the art opens up. When an art becomes too closed, its singular works reopen it and return it to its form and to its possibility of letting *no-matter-what* appear.

Artistic modernity is original in having *systematised*, in a little over a century, the problem of art genres, by disclosing the form and possibility that lay beneath these rule-bound divisions.

5. The Formation of New Arts and the Systematic Deregulation of the Ancient Arts: Classicists, Moderns, and Contemporaries

Since every art is a representational form, two representational orientations present themselves to an artwork: either the representation of the world, or the representation of the representational form itself. To represent is to make use of representational procedures and to take as a representational object either the procedures in question, or anything else.

To paint is to paint either something objective (an object, any object), or something formal (that through which one paints).

Here we define the use of representational forms that take themselves as objects as 'reflexive'. And we note that the ancient representational forms constituted in the Palaeolithic era, as we sketched above, became reflexive when their primary object became their form (their conditions of possibility) rather than *anything else*.

What we define as the 'formalisation of the ancient arts' corresponds to the following phenomenon. The ancient arts, that is, the ancient representational forms, took themselves as objects when the systematic problematisation of genres and the gradual discovery that the principle of representation was not generic but formal were made possible. The problematisation of the rules and figures of representation in the performing arts, narrative, poetry, painting, sculpture, and architecture went hand in hand with the claims of the singular work, left alone with its art, and the claims of the formal representation of our own conditions of representation (painting with our sight, music with the sonorous material of our hearing, narration with time, the voice, the subject).

The modern formalisation of the ancient arts (the movement towards abstraction and the plasticity of materials; the unveiling of the stage, bodies, and voices as presences; the return to the conditions of the work's reception) corresponds therefore to the refusal and systematic decompartmentalisation of genres, of possibilities and of impossibilities of certain representational possibilities. Therefore, modernity marks the search for a representational possibility without impossibility. This 'modern' movement of the ancient arts, which passed through the problem between representational and sacred taboos (what is not representable), the challenging of canonical (bourgeois, conventional) subdivisions, and the weakening of figures, exposed the form of an art deprived of its genre.

We will thus say that the human arts were always rule-bound forms, but that their deregulation allowed us to apprehend them as forms. This is the positive lesson of modernity that we must remember. But there is also an unspoken, negative part in modernity. The modern emancipation of deregulated art forms was in fact the ancient arts' response to the appearance of new, popular, and mass arts. The deregulation and formalisation of the ancient arts essentially derives from this formation of new arts. Examples abound. Nicéphore Niépce's and Louis Daguerre's decisive invention of photography, a new type of image which mechanically joined 'taken' and 'given', challenged pictorial forms which arranged material on a surface. Thomas Edison, William Friese-Greene, the Lumière brothers, and Max Skladanowsky invented cinematography, the art of event-images. Robert F. Outcault and Winsor McCay, creator of *Little Nemo*, invented the graphic novel, the art *between the images*, combining panel and paper, connected to modern childhood and the appearance of the popular press. Edgar Allan Poe, Jules Verne, H. G. Wells, and Hugo Gernsback invented science fiction not only as a narrative genre, but as a new art of making real things possible and placing them in time, in the future or in the past (in the case of fantasy). The detective novel is not simply a genre either, but the new art of reducing real things to possibilities, joining factual things and legal codes, the heterogeneous composition of Oriental *firasah*, the picaresque, the gothic fantasy, the emergence of urban police forces, and theories of the state of law. Recorded popular music transformed the ontology of musical sound, no longer defined by the written work but by mechanical, analogue, or digital recording, allowing us to deterritorialise folklore. Television, the composed and decomposed image, remote transmission, is not something viewers *go* to, but which *comes* to them. Video games, representations organically connected to actions – the world perceived inseparable from the perception that we have of it and from our possibility of action within it – transform games into representational forms or into an exploration of worlds, thanks to its pioneers Ralph H. Baer, Nolan Bushnell, the designer of *Pong*, and the designers of *Spacewar!*[7]

The emergence of the new arts was misunderstood by classicists (who denied the new forms an equal status with the ancient forms), by moderns (who transformed the ancient forms into introspective forms), and by contemporaries (who describe as artistic all the singular objects aspiring to this name, without further distinguishing between the human arts). Artistic movements throughout the twentieth century were fuelled by these misunderstandings and polemics. They were certainly not autonomous, but reactive. Modernity is nothing other than a reaction. It is the introspective reaction against the shift from our ancient representational forms to the emergence of new forms representing the world through the arts unnecessarily described as 'popular' or 'mass' arts.

The study of the modern introspective movement against our ancient representational forms must allow us to understand, for example, how, by breaking the monopoly of the pictorial over the image, photography led the *pictorial* art into an introspective *plastic* reaction through a series of 'turns of the screw'. All that was a *procedure* of pictorial representation turned against itself as a representational *object*. In this way, a process of artistic movements unfolded. This included explorations into visual impression (Impressionism), light (among les Nabis, for example), colour and form, the geometry of lines (Geometric Abstraction), the act and pictorial matter (Abstract Expressionism), and representation as a whole. The various conditions of pictorial representation, instead of being useful for a representation of the world, themselves became represented objects. This process, guided by the myth of advancements in the modern history of painting through the exploration of its material, led contemporaries to a feeling of the impoverishment of the representable, which is nothing other than the sensation that 'there is nothing else to paint except that through which we can paint'. Declarations of the 'death' of pictorial possibility occurred frequently, encompassed in the broader idea we had of 'plastic arts'. These declarations led to the contemporary rupture, the desire to replace a representational form declared old-fashioned with the fashions of the *presentation* of objects and events (installations, propositions, happenings).

We could describe similar movements within the framework of the ancient forms of the narrative, written music, poetry, performing arts (dance and other staged arts), or architecture.

'Classicists' believe in one way or another in mimetic representation, aiming at the presentation of the representation of the world, reality, or ideas. Unlike 'classicists', 'moderns' do not believe in representations of the world, but only in introspective representation. 'Contemporaries' do not believe in the representation of the whole, but only in the presentation and presence of things. 'Moderns' are engaged in an introspective spiral, in the process of the 'step forward' in representation which ought to further represent its own conditions of representation, exhibit them, and undo them. Consciousness of the increasingly advanced representation is its sole criterion. 'Moderns' can only diminish their representational possibilities insofar as they show their conditions of possibility, and increasingly forget the world. In the end, they must always *force* themselves towards sorrow; novelty, the work of the avant-garde, and the vanguard are henceforth behind them. 'Moderns' appear to be concerned and solemn, mixing lucidity with lamentation. 'Contemporaries' reduce representation to one effect of presentation among other effects. They believe only in singularity and plurality. They do not have a world, but only things – always new things. 'Contemporaries' must in the last instance always *force* themselves to enjoy. All that happens, all that arrives, all that is new *must* satisfy them.

6. Singular Art Objects (the Analytic Position and Contemporaries)

What are the theoretical foundations of contemporary art?

In the twentieth century, with the gradual transition from logical positivism to the Wittgensteinian 'linguistic turn', a certain spatialist and anti-historicist philosophical position emerged. This position consisted in considering artworks as several different objects that can be arranged side by side. An artwork's only mystery is that we consider it as behaviourally different from other objects. This new twentieth-century discourse introduces a 'secondary' discourse, which refuses to engage in discussions concerning the value of artworks. Rather, it attacks all currently tenable critical discourses about artworks by questioning the validity and grounds of the systematic use of concepts like 'Art' and 'Artwork'. Following the work of Morris Weitz, Paul Ziff, and William Kennick, a new field of research emerged that rejected essentialist aesthetic concepts (form, content, value) and that affirmed the primacy of objects over Art as a 'concept'. According to this position, the fact that objects are found before us is primary. The fact that one describes with certain predicates this or that object, at the expense of other objects, as an 'artwork' is secondary and must be analytically accounted for. Different theories emerged throughout the latter half of the last century to explain how specific objects attain the status of art objects: Nelson Goodman's theory of exemplification; Monroe Beardsley's theory of subjective experience; and Arthur Danto's and George Dickie's institutional theories of objects.

In one way or another, this way of thinking seeks to bring together the status of 'art object', starting with 'the bare object' [*l'objet nu*], by questioning the processes of differentiation by which, for us, some things can be distinguished from others, to the point of being considered and 'see[n]-as' works (as Richard Wollheim argues). This view claims to be external to the aesthetic value of objects, since it never engages with works. It does not express any judgement about a work's value, but remains on the threshold. It clearly intersects with contemporary aesthetic practices: object installations, conceptual art, and so on. These practices appeared tormented by the presentation of mere objects as art objects, as works. They denounced the 'essentialist' and naïve perspectives according to which processes internal to a work would transform the work into an artwork.

The contemporary's artistic problem is therefore the following: how does a unique, singular object externally attain the status of an artwork? Contemporary art feeds on such object 'success stories'. This or that object 'succeeded' in asserting itself as a work, by forcing us to 'see [it] as' a work, and by becoming a work of value.

According to the analytic position, the success and posterity of an artwork depended on its capacity to cut across the concerns of contemporary art and its market. How does an object become an art object? Jean-Marie Schaeffer's radical critique of idealist and speculative theories of art and Yves Michaud's defence of aesthetic pluralism showed how 'the artistic' was ultimately dissolved into aesthetics. The analytic position can thus be considered as a genuine *model* of understanding singular and contemporary aesthetic objects, from design to fooding to Fashion Week to performance.

Nonetheless, the limits of this theoretical model that underlies all contemporary aesthetic enthusiasm are unsettling. Analytic positions prevent us from understanding that a logic of arts and human practices exists beyond singular objects, whether or not they obtain the status of art. Unlike contemporary art objects, an opera and a graphic novel certainly do not *individually* obtain the status of artworks, but only in virtue of their belonging to a *genre*, or, moreover, to an *art*. On this view, the analytic position also blinds us to the emergence of new arts and ways of *representing*. It doesn't give us understanding of how new objects become art objects, but how new human arts were constituted from the nineteenth century onwards. The analytic position doesn't give us understanding of the relation between a work and its art. How does one explain, then, how a work *represents* its art, how every painting carries with it a representation of what a narrative is? How does a work represent the world, and how is this representation nothing but an accidental quality that enters into signification (or exemplification)? And how is an art object nothing but an *object*? This is the blind spot of the analytic position, the price it pays for formulating its problem as: 'How can an object become an art object?' The chance of this position or formulation certainly makes us sensible to the fact that an artwork is always a *thing*. But the analytic, nominalist position moves away from individual things to understand the distinction of some things as 'art things'. In this way, the fact that an art object is nothing *but* an object (but also, as we have seen, a form) remains forever a mystery to this position, if not the path of some metaphysical obscurantism.

7. Universal Arts (the Dialectical-Critical Position and Moderns)

Another position primarily consists in considering an artwork as a whole and in asking how this organic totality – a product of the human mind – can be reduced to being only a thing. It is what we call the *dialectical-critical* position. It is an essentially Germanic, and, more broadly, continental and post-Romantic tradition. The Kantian tradition makes an artwork autonomous: finality without end. Hegelian reflexivity ends the artwork as one moment in the cultural processes of spirit. The transition from Kantianism to Hegelianism marks an ongoing conflict between the conception of the artwork as, on the one hand, the imperative of an *autonomous* entity, and, on the other, the consciousness of what this entity is immersed in – culture, history, and other social determinations. One can therefore identify a certain conception of the artwork as the contradiction between the ideal of autonomy and the product of real determinations, in Marx and the critical Marxist tradition and among many continental thinkers (Marxist or not: the French tradition, from Paul Valéry to Jacques Rancière). This theoretical line leads to a non-*spatialising* – arranging artworks side by side, as in the analytic position – but *historicising* construction – arranging works in each other. This discourse, tightly bound to the European tradition of art history, claims to be *internal* (and not *external*) to Artworks, continually posing the question of 'Art's essence', a work's singularity, and the formation of 'the common' or community around the work. The analytic position focuses on art objects – by beginning from objects in general, opting for art objects in particular, and asking through which perceptive, linguistic, or institutional processes objects become considered as artworks. In contrast, the dialectical-critical position focuses on Art and the question of Art – by beginning from Art, opting for art objects, and asking how art objects, in market societies, can be reduced to objects and commodities.

Employing concepts of form, content, and value (concepts dismissed by the analytic position), the dialectical-critical position thus establishes the primacy of Art, and seeks to join Art – as a human mental process – with things. György Lukács's foundational work opened up several paths in this direction. The most fruitful paths were Walter Benjamin's concept of the aura and the examination of subjective–objective aesthetic experience, and Siegfried Kracauer and Theodor W. Adorno's concept of culture and engagement in cultural critique. These different theoretical paths intersected in cultural modernity. Questions revolved around the status of human Art as a practice within the twentieth-century culture industry developed in Western capitalist and liberal societies. This is what guaranteed the *modern* (rather than *contemporary*) position its intellectual success. If the dialectical-critical position aroused so much interest, it was because it encountered the novel, modernist concerns regarding the relation between an ideal of autonomous Art and an analysis of the cultural heteronomy of artistic productions. In this way, it made political aesthetics possible by connecting an idea of Art with a cultural diagnosis of, and political commitment to, the historical situation of human practices. Nevertheless, the dialectical-critical position ultimately led to a negative aesthetics, a strategic withdrawal, and deeply pessimistic cultural criticism at the close of the century. We are all too familiar with the monotonous discourses on the end of Art, commodification, the collapse of artistic authenticity, the triumph of simulacra, and the forgers of culture and mass art. The alliance between reaction and the ideal of Art against contemporary objects, which one finds among old modernity's polemicists and nostalgics, as well as among classicists, derives from the critical and seriously 'concerned' consciousness of a contradiction between an ideal of Art and the reality of culture. What weight does a mere *ideal* autonomy carry when confronted with a *de facto* cultural heteronomisation?

However, the dialectical-critical model is a comprehensive system of formulating the question of Art (which is confounded with the question of singular, autonomous human representations). Its response to this question, which contains a critical cultural diagnosis of modern societies, has its limits. Within this system's framework, how can one think that an art object could be an object, other than as a 'dialectical contradiction'? While the analytic position is incapable of conceiving of an object as anything *other than* an object, the dialectical-critical position fails to account for the fact that an art object is *an object*. Leaving the artwork alone in the face of culture, the dialectical-critical position makes impossible any understanding of the mediation of arts and human representational practices by dialectically opposing 'Art' – production of the Spirit – to social and cultural determinations. It often makes it difficult to fully understand the emergence of new arts, reducing them to alienated and alienating cultural practices, like jazz, graphic novels, cinema, and video games. It also prevents one from grasping the form of human arts outside of their history; one cannot atemporally define them as transhistorical representational possibilities.

Generally, faced with Art, the dialectical-critical position seems inevitably bound to the *modern*, symmetrical to the analytic position faced with singular art objects, which was inextricably bound to the *contemporary*. One cannot understand the artistic through general Art or through particular art objects. But particular human arts exist between *general Art* and *particular works*; they are differentiated human practices, like many old and new representational forms, allowing the production of works, representations in object-form. These arts are the key to every *artistic* activity relieved of the contemporary and modern dilemmas.

8. The Particular Arts

We conclude the chapter with an interpretation of the modern and the contemporary, and go beyond the potential debate between the 'nature' and 'culture' of human art, by articulating between representational *forms* (resulting from the aestheticisation of natural human functions) and representational *rules* (systems and structures of representational impossibilities particular to the internal functioning of each human culture). What is most important for us is to make each of the arts equally *possible*, and to untie them from concerns for their own actual possibility or impossibility.

The price of such an operation is to give up identifying 'Art' as such, as in the post-Romantic continental tradition, to consider human *arts*, whether old or new, as equivalent, and to establish as self-evident that what is of a human art *in particular* is of art *in general* [*qu'est de l'art ce qui est d'*un *certain art humain*].

We must therefore admit that every object which is of *an* art is of art *in general*, even if it is rule-bound in a way that neutralises its aesthetic form. Every written or oral narrative; every piece of music; all wooden, concrete, durable, or ephemeral architecture; every photograph, in a museum, a journal, or photo booth; every film, at the cinema or on television, experimental or promotional; every drawing, sketch, geometric draft, profile, doodle, or signed Georg Baselitz are equally of *an* art and are therefore of art *in general*. But some are rule-bound such that their representation is neutralised and used as a (journalistic, scientific, advertising) *sign*. Others are rule-bound as art *genres* (as figurative portraits, still lifes), or are without rules [*déréglés*] and therefore singular. It doesn't matter if we know if they 'are of art in general or not', as if it were necessary to determine some higher value to attribute to them. What matters is to what extent their representation is neutralised and to what extent it is valued.

We must attempt to articulate an interest for *all* our representations by examining the *modern* formation or formalisation of their forms and conditions of possibility (pictorial, musical, and so on), and an interest for *new* representations which came to challenge them. *Interesting* works – in all forms, old and new – are those that organically manage to produce their own criteria of assessment. We do not believe in the possibility of determining a priori aesthetic criteria distinguishing interesting works from uninteresting works. Interesting works may sometimes, though rarely, teach us what makes them interesting and distinguishes them from other works. A beautiful or good work is not an artwork which stands behind predefined criteria of assessment, but one which makes us recognise these criteria, and establishes them on its own. By affecting the form of our representation through some new representation of the world, an interesting work creates its own interest. It teaches us to appreciate it, and gives us a new method of accounting for or not accounting for its interest. On this view, a masterpiece is nothing other than an art object which, by always representing the same world, transforms the form it appears to us in.

Leaving the modern or contemporary period, we have nonetheless not returned to the classical period. We have not sounded the death knell of works or masterpieces, objects which we produce with art that affect our ways of representing the world to ourselves. But we must abandon the search for Art in self-consciousness, reflexivity, or in the so-called historical progress of representation and the exploration of its conditions, materials, and decomposition (as moderns had done). We must also abandon the search for Art in the presentation of the real or ideal world (as classicists had done). We must again learn to search for human arts without 'Art', works which, for or against rules, realise representational forms of the world.

A masterpiece is clearly not an island, an empire, or a world. Affecting its own form, that is, its conditions of representation, its art, a masterpiece always follows or breaks generic rules, clearly seen in the modern processes of the deregulation of representation. If an interesting artwork is a representation which creates its conditions of assessment, at least partially, every artwork is both *artistic* and *cultural*: artistic, since it has the form of art (its representational form), and cultural, since it has rules, any rules (its representational genre). A human art combines the formal potential of *no-matter-what* and the normative power of generic cultural rules, which objectively limit and determine the representational domain. Every work uses cunning with one as much as the other. Formally representing no-matter-what, it loses its determination and objective intensity. Generically representing, according to codes, figures, and conventions, it loses its formal singularity. It navigates near the shores between these two limits.

The artistic is therefore the expression of the human capacity to form representations. The cultural is the expression of the human capacity to determine them.

Notes

1. For instance, Louis Hjelmslev researched the characteristics common to what he calls possible 'restricted languages', which serve definite purposes of meaning, like traffic lights, a telephone dial, or a clock tower's chime, and what he calls 'pass-key languages', through which any meaning can be translated. He primarily refers to the submission of units to *rules*: 'there is a regulated arrangement prevailing in every immediate linguistic fact', Louis Hjelmslev, 'The Basic Structure of Language', p. 129.

2. 'Tema 4' from Kurt Schwitters' Dadaist sound poem *Ursonate*.

3. Stéphane Mallarmé invented this word in the rhyme of his *Sonnet allégorique de lui-même* (1868), also known as *Sonnet en X*.

4. After his Dadaist period, Hans Arp and his wife Sophie Taeuber-Arp became members of 'Cercle et Carré'.

5. Arthur Rimbaud, 'Letter to Paul Demeny, Charleville, 15 May 1871', p. 375. [Translation modified.]

6. The stringent though dated rules which define the enigmatically English classical detective novel as an authentic *genre* are set out at the end of John Dickson Carr's 'The Grandest Game in the World', pp. 323–4: '1. The criminal shall never turn out to be the detective, or any servant, or any character whose thoughts we have been allowed to share. 2. The criminal shall never at any time be under serious suspicion until the unmasking. If you haven't the ingenuity to keep his identity a secret until the end, at least pretend you have. Even if the reader outguesses you, and your thunderbolt ending doesn't come off, the effect is far more satisfying than if you apologise for your murderer by "clearing" him in an early chapter. 3. The crime shall be

the work of one person. While the murderer in some instances may be allowed to have a confederate, you will ruin your story if two or three or four people are dragged in as accomplices. The essence of a detective story is that the one guilty man shall fool the seven innocent; not that the one innocent shall be fooled by the seven guilty. 4. The crime shall be clean-cut. If a character disappears and is assumed to be murdered, state frankly what has happened to him. If he hasn't been murdered it's a pity; but the reader has a right to a clear stating of the problem.' Note that the most beautiful Agatha Christie novel, *The Murder of Roger Ackroyd*, violates the first rule, that the best Stanslis-André Steeman novel, *L'Assassin habite au 21*, clearly goes beyond the third rule, and that Dickson Carr's own masterpiece, *The Burning Court*, cheerfully rides roughshod over the fourth rule in its famous last chapter.

7. For details of this analysis, which is very crudely summarised here, and for studies on the emergence of these new arts, allow me to refer to my doctoral thesis, *Arts anciens, arts nouveaux*.

Chapter IX

Culture

1. Plural Cultures, Universal Culture, Naturalised Culture

In *Beyond Nature and Culture*,[1] Philippe Descola claims that the idea of 'culture' arose from a tension between at least two of the 164 meanings of the term catalogued by Alfred Kroeber and Clyde Kluckhorn.[2] Culture, in the singular, is defined as a distinctive characteristic of humanity, in a sense close to 'civilisation'. Cultures, in the plural, are defined as a plurality of human modes of organisation. In 1871, Edward Burnett Tylor stated that:

> Culture or Civilisation, taken in its wide ethnographic sense, is that complex whole, which includes knowledge, belief, art, morals, law, custom, and any other capabilities and habits acquired by man as a member of society.[3]

He defines culture as what distinguishes social humanity *as a whole*, and contrasts this concept with the concept of nature. When Franz Boas established North American ethnology at the dawn of the twentieth century, he defined 'cultures' as beliefs, customs, and institutions that individually characterise different societies. The meaning of cultures derives not from some primitive unity between culture and nature but from the plurality of cultures and the relations that they maintain between each other through an interplay of differences and identities.

Other possible meanings of culture exist, but its primary meaning derives from this conflict between the definition of a unified culture contrasting culture with nature, and the definition of plural cultures contrasting with each other. The problem with the determination of culture as the distinctive property of

Man vis-à-vis Nature is that it assumes that the birth of society as a whole breaks with nature and entails the emergence of (cultural) qualities absolutely irreducible to the natural movement of appearance and the establishment of this social whole on its own. But the problem with the determination of cultures, each culture having meaning only in relation to others, is also the problem of constructing structural relations between cultural systems which take nature to be a catalogue or inventory of neutral possibilities, which each cultural system could appeal to in order to yield a meaningful whole. Wilsonian sociobiology revitalised naturalism. It understood culture as a natural *effect*. Naturalism is contested by two other determinations of culture: culture as a plurality and culture as a unity, independent of nature.

In each of these three cases, the idea of culture is reduced to one culture or several cultures which are naturally connected through the concept of universality. In the case of a unitary culture, the distinguishing feature of humanity is opposed to nature. This is a humanist universality. In the case of plural cultures, each particular human culture is defined in relation to others. The differential system alone is universal. Culture as a natural effect is a set of universal human phenomena reduced to the natural or to the genetic.

The idea of 'culture' is not therefore a *formal* concept, but an *objective* concept pertaining to the universe. It is only conceivable between nature and universality. Culture is not formal, since it pertains to living objects considered *together* and not apprehended *alone* in the world. Culture is objective, connected to the inter-comprehension of objects and events in the universe. It pertains to living and animal things – particularly but not exclusively human things – insofar as they live together. Culture, more precisely, is not particularly opposed to nature, but it is what holds some sets of living animals together *between* nature and universality.

Universality is what holds for the universe, the biggest possible thing. It aims at maximum comprehension. Nature, on the other hand, does not aim at the universe, but constitutes the universe. Just as 'no-matter-what' was – in Book I – what 'entered' into a thing, nature is all that 'enters' into objects and events. Nature is therefore the minimum objective determination of the relations between objects and events. It constitutes the relations between the being and comprehension of these objects and events, their order, though it is not itself determined or constituted by anything. Nothing accounts for nature or the so-called natural laws, since nature is a concept accounting for what constitutes the objective order of the universe, though it is not itself explicable in these terms.

Nature *is* the universe in the same way that 'no-matter-what' *is in* the world. It constitutes objectivity, but nothing objective constitutes it. Therefore, one cannot say of any object, or of any relation between objects, that it *is* natural; nothing is natural. Nature is *this* object, is in *this* object, and constitutes *this* objective relation, precisely because nothing can be natural or enter into nature.

Humanity, no more than any other animal species, is not natural. Nothing of *what* animals *do* is natural in the strict sense of the term. Nature is *what makes* an animal, everything that constitutes an animal.

Moreover, everything that animals do is not cultural. Culture is not the *opposite* of nature. But when animals aim at universality, that is, aim at understanding the universe through their behaviour – particularly by representing the universe – then everything that is between the nature which is in them and the universality which they aim at is 'cultural'. In this way, one can consider culture as strong or weak (for example, symbolic cultures or material cultures).

2. Between Nature and Universality: Culture

Culture is the *milieu* between nature and universality for naturally constituted animals who attempt to constitute the universe by presenting and representing things. In this way, culture is not essentially connected to humanity. Other primates who discover new, more universal behaviours, understand more things, transmit these behaviours, and represent and present things, also possess a culture. Take the famous and controversial example reported by the schoolteacher Satsue Mito. On the Japanese island of Koshima,[4] Imo, a macaque, discovered how to wash sweet potatoes in a freshwater stream, removing soil from them before eating them. This behaviour did not exist in the neighbouring colonies, and yet, after its discovery, was transmitted from generation to generation and became widespread among local macaque groups; eight out of ten macaques acquired this technique. One may rationally think that this behaviour is in some weak and unrestricted sense 'cultural'. Feeding was natural for these macaques. The transmitted desire to eat the best possible tasting potato indicates a search for a universal, that is, for a 'possible maximum'. Between the two, the possibility of an individual act, then transmitted and inherited, connecting nature and universality, produced culture.

Many animal species have 'presentational' cultures. The human species has, in addition, a 'representational' culture, which expresses itself via rule-bound or deregulated arts.

Therefore, every set of rules that holds *between* nature and universality, through presentation or representation, is cultural. A cultural rule is the determination either of 'possible *possibilia*' (such as the washing of sweet potatoes, which was previously a nonexistent possibility for macaques) or of 'impossible *possibilia*' (such as every prohibition, which recommends not doing what one can, however, do – in games, languages, bans on incest, kinship systems, strategies of alliance and counter-alliance). It is clear that all animal behaviours which presuppose orders of precedence, of prohibition, and of dominance are cultural. Human culture, in the strict sense, is thus not something specific, but the intensification of the cultural animal, in the broadest sense. Its development is marked by new systems of rules and representational regulation: rule-bound languages, conceptual knowledge, artistic disciplines, and normative groups.

The cultural animal is clearly not opposed to nature, as early ethnologists claimed. Nor is the cultural animal opposed to universality, as relativists claimed who counted on the differential intensity between human sets of rules from one group to another, thus dissolving the possibility of a common universe. The cultural animal stands, in truth, equidistant from nature and universality.

Nature constitutes every animal. All animals aim to collectively comprehend a universe through presentation or representation, that is, to make their behaviour superlative, to direct it towards the most unrestricted possible comprehension of possibilities. All animals must construct rules. In order to separate nature from the universe, they must determine possible *possibilia* and impossible *possibilia*. And each culture is precisely what separates nature from the universe.

Nature is the objective universe. Nature constitutes the universe. But the objective universe is not natural. If it were natural, it would be compact. When animals attempt to distinguish the universe from nature, they show how culture derives from nature and universality. But only *some* cultures are between nature and the universe. The plurality of cultures is necessary for two reasons.

First, de-compacting nature and universality requires passing through a cultural intermediary. According to our logic, nature and universality cannot be obtained in a single culture, since a single culture would directly fuse nature and universe. Second, each culture is an arbitrary and contingent set of rules, of possible and impossible *possibilia*. Each culture denies certain possibilities and accepts others, such that one cultural combination can always be contrasted with another.

The diversity of cultures intensified in the human species while being neutralised in many other animal species. In order to distinguish nature ('what is in all objects') and the universe ('what all objects are'), this diversity differentiates necessity from contingency, the determination of some rules at the expense of others. All prohibitions, uses, customs, systems of alliance, and representational genres double the possibility of some relations between humans by establishing these relations as either possible or impossible. Nature is not universal. Therefore, an order of objects and events exists, but the objective universe is irreducible to the flat and undifferentiated formal world.

Philippe Descola has shown that the limit between nature and culture is cultural, precisely because nature is not an object or a set of objects and events comparable and opposable to a culture. Nature constitutes objects together – namely, living objects. Culture is a given order of these objects, bound by identifiable rules. Nature is unidirectional: it *is* things, but it *comprehends* nothing. Nature therefore does not have qualities, particulars, or limits. On the other hand, a culture has two senses. Nature constitutes each culture, while each culture constitutes a universal. A culture both *is* and *comprehends*. Universality comprehends the maximum of possible objects and events, but is not, on its own, an object or an event.

3. Culture Exists if More than One of them Exists

Cultures cannot be universally equivalent, since they distinguish nature from universality. No culture can be universal, since cultures are systematic sets of rules. And, for the same reason that there cannot be an absolutely universal language, which would comprehend all possible languages, go beyond them, and replace them, each culture is a particular selection of some possibilities at the expense of others, required to make significations function.

A culture makes the production of a *common* sense possible, through language, rule-bound representations, codes, uses, and norms, under the express condition that this culture is not *alone*. Hegel's *Sittlichkeit* fulfils this function. Culture is a particular that intervenes between nature and universality, in order for animals – and particularly human animals – to live among objects and events ordered through several different meanings.

But from roughly around the end of the eighteenth century, an increasingly powerful doubt affected culture, and raised the problem of the very extent of its universalisation. Today, culture is considered from a critical distance – for example, in Adorno's or Valéry's pessimistic stance towards culture,[5] in Jean Dubuffet's discussion of consciousness in *Asphyxiating Culture*,[6] in situationist irony against cultural commodities, or in Christopher Lasch's analyses of mass culture.[7] Here, aesthetic values and Art were always opposed to a democratic and global 'culture'. They described modernity's universalisation of culture, which made humanity compact. If only one culture exists, which directly accepts and assimilates resistant counter-cultures, then nature universalises itself and the universe naturalises itself. It follows that culture is only the passage through our nature, desires, and needs, leading to all that exists, to the growing expanse of the accessible universe. It also follows that this universe of humanity, a composite of representations, languages, customs, dress, and signs of all genres, would be absolutely naturalised, since it would be unique and determined.

Georg Simmel's tragedy of culture[8] involves not only a contradiction between our artistic representations, the works of the mind, and their social sedimentation, but also the reduction of the distance between the universe and our natural needs. This reduction would entail the unification of culture, which would merely be a weakened link between what affects us and what we aim at. Several cultures, several distinct sets of rules, must exist in order to articulate our nature and universality. The idea of a global formalised set of representations, modes of presence, behaviours, customs, and 'possible *possibilia*' is compact. The distance would then be reduced between *that which is us* and *that which we are*. If there were truly only one single culture, then there would not be any culture, but a universal Nature and a natural universe of humanity. What constitutes us would be directly attained in what we attain, such that all our works, uses, ways, or representational or presentational rules would be equally possible. And we could identify the human universe with the utterly flat formal world that lacks all cultural depth. For the distinguishing feature of every culture is to do some *particular* thing with nature in order to understand the universe.

After Claude Lévi-Strauss deplored the unification of human cultures in the twentieth century, the defence of the plurality of cultures admitted the new ideal of 'counter-cultures'. The goal of a counter-culture was not simply, as was believed, to subvert the dominant culture. Instead, it was a search for the possibility of plural cultures and the invention of alternative cultures. But with the structural reappropriation of counter-cultures into a single culture, maintaining a difference between universe and nature to avoid making humanity compact became difficult. Modern minds were plagued by this difficulty.

The difficulty above all derives from the representation of a sense of history through which human cultures would become compact. Ultimately, only a compact mind existed, but certainly not Hegel's prophesy of the absolute Spirit. A culture is not a world. Never did a culture triumph in the absolute and in solitude, for a culture is a distributive and classificatory order of relative objects. No culture exists unless several exist, unless a society of cultures exists. Universal history undermined the constitution of a society of cultures at the same time that it made possible the ideal of universal history.

Notes

1. Philippe Descola, *Beyond Nature and Culture*, p. 72.
2. Alfred Kroeber and Clyde Kluckhorn, *Culture*.
3. Edward B. Tylor, *Primitive Culture*, p. 1.
4. Masao Kawai, 'Newly-acquired Pre-cultural Behavior of the Natural Troop of Japanese Monkeys on Koshima Islet'. In this remarkably detailed report, Kawai talks about macaque 'pre-culture'. In 1959, Syunzo Kawamura talked of simian 'sub-cultures' on these Japanese islands (Kawamura, 'The process of sub-culture propagation among Japanese macaques'). Ron Amundson harshly criticises Lyall Watson's reckless use of this example and the theory of 'the hundred monkey phenomenon', according to which the 'miracle on Koshima' marks a sudden qualitative leap of some animals beyond their natural limits. See Amundson, 'The Hundredth Monkey Phenomenon'.

5. See Michel Deguy, 'Paul Valéry et la culture', who finds in Valéry the inspiration for his own critique of contemporary 'culture'.
6. Jean Dubuffet, *Asphyxiating Culture and Other Writings*.
7. Christopher Lasch, 'Mass Culture Reconsidered'.
8. Georg Simmel, 'The Concept and Tragedy of Culture'.

Chapter X

History

1. Universal History

The problem of universal history does not result from the possibility of organising the universe in time, but rather from considering time as a universe. How is it possible to grasp time – structured by the present (maximal presence), the past (weakening of presence), and the future (maximal absence) – as a cumulative order of all past instants, from the most remote to the most present? We raised this question in Chapter III of this book. Universal history inscribes objects and events in an order of comprehension, which leads to the present and points towards the future. The cultural structuring of time as if it were a universe yields two difficulties. First, temporally, the past is to the present as *less* presence is to *more* presence, and no continuity exists between past, present, and future. The future is to the present as maximum absence is to maximum presence. The past, a progressive weakening of presence, is comprehended in the present. Therefore, one can never trace a continuous arrow beginning in the past, passing through the present, and directed at the future. Second, the past is comprehended in the present, the greatest possible presence. By definition, the present is the universe (the biggest possible thing) of the past. Therefore, one can never place the past and the present together in something bigger, that we could call history, which would embody their common universe. The past is in the present – but past and present together are in nothing that one commonly calls 'history'.

The past alone remains to be ordered in history. But the present still acts as a placeholder, a universal container of the past. In truth, the past is not in history, but always already in the present.

Universal history – cultural time considered generally as a universe – cannot function unless it is identified with the present.

Universal history would already exist – what we call 'now', an immediate summation or outcome of everything that had been up to now.

However, 'now' is not enough to construct what is often called a *discursive* history of all that has occurred. One must therefore imagine a narrative that transfigures the differences between past, present, and future, in order to place them on the same plane called 'history'.

Universal history is the expression of the desire to develop time as a plane, in order to progressively make the human past, present, and future of the whole world equivalent, as if they were composed of the same stuff and could remain together in a history. The common quality that one projected onto the past, present, and future in order to historicise them is, as Paul Ricœur indicates,[1] the capacity to be placed in narration.

History is thus tied to the belief that past, present, and future, without being equally *narrated*, are equally *narratable* – that is, they share the capacity to be or become narrative objects.

2. Prophetic Consciousness and the End of History

Oracular, prophetic, and apocalyptic literature presents visions of the future. But all prophesies are representations of the future *in the future*. A prophesy is a vision of the future by a human being of the present, who describes this vision for other human beings of the present. Prophets do not merely narrate what will happen tomorrow, but they often reveal in symbolic terms 'the things which must shortly take place',[2] which will mark the end of the present time, as the *Book of Revelation* proclaims. A prophesy marks the irruption of the future in the very heart of the present, in the visual form of the negative or end of history. The future is not merely the projective place of possibilities, but the *verso* of history which imposes itself on the *recto*: 'there shall be no more death, nor sorrow, nor crying. There shall be no more pain',[3] 'the nations of those who are saved shall walk in its light',[4] 'there shall be no night there'.[5] One finds these same forms in Nostradamus: 'the young lion shall overcome the older; the blue head will inflict upon the white head',[6] as well as in Nekauba's ancient divination: 'The Roman Empire will end one-thousand two-hundred years after its founding'. But these forms can also be found in Pammenes' predictions and al-Kindi's legendary horoscope,[7] foretelling the decline of the caliphate, the loss of his constituents, and the rebirth of Islam in the year 1379 of the Hijra, that is, in 2001.

Prophesies and predictions are thus representations of the future, which describe in the *future* the reverse side of all that has occurred up to the present. Apocalypses are revelations of the future as the end of human time, in which the future appears symbolically as the very opposite of history. Prophesies, predictions, and apocalypses do not tell us about what will happen or will become a day of the past, but rather about the form and end of what has happened up to the present. They do not recall the day after, but the eternal night which threatens us at all times. This threat of the eternal night makes what is called the 'precautionary principle' function.

For Jean-Pierre Dupuy[8] 'precaution' is at best confounded with prevention, which assumes a metaphysics according to which the event to be prevented – the catastrophe – is kept at bay in a world of unactualised possibilities. Dupuy contrasts this metaphysics of potentiality and actuality with Bergsonian novelty, the irruption of an event which was nonexistent prior to its happening. Dupuy is caught in a double envelopment between a traditional conception of the future, according to which the catastrophe is foreseeable (since the catastrophe is possible before being actual), and a non-traditional conception, according to which the catastrophe is unforeseeable (since the catastrophe is only possible after having happened). He thus asks how to make a rational, enlightened decision possible when faced with catastrophe. This decision theory ought to be situated equidistant from Hans Jonas's theory of the principle of responsibility and the impossibility of thinking about the absolute novelty of an event, and from Henri Bergson's theory of the emergence of novelty and the impossibility of rational prevention.

Dupuy suggests making the future catastrophe undecidable, speaking of its consequences in the future perfect tense. According to Dupuy, only in this way will one be able to find the necessary resources to prevent it. Dupuy identifies this 'apotropaic' argument with prophetic activity, which necessitates a catastrophe in order to preclude it from happening. He recalls the figure of Jonas, son of Amittai, in the Bible, whom he associates with Hans Jonas through the homonym. God asks Jonas to prophesy the fall of Nineveh. Jonas doesn't do it, since he knows that by warning the Ninevites, they will convert, that their city will be spared, and that his prophesy will prove false – and therefore efficacious. Since Jonas was the enemy of Nineveh, he did not wish for the salvation of its inhabitants, and he knew that his prophesy would have at best prevented the fulfilment of what the prophesy announced.

For Dupuy, the dilemma of every catastrophe is that the evil prophet will be taken seriously only after the catastrophe has occurred, but it will be too late; if it is taken seriously in time, the catastrophe will not occur and the prophesy will therefore prove false.

Nonetheless, the picture of prophets that Dupuy's 'enlightened catastrophe' conjures up does not appear to inscribe the future in history. On the contrary, to consider the catastrophe is to place all human history under the condition of its end or 'self-destruction', rather than its continuation.

Therefore, prophets are those who decide that one can attribute the future to history only on the condition that they represent history's *end* – whether the end is positive (the City of God, the End of History à la Alexandre Kojève or Francis Fukuyama) or negative (apocalypse or catastrophe). Like a messiah, a prophet succeeds in thinking of history only on the horizon of its end or the determination of a final endpoint, which entails either annihilation and disaster, or success and salvation.

In contrast, the historicisation of human time appears to have consisted in considering history – against the prophetic tradition, messianism, or catastrophism – on the horizon of its own continuation, of a future which would merely be 'to pass'. This not-yet-past cultural future which will pass is the key to the (good and evil) secularisation of universal history.

Prophetic consciousness admits history only if it can see the end of it. On the other hand, historical consciousness sees history serially.

3. Historical Consciousness and the Continuation of History

From Renaissance humanism and the Enlightenment to the French revolution, through the conjunction of social criticisms of the present state, religious miracles, and prophesies, social expectations appear wherein possibilities are placed in the future and written *in the present*. Social expectations are not prophesies revealing how the world *will be*, but pictures describing how the world *is* some years or centuries later. They are not apocalypses unveiling the reverse side of our present state, but texts depicting another present state in some distant future.

In the European world of letters, these expectations were successful both as real, though warped, projections of the present situation and as criticisms of the present situation through the transposition of another possible present time in the future.[9]

Louis-Sébastien Mercier writes, speaking both of the present and of the year 2440: 'The two ages belong to the same history.'[10]

But though the idea of a history common to a present and future date becomes clear, the continuity of this history does not yet become clear. These narratives do not narrate the evolution of humanity between a present and future date. Rather, they project the present moment onto a future moment, which clarifies and reflects the present moment.

Only a century later will narratives appear that are not simply projections of the present, but projections of a unified and organised past. They are now written *in the past*. They are chronicles of the future and what happened between today and tomorrow. One passed from descriptions of a future year reflecting the present year by implicitly criticising the latter, to narratives of tens, hundreds, or thousands of years, which henceforth reflect and direct the past and all human history. One went from the present picture projected onto some future year to organised, rationalised histories projected into the future. One passed from the future moment to a conception of the future as duration and as history.

Breaking with theology, the messianic tradition, and apocalyptic discourses told or written in the future, we no longer find representations of a reverse side or end of time, but rather a continuous time which allows for the opening of a certain period of time between today and the end of time. The time interval between now and eternity is increasingly determined. After the progressive assimilation of possibilities, we witness a kind of invention of the *historical future*.

By considering time as continuous, homogeneous, uniform, and universal, we think that the future is always a past that has not yet passed. In this way, we create an image of the future as what, not yet being of history, *will be* of history, and as what, not yet being narrated, *will be* narratable.

The future then becomes a homogeneous continuation of the

past, giving it its direction and meaning. Philosophy breaks with the theory of an ahistorical origin, conceived as the reverse side of history, and with the myth of origins, replaced by a homogeneous future in the past. It is no longer an ahistorical myth which gives meaning to human history. It is the future that is to become historical.

In the French, German, and Scottish Enlightenment, a profound mutation occurred in the intellectual domain through the formation of 'philosophies of history' (the expression is Voltaire's) against Thomas Hobbes's and Jean-Jacques Rousseau's contractualism: views of history as an empirical chaos of facts and views of an ahistorical genesis of humanity.

Against theology and Rousseau's ahistorical contractualism, Voltaire is doubtless the first both to conceive of the idea of a genuine universal history which cannot be reduced to a series of military events, and to confront religious narratives of the formation of humanity.

Voltaire's concept of history is disorderly: 'a chaos of events, of factions, of revolutions, and of crimes'.[11] Condorcet also combated ahistorical contractualism. He considered it as one of the sources of the Terror's fanaticism, which he was the victim of. He presented a well-ordered picture of this universal history, which does not limit itself to the particularity of peoples or to the picturesque plurality of habits: 'It is an historical picture of the progress of the human mind that I try to sketch; and not the history of governments, laws, habits, customs, and opinions, among the different peoples who had successively occupied the globe.'[12] This organised, universal picture of human progress is meant to be 'the history of a single people'.[13]

The essential question then becomes that of the *orientation* of the picture, and, consequently, of the future direction this progress is supposed to organise from the picture's otherwise chaotic facts. To explain this orientation, Condorcet takes up the Rousseauist concept of indefinite perfectability, but historicises it. Humanity self-perfects and will self-perfect. Condorcet then opens up the problem of a history of the *future*:

> If man can, with almost complete assurance, predict phenomena when he knows their laws, and if, even when he does, he can still, with great expectation of success, forecast the future on the basis of his experience of the past, why, then, should it be regarded as a fantastic

undertaking to sketch, with some pretence to truth, the future destiny of man on the basis of his history?[14]

What is sometimes called the 'Scottish school' presented a hybrid version of this unprecedented project. After David Hume, a heterogeneous group of thinkers like Adam Smith, William Robertson, Adam Ferguson, Dugald Stewart, John Millar, and Henry Home generally take Condorcet's rigid picture to be a natural history of humankind that assimilates cycles and expresses doubts about the destiny and future direction of this history.

The liberal Ferguson criticises Rousseau and the absurd, ahistorical state of nature, on the grounds that all historically successive states of humanity are equally natural and the state of nature is everywhere:

> Such is the state of nature relative to the human species; and, in this, as in every other progressive subject, the present being intermediate to the past and the future, may be different either. Each is a part of the whole; and neither can, with any reason, be said to be more natural than the others. It cannot be said, that it is more natural for the oak to spring from its seed than to overshadow the plain; that it is more natural for water to gush from the land in springs than to flow in rivers, and to mix with the sea.[15]

The problem becomes that of giving 'an accumulative view of its movement throughout'.[16]

This history is *uniform* and not simply *universal*. Complementing Ferguson, Robertson writes that 'in similar circumstances, the faculties of the human mind hold nearly the same course in their progress, and arrive at almost the same conclusions'.[17]

One can therefore imagine projecting this schema onto future peoples.

Ferguson, like all the Scottish school thinkers, refines the schema through the description of ages, periods, and cycles within this continuous history: the ages of hunter-gatherers, shepherds, agriculture, and commerce. In this way, he considers that growth 'in perfection, and [. . .] without end'[18] is linked to the development of the conditions of exchange and of production: commercial expansion, division of labour, and technological progress. But this progress constantly rubs up against morality, and is inevitably accompanied by moral decline. Progress must therefore pay the price of material evolution and compensate for it in some way. The 'admirable virtue' of the Ancients' patriotism becomes obsolete during the development of international commercial forms.

Ferguson then discovers an aporia between two subjects of history: the citizen and the individual. The latter's progress leads to the former's decline.

After Ferguson and Home,[19] doubts emerged about history's exact orientation, which now changes according to the standpoint adopted. Isaak Iselin, the author of *On the History of Humanity*,[20] is indifferent to these doubts. After Leibniz's theodicy, Iselin examined how evil could be historically conceived as a good. Like the above-mentioned philosophers who were opposed to Rousseau, Iselin sought to produce a history of humanity through the facts and prescribe a certain number of historical cycles, identified with peoples and geographical territories; the subjects of history ranged from the Orient to the Mediterranean to the Nordic West. Iselin makes each historical period correspond to an age of life (childhood, adolescence, and adulthood) and to a type of government (Oriental despotism, republic, and enlightened monarchy). These governmental modes do not simply follow one another in a logically deductive order (as in Aristotle) or as geographic or climactic possibilities (as in Montesquieu). Rather, they follow from each other in the concrete historical succession of facts. Bertrand Binoche claims that this well-ordered succession allows Iselin to be 'the first to give an homogeneous representation of the future, a horizon of expectation'.[21]

The main point is that, struggling against the apocalyptic theologies of his time, Iselin presented a universal, rationalised, directed, and homogeneous view of history. It was henceforth possible to pass from an order of the past to a rational representation of the future of humanity.

This problem haunted thinkers such as Johann Gottfried von Herder, who denounced both the dogmatic belief in continuous progress and the denial of access to cultural differences. It evokes the *price to pay* for so-called progress, the orientation of the history of humanity. In the sequence that includes the Oriental, the Egyptian, and the Greek succeeding one another, innocence is lost and replaced by loyalty, which is in turn lost and replaced by ruse and reason, always at the price of the progress of civilisation.

The problem of history's ultimate orientation and the series of cycles discerned from a human past take centre stage. Herder asks, 'In what direction should we order history? In what direction should we connect everything together?'[22]

4. Progress, Fashions, and Seasons

The spectre of *directional* universal histories still haunts Oswald Spengler's and Arnold J. Toynbee's work as well as Fernand Braudel's three levels of time and Robert Bonnaud's 'noosphere' in *Le Système de l'Histoire*.[23]

As the adventurous colonial exploration of the earth gave paradoxical unity to human space, it was quite necessary that human cultural time also unify through the levelling of the formally incomparable past, present, and future. The desire to describe universal history as a flattening of the past, present, and future through pictures and narratives – through the secularisation of both a future destined to become present, past, and narratable and a potential past present [*présent passé en puissance*] – led to Hegelian, Marxist, Comtian, and Darwinist universal narratives. Postmodernism, as we know, contested these Lyotardian 'meta-narratives'.

The desire to be done with history is, however, certainly inscribed in the very structures that it claimed to break with. The idea that we have gone beyond a certain belief in history is connected with the view of our time as an additional history. On this view, the past is history, the present is the end of history, and the future is the invention of other histories and narratives of human time. Jocelyn Benoist claims in *Après la fin de l'Histoire* that the whole is a meta-history.[24] Since historical consciousness emerged, attempts to go beyond history have continuously been written and narrated as histories squared [*histoires au carré*]. One never escapes from history.

While history must universalise to give support to the unification of human cultures, a contradiction appears between the structure of time and the very structure of the universe.

The universe is the biggest possible thing, that comprehends objects which comprehend each other in order from smallest to biggest. To universalise is therefore to order from what comprehends the least to what comprehends the most. On the other hand, time is the articulation of the past (which is comprehended in the present as a weakened presence is comprehended in a maximal presence), of this present, and of a future (or maximal absence, which is also the present's negative and form). Therefore, the past has an objective structure similar to that of the universe; but the present and future maintain a non-objective, formal relation. The present is to the future what a thing is to the world, what a thing is to its form. Time thus combines an *objective* relation (between past and present) and a *formal* relation (between present and future). Universal history's attempt to construct the totality of human time as a universe comes up against the formal relation between present and future. Despite all attempts to assimilate the future into historical narrative, the future systematically breaks the structure of the universe of historical time.

The structure of time stands between a formal structure and an objective structure. The future makes all presents equivalent. All presents, including *past* presents, have had a future and remain within the same future. Since the future exists, each infinitesimal part of the past, each second and each thousandth of a second, are formally equivalent to the present, since each moment of any duration is *alone and equal* before the future, as each thing is *alone and equal* in the world.

The formal structure of the relation between present and future thus short-circuits the order of the objective accumulation of the past – seconds and minutes that are linked together, one after the other. Formally, each instant is equal 'before the future', since the future is the same for every past or present moment: a maximal absence. Formal equality thus short-circuits objective historical accumulation and prevents the constitution of a universal history, whether it is a Marxist, Darwinist, or any other kind of universal history.

To take up Herder's picture, this means that it is necessary to think in and through history, against it, such that all that is gained, all progress, is balanced by an equal loss, like a ship that abandons behind it what it gained by advancing. Universal history cannot formally be an absolute progress because both objective and formal time extend beyond accumulative history to the formal equality of all instants. If there is an objective progress of humanity that lives better, knows more about things, lives longer, less violently, and more consciously, then this progress must only be objective – and not formal – that is, it must remain local. Since each one of the earlier instants must be equivalent to the present, progress must be balanced by a loss and allow formal equality. Since my historical moment would be compact if it were absolutely more and better than that of a human being of the Middle Ages, human consciousness always suspects that what was gained on one side was lost on the other. This equilibrium is essentially realised in the feeling of *nostalgia*, which is not the wound of loss, but the necessity of feeling equal to what is no longer and to what is neither more nor less than what one was, than what always was. 'Golden age' nostalgia, reactionary politics, Proustian fleeting time, and impressions of bygone orders (the Greek cosmos, feudalism, the Renaissance, or the glory of the sixties) embody the movements by which humanity reestablishes history as a plane of equality. Every era that knows itself to be making progress, to be the result of progress, produces incomprehensible nostalgia – since what one must gain objectively (in assurance, prosperity, justice, life expectancy), one must lose proportionally. Not only can a historical being not avoid this equilibrium of cumulative history through a feeling of loss, but a historical being is only a historical being insofar as it articulates objective progress and formal equality, and therefore the equilibrium by the feeling of a loss. A historical being is a being who knows that one loses what one gains, who believes in progress only to experience the melancholia of it.

The concept of progress only partially allows a universal history, since it is reduced to an accumulation of knowledge and experience and to a directional evolution, and self-compacts. Two other concepts, in the absence of which no history exists, correspond to the concept of progress: the concept of fashion and the concept of seasons.

While progress is the linear or dialectical no-return, seasons are a *return of the same* and fashions a *return of the different*. Fashions and seasons objectively compensate for all progress. They structure a possible non-compact history and make a plane of equality of all moments possible. Seasons project onto the course of time the repetition of identical and regular cells that identify returns of unchanged moments in human time: autumn, winter, spring, and summer in Western culture; the dry and rainy seasons in parts of Asia and elsewhere. Since the emergence of agrarian societies, seasons have structured the impression of natural time. After urbanisation, it is repeated in school, political, and sports calendars, guaranteeing the temporal existence of the *same*. No human complaint is more superficial and at the same time more profoundly revealing of our anxiety than the eternal complaint: 'there are no more seasons'. For, if there are no longer any seasons (in the formal sense, and not merely in the calendrical sense), then humanity would live in universal history, in an indeterminate progress, and in a cumulative newness – like a transient God abandoning humanity. Humans would always be absolutely superior to the humans that preceded them, but infinitely inferior to those that will come after them. Who can live while thinking that they are *absolutely* superior to those who lived before them? Who can live while thinking that they are *absolutely* inferior to those who will live after them? Formally, I must be something like a human being of long ago, and a human being of tomorrow must be something like me now. If I become the number of a series that continues without obtaining formal equality with what precedes and what follows, nothing makes sense any more, for everything has but one, unique sense: the sense of progress made compact.

While seasons allow the return of the same, fashions allow the return of the different. Fashion is not a superficial structure of time. It is the possibility that something which makes unfashionable what existed before will be made unfashionable by what exists after it. It is this something that returns to every moment. In this way, what was unfashionable returns to make unfashionable what made it unfashionable. Fashion is an endless revenge of the dead on its murderer. Fashion is the executioner assassinated by the victim, who becomes the executioner in turn. Phenomena of fashion are often the subject of mockery, above all when they are blown up out of proportion or seem to have something movingly superficial about them. But Baudelaireans have always known that fashion saves us from progress.

Seasons – the return of the same, an unchanged schedule or series – and fashions – the return of the different, things that overcome and are overcome – are images associated with progress, required for the existence of history. Every history is an interaction between progress, fashions, and seasons.

5. Objective Progress and Formal Equilibrium

Since recycling is structurally a part of every history, no dustbins of universal history exist.[25] Certain theorists love to believe that the things, ideas, and people that they hold in contempt will absolutely disappear through history. But this plausible argument is *false*. Everything that historically tends to disappear also tends to reappear. Nothing gives more power to an idea, for example, than its historical eclipse, its forgetting, or its placement in the cultural minority. Since every historical object is also a thing, it is never reduced to nothingness. It always has a chance to reappear. And even the worst, once it appears, never ceases to be capable of being.

'History [. . .] is a nightmare from which I am trying to awake',[26] said Stephen Dedalus in James Joyce's *Ulysses*. Yes, surely something nightmarish exists in every history, since it simultaneously guarantees the possibility of local progress (through the duration of our life, social justice, in the beauty of artworks, health, the conditions of life, and the realisation of hopes) and the necessity of a flattening of all moments and all that was. Evils that appear in history are forever possible; they never cease being possible; and we have to make do with them *forever*.

But the formal flattening of all that appears is also the condition of objective progress. Progress is an accumulation of objects and events in an idea, as if objects and events were one day able to fulfil and attain this idea. For this reason, *objective* progress only exists through accumulation. Formally, nothing can progress, since everything is equal. Progress is thus strictly relative to an idea, however big or universal it may be. That humanity progresses towards a longer life, for example, seems indisputable, but without any guarantee. However, this idea of increasing life expectancy on its own constitutes progress. Progress exists only in ideas, and, formally, these ideas are equal things, which are never *absolutely* either more or less than others.

Since all progress is objective, it is also an inequality. What takes part in accumulation is always less than what will take part in the realisation of the idea towards which it progressed. Kant realised that the inequality between past and present inherent in all progress is a sacrifice (for future generations). But this can take place only against the background of a formal equality. Whoever holds to the moment of realising historical progress loses the struggles of those who aimed at this realisation. All talk of pioneers, all monuments, all human commemorations are generally empty gestures that objectivise the loss that those who live at the end of some progress owe vis-à-vis those who were the means of this progress. For the latter were thus caught in objectively inferior historical conditions: a more difficult material life, a lower life expectancy, and so on.

The progress of human culture derives from the increasing

comprehension of the cultural by a unified global culture – connected to the realisation, through exploration, colonialisation, and exchange, of the *finitude* of our planet, the map of which, since the Pacific's marking with buoys and the Polar conquest, no longer has any *blanks*. But this objective geographic progress of knowledge and circulation is connected to a loss, through fashions and seasons (habits, customs, linguistic returns that were thought lost). This loss in particular makes human culture, which is increasingly more universal, have increasingly less different universals – or, more precisely, different *accesses* to universality.

History is not merely the unified time of human cultures, which becomes a single, spatially unified universal culture. It is also the human equilibrium of this time. History does not accompany the course of time, but, rather, *accentuates* it objectively (through progress) and *compensates for* it formally (by establishing a plane of equality of all moments).

Human culture increasingly comprehends all human cultures and becomes increasingly more universal. However, what it gains historically in a greater universe, it loses in a plurality of universes. It gains a universe which *is* more, but it *has* fewer different cultural universes. Conversely, distinct human cultures made humanity gain more different universes, but universes that were less. We call this the principle of historical equilibrium.

This equilibrium is a plane of equality on which things are not ordered through accumulation, or cultural or historical hierarchisation, but through the possibility of the equal value of things beyond rules and progress. This brings us to the economy of objects. The *economy* is what establishes a possible plane of objective interchangeability, short-circuiting the cultural order (in space) and the historical order (in time).

Notes

1. 'Time becomes human time to the extent that it is organised after the manner of a narrative', Paul Ricœur, *Time and Narrative*, p. 3.
2. *Book of Revelation*, NKJV 22:6.
3. Ibid., NKJV 21:4.
4. Ibid., NKJV 21:24.
5. Ibid., NKJV 22:5.
6. Nostradamus' quatrains are legion on the Internet.
7. The standard, though dated, reference for most of these examples

remains August Bouché-Leclerq's *Histoire de la divination dans l'Antiquité.*

8. Jean-Pierre Dupuy, *Pour un catastrophisme éclairé*, p. 150.

9. Louis-Sébastien Mercier's *Memoirs of the Year Two Thousand Five Hundred* (1771); Herbert Croft's *The Abbey of Kilkhampton, or, Monumental records for the year 1980* (1780); Karl Heinrich Wachsmuth's *Das Jahr Zweitausend vierhundert und vierzig* (1783); Johan Herman Wessel's *Anno 7603* (1785); Restif de la Bretonne's *L'An deux-mille* (1789); Sylvain Maréchal's *Le Jugement dernier des rois* (1793); Daniel Gottlieb Gebhard Mehring's *Das Jahr 2500* (1794). Many of these texts are available in French on gallica.fr.

10. Mercier, *Memoirs of the Year Two Thousand Five Hundred.*

11. Voltaire, *Essai général sur les moeurs et l'esprit des nations et sur les principaux faits de l'Histoire*, p. 905.

12. Condorcet, *Tableau historique des progrès de l'esprit humain (1772–1794)*, p. 466.

13. Condorcet, *Sketch for a Historical Picture of the Progress of the Human Mind*, p. 9.

14. Ibid., p. 173.

15. Adam Ferguson, 'Of Man's Progressive Nature', p. 203.

16. Ibid., p. 200.

17. William Robertson, *The History of America*, p. 384.

18. Ferguson, *An Essay on the History of Civil Society*, p. 199.

19. In the *Sketches on the History of Man*, Henry Home describes four stages of human history: first, isolated hunter-gatherers; second, societies formed around herds of domestic animals; third, an agricultural activity necessitating commerce, work, and possibly slavery; and fourth, the migration to ports and merchant cities, and civil constitutions. Home projects these four stages on the geography of Scotland and on several other territories.

20. Isaak Iselin, *Über die Geschichte der Menschheit.*

21. Bertrand Binoche, *Les Trois Sources des philosophies de l'histoire (1764–1798)*, p. 166.

22. Johann Gottfried von Herder, *Outlines of a Philosophy of the History of Man.*

23. Robert Bonnaud, *Le Système de l'Histoire.*

24. 'What connects one discourse [on the end of history] to another – for example, Derrida commenting on Fukuyama – is a common operation: history, precisely, bears its own end', Jocelyn Benoist and Fabio Merlini, *Après la fin de l'Histoire*, p. 20.

25. In 1917, the day after the Bolshevik seizure of power, Leon Trotsky

took the floor and shouted at the delegates of the leftist parties still hostile to the Revolution: 'You are pitiful, isolated individuals! You are bankrupts. Your role is played out. Go where you belong from now on – into the dustbin of history!'

26. James Joyce, *Ulysses*, p. 34.

Chapter XI

Economy of Objects

1. Utility

The future of the economy is the future of the *utility* of objects. Utilitarian thinkers sought to construct a formal distribution channel of uses, curtailing the systems of cultural rules and historical progress.

Utilitarianism was a minority position in nineteenth-century English philosophy. After many twists and turns, it gradually spread across all branches of modern knowledge: economics, animal ethics, morality, political science, and law. This 'consequentialist' moral theory focuses on an action's consequences, and not on an action's intention or intrinsic value. The theory recommends acting so that every being's well-being increases. It is not egoistic (since it does not concern the value of my own well-being), but concerns the *calculation* of the values of human actions. Utilitarianism desubstantialises both actions and things in their relation to the sentient and moral beings that we are, and opens up an evential and objective network. The value of events and objects depends on the way in which they contextually affect surrounding events and objects; their value does not depend on some kind of essence or value intrinsic to things or beings.

This utilitarian world of exchangeable and calculable things and events may appear to be the flat and formal world of Book I. In fact, as we will demonstrate, this utilitarian world is merely an economic approximation of our flat and formal world. The utilitarian world curtails history's objective accumulation. Contrasting this world with a moral, sociological, or anthropological state of exception is an empty gesture. Instead, one must play it at its own game, by determining how its desubstantialisation of used and exchanged things always remains incomplete.

303

Jeremy Bentham's hedonist utilitarianism is a moral *economy* that consists in maximising the well-being of the greatest number of persons. It is a system of value equivalence that operates through the compensation and optimisation of all potential losses with higher gains. David Hume and Claude Adrien Helvétius inspired Bentham to present a moral economy in which a thing's or an action's value depends on an addition to or a subtraction from the sum total of well-being within which the thing or action is bound. Benthamian ethics first limits itself to individual or collective social behaviours. It then models utility as an essential value of things and of human actions, through a general economic calculation of the happiness of the totality of beings who take part in the whole. In our terms, it is a calculation relating objects or events to their universe:

> By the *principle of utility* is meant that principle which approves or disapproves of every action whatsoever, according to the tendency which it appears to have to augment or diminish the happiness of the party whose interest is in question [. . .] By *utility* is meant that property in any object, whereby it tends to produce benefit, advantage, pleasure, good, or happiness.[1]

Utility is therefore the potential of each thing involved in a human relation to positively contribute to and affect the economy of all sentient beings – in other words, to augment pleasure and to diminish global, abstract suffering:

> Nature has placed mankind under the governance of two sovereign masters, *pain* and *pleasure*. It is for them alone to point out what we ought to do, as well as to determine what we shall do. On the one hand the standard of right and wrong, on the other the chain of causes and effects, are fastened to their throne.[2]

Benthamian principles represent a specific idea of human nature that reduces human sensibility to pleasure and pain, and models human activity through an economy and calculation of what increases pleasure and diminishes pain. Every loss is and must be compensated for by a more important gain in absolute value. Utilitarianism may be the best picture we have of a plane or flat reason, levelling the topography and accumulation of all histories.

2. Flat Reason

John Stuart Mill was the son of one of Bentham's followers, who raised him in accordance with the strict rules of *early* utilitarianism. Mill was arguably the most significant critic of the Benthamian use of the principle of utility. He experienced internally the psychological limits of behaviour modelled on a rational norm of calculating our pleasures and pains. Mill promoted an *indirect* utilitarianism, which takes utility as the evaluative and non-descriptive norm of our actions. Mill's indirect utilitarianism considers the maximisation of the sum total of well-being as the evaluative criteria of our actions, and not merely as the cause for our actions, impulses, and cognitive life. In this way, he made the utilitarian economy of human actions more flexible: 'I never indeed varied in the conviction that happiness is the test of all rules of conduct, and the end of life. But I now thought that this end was only to be attained by not making it the direct aim.'[3]

Utility – that is, the optimisation of the sum total of happiness – thus remains the yardstick of all values, and not the cause which sets all our actions in motion. Mill prefers to think that there are a rich variety of human reasons to act, but utility is the ultimate 'criterion'. Mill thus structures the plurality of human reasons and the unity of reason on which they must be modelled.

Through the extension of use-value, Mill establishes a portrait of restricted utility which reduces human operations to the direct and mechanical search for a quantitative gain in abstract well-being. Bentham's rules:

> are, therefore ([he] thought), favourable to prudence and clearsightedness, but a perpetual worm at the root both of the passions and of the virtues: and above all, fearfully undermine all desires and all pleasures which are the result of association, that is, according to the theory [he] held, all except the purely physical and organic: of the entire insufficiency of which, to make life desirable, no one had a stronger conviction than [he] had.[4]

In other words, the Benthamian economy of pleasures and pains analytically accounts for human operations, except that it holds that the very desirability of life for whoever lives it is trivial. What is important – the very condition of life – becomes a trivial remainder in life, the unquantifiable value of the existence of whoever must be capable of quantifying and calculating what she gives and receives. According to Mill, Bentham presents a model of humanity that restricts humanity to a balance of pleasures and pains. Self-interests and interests for other beings order human actions.

> Man is conceived by Bentham as a being susceptible of pleasures and pains, and governed in all his conduct partly by the different modifications of self-interest, and the passions commonly classed as selfish, partly by sympathies, or occasionally antipathies, toward other beings. And here Bentham's conception of human nature stops.[5]

What Benthamian utilitarianism lacks is the conception of a value that escapes the calculation of equivalence between what is lost and what is gained and the compensation of the former by the latter. In other words, it lacks something that would be valued on its own. Distantly echoing Aristotle's opposition between *praxis* and *poïesis*, Mill understands the necessity of a value within utilitarian calculation, but valued on its own, not by equivalence and interchangeability: '[Bentham] faintly recognises, as a fact in human nature, the pursuit of any other ideal end for its own sake.'[6]

For Mill, the mechanisation of Bentham's *flat* reason can only account for human associations and exchanges as atomic compositions and decompositions by appealing to gained pleasure and lost pain:

> Accordingly, Bentham's idea of the world is that of a collection of persons pursuing each his separate interest or pleasure, and the prevention of whom from jostling one another more than is unavoidable, may be attempted by hopes and fears derived from three sources – the law, religion, and public opinion.[7]

Mill concludes, 'a philosophy like Bentham's [. . .] can teach the means of organising and regulating the merely [*sic*] *business part* of the social arrangements'.[8] Benthamian utilitarianism is carried out in a pure *economy*. Mill's criticism manages to include humanity's utility in what does not fall within Benthamian utility. By recognising in human nature the reality of impulses and forces which, as psychological causes, are irreducible to the search for calculable interest, and which are valued only because they are unquantifiable, Mill includes values, which are equivalent only insofar as they are *not* economic, in the economy of 'the merely [*sic*] business part of the social arrangements'. Here is the paradox. Mill discovers that real human reasons exist only insofar as they are not directly the product of a reason which orders and determines the value of our actions. We do things for reasons which are not the reasons that compel us to do them. We act according to several different interests, which are not always the interests that compel us to act.

In this way, Mill separates our indirect motives, which are a product of psychology, from calculable interest, which rationally and objectively governs our acts. Calculable interest is ripe to be a product of the economy which constructed itself, and will progressively incorporate indirect motives. The history of this incorporation of the 'non-economic' into an economy of use interests us here.

3. Production, Consumption, and the Question of Luxury

Classical political economy consists in modelling the relations between humans and things. According to this model, what humans do to things falls under either *consumption* or *production*. And what things do to humans falls under either *pleasure* (that one seeks to increase) or *pain* (that one seeks to diminish).

Consequently, according to the early systematic (so-called) scientific writings on value and money, political economy depends on the formation of a channel between consumption and production. Adam Smith tried to establish a positive connection between the two, which he called *wealth* or *enrichment*. Smith expressed a common conviction of the time, which had the appearance of flatness. He assumes that 'consumption is the sole end and purpose of all production'.[9] This maxim, though not directly aimed against saving, clearly attributes to human action the function of expending what it produces. Everything that humans add to the world of things is meant to be consumed, expended, that is, in a certain way, lost. We are far from Aristotelian considerations on contemplation (*theoria*) as the highest practice of human activity, which obtains its end in itself and, by definition, does not touch upon things, neither destroying them nor even affecting them.

If human production is carried out through consumption, then consumption must also be carried out through production. The loss of what was gained must be turned into gain: a gain in productivity, activity, and well-being is only one condition in the increase of production realised through increased consumption. Thomas Robert Malthus, David Ricardo, François Quesnay, and Karl Marx marginalised the classical problem, seeing this only as a more or less thorny residue. The classical problem concerns the part of consumption not modelled in production – what the classical economists called 'unproductive consumption'. Adam Smith named them 'luxuries', and contrasted unnecessary commodities with necessary ones, which are 'not only the commodities which are indispensably necessary for the support of life, but whatever the custom of the country renders it indecent for creditable people, even of the lowest order, to be without'.[10] What will later be called 'basic social welfare' by definition combines *natural* necessity (the minimum required to maintain individual human life) and *social* necessity (what a society considers indispensable for every individual hoping to be included and appear 'creditable' in this society). Everything that goes beyond inextricable natural, social, vital, and cultural necessity is defined as 'luxurious', that is, as a loss without immediate gain.

During the Enlightenment, it was important to take the moral and/or social theories of luxury into account. These theories evaluate luxury's value with regard to transcendental, essentially religious, values. The economic theories evaluate luxury's use-value, the gain, or lack thereof, in spending beyond the necessities of what one could have to gain therein.

Joseph Schumpeter quite rightly reminds us that:

> The confusing and confused mass of contradictory opinions on luxury may be straightened out, first by discarding, as not relevant to our subject, however interesting from other standpoints, opinions that are (a) primarily morally motivated, in which case a writer may be 'against luxury' even if his economic argument leads him to attribute 'favorable' effects to it, (b) clearly traceable to bourgeois resentment against 'high living', especially in the 'aristocratic' stratum.[11]

The assumptions economists make about the function of luxury and unproductive consumption are diverse, and at times astonishing. For Hume, for example, high-level consumption allows the luxury commodity-producing industries to appear in the eyes of the industrialists as, if necessary, a 'store-house of labour'.[12] For Bernard Mandeville, luxury is, if necessary, a reserve of workers, and resembles a variety of private vices and the selfish search for individual interests, which becomes a public good by making society function.[13] In his *Théorie du luxe*, Georges-Marie Butel-Dumont makes a comparable argument.[14] Malthus and others nevertheless contrast luxury with savings, going so far as to see, like Adam Smith, luxury as a 'ruinous expense' (a 'dis-saving'). Economists then side with those who long ago enacted sumptuary laws in order to prevent some from living above their station, and to prevent their downfall in a courtly society which sometimes compelled high-ranking officials to appear to be economically of higher social status than they were in reality.

This contradiction points to the difficulty of understanding the interest of disinterested consumption or an expense which does not immediately and socially turn into a gain in production – in the way that production turns into consumption for early classical economy.

Nonetheless, by redefining the very act of consumption, classical theories managed to assimilate expense and loss as an economic use-function.

4. Loss and Gain

In the seventeenth chapter of his *Cours complet d'économie politique*, published in 1840, Jean-Baptiste Say defined consumption as an essential loss. For humans, things present their usefulness as appropriate responses to the assumed needs of human nature: 'The common feature of all riches is their utility, or, if you prefer, the property useful to the satisfaction of needs given to us by nature and social customs.'[15]

Smith understood that the distinguishing feature of utility – the capacity of things to fulfil natural or social human needs – is that its only possible end is its destruction. Humanity's consumption of a thing's value destroys a thing's value. In the *Philosophy of Mind*, Hegel claims that the difference was between alimentary consumption, which supposes the destruction of the consumed thing, and aesthetic consumption, which, through contemplation, preserves its object.[16] Nevertheless, from an economic point of view, in the age of the mechanical reproduction of art objects, even the works' values are lost in their consumption; a 'consumer' is not prepared to pay the same price for a copy (of a book or a record) that she already owns, unless the culture industry finds a means of inventing a 'value added', in marketing terms, to the reproduced copy. If an artwork's value is not destroyed by its consumption, then, unlike other kinds of commodities, *copies* cannot be consumed without their value deteriorating, and then being lost, through this consumption. Say continues:

> We cannot make use of the utility which resides in social riches, without partially or entirely destroying their utility, and consequently without partially or fully deteriorating or destroying their value. We completely destroy the value of the food which nourishes us; and each day we partially destroy the value of the dress which clothes us. This destruction of value is called consumption.[17]

Consumption is classically defined as similar to the theoretical assimilation of expenditure, loss, and negativity into the economy's positive processes. The destruction of value through consumption compensates for humanity's production of value. Say and other classical theorists viewed the loss of value as an inverse function of production; expenditure is thus rationalised and can no longer be viewed as 'pure loss'. Expenditure logically responds to production. In Say's words, 'To produce value was to produce wealth. By consuming value, one destroys wealth. Production was a gain. Consumption is a loss.'[18]

However, while classical economic theory aims at the progressive development of a conceptual model of value, which gradually assimilates and rationalises all social and individual phenomena, in nineteenth-century political economy, a waste or residue of absolute loss remains. No matter how much consumption was conceived as destruction, this destruction allows production and maintains the economic cycle. Can we conceive of destruction not as *reproductive*, but as *unproductive* – as a consumption that causes loss and no reproduction? Say thinks that the terms are vague, if not unsuitable. All consumption, which is a destruction, can either fuel production or appear unproductive. But consumption which *appears* unproductive, since it merely satisfies a human need, at least produces a real satisfaction of experienced needs. In addition, consumption (of energy, of primary matter) which *appears* reproductive is not directly reproductive, since it is only the condition, or indirect means, making possible a future production, the cause of which will be labour or capital investments.

You well know, gentlemen, that one can compensate for it in two ways: either through the well-being resulting from a satisfied need; or through the production of wealth equal or superior to the consumed value. From this, unproductive or pointless consumption and reproductive consumption [. . .] Considering things thoroughly, these designations are far from being perfect. Consumption which satisfies one of our needs is neither unproductive nor pointless, since it produces satisfaction which is a real good. On the other hand, it is not reproductive consumption which produces, since, in reality, productive services – that is, industrial, land, and capital activity – are the only means of production.[19]

Reaching its peak in Say and Marx, classical economic theory assimilated loss into its definition of consumption. It perceived in advance that reproductive or unproductive consumption contained both a sense of destruction, which is not directly a production, and a sense of loss, which is always already a gain: the satisfaction of a need on one side, and the indirect means of an embryonic production on the other. Therefore, the great economic models do not really distinguish between unproductive consumption, pure loss, and reproductive, functional consumption. Instead, they distinguish within all consumption, understood as a destruction of value, an unproductive part of expenditure without compensation and a functional part that is directly or indirectly reproductive.

What is clear is that the idea that all economic destruction of value and all consumption, even if it is not a priori meant to become the condition of a compensating production, appears functionally and a posteriori as a gain. The economic models reserve a new place for the idea according to which economic negativity, loss, is a functional fraction of the mechanism of every capitalist economy and the condition of its evolution, through the replacement of older elements of production with new ones. Schumpeter calls this 'Creative Destruction'. He analyses the capitalist dynamics of the replacement of some conditions of production with others, old markets with emerging markets, old tools of production and creation with new ones.

[T]he history of the apparatus of power production from the overshot water wheel to the modern power plant, or the history of transportation from the mailcoach to the airplane. The opening up of new markets, foreign or domestic, and the organisational development from the craft shop and factory to such concerns as U. S. Steel illustrate the same process of industrial mutation – if I may use that biological term – that incessantly revolutionises the economic structure from within, incessantly destroying the old one, incessantly creating a new one. This process of *Creative Destruction* is the essential fact about capitalism. It is what capitalism consists in and what every capitalist concern has got to live in.[20]

5. Economic Desubstantialisation

On our view, the history of Western economics is closely tied to the progressive assimilation of a value's negative side into its positive side – its loss into gain, its destruction into creation, its expenditure into production. By turning away from a thing's value of *production* and turning towards the *consumption* of products, beyond the classical debates, the economy modified its logic of irrational expenditure, going so far as to make it a function of the determination of every economic value. The turning point began when several marginalist theorists, according to economic legend, simultaneously discovered the principle of 'marginal utility' in England (William Jevons and Alfred Marshall's neoclassical tradition), Austria (Carl Menger and the Austrian school), and Switzerland (Léon Walras, and then Vilfred Pareto in Italy). The simultaneous discovery corresponded to the modelling of a desubstantialised economic value, which no longer appears as a function of humanity's needs, the use-qualities of things, or their rules of exchange, but as a surplus function of a thing's value in relation to a consumer. Pareto very plausibly argues that the new marginalist school breaks with classical economics. Marginalism studies neither the relations between *humans* and *things* (according to very general natural laws) nor the relations between *humans* and *one* thing (by appealing to a product's supply and demand), but rather the relations between *one* human at any given moment and *a specific unit* of a thing at this same moment.[21]

Marginalism consists not in seeking the value of *one* glass of water, but rather the value of $x + 1$ glass of water, knowing that the consumer has already consumed x glasses of water, and attempting to estimate the value of an additional unit of the object 'glass of water' for this consumer. The unit and identity of this object is not guaranteed, since its value depends on its order in a sequence of consumption. The glass of water thus appears shattered like a

Cubist painting in a series of supplementary glass of water units, their value declining as their quantity increases. Jevons claims that 'the value of a divisible product is [. . .] measured not by its total utility, but by the intensity of the need that we must have more and more of it'.[22] Hence, the value of an *additional* thing is a function of consumed things of the same kind, the value of which was destroyed or deteriorated through its consumption. Unlike in Ricardo, for example, the quantity of work positively added to a commodity is no longer what determines its value. Rather, the function of the commodity's relative consumption negatively determines its contextual value by gradually deteriorating it. In marginalism, modern economic value is a function of *consumption* (destruction and loss) and not of *production* (positive creation of value).

Utilitarianism ignored the phenomenon of value loss or expenditure. Marginalism considered expenditure as a residual phenomenon. Later, expenditure became functional and essential to the determination of the modern economic value of commodities.

6. Economic Aggregate Serviceability and Unserviceability

We think that the economy historically aims at using increasingly more expenses and at the destruction of value, not as counterexamples, but as exemplary manifestations of the modern model of formal economic value. In doing so, unlike narrative histories ordering time as a universe and a cumulative factual order, they construct novel flat worlds, planes of the circulation of value.

Marginal value is a thing's surplus over itself: an additional glass of water; a third pair of sneakers when one already possesses two pairs. Schumpeter claims, however, that this surplus that determines the economic value attributed to things is not *psychological*, but instead is assimilated as a paradoxical element in twentieth-century theoretical formulations.

Thorstein Veblen shows how the mechanisms of the contemporary economy assimilated the surplus of value of a thing over itself, not as a function of its value's *deterioration*, but rather of its value's *augmentation*. Spending more on a thing than it is actually worth increases its value. Use-value is not an objective kernel of a thing's value on top of secondary surpluses of its exchange-value. It became essential to our market evaluation of things to spend more on them than they were worth. In this way, we no longer know how much things are 'really', 'objectively' worth.

> Goods are produced and consumed as a means to the fuller unfolding of human life; and their utility consists, in the first instance, in their efficiency as means to this end. This end is, in the first instance, the fullness of life of the individual, taken in absolute terms. But the human proclivity to emulation has seized upon the consumption of goods as a means to an invidious comparison, and has thereby invested consumable goods with a secondary utility as evidence of relative ability to pay. This indirect or secondary use of consumable goods lends a honorific character to consumption, and presently also to the goods which best serve this emulative end of consumption. The consumption of expensive goods is meritorious, and the goods which contain an appreciable element of cost in excess of what goes to give them serviceability for their ostensible mechanical purpose are honorific. The marks of superfluous costliness in the goods are therefore marks of worth – of high efficiency for the indirect, invidious end to be served by their consumption [. . .] This indirect utility gives much of their value to the 'better grades' of goods. In order to appeal to the cultivated sense of utility, an article must contain a modicum of this indirect utility.[23]

Veblen again distinguishes between a product's *direct* utility and its *indirect* utility, which is nothing other than the unserviceable part of an expenditure that the consumer is prepared to include to pay more for it than what it is worth, so as to lend a 'meritorious' and 'honorific' character to her act of consumption. Unlike the potlatch dear to Marcel Mauss and Georges Bataille, this is not a 'total social fact', but an economic variable that enters into the equation of a thing's economic value.

A commodity must therefore be organically included in the expended quantity of work to give enough 'indirect' value (pure lost value) to the commodity's 'direct' value. A commodity defies being a necessary commodity and acquires enough inaccurate and unnecessary value to have economic value for us. Veblen continues: 'Goods, in order to sell, must have some appreciable amount of labour spent in giving them the marks of decent expensiveness, in addition to what goes to give them efficiency for the material use which they are to serve.'[24]

However, Veblen points out that the function of a commodity's 'indirect' value is not to have a function and to be in surplus over a thing's very value. It becomes difficult if not impossible to take into account the direct value, a thing's utility, and its indirect value, the necessary expenditure, in order to give it a value that defies necessity. In this way, a thing becomes valuable, 'honorific':

> The habit of looking for the marks of superfluous expensiveness in goods, and of requiring that all goods should afford some utility of the indirect or invidious sort, leads to a change in the standards by which the utility of goods is gauged. The honorific element and the element of brute efficiency are not held apart in the consumer's appreciation of commodities, and the two together go to make up the unanalysed aggregate serviceability of the goods.[25]

This 'aggregate serviceability' is important. After the turns taken by twentieth-century economics, marginal value corresponds to a function of the commodity's consumption and a function of surplus of a unit of this commodity over itself. The 'positive' value created by the work of commodity production (in Ricardo and Marx) can no longer be distinguished from the value of a thing in excess of its utility. Hence, the economic utility of a thing vaguely indicates its 'positive' value, its direct utility, and the value that consumption assigns to it in excess, through pure expenditure.

Was the contemporary economy on its own capable of realising the 'counter-economies' studied in the anthropology of the gift and potlatch that show humanity's cultural resistance to the historical movement of a single (and globalised) economy? Classical economics once modelled an equilibrium of gains and losses, production and consumption, on humans seeking the useful and beneficial. But modern economics assimilated a 'pure negative' loss [*la perte 'pour rien'*] into a gain, expenditure into the economy, and the destruction of value into creation and economic production. Modern economics is not opposed to the anthropological reality of expenditure, the sacrifice of value, and pure loss. It effectively assimilates, on all levels, the unserviceable in the constitution of the serviceable, the ceaseless modification of expenditure without equilibrium into a gain of value. Older economies centred on production were caught off-guard by cultural counter-economies of expenditure, the gift, sacrifice, or the intrinsic value of persons. But modern economies centred on consumption as destruction – which constitute value through a function of consumption and organically assimilate unproductive consumption into the direct utility of commodities – render inoperative the historical demand for counter-economies, values resisting the economy, or values having value on their own or in pure loss.

In short, it is unclear how we can today contrast the conception of humanity as the realisation of the unproductive and unserviceable with a unified and unifying economic logic, when the latter continuously assimilates loss, expenditure, and non-interest in order to constitute the economic value of things. The subversive import of a 'counter-economy', negatively grounded on economic interest and calculation, is immediately neutralised by accounting for this negativity as essentially given in the positive value of things bought and sold.

7. Replaceable Value and Irreplaceable Value

The objection is the following: if a thing's economic value consists in its essential *replaceable* value (a thing is equivalent to one or many things), can one still assume an *irreplaceable* value of things, and, if so, according to what criteria?

A thing's value may be its equivalence to another thing or some quantity of any other thing (its economic value), but it may also be its irreplaceability. If a thing is beautiful, this does not mean that it can be replaced by any other beautiful thing. What determines the value of its beauty is not that this thing is *beautiful*, but rather that *this thing* is beautiful.

Now, the problem of a thing's irreplaceable value is that it always grounds its replaceable value. For example, by adding sentimental value to an object, one makes this object irreplaceable: I keep this hat and will never exchange it for anything else. But an object is irreplaceable only to the extent that its irreplaceability increases its value and makes it replaceable with something more than it is worth: during an auction at my death, if I am famous, the hat's economic value will be the sentimental value that I attributed to it. The problem of irreplaceability is that it always increases the replaceable value up to a *breaking point*.

In this way, we can reinterpret all modern political attempts to propose a 'counter-economy' and a theory of non-commodities. Persons, gifts, the commons, and 'expenditures' are in fact ideals of an absolute surplus value, in contrast with a counted value [*valeur de compte*], of all replaceability: 'this is not a commodity', 'that is not for sale', and other contemporary slogans. What is captivating about the potlatch, the phenomenon of the gift, and pure negative loss, is that wealth is negatively expended: the value added to something exceeds any equivalence. In all political 'counter-economies', humans secretly seek, beyond economic calculations, to spend to such an excessive extent that the value lost is neither the opposite of a gain nor replaceable, but is valued for itself. The ancient search for a *praxis* valued for itself gave way, in modernity, to the search for a practice valued for itself which would exceed any possible 'equivalent' value. This is seen often in the anti-economic ideal of an uncounted value, where no thing is capable of being equivalent to another (a table is worth three chairs), but each thing exceeds any equivalence.

This ancient inquiry into a *praxis* valued for itself, not 'equivalent' to Aristotelian *contemplation*; Edgar Allan Poe's search for a 'mobile without motive', for an act valued for itself, for something against its own self-interest (what Poe called *perverseness*[26]); Bataille's desire for a counter-economic value that exceeds all equivalence (*expenditure*); the traditional values accorded to sacrifice; the recurrent slogans opposed to the world's 'commodification' – all these are examples of the continuous hopes to find an irreplaceable human value.

But the distinguishing feature of the modern economy is that it gradually assimilates irreplaceability by making it the element that increases a thing's replaceable value and by defining the counted value of commodities by a surplus value. What exceeds a commodity's utility and expends itself in consumption increasingly becomes a part of the counted economic value of commodities. Economic rationality turns unserviceability into an organic element that increases a thing's utility. It considers unproductive expenditure as an essential element that contributes to the maximisation of the production of a thing's value. Henceforth, it becomes quite difficult to contrast a thing's economic replaceable value with a thing's irreplaceable value in itself, or to contrast the consumption of things for our needs or our pleasure with irrational and disinterested expenditure.

8. Counter-Economy of Persons (Morality)

Historically, we can identify at least three attempts to establish another value of things or beings, avoiding replaceable value and counted economic value. We find the idealist and moral attempt in Immanuel Kant's *Groundwork of the Metaphysics of Morals*.

Kant takes great care to distinguish between the 'price' of things and the 'dignity' of things (in fact, of rational beings). A thing's 'price' refers to its exchange value or its affective value, while 'dignity' alone can plausibly and rigorously be called an *absolute* value. The distinction rests on the fact that '[w]hat has a *price* can be replaced by something else as its equivalent; what on the other hand is raised above all price and therefore admits of no equivalent has a *dignity*',[27] that is, an 'intrinsic value'.

Kant distinguishes a value without an end in itself, which is absolute and rests on the irreplaceability of what it is the value of, and an economic 'price', which assumes a thing's replaceability (via a sum of money) by some amount of any other thing. Kant tries to short-circuit the economic value of things, the counted value, and the replaceable value, through the value of 'dignity'. This non-economic value, in the sense that it cannot allow the functioning of a reciprocal exchange or replacement channel of things by other things, guarantees the irreplaceable singularity of a being, its departure from every economic channel.

Kant reserves counter-economic value strictly for *persons*, for all rational beings. Ultimately, persons alone are situated outside the economic channel of replaceability, the equilibrium of gains and losses that is a *person*. If such a principle provides the foundations for the classical critique of slavery, for example, then economic modernity – from Marx's definition of wage labour (which consists not in selling one's person, but the labour power of the person, who possesses nothing else) to modern service economies (which consist in making money from a person's skills: for example, his availability as receptionist or her image as consultant) – raises serious problems at the Kantian limit situated between persons valued by dignity and things or actions with a price. Do prostitutes sell themselves as persons? Do they make money from the sexual availability of their bodies, their personhood? Do they attain their dignity by reducing it to a price? Or do prostitutes always sell a service of their person, a facet of their being, a capacity and a skill, not harming their dignity (like a master does a slave), but simply fixing a price for some of their services? Questions like these arise frequently in contemporary ethical debates.

By fixing the limit between counted economic value and excess value, which goes beyond any price or replaceability – in a moral perspective by establishing a *distinguo* between persons and objects – is to blind oneself to the numerous intermediary levels between *persons* and *things* in the modern universe. A person's services or skills are irreducible to persons and things. They represent intermediary events – like each wage labourer's labour power, a person's potentiality to act – but not persons or material objects themselves.

No value of anything can exist *in itself*, otherwise it would be compact. And what is a person for Kant if not a compact thing, since the dignity of this compact thing is acquired only at the price of its absolute absence of equivalence? What is absolutely equivalent to nothing except itself self-compacts as an object, and has no chance of functioning, for example, as an event. Personhood is an object that cannot become an event (like when I play a role, for example). Personhood prevents us from conceiving of dignity as a comparative value and exchange value given to a self-event [*événement de soi*]. Now, for the most part, the economy depends on the possibility of exchanging persons as events (services, labour time, functions, modes of a person's presence), and formalises what the Kantian distinction compacts.

9. Counter-Economy of the Gift (Social Sciences)

A second modern solution was proposed in order to resist economic reification. This solution was not *moral*, but *sociological*, and consisted in differentiating between an economic, calculable, counted value and a social, symbolic value – an excess value, a product of the 'total social phenomenon', irreducible to the calculation of economic gains and losses. Marcel Mauss, Émile Durkheim's executor and one of the founders of the continental social sciences, defended this solution.

In *The Gift*, Mauss argues for the necessary existence of 'total social phenomena'. Total social phenomena have no economic values, precisely because they contain these values as elements among other elements. The Kantian moral strategy consisted in distinguishing and opposing the economic value of price and the absolute value of dignity. For Durkheim and Mauss, the strategy of the social sciences consisted in encompassing economic value, equivalence, and replaceability not by a transcendental *value*, but by a total *phenomenon* involving the whole society, which contains economic phenomena among other phenomena.

In these 'total' social phenomena, as we propose calling them, all kinds of institutions are given expression at one and the same time – religious, juridical, and moral, which relate to both politics and the family; likewise economic ones, which suppose special forms of production and consumption, or rather, of performing total services and of distribution. This is not to take into account the aesthetic phenomena to which these facts lead, and the contours of the phenomena that these institutions manifest.[28]

For Mauss, the phenomenon of the *gift* is a particular, striking example of the 'total social phenomenon' encompassing economic values. The gift is both the principle and the reverse side of the contemporary economic exchange of things, on account of 'the so to speak voluntary character of these total services, apparently free and disinterested but nevertheless constrained and self-interested'.[29]

He turns to primitive or archaic institutions within which this 'total social phenomenon' of the gift is expressed. Mauss develops his conception of this voluntary loss of value and property without equivalent economic remuneration in order to sketch a brief genealogy of the market economy. He suggests reducing the market economy to a particular moment in the history of exchanges between humans and human groups:

> In these societies we shall see the market as it existed before the institution of traders and before their main invention – money proper. We shall see how it functioned both before the discovery of forms of contract and sale that may be said to be modern (Semitic, Hellenic, Hellenistic, and Roman), and also before money, minted and inscribed. We shall see the morality and the organisation that operate in such transactions.[30]

Mauss proposes a 'counter-economy' in the sense of a general economy in which the market economy, resting on counted value, money, equivalence, and the replaceability of things, is only one particular, recent example:

> In the economic and legal systems that have preceded our own, one hardly ever finds a simple exchange of goods, wealth, and productions in transactions concluded by individuals. First, it is not individuals but collectivities that impose obligations of exchange and contract upon each

other. The contracting parties are legal entities: clans, tribes, and families who confront and oppose one another either in groups who meet face to face in one spot, or through their chiefs, or in both these ways at once. Moreover, what they exchange is not solely property and wealth, movable and immovable goods, and things economically useful.[31]

The strategy of the social sciences consists in making the replaceable value the counted value, which assumes the equivalence and equilibrium of gains and losses, a very particular case of a phenomenon that falls within the scope of *fact* rather than of value: the gift, expenditure, loss, and the voluntary destruction of value binds another human group.

Sometimes gifts appear as functional phenomena without any ends in themselves, systems of social constraints that, lacking any quantifiable, calculable, monetary value, have values intuitively known by the social agents within the economy of human exchanges. However, Mauss applies his concept of the gift to our societies as a critical tool of economic rationality. He gives us a glimpse into an ideal of the gift as the source of values different from economic, interested, and interesting values. He acknowledges a contemporary world given over to counted value, utility, and calculation. He then presents the gift as a value emblematic of humanist resistance to commodification: 'Fortunately, everything is still not wholly categorised in terms of buying and selling. Things still have sentimental as well as venal value [. . .] We possess more than a tradesman morality.'[32]

Mauss presents the gift as a value that falls under another logic, anthropologically more profound and total, lost by modernity. As an early twentieth-century militant, he defends humanist and socialist values:

> Thus we can and must return to archaic society and to elements in it.
> We shall find in this reasons for life and action that are still prevalent
> in certain societies and numerous social classes: the joy of public
> giving; the pleasure in generous expenditure on the arts, in hospitality,
> and in the private and public festival. Social security, the solicitude
> arising from reciprocity and cooperation, and that of the occupational
> grouping[33]

Not only *can* one return to lost, economically unrestricted, and archaic 'total social' values, but one *must* politically respect these values, which mysteriously correspond to the social phenomenon that Mauss analyses. How did this 'phenomenon' become a 'value' to uphold in present-day society? The mystery is why one would want what we think of as social *phenomena* in Amerindian societies to return as *values* (mutuality, solidarity, free gifts, and so on).

Mauss gives the impression that the general economy of gifts contains and extends beyond the economy of 'utilitarianism', interest, equivalence, and replaceability of things: 'Several times we have seen how far this whole economy of the exchange-through-gift lay outside the bounds of the so-called natural economy, that of utilitarianism.'[34]

He acknowledges that our society historically aims at the success of economic rationalisation, but leaves a remainder of values of utility, interests, and the compensation of each gift by a gain: 'The victory of rationalism and mercantilism was needed before the notions of profit and the individual, raised to the level of principles, were introduced. One can almost date – since Mandeville's *The Fable of the Bees* – the triumph of the notion of individual interest.'[35]

For Mauss, the recent history and rationalisation of the economy into a system of counted values, of the value of a calculation of gains and losses around our interests and material needs, marks some 'betrayal' of humanity's essence:

> It is our western societies who have recently made man an 'economic animal'. But we are not yet all creatures of this genus. Among the masses and the elites in our society purely irrational expenditure is commonly practised. It is still characteristic of a few of the fossilised remnants of our aristocracy. *Homo oeconomicus* is not behind us, but lies ahead, as does the man of morality and duty, the man of science and reason. For a very long time man was something different, and he has not been a machine for very long, made complicated by a calculating machine.[36]

Here we find the criticism made against the utilitarian economy that reduces humanity to calculation and to a single *flat* reason confounded with its self-interested machinery. Nonetheless, Mauss's 'counter-economy', like the Kantian moral distinction, meets with several difficulties. First, Mauss must assume that the gift is a ('total social') phenomenon to particularise the economic value and reduce it to the level of a single, more or less recent, element of this factual global system. But when coming to his contemporary diagnosis, he must then deny economic reason what he grants to the total social phenomenon and the gift. Since, for Mauss, modern economic reason, the calculation of interests, losses and gains, became totalising and exclusive, he opposes it to the (archaic but still present) gift, open social exchange, economic disinterestedness, expenditure, and all that goes with it (organic solidarity, mutualism, and so on) as a *value*. He shows us why and how a *phenomenon* that encompassed and particularised a value (economic value) can and must become a *value* that cannot be a total phenomenon (economic reason, the calculation of utility and interests). Why can't the 'total social phenomenon' analysed by so many be considered a political value of contemporary social militancy and resistance?[37] If the gift can be considered as a 'total social phenomenon', why can't economic reason be considered, in light of its historical evolution, a 'total economic phenomenon' (which encompasses its negative)?

Mauss is ultimately forced to defend archaic values faced with the economic reductionism that he fears, to such an extent that the transformation of utilitarianism and political economy into total economic reason leaves no other choice for the social sciences than a problematic reaction and resistance as soon as it concerns expressing not the phenomena, but the values contrasted with economic value, through an alchemy, a transformation of *leaden facts* into *golden values*, always hindering anthropology and sociology.

10. Counter-Economy of Expenditure (Anthropology)

At the limits of the modern sociological solution to the problems raised through Western and global economic rationalisation, we come to the third modern solution: the 'accursed' response to the reduction of human reason to the calculation of a thing's exchange, compensation, and replaceable values. This is the solution sketched out in Georges Bataille's 'The Notion of Expenditure'.

Bataille borrows his strategy from Mauss. He contrasts the economic rationalisation of human actions with a deeper negative reason outside of human actions. The gift, the primary figure of expenditure, is a phenomenon of voluntary loss and of the destruction of value, in which responsibility passes from the donor to the recipient. In this way, the gift is not a calculated value which compels one to respond to some loss by an equivalent compensatory gain. Rather, it allows an excess value to circulate socially: 'The gift must be considered as a loss and thus as a partial destruction, since the desire to destroy is in part transferred onto the recipient.'[38]

Bataille opposes the 'counter-economy' of the symbolic circulation of value (through losses and gifts) to the market economy of calculation, which indiscriminately combines primitive utilitarianism, the principles of political economy, and the foundations of the market economy. Rationalised economic exchange requires a model through which *losses* and *gains*, *consumption* and *production* counterbalance each other, compensate for each other. But in the counter-economy of the gift, loss, and expenditure, the basic human value is surplus value, rather than counted value.

'The very principle of the function of production requires that products be exempt from loss, at least provisionally. In the market economy, the processes of exchange have an acquisitive sense.'[39] Bataille remains close to Mauss's theory. But, by passing from an analysis of archaic systems to a modern and historical diagnosis, Bataille distances himself from Mauss's position, since the latter must sociologically link together phenomenon and value. In more colourful language, Bataille conceives of the discharge of energy and of value, and productive uncompensated loss, less as elements of social solidarity, a total social phenomenon, like Mauss, than as a *principle* of the organic functioning of human life. Acquisition, exchange, and production are merely the means of subsistence and maintenance of human life. The ends of human actions, when they are maintained in this way, are the exact opposite of these means: the discharge of force and the loss of value.

> The immense travail of recklessness, discharge, and upheaval that constitutes life could be expressed by stating that life starts only with the deficit of these systems; at least what it allows in the way of order and reserve has meaning only from the moment when the ordered and reserved forces liberate and lose themselves for ends that cannot be subordinated to anything one can account for.[40]

What do human beings seek in this discharge and loss, which is against conservation and the economic reproduction of their means of subsistence? 'It is only by such insubordination – even if it is impoverished – that the human race ceases to be isolated in the unconditional splendor of material things'.[41]

What they seek, quite simply, is the loss of value: 'the creation of unproductive values'. It is also the possibility of founding values that are not *equivalent*, but which *exceed*, and therefore preclude the replaceability of things by each other for us. But these values are valued by themselves and by their excesses over everything else. Excess values are what allow human beings to distinguish themselves from the formal flatness of the world of material things. The cry of all these 'counter-economies' is to flee from our flattening to the level of things.

As in Marx, the aim is therefore to avoid reification and the contamination of our being by the being of the material things we produce and consume. So long as human beings continue to exchange things with each other by calculating them through their equivalence or interest, they remain things among things. By fully comprehending an excess value, a non-equivalent value, through countless expenditure, and by defining a value that no gain, interest, or benefit of any sort can compensate for, human beings extract from the world of interchangeable things something which, like Aristotelian 'sovereign good', is equivalent to nothing, but is valued by and for itself. From Marx to Bataille, only human beings can situate themselves outside the world of things. Because humans are afraid of things, in this tradition, they imagine themselves free only outside of their domain.

Aristotle's 'sovereign good' was employed as an end both for itself and for all other means, for all intermediary ends. The competition of a totalising economic reason, which, via utilitarianism, first annexed the good to utility, led to a series of modern responses. Kantian morality situates persons outside the world of things, where things have a price and are, in principle, exchanged through moral imperative. The social sciences situated the total social phenomena outside the economic world of things. And Bataille's singular undertaking situates humanity outside the economic world of things through practices of expenditure and uncompensated loss.

Bataille's anthropological 'counter-economy' is emblematic of modernity's agony over the reduction of human reason to the economic reason of interests, the calculation of gains and losses in all things. It overthrows the order of priorities between necessities and the inessential, between the conditions, means of subsistence, and value of human existence. Counted economic values, values of calculation, are reduced to means guaranteeing life's necessities; they always exceed utility and necessity, which embody life's 'value in itself': 'Men assure their own subsistence or avoid suffering, not because these functions themselves lead to a sufficient result, but in order to accede to the insubordinate function of free expenditure.'[42]

Bataille defines expenditure as a value of life *in excess* of all that may count for us. According to him, humans would manifest the primary, and not secondary, importance of this excess over the necessities of existence through countless expenditure and the discharge of energy and value beyond any possible compensation or economically rational equilibrium.

The problem is that it is precisely this counter-economic expenditure which became the core of the contemporary economy of objects. But what once situated us outside of objects, today reduces us to objects, and marks the failure of all Romantic, moral, Marxist, sociological, and anthropological counter-economies.

11. Failure of Counter-Economies

In his short book, *Globalization and Its Enemies*, Daniel Cohen examines recent studies of the composition of the value of a pair of Nike sneakers: for a pair sold at $70 in 2001, the person who made them (very likely in Indonesia) earned $2.75. If we add up all the costs of making them, their manufacture costs a total of $16, while the wholesale price, which corresponds to the selling price to the distributors, was $35.50 at the time. That means that the manufacture of such an object only contributes to *half* its price. The other half corresponds to the value in excess of the shoes, in the price of the consumption of the shoes, and not in its production. To the positive value of the shoes as material objects is organically, inextricably added the value of loss, the expenditure included in the brand, which raises its price to maximise the reputation of the shoes. The other half of the price of the pair of shoes corresponds to the expenditure that consumers must commit to so that the object exceeds its own value, and thus becomes *valuable*:

[An object like] Nike's Air Pegasus shoe costs as much to produce as a social object as it costs to produce as a physical object. That is, the promotion costs just as much as the manufacturing [in Indonesia]. In light of this, it can be said that one purchases the image, or the concept, as much as one purchases the product [the object itself].[43]

Cohen argues that by analysing the functioning of the 'new economy', notably through the Internet and free service models, the consumer does not in fact pay for the price of objects. In the old economy, the consumer paid the producer for the service that the producer gave to the consumer. In the 'new economy' models, a channel or service obtains its price through advertising. Price has nothing to do with the channel's or service's production of the good, but instead with a derived object: capturing the attention of the consumer. A pure economic loss must be given to the consumer in order to capture their attention and to indirectly make the expenditure involved profitable. This economic model of valuation is not so much exchanged-based or contractual as gift-based: 'As DeLong and Froomkin humorously note, the business model of the new economy renders the gift economy more effective than mercantile trade.'[44]

This claim is clearly unforgiving towards the counter-economies described above; it indicates their failure and underestimation of *formal* economic rationality.

12. The Economic Assimilation of the Negative: Towards The Flat World

Modern counter-economies embody humanity's cultural resistance to the universalisation of an economy of objects. However, the problem with them is that they are continuously undermined by the successive waves of the theoretical and concrete economy of the twentieth century. They were conceived as a war machine, countering utilitarian political economy and centring on phenomena of production. The enchanting ideal of counter-economic values of expenditure, loss, and the destruction of value was humanity's claim to its singularity among material things. But they failed in the transformations of the global economy. An economy of *production* became an economy of *consumption*, an object's value being a result of the function of consumption and the destruction of value. The utility of things is no longer a positive utility, grounded on the necessary work required in their production, but rather an indivisible aggregate of positive, direct utility and indirect utility, which derive from the consumption of things and the assimilation of unproductive expenditure as a function maximising economic value and the price of commodities. In the same way, the self-critique that shaped the history of utilitarianism, the passage from Bentham's hedonist utilitarianism to Mill's more complex indirect utilitarianism, which could assimilate unquantifiable values as essential givens into the calculation of interests, prevented anthropologists from obtaining 'another value'. Economic rationalisation governed this logic of other unproductive values, and included them in the composition of economic values.

In another register, Poe wrote in 'The Imp of the Perverse'[45] that the 'perverse' is the principle of counter-psychology, a primitive attribute of human minds, outside the flat logic of interests, duty, and the search for well-being. The perverse was ironically assimilated throughout the twentieth century through the rationalisation of scientific psychology. In various branches of psychology and psychoanalysis, the perverse was an acknowledged motor of human minds. Everyday, common discourses recognised the (mis)understood role of the perverse in our least actions and behaviours.

What leads to the 'perverse' also leads to the marginal logic of 'expenditure', loss, and the destruction of value. Perversity is included in the functioning of the economy, becoming an affective part of the most common discourses and practices. It actively takes part in the formation of the replaceable economic values of things. It resides in our modellable and modelled economic behaviours. Our relationship to consumption included the function of expenditure, loss, non-compensation, and the search for the useless and the unnecessary in our economic acquisitions. Likewise, our psychologies assimilated the relative place of perversity, of rational actions that run counter to the good, duty, and any psychological *nomos*. We have genuinely normative discourses on the necessary part that perversity plays in our motives and intentions. Likewise, we know and discuss the part played by pure discharge, expenditure, and the search for what cannot be compensated for in the economic logic of consumption, the everyday acquisition of things, and the calculation of their price.

Our economy carries within its core what the ideal of expenditure was supposed to be able to oppose: the values of things paid for and exchanged – the services, objects, and events which we continuously convert into cash – carry in themselves a kernel of non-utility, non-necessity, loss, and expenditure. These values do not correspond to our economic practices that seek out necessities, subsistence, interests, or the satisfaction of our needs, but instead to the valuation of things in excess of their utility and interest. This encourages the formation of their economic value through sacrificial consumption, through an expenditure that appears to many at least as much a productive compensation, the search for well-being, as a means of psychological discharge, pure expenditure, ritualised, for example, in modern shopping habits.

We can fret and moan before this assimilation of the marginal logics of expenditure and loss, from psychological discharge to the rationality of the consumption-centred economy. We may also think that a defence of values other than economic values is not subversive, and that there remains to be found another means of relativising total and universalising economic reason, the *replaceable* value of things.

Undoubtedly, to see beyond, we must emphasise the replaceability of things, maximise it – rather than unsuccessfully attenuate or minimise it at all costs.

Notes

1. Jeremy Bentham, *An Introduction to the Principles of Morals and Legislation*, p. 2.
2. Ibid., p. 1.
3. John Stuart Mill, *Autobiography*, p. 144.
4. Ibid., p. 142.
5. John Stuart Mill, 'Bentham', p. 94.
6. Ibid., p. 95.
7. Ibid., p. 97.
8. Ibid., p. 99.
9. Adam Smith, *An Inquiry into the Nature and Causes of the Wealth of Nations*, p. 28.
10. Ibid., pp. 328–9.
11. Joseph A. Schumpeter, *History of Economic Analysis*, pp. 324–5.
12. David Hume, 'Of Luxury', p. 29.
13. Bernard Mandeville, *The Fable of the Bees*.
14. Georges-Marie Butel-Dumont, *Théorie du luxe*.
15. Jean-Baptiste Say, *Cours complet d'économie politique*, p. 197.
16. G. W. F. Hegel, *Philosophy of Mind*.
17. Say, *Cours complet d'économie politique*, p. 197.

18. Ibid., p. 198.
19. Ibid., p. 201.
20. Joseph A. Schumpeter, *Capitalism, Socialism, and Democracy*, p. 83. Our emphasis.
21. Vilfredo Pareto, *Manual of Political Economy*.
22. William Stanley Jevons, *The Theory of Political Economy*.
23. Thorstein Veblen, *The Theory of the Leisure Class*, pp. 154–5.
24. Ibid., p. 158.
25. Ibid., pp. 156–7.
26. Edgar Allan Poe, 'The Imp of the Perverse', p. 827.
27. Immanuel Kant, *Groundwork of the Metaphysics of Morals*, p. 42. Our emphasis.
28. Marcel Mauss, *The Gift*, pp. 3–4.
29. Ibid., p. 4.
30. Ibid., p. 5.
31. Ibid., p. 6.
32. Ibid., p. 83.
33. Ibid., pp. 88–9.
34. Ibid., p. 92.
35. Ibid., p. 97.
36. Ibid., p. 98.
37. 'But to note the fact is not enough. One must deduce practice from it, and a moral precept', explains Mauss (ibid., p. 87). That is the problem.
38. Georges Bataille, 'The Notion of Expenditure', p. 122.
39. Ibid., p. 123.
40. Ibid., p. 128.
41. Ibid., p. 128.
42. Ibid., p. 129.
43. Daniel Cohen, *Globalization and Its Enemies*, pp. 57–8. [Translation modified.]
44. Ibid., p. 60. Here Cohen cites J. Bradford DeLong and Michael Froomkin's 'Old Rules for the New Economy'.
45. 'In the sense I intend, it is, in fact, a *mobile* without motive, a motive not *motivirt* [. . .] or, if this shall be understood as a contradiction in terms, we may so far modify the proposition so as to say, that through its promptings we act, for the reason that we should *not*.' Poe, 'The Imp of the Perverse', p. 827.

Chapter XII

Values

1. Flat World and Variable Intensities

Picture a flat, valueless world.

This is a world where nothing is more beautiful than another thing, where truth is no different from fiction, where fictions, illusions, and contradictions have some actual value, and where what is evil is not negative and subtracts nothing from the world. Each thing is *equally* in the world. This is clearly the formal world of Book I. Not only is this world possible, but it is the only *world*. Nonetheless, this world is not the objective and evential *universe* in which we live together as objects exchangeable and replaceable with other objects. It is the world where each one or each thing is alone and equal.

The flat, valueless world is a world devoid of intensities. Nothing is either *more* or *less* than another thing. Everything is equal.

The formal world is without intensity. The objective and evential universe includes variable intensities, lives, and works. Whereas no thing can formally be either more or less than another thing, the universe is filled with objects that are objectively either more or less than others. This not only means that objects and events materially and symbolically comprehend and augment each other; it means that each object is likely to be either more or less *that which it is, in that which it is,* and *for that which it is.*

In the objective and evential universe, nothing is flat. Everything possesses a continuous, intensive depth, since the extension of the objective and evential division is doubled by either more or less being or comprehension, which has no formal meaning, only an objective meaning. All objects are likely to be either more or less *beautiful,* either more or less *true,* or either more or less *good.*

The formal, flat world is the condition of possibility of the

331

objective and eventual universe, obtained through our access to 'no-matter-what'. The formal world neutralises the relative intensity of objects and events. Intensity has no formal meaning. Nothing is *formally* more beautiful, more true, or better than another thing, since each thing is formally alone and equal. The meaning of intensity is thus altogether *objective*: what we call 'values'. Each value of an object or event, whether it is an aesthetic, economic, logical, ethical, or utilitarian value, is altogether objective, since it pertains to objects rather than to things in their relation to the world.

This objectivity of values is immediately made implausible by the relativity of values that the modern economy reinforces. In reality, there are no *values*, only *valuations*. The values of objects connected to an economy, to an exchange system of these objects, which we analysed in the previous chapter, would thus be dependent on the values that one attributes to them. The source of each value is obtained through humanity's collective or individual projection of its interests onto things of the flat world. The replacement of values by economic valuations consists in combining the objective with the formal. The non-human objective universe is conceived as the flat, formal world. In contrast, human actions produce a topological interface of intensities in the universe of surrounding objects. On this view, nothing has value *in itself*. Nothing is beautiful, true, or good, except in relation to the human actions that attribute values to other objects. Beauty, one might say, is in the eye of the beholder, good in the interest of the one who defines it, truth in the mouth of the one who speaks it. This is entailed by an economic conception of objects.

The fundamental error of theories of *valuation* consists in claiming that the non-intensive, indifferent, flat world is not the world (which comprehends each stone, each human being, each consciousness), but instead a part of the universe which comprehends non-human objects (that is, all objects except humans). This 'flat universe' conflates the formal (flatness, indifference) with the objective (the objective difference between human and non-human); it is the economic playing field on which human actions produce valuations. We may call this the economic plane of *relativity*. The Beautiful would depend on the era or on the historical evolution of the canon of beautiful works. Examples are Peter Paul Rubens's full flesh tones, the beardless beauty of Japanese taste, or the fashion of anorexic models, how one distin-

guishes revealed truths, scientific truths, or what is good for the
lion, which is apparently not good for the antelope. The relativity
of *valuations* derives from the fact that we attribute all intensity
of values to those who make values, by situating intensity outside
what is characterised by the attributed value, which is like a flat,
passive, and undifferentiated matter.

However, the problem with the economic *valuation* model is
twofold. On the one side, this model always assumes an underly-
ing dualism between a part of the flat universe without intensity,
awaiting its valuation or devaluation, and a part of the active
universe, which is the source of all intensification and evaluates or
devaluates according to its potential, interests, or orientation. On
the other side, this model attributes all intensity to the donor and
no intensity to the receiver, so that the intensive object continues
to have *replaceable* value.

This *vaguely* economic model is never entirely consistent, and it
is necessary to play it at its own game; the assumed source of the
valuation of things (for example, individual interests) is as much
something (replaceable and exchangeable) as the evaluated things.

By distinguishing between a part or mode of the universe passively receiving variable intensities given to it, and a part or mode
of the universe which produces and projects variable intensities,
one makes the error of formalising objective things and of objectivising formal things. The world – what comprehends each thing
– is merely flat, without intensity, equal. The universe of objects,
which comprehend each other, is never flat; when things are
together, nothing is flat. The universe of objects therefore becomes
compact through the determination of a universe opposed to
humanity and its interests, which would receive values without
having them by itself. In the universe, everything already has value
in some way before one gives it value, since objects are not alone
in the universe, but among objects. Objects are therefore always
either more or less. On the other hand, by formalising the objective universe, a non-formal distinction is made between *donors*
of value and *receivers* of value. Nonetheless, no *formal* difference
exists between active and passive things, between naturing and
natured, between human and non-human: in short, between all
that divides the universe into *evaluating* and *evaluated*, into intensifying and intensified. Formally, only things exist equally, since
they are equally in the world – and exchangeable.

Every *economic* model maintains an objective part (human

nature, psychology) within its formal world of things. This is its Achilles heel. Economic models are never completed by maintaining a semblance of difference between the subject of valuation (human interests, human nature) and the object of valuation (all things exchangeable with others). It is necessary to prove more royalist than the king and more economical than the economy; the source of the value of exchangeable things is neither more nor less of something than the things in question. It follows that non-things, subjects, consciousness, interests, structures, or models of equilibrium do not give things their value, but that their value is *situated in the things themselves*.

By crossing the economic channel of objects, we situate ourselves outside it, but not by blocking the channel with 'authentic values' such as persons, sacrifice, dignity (which were easily integrated into the economy of objects).

But if only comparable things exist, without any privileged centre of valuation of these things, then the value of objects and events belongs in some way to the objects and events themselves. The mirror image of my interest or desire to find something beautiful is not what makes something beautiful. Rather, we find beautiful that which is beautiful. If one finds beautiful that which is *not* beautiful – if this value that we attribute to faces or landscapes was merely a valuation by the one who finds the faces or landscapes to suit their taste – then everything could be *equally* beautiful, since anything that I find beautiful can be replaced by another thing that I find beautiful. Valuation allows us to conceive of the *replaceable* value of things, which connects equally evaluated objects. Now, when we find something beautiful or claim that something is true, we attribute an *irreplaceable* value to it. Value makes something singular, while economic valuation yields particulars.

If I find a face beautiful, then I evaluate it, I project onto it criteria or qualities which are not its own, but which belong to my history, culture, interests, perspective, and nature; so I attribute a replaceable value to this face. It can be replaced by any thing that I judge as equally beautiful, or that my culture, class, tastes, or species judges as equally beautiful.

But if I find this face beautiful, I merely acknowledge something situated in it, which is necessarily for me a beauty that the face conceals, so I give a replaceable value to this face. I understand through its beauty what belongs to it.

All value is therefore situated at the crossroads of the replaceable and irreplaceable. Value is the intensity of objects and events.
Value allows their *comparison* (in terms of 'more' or 'less') or
their exchange (in the economic channel), and their *singularity*,
their differentiation, and the determination of what makes them
irreplaceable. The value of things is both what makes possible
the exchange of one thing for another and what precludes the
exchange of one thing by another.

This tension derives from the fact that the intensity of objects
and events resides neither strictly in evaluating actions nor in
objectivity (an *in-itself* of things). What is beautiful owes its
beauty neither to the one who finds this object beautiful nor to the
object which would be beautiful by itself. All value is paradoxical
in this way: what I find beautiful or true or good, I 'find' beautiful, true, or good; I do not 'attribute' beauty, truth, or goodness
(any more than I am 'attributed' beauty, truth, or goodness), but
I discover beauty, truth, or goodness in objects even though these
values are not intrinsic to the objects.

The Beautiful, the True, and the Good are not qualities of
objects, included inside the objects. They are *intensities situated in
the objects without the intensities being there.*

Value is irreducible to valuation or substantial value. This is
why each value reveals the ambiguity of the replaceable and irreplaceable in modern economic models. Since the value of things is
not intrinsic to things, like other qualities of things (their colour,
weight, or elements), and since the value of a thing is its intensity
and not its extension or division, this value does not belong to the
thing. Rather, values make things comparable to and replaceable
with other things. But since a thing's value is not attributed to
this thing, as if there were a conscious action projecting an external interest onto its concrete expression, this value can only be
situated in the thing, which makes the thing incomparable to and
irreplaceable with another thing.

Values – the intensities of things – are antagonistic. Values
are non-extensive and correspond to an object's or an event's
possibility of being either more or less what it is, either *greater*
or *lesser* what it is. But the intensification of things belongs
neither to things nor to the one who evaluates them; intensities
are situated in things without those intensities being there. When
one claims that a face is beautiful, the face is doubled by itself,
as if it were intensely what it is. Intensification consists of rules

and norms that are partially natural and partially cultural. But the intensification is always of the thing's identity; a face, which is what it is, has *value* if it becomes either more or less itself. Someone must activate it and *find* it beautiful; beauty becomes the transformation of what something is into a relative intensity, into something either more or less itself. The intensification of what constitutes this face (which belongs to the face, and not to the one who sees the face), in various degrees that this face does not control, is activated by the seeing. The beauty of a face is thus found by the seeing, though the beauty of the face is nothing other than the face itself. What the seeing finds is intensified: what is irreplaceable about the face. But what the face acquires is some intensity, a measurement or gradation of beauty. The face has something either more or less beautiful, which allows us to compare this face with another face. The evaluated face becomes comparable and exchangeable with another (for example, the hesitant lover who must choose between two faces), included in some economy, which involves the interplay of exchangeable values.

As we saw in the previous chapter, since at least the nineteenth century, the diagnosis of the crisis of values has corresponded to the replacement of substantial values with formal values. It is the expression of the progressive victory of replaceable values over irreplaceable values, of formal values (useful, economic values) over ancient substantial values (the Beautiful, the True, the Good). However, values are neither substantial nor formal. They are objective.

The 'crisis of values' consists in the progressive compacting of the two senses of every value, as if it were a problem of opposing values: on the one side, irreplaceable values in the things themselves; on the other side, economic, replaceable values in human beings' relations to things through their exchange. The compact solidification of lost values – the Beautiful, the True, and the Good – as if they were values in themselves, gave way to the compact solidification of particular values – useful, economic values. Whether one bemoans this or rejoices in it, this historical progression is in fact a misinterpretation.

The Beautiful, the True, and the Good do not resemble substantial values, nor are they reducible to the economic replaceable values often attributed to them. They are objective values situated in the objects without these values being there.

2. The Beautiful

What does one find when one finds something beautiful?

In *Aesthetic Theory*,[1] Adorno addresses the problem of natural beauty. He cites Wilhelm von Humboldt, who reproached a landscape for not being beautiful enough because it lacked trees. While these words might seem ridiculous, since they reproach a landscape for being what it is, in Adorno's ears they have a particularly interesting ring to them: aesthetic judgement appears to correspond precisely to the possibility of intuiting the difference beneath the natural mask of a thing's identity and how 'it could have been otherwise', how it *ought* to be different from what it is. Every aesthetic judgement is based on the possibility of this implicit reproach, otherwise nothing can be beautiful. We must understand that it could have been different, that it could have been what it is differently, and that it is ugly if it is insufficiently what it is.

The Beautiful would then be some intensity attributed to the identity of a thing, which could be different from the way in which it is. What does one compare a thing to when one claims that it is insufficiently itself? What does one compare a landscape to when one claims that it lacks the trees that would really make it beautiful?

The first possible response to this problem defines what the Beautiful is: an Idea.

A brief survey of the Western philosophical tradition allows us to glimpse a clear *desubstantialisation* of this idea. First, the Platonist *eidos* – the Idea towards which Diotima of Matinea's dialectic of love leads, from the love of beautiful bodies to the love of the beauty of bodies, and then to Beauty itself – is an *in-itself* through which the things that take part in it exist. For Plotinus, when the soul rises from sensible beauty to supreme beauty, from the many to the one, the subject unites with the object, the eye with what it sees: 'seeing and seen are one'. What is ugly is all that is not governed by form, all that is not one, and all that does not correspond to its Idea. The Beautiful as an Idea is therefore the Beautiful in itself, the direct correspondence of what is One to itself. Many things imperfectly take part in this Idea, since the Platonist and Plotinist Beautiful is a compact Beautiful; it is the very embodiment of compactness as a value.

An intensive compactness – a self-saturated substance, something having the most possible amount of selfhood – the Beautiful is the Idea of compactness as a value. All that leads to compactness leads to the Beautiful, that is, self-absoluteness.

The history of ideas and sensibilities in the Renaissance, Romanticism, and post-Romanticism is the history of the problematic construction of this Idea of the Beautiful into a mere 'ideal' of the Beautiful. Held as self-immediacy, the Beautiful is progressively understood as what is lost, and henceforth inaccessible. The world of things takes place in self-distance, and prevents the calm conception of its idea. The active nostalgia of this becoming-ideal idea persists: a necessary, inaccessible concept, glimpsed but concealed, tainted with a sensation of weakening or collapse, which trembles in Marsilio Ficino's lines and Michelangelo's marble statues, only to fail in the Baudelairean Ideal. Charles Baudelaire's work sought to give an account of this idealisation of the Idea. The Beautiful is no longer sufficient to give an account of aesthetic experience of the plurality of judgements, with the rise of democratic sentiment oppressing the poet, and of things, which are introduced between themselves. Aesthetic experience reveals that the Beautiful as an idea of self-immediacy is compact, in the image of the impenetrable blocks that haunt symbolist and Mallarméan poetry. The figure of the dandy, who represents the aesthetic aristocracy in the democratic world of things, is the personal crystallisation of the ideal of the Beautiful – both the abandonment of the possibility of the Idea of the Beautiful and the defence of its subjective necessity. In order to maintain the cosmic possibility of compactness, like the Greeks, in dandyism one must defend the Beautiful's problematic subjective necessity. The Beautiful is no more than what must be directed at as the Idea of the substantial self, without objectively being it.

Philosophically, this aesthetic ideal of the Beautiful, which replaced the dethroned Idea, expresses itself as the subjective Idea in Kant's Third Critique:[2] the Beautiful is what pleases universally, but it is without a concept. Therefore, the Beautiful is not relative, since I must rationally require someone to find beautiful (and thus find beauty in the thing) what I find Beautiful. I cannot have a concept of the Beautiful, since it is only derived through the free use of my faculties, the understanding, and the imagination, and without rules. It is an agreement connected to the perceived object, determined neither by sensory motives nor by a conceptual interest. The Kantian universal without a concept attributes a form of contentless substance to the Beautiful. The Beautiful, which is merely a subjective Idea, is the self-correspondence which anyone can find in things, but without the concept of an end and without the pleasant element of the sensation. For Kant, the Beautiful is neither a judgement of objective utility (external finality) nor a judgement of objective completeness (internal finality), but becomes a mechanism which is supposed to maintain the possibility of value judgements of an object in relation to itself, neither strictly for me nor in reference to what constitutes it. Self-relation is then possible between inside and outside, situated between what the object is in (my use of it, what I make of it) and what is in the object (its organic structure). The possibility of the Beautiful is maintained in this between-the-two. In other words, the possibility of objects that can be judged without a concept is proof that objects are either more or less beautiful, either more or less themselves.

However, by formalising and desubstantialising self-correspondence in this way, and by guaranteeing the loss of the Idea of the Beautiful as a model substance, Kant presents a weak, undetermined beauty, like a sheet of glass between itself and itself, a minimal intensity which Hegel resolidified. Henceforth, rather than being reduced to the Idea of compactness as self-immediacy, the Beautiful unfurled through a series of determinations. Hegel submitted this series to the processes of Spirit, to History, and in the nineteenth century, the series was divided between culture and nature.

In Franz Boas' ethnology, the Beautiful is a cultural concept that is neither the universal aim of artistic creation nor the model idea of self-relation, but simply the determined technical mastery of a form. Boas claims that style exists when form goes beyond an object's mere function.[3] Style depends on a cultural and spatially restricted structure. For Boas, there are two ways of representing space: either by referring to sight, or by representing objects as they appear to the mind. These two ways involve two very distinct criteria of beauty: the correspondence between the object's form and function.

The Beautiful became a concept with a plurality of uses. It no longer meant self-correspondence, but the correspondence of a form to an object according to modes that depend on cultural determinations. The substantial Beautiful, formalised by Kant, is no longer a Self, but rather the difference between form and

object, making possible several cultural configurations and variations, which ground the 'distinction' of taste for Pierre Bourdieu.

The *cultural* Beautiful was ascribed the function of explaining
differences of taste between individuals and societies. In modernity, it falls to the *natural* concept of the Beautiful to give an
account of their supposed *identity*. From Humean naturalism to
Darwinian evolutionism, the naturalist concept of the Beautiful is
relative: it pleases only through its tendency to provoke utility or
pleasure. Its utility is combined with secondary sexual characteristics, the development of an aesthetic instinct, bodily sensations,
colours, forms, sounds, and so on.

The Beautiful clearly underwent a process of desubstantialisation and formalisation. Again, it was defined first as an Idea,
then as an ideal, then as a subjective idea, then as a mere form of
an object's self-intensity, then as a concept, then as the relationship between form and object, then as a cultural concept or a
naturalised concept. In the West, *that which* the Beautiful *was* was
emptied insofar as *that which was* likely to be beautiful expanded.

The crisis of the substantiality of the Beautiful derives from
expanding the spectre of what is likely to be judged beautiful. In
the end, *what can be beautiful* displaced *what the Beautiful can be*.

Romanticism's assimilation of ugliness, Victor Hugo's union of
sublimity and vulgarity, the taste for monstrosity, and the beauty
of ugliness are clearly symptoms of a sensibility that sought primitive values and that weakened the modern understanding of the
idea of the Beautiful. But at the same time, the Beautiful increased
its extension. The nineteenth century carried out the reversal of
what was situated outside the Beautiful: the Baudelarian eternal
and ephemeral halves, and assimilation of the contingent and the
ephemeral, the Rimbauldian resentment against beauty placed on
its knees and insulted, Nietzsche's promotion of the Dionysian,
and Oscar Wilde's[4] denial of absolute beauty and the beautiful
in itself – all these clearly contributed to the formalisation of the
Beautiful. It is no longer a problem of determining the Beautiful
as a self-to-self relation in and through harmony, unity, symmetry,
and so on, but of understanding as Beautiful everything that can be
intensely what it is. Artistic modernity accompanies this change:
Pablo Picasso and Willem de Kooning's dissonance, fragmenta-
tion, and twisting of the norms of the representation of feminine
beauty. Contemporary artists also realise this change: Robert
Filliou's[5] placement of the 'well made', 'badly made', and 'not

made' on an equal footing; Jean Dubuffet's[6] praise of awkward-
ness, luck, the involuntary, and the non-technical. The Beautiful
is ultimately no longer either a substance or an Idea. It is, instead,
the intensified form of everything that is itself. Beautiful things are
things that can be themselves more than other things: aesthetically,
modernity adjusted and popularised this form through the rhetoric
of fashion and look, the assimilation of freaks, beatniks, punks,
the valuation of everything that is self-sufficient, self-advancing,
self-intensifying as novel beauty.

Horror and gore films, far from being the sign of moral decline,
are one of the points of the movement by which the formal beauty
of everything that escapes beauty was incorporated into beauty:
deformation, monstrosity, the dreadful, and the unnamable. They
present moral and physical Evil as an aesthetic object with a strong
intensity, giving it a form of beauty, taking part in the historical
distinction between the Beautiful and the Good, which became
confounded in the compactness of value in itself. Nonetheless,
objections to horror films conflate Good and Evil, but horror
films do not conflate them. Horror films remain moral insofar as
they distinguish Good and Evil and show that even Evil cannot be
precluded from sometimes being beautiful as an 'intense thing'.
Objections to horror's aestheticisation take the side of substantial
value (and confound the Beautiful and the Good) against its formalisation. The objection is that any intensified thing cannot be
held as Beautiful. But the modern incapacity to provide substantial
criteria of the Beautiful against this formal Beautiful, which does
not lead to the Idea of the Beautiful and to its compactness, makes
this resistance a mere *reaction*. The formalisation of aesthetic
value continues to hold.

What can be beautiful or ugly? A body, a face, a body part, an
animal, a vegetable, a mineral, a landscape, the sky, an act, an
artwork, an artisanal object, and so forth.

Any thing can be beautiful or ugly: for any thing does not correspond to a norm of selfhood, but is itself *intensely*. The problem
with this contemporary representation of the Beautiful is that it
replaces an ancient, compact Idea of the Beautiful (Plato's and
Plotinus's Beautiful) with self-compactness. Since any thing can
be beautiful if it is intensely itself, the Beautiful is what makes
any thing distinct, original, singular, and what assures the interchangeability of things, since the reduction of the Beautiful to the
'intensely itself' makes beautiful things exchangeable with each

other. What resembles a beautiful human, because it is intensely itself, more than another human or than a potato (as in Henri Cueco), which are beautiful because they are themselves at the highest point?

The Beautiful transformed as a value through the gradual extension of what can be beautiful and the corresponding reduction of what the Beautiful is. In this way, the compactness of the ancient Beautiful as a substantial irreplaceable value made way for the compactness of the modern Beautiful as a formal self-replaceable value.

The meaning of the Beautiful as an objective value must be decided between the two. It is the intensification of this thing. The Beautiful is the transformation of a determined thing with greater or lesser intensities through natural, cultural, and individual processes, through which one compares the thing to what it could have been and to what it could be. A thing's beauty is its value insofar as one can find in it the potential to see another thing as what it is, and as one compares the thing to what it is not. A thing's beauty is the value that it takes when one finds or does not find in it something more and better than itself, or not more and better than itself.

Everything that is *something* can therefore be either beautiful or ugly. As an objective relation, $2 + 2 = 4$ is neither beautiful nor ugly, but it can be aestheticised, since I can make an object of it. What escapes the beautiful and the ugly, the value of something's intensification, is the relation between the being and comprehension between two objects, which is neither the ugly nor the beautiful, but either *true* or *false*.

If to find the beautiful is to find something (and to intensify it), to find the truth is to find a relation between objects (and to intensify it).

3. The True

It may be strange to consider truth as an intensity. Normally we think that a proposition is either true or false. In the twentieth century, heterodox logics rejected the law of excluded middle, which in Poland produced logics intensifying the values of truth and falsehood.

We do not defend any of these logics, but only attempt to determine what can be true or false, and why the true revealed its intensive character by desubstantialising, like the Beautiful.

Things cannot have intensities of truth or falsehood. Things can only have aesthetic intensities, since we find them to be either more or less what they are. The difference between the Beautiful and the True, which are irreducible to each other, consists in their application. While things exist entirely in the Beautiful, the True always concerns the being and comprehension of *objects*. What is true and false is never something. But falsehood is in truth and truth comprehends falsehood.

There is truth only of what is *present* (or absent), and not of what *is*.

Truth is the possibility that the relation between two objects can be reinforced or redoubled. To say that it is true that I have stolen money from a wallet is to distinguish the fact that I have stolen money from the wallet from the fact that I have not stolen it, by redoubling the former by a value, an intensity, which makes it *more* than the latter. However, the fact that I have not stolen the money from the wallet *is* not less: it *is* untrue, it *is* fictional, and it *is* illusory. Perhaps it is even beautiful. Formally, it is *equal*, whether I have stolen from the wallet or not. The two events are equivalent, even if they are different things (a real fact and a fictional fact). Truth is what intensifies one of the two events by redoubling its being. One fact is more than the other. Falsehood diminishes the intensity of an event's being, while truth accentuates it.

Truth is an intensity because it never has the power to reduce falsehood to nothingness. The fact that it is true that I stole money from the wallet diminishes the intensity of being false, but it does not reduce being false to nothing. The fact that I have not stolen money from the wallet is always something; in short, its falsehood weakens it.

Truth is thus what reinforces the being of an event, the relation between objects, while falsehood is what weakens it.

But the crisis of substantial truth corresponds not to challenging truth through falsehood, but rather to the appearance of weakness joined with the strengthening of truth.

For example, in ancient scepticism, the proof of truth could always undergo the production of the equal value of the affirmation and negation of a determined proposition: time is finite or infinite; matter is divisible or indivisible. A symmetric relation exists between the truth and falsehood of a proposition. In the

modern context, the case is different: doubt concerns not the truth
of the relation (for example, if this cat is black or not), but rather
our *relation to this relation*. The relativisation of the truth of a
proposition does not derive from the possibility of the truth of the
opposite proposition, but from our relation to this proposition:
you say that this cat is black, but it is *you* who says this.

The second crisis of truth derives from the dissolution of its
terms: truth places objects in a relation that can continually be
questioned. You say that the cat is black, but who tells you that
this black is black? What is a cat? Not a feline? Not a York choco-
late or a Norwegian forest? Who tells you that it is not its coat
which is black, and not the cat itself which is black? Is everything
in blackness? No. What proves its blackness? Did you see it? Was
it not genetically modified? 'Is' it really black?

The crisis of truth, its desubstantialisation, is twofold. On the
one hand, our relation to the true relation is doubted. On the other
hand, things placed in relation by the true relation are objected to
and challenged until they slip through our hands and disappear like
sand. Since the truth reinforces the relation between two things, its
modern state of crisis does not correspond to a frontal attack on
truth through falsehood or the true relation itself, but performs an
attack on the flanks. It is our relation to this reinforced relation,
things placed in relation by this relation which are weakened by
the reinforcement distinct to truth. On one side, one will say that a
truth is only ever *my truth*: it is my relation to this relation; others
think differently, and it is their right to do so, one will say. On the
other side, one will object not to the true relation by itself, but to
the things placed in relation. Of course Elvis Presley is dead, but
was Elvis the Elvis who is dead? This is the key to every contemporary 'conspiracism', every conspiracy theory; it does not perform a
frontal attack on truth, but a flank attack.

The two objections which mark the crises of substantial truth
are therefore lateral objections. They do not concern a relation's
existence or nonexistence, but the relativity of the subject for
whom this relation exists, and the very identity of objects placed
in relation.

Truth was first attributed to thought since it was conceived as
substantial. Truth is presented as a content or corpus of truths,
embodied in sacred myths and revealed truth. Here it is a truth
absolutely independent of our relation to this truth or corpus
of truths in themselves. Its specificity does not change through

time and events, but must be interpreted to be applicable to what appears to us. A revealed truth is a truth without relation, requiring a human being to *itself* construct its relation to this truth in itself in order to interpret it, make it meaningful, and place it in relation to reality. It is a truth (the Trinity, the Prophet's words, the Buddha's teaching, Shintoism's creation of the world) which is fixed in itself and can become changeable only for and through our interpretation.

Truth is gradually displaced, while thinking interprets what happens and gives truth a value in relation to a given corpus of truths.

But this realignment between thinking, which interprets a body of truths, and changing reality necessarily became truth's centre of gravity, which was gradually displaced outside revelation. Truth became *adaequatio rei et intellectus*, a sought-after coincidence between intellect (knower) and things (known).[7] Truth is then not a series of propositions, but the relation between truth that says *that which 'is' is* and falsehood that says *that which 'is not' is*. This relation is at the heart of the Aristotelian and Thomist medieval controversies. It yields a truth that is not prior to its relation to things, but derives from this relation. It was therefore necessary for the conditions of its verifiability to be distinguished from the conditions of its verification, by differentiating a formal truth, which is a context and linguistic expression of truth-conditions, from the factual truth, which is the adequate relation between a context and what is actually characterised therein. However, Kant claimed[8] that if I must compare my knowledge of things to things, I can only do so through my knowledge of things, since adequation cannot be a universal characteristic of truth as regards its *content*. Adequation, which for Kant became the relation between knowledge and the universal and formal laws of understanding, is nothing but the necessary and insufficient truth-condition, or 'negative condition' of truth – and transcendental logic cannot venture any further.

Truth is thus internalised as a *formal* thought-relation, without any content-relation. This internalisation of truth as a thought-relation leads to attributing truth to the language which contains the formal conditions.

Modern considerations of truth as a logical condition or function (Wittgenstein) object to the relation between substance and predicate in favour of a propositional relation. The law of excluded middle alone remains substantial and not merely functional. At the beginning of the twentieth century, objections to the law of excluded middle arose. Faced with L. E. J. Brouwer's intuitionism, Bertrand Russell claimed that the desubstantialisation of excluded middle and the prospect of non-standard logics essentially consist in confounding the truth and the known. But what is the status of that which one does not yet know the truth about, of that which one says is true but which one may later say is false, or vice versa?

In modern logic, what substantially subsists in the relation between truth and language is confronted with the passage of time. Eternal Cartesian truths give way to the crisis of a modern history of truths. Nicolas Malebranche could claim that I know that $2 + 2 = 4$, and that I must love my friend more than my neighbour.[9] But George Orwell considered the possibility, in *Nineteen Eighty-Four*,[10] that $2 + 2 = 5$ if the Party deems it so. And since human sensibility changed, Curzio Malaparte could honestly claim, in *The Skin*, to have preferred his dog Febo to all his friends.[11] The history of scientific truths, which Thomas Kuhn considered as so many successive paradigms, and the questioning of the status of Greek myths or truths of other peoples gave way to the modern assumption that a history exists, histories of truths, attributing truth not to the eternal but to the relative.

First, a body of truths became a relationship between intellect and things, then truth was internalised in thought and formalised in language, and then became less a relationship than a relation, and less a relation than the relative par excellence. Truth is no longer considered as a substance, nor even as a substantial relationship, but refers to a meta-relation ad infinitum. Truth changes according to cultures, languages, logics, discourses, and persons. Assimilating the relativity of relationships, it was necessary to make a meta-relation true.

Then, truth went away.

Truth remains as an objective relationship, but our relation to this relation is mediated by the relativity of our culture, our uses, our tastes, our interests, and so on. Things that truth relates to dissolve. For example, historical revisionism is typical of the strategies wielded against truth. A fact is not denied, but everything that enters into this true fact is dissected, dissolved, and contested to such an extent that truth becomes a *weakening force*.

By attributing truth-values to a relation, one defends this relation from any other possibility and strengthens its solidity in order to weaken opposing relations. By evaluating this relation, by determining a truth, one effectuates an architectural work that strengthens certain articulations of the objective and evential world. Above the formal flat world, truth is the cement that solidifies certain connections at the expense of others. But by safeguarding certain relations (for example, the fact that the Nazi authorities planned and accomplished mass exterminations of Jews in World War II), one immediately weakens the relational terms. The fact is accepted, but each object that enters into this relation is weakened. Why only mention exterminations 'of Jews'? What does one mean by 'mass'? Was there really a 'plan'? It is not falsehood that opposes truth here, but the weakening of terms in the reinforcement of relations.

Truth strengthens a relation between objects and events of the world, but having done so, it discloses and exposes what is placed in relation. To find a connection between two things is to find what both strengthens them and reveals their Achilles heel.

The modern crisis of truth is due to this paradox: after desubstantialisation, truth as a strengthened formal relation jeopardises what it safeguards the connection from. Becoming for us a meta-relation, a relational relation, mediated by the relativity of our language, our era, our culture, and our uses, truth is a way of relating to the way in which things relate to each other.

All that is true became weak.

Truth is no longer substantial, nor is it a body of revealed truths, or a thought's or language's relation to things. Rather, it is a relative relation, a relational relation, which is not threatened by falsehood, but instead by the problem of *the very truth of truth*.

In safeguarding the relations between certain objects of the universe, truth exposes these objects even more, and nothing is open to doubt except that which enters into a truth. It is symptomatic that the greatest contemporary scepticism is tied not to doubtful affairs, but rather to particularly well-attested events; doubts about the attacks against the World Trade Center and the Pentagon on September 11 demonstrate the weakening force of truth. The more one demonstrates the truth of a relation (that two planes struck two towers which fell and were filmed), the more the elements of this relation are doubted. What if something other than the planes caused the collapse of the towers? What if explosives caused their collapse? What if the American Secret Service, which still had some of their offices in the towers, financed or encouraged this attack? Why did the towers fall in *this* way? What if the responsible parties were not the responsible parties and the victims not the victims?

In truth, one never really doubts what is doubtful, but only what enters into a truth; doubt is excited by truth, like a child's burning desire to knock down a house of cards.

4. The Good

If the True is the value of the relation between the being and comprehension between objects, the Good is the value of an object *for* another object. The problem of the Good is not that of knowing whether or not an object is in another object, but of knowing whether this object augments another object or diminishes it. What augments its universe is good and what diminishes it is bad.

Like any value, the ethical value of the Good is not formal. Formally, each thing augments that in which it is and nothing ever diminishes. An object which is in another object always augments this object. Formally, the Devil's possibility, the great dictator's existence, trickery, rape, murder, genocide, the vilest cruelty, and the suffering of all living beings augment the universe. They are additional things, since formally each thing equally counts as one.

Good is an intensity insofar as objects can be augmented more than they are through what they comprehend. By judging something as bad, one judges that its existence diminishes what it is in, and that its nonexistence augments the state of objects. Good exists only *for* a thing, since augmenting or diminishing exists only for the augmented or diminished thing through some object or event. The Rwandan genocide is certainly an evil event for Rwanda and for all of humanity. Two thousand years from now, if all of humanity disappears, the Rwandan genocide may not be evil for the universe, since there would no longer be anything for which this tragic event could be evil.

Nonetheless, since objects and events are in each other, Good and Evil are not relative. They are related to an augmented or diminished thing through this or that object or event, but they can also relate to the universe, to the biggest possible thing. Thus, it may be that *universal* Good and *universal* Evil exist, even if neither *formal* Good nor *formal* Evil exist. The extinction of the human race or life in general would clearly be a universal Evil, since it would deprive the universe of life's every objective and evential intensification. The preservation of life and humanity are universal goods, though they are not formal goods – formally, it may be that the human species' disappearance would lose equal amounts of Good and Evil.

According to the Christian formula, Good is overabundance. It is the augmentation of augmentation. Every object augments the universe, but a good object augments and intensifies this augmentation, whereas a bad object augments the universe with something *less*. However, since Good and Evil are values and cannot be formal, an objective or eviential Good cannot sufficiently augment the universe to the point of annihilating bad objects. Good never augments the augmentation of an object to the point of making it an absolute object, and Evil never diminishes an object's entering into the universe down to nothingness.

To do Good is to augment the objective universe, a set of objects and events, more than the mere existence of this object augments this universe. Everything that does more than bring mere existence to the universe is good. Everything that overflows from the mere fact of existing and strengthens a community of living beings, a set of objects, is good.

Whoever does Good must know that nothing formally guarantees that doing Good is good. All ethical behaviour derives from the knowledge of its non-formal character. By doing good, I lose the guarantee that the Good is good, because, formally, the Good is neither good nor bad. To care for a wounded animal can be good, insofar as it is an act which augments the community of living beings around me. But if I ask if it is good to augment this community of living beings, I will never find ethical criteria that are reducible to my own criteria. If it is good to augment the universe rather than to diminish it, it is because to augment the universe is not good (but is not bad either). The foundation of compact criteria of the Good, which G. E. Moore criticised,[12] is marked by the desire to determine a Good of Good, to define how *it would be good to be good.*

This 'good Good' appears as the Sovereign Good in Western antiquity. The Sovereign Good is a substantial good in itself, not the Good for a thing, however big, but the Good in itself, both universal and formal.

The problem of compactness is that it tends to unify everything that self-compacts; the ancients confounded substantial values. How can one distinguish the Good, the Beautiful, and the True when they are confounded in the One, Plotinus's *apex* of value compactness? The more that the Good is compact, in itself, absolute, the more it is unified with the True and the Beautiful. The crisis of the desubstantialisation of values is nothing other than the attempt to distinguish values and to go beyond the ancient compactness of a true and beautiful Good. To distinguish the Good from the Beautiful, it was necessary to think of the Good as a relational value. This relational value does not concern one thing alone (it is neither true nor false), but what exists *between* two objects. By assuming that something is beautiful or ugly, but not good or bad in itself, one distinguishes the Beautiful from the Good. Then, to differentiate it from the True, it was necessary to add that the Good corresponds to the intensification, not of a relation between objects, but of the orientation of this relation.

Epicurus and Diogenes Laertius's economy of Goods[13] was the first to desubstantialise and transform the Good. The passage from the absolute Good to the relational Good distinguished the preferable in itself from the preferable in light of another thing. The Good is what I must choose and prefer; other goods are those that I choose in light of the Good.

The next transformation occurred through the passage from the relational Good – liable to stratification from the Good for another thing to the Good for itself – to the Good chosen object. Offered the choice, Cartesian Good organises a formal equality and its opposite and an objective superiority, because it is one possibility among others for subjectivity, but at the same time the only possibility which is necessary.

The Good was at first an object. Then Søren Kierkegaard made the Good the result of a choice. Utilitarianism reduced the Good to formal augmentation. It was not substantialised but formalised; it is what augments pleasure and diminishes the suffering of active, sentient creatures in the universe.

First an absolute, then a relation, and then a choice, the Good becomes 'most' formal for us. Like every value, the Good passed from substantial, undifferentiated compactness to formal differentiation through its connections to the replaceable value of things. The modern Good, confounded with utility, is the calculated augmentation of pleasure for living things – that is, a quantity which allows the comparison and interchangeability of events, of decisions, and of facts. 'Another view of the Good'[14] remains, faced with the conflation of desubstantialised Good and utility, which more or less ties it to the Good: self-realisation, an adventure, an ethical way of being one's own author and/or of taking care of others.[15]

Ancient Sovereign Good was a compact Good; the useful Good of contemporary utilitarianism is also a compact Good. The ancients did not differentiate the irreplaceable values (the Beautiful, the True, and the Good) within a substance; utilitarians confound all values into an exchangeable value included in the implacable logic of the economy of objects. While the logic of the economy of objects strengthened exchangeable values, resisting the moral, sociological, and anthropological attempts to make an absolute exception of it, Western history carries with it the desubstantialisation of irreplaceable values, which were formerly left undifferentiated in an untenable and compact substantial value.

We now have a response to our question concerning the principle of the historical unification of cultures through some relation to interchangeable objects. The modern processes of the desubstantialisation of values was compelling – and it caused the historical universalisation of an economy of objects – because it de-compacted the intensities of objects and events by differentiating the Beautiful, the True, and the Good. But we must understand that these processes ended up betraying themselves, since they resulted in a compacting of the exchangeable value of things.

We've come full circle. The modern processes of the economy of objects associated with the development of utilitarianism, after having freed the ancient Beautiful, True, and Good through their desubstantialisation and differentiation, compacted all these values into a single economic exchangeable value.

5. Desubstantialisation of Values and Universal Intensification

All values stand between a single compact, substantial value, which tempted the Greeks and traverses the myths of numerous peoples, and a single economic value, which makes things interchangeable and exchangeable, crystallising during the Victorian era of utilitarianism and progressively dominating the Western and contemporary world.

Values are meaningful only if we understand them as between these two senses. The value of things is neither formal nor substantial. It yields neither an irreplaceable thing nor interchangeable things. It is absolutely pointless to either make something singular or to count and compare it with others. The value of things functions in two senses, between these two impasses.

The Beautiful lost in comprehension what it gained in extension. By assimilating the ugly, horrible, formless, ephemeral, dissonant, and different into the Beautiful, the Beautiful is not the idea of compactness, of an immediate self-relation, but rather the intensification of all that is something. The formalisation of the Beautiful gradually led to making it a mere self-intensity – what is the greatest possibility itself is beautiful.

In the same way, the desubstantialisation of the True, this weakening force, through its distance from the relational relation and its relativisation, led it from a body of revealed truths to a realignment between thought and things, and then to an internal relation between thought and knowledge, an internal relation relative to uses, cultures, and interests. Finally, the True became the reinforcement of the relation between objects that exposes and weakens the relational terms.

The Good underwent a similar process of desubstantialisation. The substantial Sovereign Good, indistinct from other values, was compact. It then distinguished itself as a directed relation, as a relational Good. Finally, the Good was conceived as the augmentation of the augmentation of the existence of objects in the universe. What augments the universe by augmenting it is good; what augments the universe by diminishing it is bad. But the relativisation of this Good, and its use in the economy of objects, led to a compact, useful Good at the foundation of the modern economy of objects.

Substantial irreplaceable values – a thing's non-exchangeable, non-economic value in itself – were made impossible. We cannot recuperate them by conceiving of ethical states of exception, like Kant, or social states of exception, like Mauss.

We cannot appeal to states of exception simply by affirming that human persons are not things or that love is a value which does not convert into cash. Human persons and love are things. But they can be neither substantial values (a Beautiful, a Truth, or a Good in itself) nor formal values (an exchange value or counted value). In reality, the value of things is *objective*.

Values are qualities of things that we find in them without them being there. They mark the transformation of things into variable intensities. Each thing receives with its value what makes it simultaneously exchangeable with another and irreplaceable. Like any other thing, human beings have values. Like things, they are beautiful or ugly. In their relations with other objects, they are true or false. In relation to their environment, the earth, or the universe, they are good or bad. Values intensify them, give them depth, and uproot them from the flat world. They transform their determinate extension into an interplay between more or less variable values, which give them their irreplaceable singularity. At the same time, the values that humans have make them comparable to other things and restricted to possible calculations of their worth in relation to other species and other things, since their values also provide them with pictures of their relative identity.

A dead universe would not be formally flat, but neutralised. Life unquestionably intensifies, increases, and empties the depths of the universe. Living beings find things beautiful or ugly – that is, either more or less than what they are. They find relations true or false – that is, strengthened or weakened. They find good and evil – that is, augmentations that are overabundant or impoverishing.

Living things give (aesthetic, alethic, and ethical) values to the universe, but they find these values only in the universe itself. Values are objective; living things are content with intensifying them.

Notes

1. 'Wilhelm von Humboldt occupies a position between Kant and Hegel in that he holds fast to natural beauty yet in contrast to Kantian formalism endeavors to concretise it. Thus in his writing on the Vasks [. . .] he presents a critique of nature that, contrary to what would be expected one hundred and fifty years later, has not become ridiculous in spite of its earnestness. Humboldt reproaches a magnificent craggy landscape for the lack of trees [. . .] Yet this naïveté, which does not delimit the use of human taste at the boundary of extrahuman nature, attests to a relation to nature that is incomparably deeper than admiration that is content with whatever it beholds', Theodor W. Adorno, *Aesthetic Theory*, p. 93. Later, Adorno offers this formula: 'Natural beauty is the trace of the nonidentical in things under the spell of universal identity', ibid., p. 95.
2. Immanuel Kant, *Critique of the Power of Judgment*.
3. Franz Boas, *Primitive Art*.
4. 'A subject that is beautiful in itself gives no suggestion to the artist. It

lacks imperfection.' Oscar Wilde, 'A Few Maxims for the Instruction of the Over-Educated'.

5. Robert Filliou's exhibit, *Le Principe d'équivalence: bien fait – mal fait – pas fait*, opened at Alfred Schmela's gallery in Düsseldorf in 1969.

6. Jean Dubuffet, 'Notes pour les fins lettrés'.

7. Before the conformity of the concept to the object takes the form of truth in consciousness, the addition of an intellectual judgement is required, which carries things in it, and which happens to confront them, so that truth marks the conjunction of this intellectual motivation with an object distinct from it: '*Quid sit veritas?* [. . .] *Adaequatio rei et intellectus*', Saint Thomas Aquinas, *De Veritate*, first question, first article. In the *Summa Theologiae*: '*Per conformitatem intellectus et rei, veritas definitur*', first part, sixteenth question, article two. See Michel Nodé-Langlois, *Le Vocabulaire de saint Thomas*.

8. Immanuel Kant, *Critique of Pure Reason*.

9. 'I see, for example, that twice two is four, and that my friend is to be valued more than my dog; and I am certain that no one in the world does not see this as well as I', Nicolas Malebranche, *Elucidations of the Search After Truth*, Elucidation X, p. 613.

10. Winston Smith asks in the third part if the State has the power to define this formula as true. A leader explains to him that the Party can do so 'in certain circumstances', which seems to mean that it can manipulate what is attributed to it with mathematical knowledge, but not create mathematical knowledge from beginning to end. At the end of the book, Smith writes the equation '$2 + 2 =$' without giving a response to it (in the original version), or by assimilating the lesson of the Party and writing the anticipated '5' (in the French version). This cultural difference between the two versions is in itself a novel symptom of the weakening of truth. See George Orwell, *Nineteen Eighty-Four*. The individual's challenging of the truth of '$2 \times 2 = 4$', rather than the collective institution's, also appears in Fyodor Dostoyevsky's *Notes from Underground*, wherein both the protagonist and society contest the concept of absolute truth, which oppresses in the guise of a universal formula.

11. Curzio Malaparte, *The Skin*.

12. George Edward Moore, *Principia Ethica*.

13. 'Of things indifferent, as they express it, some are "preferred," others "rejected." Such as have value, they say, are "preferred," while such as have negative, instead of positive, value are "rejected."'

Diogenes Laertius, *Lives of Eminent Philosophers*, Book VII, 105, p. 211.

14. This is the title of Emmanuel Halais's work, *Une autre vision du bien*, which takes note of the end of the 'mythologies' announced by Cora Diamond, without giving in to the contemporary egoism which reduces an ethical individual to an atom.

15. See, for example, the desubstantialisation of the 'Good', against the myths of empiricism, post-Kantian idealism, utilitarianism, existentialism, and behaviourism, and also the refutation of uncommitted 'meta-ethics', in Iris Murdoch's *The Sovereignty of Good*.

Chapter XIII

Classes

1. To Value, to Classify

The universe is both *valued* and *classified*. Valuation and classification are the two fundamental actions which give order to the universe. By valuing objects and events, one intensifies things with either more or less of the Beautiful, the True, and the Good. By classifying objects and events, one does not consider the intensity of things, but their extension and the way they belong to other objects or events.

An object is never alone in a thing which comprehends it, because only things are alone. An object which is red is never alone in redness. A being which is human is never alone in humanity. Someone who is a believer is never alone in their belief.

The relation between several objects which are together in a thing that comprehends them is no longer a value relation, but a *class* relation.

To classify objects is to define their way of being in something together.

Every class determines a common membership, an *extension* to objects or events, whereas a value determines an *intensity* of these objects or events. The scientific classification of material elements into orders of scale, causal series, or temporal sequences, demonstrates the need to order not values, but common elemental membership. However, the classification of living things and humanity leads to class conflicts. For, if an object is in some class, that is, in some relation with other objects comprehended in the same thing, it can also be in *another* class, enmeshed in other relations with other objects, since it is also comprehended in another thing. While the classification of non-organic objects essentially depends on common characteristics which are unlikely to conflict, the distinguishing feature of living things and humanity is to produce class memberships which increasingly overlap each other. Humanity does not classify itself in the same way as it classifies the non-organic: its classes inter-comprehend rather than juxtapose each other.

In addition to genders, which we will address in the next chapter, three primary classes divide humanity: (1) classes of origin, which divide up everything that a human being derives from, including her biological lineage, family, and ethnicity; (2) classes of ideas, which divide up what a human thinks, believes, or identifies with; and (3) classes of action, which divide up what a human does, including her social activities, her way of living or of survival, and her interests.

The solidification of the first kind of class produces models of individuals defined essentially by their origin, which crystallises in the transformation of classes into *races*. The solidification of the second kind of class produces individuals defined essentially by ideas, beliefs, or knowledge, which crystallises in the transformation of classes into *sects*. The solidification of the third kind of class produces individuals defined essentially by their interests, which crystallises in the transformation of classes into *social classes* or *classes of interests* – 'classes' *tout court*, in the Marxist sense of the term.

Each process marks the transformation of a class into a compact class, without this compactness being immediate. Racism reached its theoretical apex of compactness near the end of the nineteenth century, although it has appeared in numerous guises throughout history. For example, Pierre-André Taguieff analyses the notion of 'racialism'[1] in Ernest Renan[2] and Arthur de Gobineau.[3] First, human history traces the overlapping of class divisions of origin, at times including racism, which may be defined as the division of humanity exclusively according to biological or cultural classes of origin. Second, it traces the overlapping of class divisions of ideas and beliefs, at times including sectarianism, from philosophical sects to religious schisms, from party struggles to excommunications by aesthetic groups. Third, it traces the overlapping of class divisions of interest, including the universalisation of the Marxist class struggle.

A *compact* class is a class in which the thing that comprehends objects of the same class becomes the class itself. Two objects which are in the same thing are not in the same class. They are in the same thing *through* a class relation. Two human beings, for example, who are members of the Gurunsi tribe that the colonists called 'Frafra' (a term derived from a polite expression meaning 'how is your work?') share a set of customs, practices, technologies, habits, representations, and beliefs which compel them to maintain a self-identical relationship. But if the class of origin becomes compact, including *race*, then the two human beings in question will be nothing but 'Frafras' for the explorers and colonists of Burkina Faso. *All* of their customs and *all* of their representations will classify different Gurunsi individuals as 'Frafras', in such a way that they will not live in a customary and representational community, but in an ethnic identity.

Class compactness (which, in Marx and Lukács, positively corresponds to class consciousness) is *being* what one *has* in common with others, or more precisely no longer having an identity shared by others, and being *merely* what one shares with those that are like us.

Ethnic or racial identities are processes making that which human beings are compact. They are ways of requiring that someone be essentially what they share with others: a (biological or cultural) origin.

Human identities of ideas or beliefs, when they self-compact, also consist in making a being be what it can share with others: a revelation, knowledge, faith, or idea. Every philosophical sect, church, and political party tends, in some way, to make its class of individuals compact. This does not mean that they succeed in doing so, but they lead to this compactness, which can only function if it also works against itself. What leads to a sect, a part of humanity which encloses its idea within itself, is a community of ideas which gradually prevents its members from being parts of another class, that is, from also having an identity different from that of the idea which founds the sect.

The social class or class of interests becomes compact when it determines every other type of membership to the point where anyone who is a member of a social class cannot belong to something else without this thing being derived from that social class. The tension in Marx's work, for example, results from the dialectical effort to produce a theory of humanity with determined and determining classes, but without making these classes compact.

2. Classes of Origins, Classes of Ideas, Classes of Interests

In the final unfinished pages of *Capital*, Marx tried to redefine classes. He resorts to the exposition of a problem emphasised later by Joseph Schumpeter and Raymond Aron. The sociological definition that he appears to give of social classes tends to split up social divisions into as many wholes as there are interests (especially professional interests). The heuristic and political definition of social classes tends to divide into three major classes, one of which is progressively situated outside of history (landowners), leaving the two other classes comparable through a dialectical materialist logic.

Marx writes that:

the owners merely of labour-power, owners of capital, and landowners, whose respective sources of income are wages, profit and ground-rent, in other words, wage-labourers, capitalists and landowners, constitute then three big classes of modern society based upon the capitalist mode of production.[4]

He then derives from this triad a definition of social class:

The first question to be answered is this: What constitutes a class? – and the reply to this follows naturally from the reply to another question, namely: What makes wage-labourers, capitalists and landlords constitute the three great social classes? At first glance – the identity of revenues and sources of revenue.[5]

Marx establishes the class of actions as the primary class of human society: income relations and sources of income relations, how everyone obtains the means of maintaining life either through rent, work, or capital, which divides social humanity and individuals in the social domain of the modern capitalist world. Marxism neutralises the division into classes of origin, which leads to a game of false divisions, requiring the proletarian unity of all individuals, and reducing identities of social *being* to illusory identities of social *doing*. The division into classes of ideas is split into two possibilities: false consciousness, like opiated religious consciousness, producing illusory communities; and true consciousness, class consciousness, which politically allows the only true class of ideas, 'communism' – that is, the identification of individuals with an idea corresponding to social truth, to the division into classes of interests, to the class struggle, and to its deeper meaning.

Marx has three divisions: authentic classes (social classes), inauthentic classes (biological or cultural classes of origin), and both authentic and inauthentic classes (classes of ideas, emancipatory consciousness, and false consciousness). But the division of authentic classes which allows the valuation or devaluation of the other two is itself ambiguous. Marx continually tries to transform the compactness of his social division of classes into a dialectics, but he cannot solve the problem by reducing actual classes to the modern triad of landowners, capitalist property owners, and the proletariat. Another more precise standpoint exists from which Marx thinks that he is able to distinguish differences of interests within the same income class:

> However, from this standpoint, physicians and officials, e.g., would also constitute two classes, for they belong to two distinct social groups, the members of each of these groups receiving their revenue from one and the same source. The same would also be true of the infinite fragmentation of interest and rank into which the division of social labour splits labourers as well as capitalists and landlords – the latter, e.g., into owners of vineyards, farm owners, owners of forests, mine owners and owners of fisheries.[6]

Capital ends on this observation, which is open to interpretation. Marx's work doesn't solve the difficulty, but it indicates the risk involved in the production of a compact theory of classes – a temptation which follows in the later history of Marxism – and the necessity of ascending and descending along each class from infinite pluralisation to formal unification.

Marxism as a fundamental theory of classes is caught in a stranglehold: the necessity of reducing class relations to political and historical conflicts (which allow us to make the struggle meaningful and history readable) and the impossibility of doing so. By reducing class relations to a triad leading to a dualism, Marxism becomes a compact theory. In Marxism, classes of origin are denied and immediately assimilated into the production of racist or racialist constructions. Moreover, classes of ideas are reduced to the problem between authentic communist consciousness and its opposite (and, therefore, the community of ideas is indexed on the true or false recognition of the social division of classes). But – and Marx senses this in the final paragraph – to accept as such the possible dissolution of classes in the infinite plurality of professional interests and social functions, with some spirit of finesse, would not be to make class compact any more, but rather to dissolve it in a nominalism. Ultimately, there would no longer be anything except individual interests, and the only real class would be the class corresponding to each social individual, to her *particular* activities and interests. Moreover, a number of Marxists wrongly or rightly identify the theoretical foundation of *liberalism* in this nominalism which reduces classes to social individuals.

In fact, Marxism is caught between the dissolution of social classes, including the more or less fantasised atomistic liberal class, and the compactness of social classes reduced to a more or less dialectical gigantomachy between the proletariat and the property-owning classes, as the primary and ultimate division of all human divisions.

3. We

This difficulty of producing a concept of class between the individual and the compact class is not specific to Marxism. *Every* theory of class is confronted with the same formal difficulty. It is the case with racialist theorists, who are trapped between the dissolution of races (or what Gustave Le Bon[7] calls interracial mixing) and the projection of entirely theoretical and conceptual races (such as the Caucasian or Mongolian races, which are big things, encompassing too many differences to subsist as such). It is also what appears in every culturalist theory. How can cultures be identified as classes of origin? How can one avoid their dissolution into the different facts and acts of each individual? How can one avoid compacting cultures into all-too-big civilisations, which are nothing but theoretical unities, as in Spengler?

This entails the modern problem of identifying a 'we'. Who are 'we' and who do we speak for politically? On this side of the human species – threatened to dissolve into a 'we' of animals, a 'we' of living things, or a 'we' of natural things – human classes gradually struggle to remain the concrete expressions par excellence of first persons in the political plural. The Marxist's 'we' – formerly guaranteed by the concept of 'proletariat' (linking class to the universal) and indexed on the undeniable reality of the working class – sociologically breaks apart (public employees, temporary workers, the unemployed) and philosophically blurs (the exploited, oppressed, dominated, or subaltern). The racialist's 'we' decomposes downstream in the ethnic whirlpool, disintegrates upstream in the geneticist's genealogical trees, and tries to stabilise through traditional and cultural permanence. The 'we' of the sectarian of ideas also fails to discern the difference between those who truly believe (in anything), those who believe a little, those who believe in several sometimes incompatible ideas, those who believe without practising, those who believe without even knowing they believe, and so on. Classes – between the individual and the universal – and the political 'we' are no longer guaranteed. What did this 'we' become? What does it comprehend? Which class does it represent?

Nonetheless, it is quite necessary to classify objects which are in each other – humans and other objects – since class cannot be dissolved into an individual thing, nor be condensed in a specific universe.

A class is a minimal relation between objects which have a common way of belonging to the same thing. This relation can be minimised until it is almost confounded with each object. It can also be maximised until it is confounded with the thing which comprehends all these objects. In the first case, class leads to the individual without reaching it, for class is always a relation between two objects, and a relation with a thing. The nominalist or ultraliberal mistake is therefore to think that they can dissolve every class simply by keeping the individual. But an individual object is never alone in a thing that comprehends it (since only a thing is alone in the world): no human is alone in humanity, no peasant is alone in the peasantry, and so on. Therefore, human social divisions can never divide solitary things, atomistic individuals, in the human universe, but only objects together, connected objects, individuals in classes. Since society is not the (formal) world but an (objective) universe – that is, a big thing – individuals are metaphysically not alone in society like each thing is alone in the world. Social beings can only be in society *together*. To reduce classes to individuals is therefore a compact way of thinking, since it would be to consider the social universe as a metaphysical world where everyone would be equally alone. Society is a big thing where everything always goes in pairs, and therefore in relation to classes.

In the second case, the mistake – which preoccupied the history of Marxism – consists in confounding these classes with that in which individuals are located. Workers are not in the working class. They are in a way of life, a set of uses, constraints, possibilities, and values, which group them together *through* some relation, which we can call the class of workers. But to place workers *in* the working class, either to dominate or control them, or to emancipate them, to allow the trade unionist, cultural, or political emergence of class consciousness, is to produce a compact identity. A working individual will no longer be capable of identifying with anything except what they have in common with other working individuals. They will be like a Christian, Jewish, or Muslim individual to whom one does not attribute being Christian, Jewish, or Muslim by being another thing, but being *only* that which all Christians, or all Jews, or all Muslims are. Identitarian compactness is the constitution of an individual identity by what is common. By self-identifying with one's class, whether it be ethnic, of thought, of belief, or of interest, one reduces one's self to what everyone identically shares with others.

A class never has an operative sense unless it has two senses. One may reduce a class to the individual, without ever touching the individual, which is neither in the class nor a class in itself. One may enlarge a class to a general concept, without ever touching the universal, which is not a class, but the big thing in which the objects to classify reside.

But an individual is not comprehended inside a class, as a holist may be tempted to believe, nor is an individual outside a class, as a nominalist may be tempted to believe. Identities between individual things, and not the individual things themselves, are classified. It is what I have in common with other individuals which grounds my social class, such that *I* am not in this class, but *what I have in common* with others is in the class. Nonetheless, the individual is not an absolute atom which escapes classes either. As an individual, I am between several classes, between several memberships, some being objectively more determining than others. As an individual, I am neither reducible to being the member of a class which comprehends me nor irreducible to all classes, like a free electron without determination. I overlap different classes, reduced or enlarged – classes of inheritance, of ideas, of thought, of belief, and of action. My individual identities may appear ordered or contradictory, but they are above all overlapped and overlapping. I am never in any one of these classes alone: culture, society, community of ideas, family, group of interests, professional body, or cultural domain. Rather, *what I have in common with others* is in these classes. Domains of membership take shape in this way. Sometimes they are continuous (continuity exists, perhaps, between my cultural domain and my familial origins), and sometimes they are discontinuous (there may be a gap between my class of interests and my class of beliefs). The individual is really what is least undivided, the division of the same human thing between (occasionally) overlapping and contradictory classes.

Notes

1. Pierre-André Taguieff, *La Couleur et le Sang*.
2. Ernest Renan, *The Future of Science*. In contrast with Gobineau, Renan conceives of a homogeneous humanity, with a few exceptions, because race is a primordial human class at its origin, but its importance tends to be effaced with history.
3. Arthur De Gobineau, *The Inequality of Human Races*.
4. Karl Marx, *Capital*, Volume III, Chapter LII, p. 885.
5. Ibid., p. 886. Raymond Aron comments on the relationship between the dialectical division of society and pluralist sociological theory: 'Pluralism in concrete capitalist societies, apart from the question of ground-rent, results from the disparity between the formal ideal-type of a society exclusively defined by, on one side, landowners, capitalists, entrepreneurs, and, on the other side, wage-labourers, and the complex and concrete societies, where capitalists as well as wage-labourers appear in multiple forms or instances. What is interesting or problematic about the sociological theory of classes, in Marx's thought, is the disparity between the economic ideal-type and lived social reality in its plurality', Raymond Aron, *Le Marxisme de Marx*, p. 714. Aron claims that it is possible to define classes by their place in the processes of economic (and not merely material) production, and by the origin of incomes, which are the expression of the processes of capitalist production. On the other hand, he leaves open Schumpeter's problem of the organisation between macroeconomically defined classes which are almost formal types (landowners, capitalists, and wage-labourers) and the many groups socially distinct from capitalists and wage-labourers, who may wind up sociologically wearing away at and dissolving economic classes. The problem is disconcerting for Marx, who goes to great lengths to avoid class compactness in his own system.

6. Ibid. Here the manuscript breaks off.
7. Gustave Le Bon was fond of not abandoning race to the *particularising* influences of the milieu. According to him, a race can be affected only by crossbreeding with neighbouring races (with too-distant races, the result is disastrous); a race, like every class, is caught between its nominalist and individualising dissolution (if it must take into account the particularities of every milieu and cultural subsystem) and its abstract inflation to the level of the species. See, in particular, Gustave Le Bon, *The Psychology of Peoples*.

Chapter XIV

Genders

1. The Stratification of Genders

Genders are classes which have this particular characteristic: they are not divided and redivided on the same level, but they divide several different universal levels. Classes group together and exclude objects and events inside the same universe on the same plane. Genders group together and exclude objects and events inside the same universe from plane to plane.

Classes section and arrange the universe at any given level. Genders divide the universe into different levels.

The relations between human groups of interests or ideas are class relations because the relations are strictly located *between* them. The relations between man and woman are generic relations insofar as they are relations between man and woman on the one hand, and humanity (which is shared between man and woman) on the other hand. Anyone who thinks that the proletariat and bourgeois social classes, for example, are sufficient to yield the social universe, which reduces to them, must claim that the relation between the proletariat and the property-owning class is in fact the relation between society and these two classes, as much as between these two classes. In this way, one often solidifies classes into genera and conceives of society *generically*. Conversely, genera may be thought of as the primary classes, as Engels does.[1] However true this may be, classes are instances caught between the individual and the generic. Whoever wants to dissolve them makes them lose their meaning in the multiplicity of individuals; whoever desires, on the contrary, to attribute substance to them constructs them as genders of society or as their principle of generation.

The structure of classes locally crystallises into relations of origin, ideas, or interests. Genders are constructed in sexed rela-

366

tions. No gender exists except sexed gender. We have already addressed the problem of 'art genres'. But an object's genre becomes interesting for humanity through the problem of the human species' genders, which includes problems of sexual reproduction and of sexual difference.

Genders of living things, and more specifically of human living things, represent a cross-section of several levels of distinction between objects comprehended in each other. Genderedness [*généricité*] often takes a discriminatory form, or, at best, a redistributive and complementary form, that groups together the *de jure* differences and inequalities between man and woman. After the French Revolution and in the German Marxist tradition, the nineteenth century saw a period of demands by suffragettes and European revolutionary parties for gender equality. Henceforth, the necessary question arose of how to express either a (natural) difference or a (cultural) differentiation through and in this equality. Some began to deplore masculinity being disconnected from man and called for the return to a compact masculinity, that is, to the identification of masculinity and man as *vir*. Others tried to overcome feminism from above by questioning the very existence of genders, in favour of singular realities and individuals without a priori genderedness. Some tried to reunify the different gendered levels by deriving masculine and feminine characteristics and behaviour from genetics or reproductive functions according to an evolutionary logic. Others hoped to deconstruct the different gendered levels from the top downwards by beginning from what individuals do with their identities and using this singularity to argue against the universality of distinctions between the sexes.

Today, on the one hand masculinity and femininity are conceived as symbolic, cultural roles, masks worn by individuals to act out those roles, whatever their sex or sexuality. On the other hand, a picture is drawn deriving a man's distinguishing features from Mars and a woman's from Venus, and adding that the latest scientific research 'completely accords with' and 'proves that' women have a stronger olfactory perception, are objects of the imagination's fantasy, multitaskers, more faithful, and seek out stability, and that men have a stronger visual perception, are more unfaithful, more violent, attached to physical beauty, and so on. This is the naturalist *doxa*. The nominalist *doxa* is conjoined to it. According to nominalists: you are individuals; your genders are merely evening gowns with which you can act out your role by accentuating your femininity or masculinity, your yin or yang. They are only constructed functions. It is well known that they vary from one society to another, that in our society they vary from one person to another, and that in each person they vary from one existential moment to another.

Between these two interpretations of gender are situated a series of levels from the top down and from the bottom up, which define the karyotype, phenotype, and symbolic relations. If 'man' and 'woman' are two human genders, they involve three other gender relations: the relation between genetic sexes determined by the karyotype; the relation between genital sexes determined by the phenotype; and the relation between masculine and feminine determined by the symbolic order of things.

2. Gendered Levels and Domination

For our species, genders correspond to a relational stratification or series of levels of gendered differences that theories of gender determine either from the top down or from the bottom up:

- the first difference, at the lowest level (for the time being), concerns what is in a human individual: the genetic gender difference between the XX and XY chromosome pairs;
- the second difference, at a higher level, determines what makes an individual from what is an individual: the genital difference between male and female;
- the third difference, at higher level again, determines what an individual is from what makes an individual: the cultural difference between man and woman;
- the fourth difference, at an even higher level, determines what an individual makes with what it is: the symbolic difference between feminine and masculine.

Two opposing views can follow from this stratification of human genders. The first is the 'naturalist' view, which begins at the lowest level, genetic difference. The naturalist view yields a series of determinations, step by step, from level to level. They construct the opposition between male and female as a series of reproductive functions based on genetic difference. They then construct the cultural difference between man and woman based on the functional and evolutionary difference between male and female.

They construct lastly the symbolic difference between masculine and feminine as effects of the relation between man and woman. The second view is the (gender studies) 'nominalist' view, which determines genders merely as effects of the non-natural construction of active subjects and singular beings who give themselves genders. Individuals attribute to each other masculine and feminine properties, and culture solidifies them into the substantives 'man' and 'woman', which are retroactively constructed as the male's and female's natural reproductive functions yielded by an archaic genetic difference.

The naturalist ascends from the lowest gendered level to the highest gendered level. In other words, they construct individual difference from specific difference. The nominalist descends from individual difference to specific difference. In other words, they deconstruct individual difference down to specific difference.

But what is played out in this force relation [*rapport de force*] is not simply a unilateral misinterpretation of two movements of thought, but also a game of domination. Some gendered levels consist in objective differences (extensive differences), while others consist in value differences (intensive differences). In this way, the relation between XX and XY is a relation between two objects – which are not necessarily exclusive, since it is possible to consider XXX and XXY groups and other rare but extant groups. On the other hand, the relation between male and female is an intensive relation between two functions. The individual *becomes* male or *becomes* female through a continuous process from the embryonic stage to at least the pubescent stage, wherein one becomes either *more* or *less* male or female. Male and female, counter-intuitively, are to be conceived not as objects but as events: 'becoming-male' and 'becoming-female'. The relation between man and woman is again an objective relation. Man and woman are cultural objects – again non-exclusive, since one can be androgynous – but are nonetheless objects, since 'man' and 'woman' cannot be either more or less man or woman. The relation between masculine and feminine again embodies an intensive, evential pair of values – one *is* not feminine or masculine, one *makes* something either more or less masculine or feminine.

The nominalist descends from masculine and feminine as an evential pair of values, and thus of relative intensities, to objective genetic difference. What is at stake is the dissolution of every objective gender relation into an intensive, *evential* relation. The naturalist ascends from the objective genetic difference between XX and XY pairs to the masculine–feminine relation. Naturalists aim to solidify every intensive relation, which can be either more or less, into a determined *objective* relation.

Neither of these two views on its own entails gendered domination or gendered emancipation. The naturalist, who ascends the objective relation, determination by determination, to the intensive, evential relation, is not necessarily led to legitimate either masculine domination or, as some believe, to naturally justify man's superiority over woman. Some naturalists do so, but this is not contained in the naturalism of their approach. What is at stake for the naturalist is the production of an effect of continuity between the difference contained in what is an individual (therefore, in its nature) and the difference which appears in what individuals make from what they are (therefore, in cultural or individual acts). Conversely, every nominalism which deconstructs *objective* gender, by descending from the evential difference between what makes itself masculine and what makes itself feminine to the objective difference between chromosome pairs, is not necessarily emancipatory. Gender nominalism's aim is to determine the objective gender difference (natural and genetic difference) through the intensive, relative, evential difference between masculine and feminine values.

Processes of 'domination' play out inside the mechanism common to both the naturalist ascent and to the nominalist descent, in the articulation between gendered levels. Domination is not the determination of a level by a higher or lower level – which plays out in the opposition between the naturalist and the nominalist – but, rather, the confounding of a given level of extensive difference with intensive difference. If, by determining the objective difference between man and woman, I group together in this difference the evential relation of masculine and feminine values or the intensive relation of male and female functions, I confound two or three gendered levels. I no longer claim that a male human is a man or that a man can be masculine or feminine, but maintain that a man is male or that masculinity is the distinguishing feature of a man who is male. One then confounds an objective difference with intensive differences, by making some intensities (intensities of masculinity, intensities of 'becoming-male') extensive, and by attributing given intensities (to be a man is to be particularly masculine) to an extension (man opposed to woman).

3. Man/Woman

All gendered domination implies the conflation of an *extensive* gendered level with an *intensive* gendered level. Here an extensive equality exists between man and woman and an intensive inferiority of woman exists in relation to man. Woman as a reproductive condition of man is identified with the lower level of the female. Woman is conceived as equal to man, but as *less* man than man. For example, in Plato's *Timaeus*, woman is presented as determined to be like man, but less complete:

> According to our likely account, all male-born humans who lived lives of cowardice or injustice were reborn in the second generation as women. And this explains why at that time the gods fashioned the desire for sexual union, by constructing one ensouled living thing in us as well as another one in women. [In this situation, it is clearly only men who are complete human beings and who can hope for ultimate fulfilment; what a woman can hope for at best is to become a man.][2]

Determined by the functional relation between male and female, the gendered relation between man and woman is often established, as in Plato, as a relation of unequal equality. Man and woman are considered as formally equivalent, with mixed extensive and intensive functions, but are equivalent only insofar as man is *more* and woman is *less*. The most common argument consists in thinking that woman is as equally *less* as man is *more*; both are therefore intensive functions considered as equal objects.

Domination is therefore founded on the combination between the distinction of two objects and the comparison of two values. The two objects allow the possibility of equality, without which the difference and comparison become impossible. The two intensities allow the possibility of inequality, of the superiority of one over the other. For man is never thought of as *absolutely* superior to woman, but as having an identity equal to that of woman: man's identity is superior, woman's identity is inferior.

Aristotle was among the first to conceive – with all the substantiality that the conception of an unequal gendered difference requires – of a relation between man and woman which divides up an ontological relation equal in its structure and unequal in its determinations: man is identified with active form; woman is identified with passive matter. Thus, through the twofold detour around the natural determination of male and female functions (strength against gentleness, for example, since 'with all other animals the female is softer in disposition'[3]), beyond and beneath man and woman, Aristotle constructs the model of a dominant gender relation. In this type of model, *domination* is not absolute superiority, but equal superiority. Absolute superiority is only a pure potentiality. Domination is the conception of a formal condition of equality through which individuals may consider each other equals only insofar as one is superior to the other according to certain determinations. Here, through the natural determination of the genital sex (the reproductive function) conjoined to the symbolic determination of masculine and feminine principles,[4] the man/woman relation is presented as a gender relation of domination. Aristotle claims that the female is 'softer' in order to show that the female 'becomes more quickly tamed' and therefore that what she knows how to do better than the male is submit, that is, acknowledge her inferiority. Woman obtains her identity, formally equal to that of man, only in an inferior content. Man obtains his formal equality with woman only in a superior content.[5]

The gender relation in the human species is the relation par excellence that allows processes of domination to appear. Superiority obtains its condition in formal equality, in such a way that an individual cannot grasp their identity other than as either *less* or *more*. Domination is a process of differentiation through which objects can be equally different only on the condition that they are conceived as variable intensities. It is therefore necessary that one of the two objects, to distinguish itself from the other and to be formally equal to it, is *less* than the other while the other is *more*. Here, woman is equal to man insofar as she is less what man is more; and man is more man than woman. Man is identified with human being. Woman is *formally* as human as man if she is less man than man, who is more himself, that is, *objectively* more human. Domination cannot function without this articulation between equality and inequality.

Simone de Beauvoir captures this well:[6] woman, caught between the female (nature) and the feminine (idea), is established in relation to man who, defined partly by the male and partly by the masculine, has the capacity to be both gender and species. The male and masculine man is every man, in such a way that the woman, who is less in gender than man (the negative of man, privation, and so on), although equal in humanity to man, is lacking humanity, once humanity is redefined by the male and masculine man.

In fact, most religions, the jurisdiction of most states until the nineteenth century, scientific theories (like those concerning the size of the brain, which we still find in Émile Durkheim, influenced for a time by Le Bon[7]), and artistic representations made use of gendered models through domination. In all these domains an idea of gender will be reconstructed – an idea which will of course never lead to the *absolute* superiority of man over woman, but instead to the contradictory conception of a domination which is both equal and unequal, symmetric and asymmetric, an aggregate of several gender levels: masculinity reduced to man, determined by the male; femininity reduced to woman, determined by the female. Intensive objects are therefore paradoxically conceived: all-too-manly men, all-too-womanly women.

In contrast with what historical revisionists may sometimes claim, the great monotheistic religions have not unilaterally oppressed woman, but construct a contradictory picture of her, give her a status in humanity, through the status of personhood and through images of Mary, of Mary Magdalene, of Aisha, all while refusing her the status of *complete* personhood in which she takes part, but that she cannot have. Monotheistic religions construct woman by making woman *take part* in humanity (which marks an important historical progress), but by prohibiting her from *being* this humanity. A woman is thus a person who takes part in humanity, but is not a person. The religious identity of woman is ambiguous in that it allows woman to be *a particular* human [un *homme*], but prevents her from being humanity *as a whole* [l'*homme*].

Gendered religious domination, like philosophical domination, consists in making gender equality for woman contingent upon her lack of access to the species. Woman is woman equal to man only if woman is a gender (a particular of humanity), while man is man equal to woman only if man is the species (a universal of humanity). The objects that man and woman are, are therefore established in gender by an extensive equality (one considers man and woman as two equal and complementary sides of humanity) whose condition is in an intensive inequality (man realises himself only in the universality of the species, woman realises herself only in the particularity of gender).

It is as if human beings, in order to conceive of two different genders, can no longer conceive of anything except a species-gender (man) and a gender-gender (woman).

The construction of this genderedness through domination leads to schizophrenic subjectivities. Every woman is trapped in a femininity that both prevents her from being herself and allows her to be herself. Woman's negation of her gender in order to access equality leads to an identification with man, established as a gender which is more than a gender (a species-gender). Woman's acceptance of her gender in order to obtain differential equality leads to the acknowledgement of a gender which is only a gender, and which never realises itself in the species. Beauvoir describes woman, characterised as the second sex, as less, as relative, as incomplete, as particular, as closer to nature, as more corrupted and more corrupting, who is other. In short, woman is simply reduced to being a particular gender, while man is not only a gender, but the universal gender.

The only solution that could disconnect the idea of gender from that of domination consisted in regressing from the relation between man and woman to what reconnects male and female, in order to again obtain the difference in levels between each of them, to distinguish the *extensive* difference between man and woman from *intensive* differences between masculinity and femininity and male and female.

4. Male/Female

If the construction of the difference of reproductive functions yields the gendered difference man/woman as *domination*, then the former difference is, if not natural, at least trans-species.

The difference between male and female is one of the most interesting ethological objects. By observing the variations between genders from one species to another and understanding them from a Darwinian interpretive framework, the genital gendered level can be mapped. For this purpose, one assumes that, within the same species, genders develop different strategies and that these strategic differences express themselves through distinct characteristics and variable behaviours.

For example, with respect to gorillas, Alexander Harcourt summarises the fundamental idea of neo-Darwinian interpretations of gendered difference:

A fundamental dichotomy between male and female partially provides us with an explanation. Once a female has mated and is impregnated, there remains little to do to increase her reproductive success, other than to assure her offspring's survival. On the other hand, a male's reproductive success depends largely on the number of females that he will mate with. In short, females act on the quality of the descendants, but males opt for the quantity of descendants.[8]

A female chimpanzee can have her first child at 13 years, give birth every five or six years, and has a reproductive period of twenty-five to thirty years, which allows her to have five or six direct descendants at most, if they all survive. On the other hand, a male can impregnate a female once a year.

We know that this difference of reproductive possibility has consequences on sexual and non-natural selection, which has an influence on secondary sexual characteristics like the proverbial peacock's tail: the female must be seduced and the male must seduce. Here again, male and female are conceived according to the difference between activity and passivity, like that projected onto the man/woman pair.

If a female primate wants to produce 'high-quality' direct descendants, it is better for her to mate with males of good quality. The ability to fight is proportional to size and to the state of health, two parameters in large part determined genetically, which appear as selective advantages for males. Numerous species, like seals, appear to essentially adopt the strategy in which the female chooses the largest and healthiest male as her primary candidate. The well-nourished and cared for offspring become strong and healthy in turn. But education is as strategically important, in this perspective, as genetic determination. Therefore, a female primate may sometimes mate first and foremost with conquered and subordinate males who, losing their capacity to conquer other females, can help them raise their offspring.

The analysis of the male/female gendered level involves a more complex logic than it appears; that the gendered relation between male and female is determined by reproductive strategies does not immediately entail that the advantage is given to he who takes advantage in the *first degree*. The selective logic has various degrees, like all logics of interests. A particular quality may be superior to a particular defect, or conversely. Sexual selection thus involves many strategic reversals.

Some male baboons that join a troop will take care of a female and protect her current offspring, so as to assure the mother that he will be a caring male for her future offspring. Therefore, a strategy is never a simple strategy: a female may genetically prefer a strong and dominant male, but prefer a dominated or weaker male from the 'educational' point of view.

It is still difficult to determine one strategy from one reproductive maximisation principle, in order to determine the formation of differences between males and females. However, it seems that the difference between male and female obtains its natural reality, from species to species, through the constant divergence of reproductive strategies between males practising polygamy and females constrained by the difficulty of raising their offspring alone. Ninety per cent of birds are monogamous, but only 5 per cent of mammals are monogamous. Fifteen per cent of primates are monogamous. For the remaining 85 per cent of primates, polygamy, as a result of unequal distribution [*répartition*], entails a struggle between males for access to sexual partners. It seems that the more a species is polygamous, the more sexual dimorphism is important. The difference is more pronounced; since males must struggle among each other, they must be physically larger and stronger than others.

However, like all articulations between an *extensive* difference and an *intensive* differentiation, between being and becoming, the animal genetic and genital articulation proves to be the rule as much as the exception. The gap between the two, that is, the relation between a coincidental (and not 'normal') expression and an accidental (and not 'pathological' or abnormal) expression, allows the conception of the difference between being and becoming, between objective genetic difference and evential genital difference. When genital sex expresses genetic sex, they coincide and the expression of one by the other is internal. When they do not coincide, the genetic influence on the genital is counterbalanced by an external environmental influence.

Genital sex is formally contingent. It depends on external developmental conditions and genetic programming. The fertilised sexual egg is always indifferent or bivalent. If genital sex depends on a hormonal mechanism, one can experimentally cause a more or less stable sexual inversion by administering hormones to an embryo. The relation between genetic sex and genital sex is not immediate, but articulated by a number of physiological and hormonal mediations, which may reverse, slow down, or accelerate each other.

If genetic sex is *discrete*, then genital sex is *continuous*.

For example, the female Echiura spoon worm has a proboscis to collect food. The male is microscopic, does not have a proboscis, and lives as a parasite on the female. Settling on the female's proboscis, he descends into her digestive tract, then settles into her uterus where he fertilises her eggs. The same larva can produce a male or a female. If the larva remains free, then it develops into a female. If it settles on the proboscis of another female, then its development is impeded and it produces a male. Therefore, it is the proboscis of the adult female which produces the inhibitory substances of male differentiation. Here, sexualisation is not genetic, but clearly depends on external factors.

An animal always has a more or less lengthy period of sexual bivalence from the genital point of view. For hermaphrodites, this period lasts their entire life. For gonochoristic species, this period most often terminates during embryonic life. Although one of the two sexes definitively or only intermittently settles, the determination of genital sex from genetic sex is always realised through the contingent influence of internal (hormonal) and external (nutritional, temperature-based) factors.

5. XX/XY

In living gonochoristic beings, whose different individuals have genital organs, does a direct, immediate correlation exist, if not between *genital* sex and *genetic* sex, at least between *genetic* sex and a *chromosome* pair? Michèle Fonton, Évelyne Peyre, and Joëlle Wiels offer a response to the question in their short article, 'Sexe biologique et sexe social'.[9] Animal biology, genetics, and molecular biology provide a response to the problem of biological sex determination. But the processes of sex determination, the formation of gonads into internal genital male or female organs, are extremely complex. Gonads, endocrine glands, are controlled by the encephalon via the hypothalamo-hypophyseal complex and, through hormonal production, influence the phenotype by affecting the differentiation of 'sexual characteristics'. These sexual characteristics modify bone morphology among other things.

But is genetic sex on its own directly connected to the genetic determination of sexual chromosomes?

In 1923, Theophilus Painter demonstrated the existence of heterosomes ('sexual chromosomes') in the human species, but it was only at the end of the 1950s that Jacobs would establish a connection between the presence of the Y chromosome and the masculine sex. During the first six to seven weeks of the embryo's life, the fetus contains undifferentiated gonads, which later develop into ovaries or testicles. Subsequently, through the hormonal production of these gonads, embryonic germ layers (Müllerian ducts, Wolffian ducts) develop into male or female genital organs. But if hormones and, indirectly, the chromosomal formula determine the formation of sexual organs, the experimental possibility exists for rat or rabbit embryos, for example, to develop either into males in the presence of testosterone or into females in the absence of testosterone.

What exactly is the signal which allows the embryonic gonads to develop into ovaries or testicles? The search was for one or several genes located on the Y chromosome exclusively, which would govern the testicle's development – what is called the Testis-Determining Factor, or the TDF gene.

In 1964, the existence of male XX individuals was discovered. Later, the existence of female XY individuals was discovered. Henceforth, the irregularities of sexual chromosomal pairs, in these rare cases, challenge the absolute determining factor of the Y chromosome as the ultimate factor producing the male gender. Naturalists sometimes neglect these exceptions, since, as good Aristotelians, they are interested in the normativity of 'in most cases'. On the other hand, nominalists study them and recognise above all singular existences. They see in a particular case the occasion to make rules or norms particular (and not universal). Faced with these particular cases, another scientific hypothesis consisted in grouping together the determining factors of the male individual's development, not with the presence or absence of the Y chromosome as a whole, but with a molecule associated with it, the H-Y antigen. Until the mid-1980s, the theory held. However, a set of arguments dismissed the problem. In 1982, Willys K. Silvers showed that the H-Y antigen in fact splits into *two* very distinct antigens. A series of experiments cast doubts. Some XY female mice express the H-Y antigen, while some male mice do not express it. Some birds have the antigen corresponding with H-Y (H-W at the time) on the gonads of ZZ male embryos 'feminised' through the injection of hormones. Therefore, the antigen is correlated with the *development* of the feminine sex among birds, although it is not the *cause* or deciding factor of it.

Since research into an exact determination of the genital gendered level by the genetic gendered level resembles a continuous search for increasingly more particular and occasionally *ad hoc* elements, another theory soon appeared. It was no longer the Y chromosome, nor the H-Y antigen, but two genes, ZFY and SRY, which were responsible for the passage from one gendered level to another. But the appearance of rare cases soon also made this theory untenable.

Recent research into an absolute TDF is not always successful. Research has become more refined concerning the relation between the genetic gendered level – the difference between chromosomal pairs, the transport of antigens, the presence of this or that gene, the expression of this or that amount of protein – and the genital gendered level – the more or less male or female development of an organism. But the more the relation becomes sharpened, the more the articulations between extensive gender relations and intensive gender relations become more complex and blurred. Various possible genetic factors intersect to explain the passage to a higher level of differentiation between male and female. This differentiation must still join the objective difference between the two complementary reproductive functions, then express itself for the human species in the relation between man and woman, before individuals culturally, historically, or voluntarily self-construct a more or less masculine or feminine secondary identity through their being a man or a woman.

Genders are therefore stratifications of identities and differences within living things. For the human species, human objects distinguish each other inside their species through multiple layers of gender relations. Levels accumulate without any one of them being reducible to a lower or higher level. Human genderedness is not compact, but layered.

Genders classify objects and events into levels. No absolute determinism exists from one level to another (whence the formal importance of *exceptions*), because it is meaningless to purely produce an evential difference from an objective difference, and conversely. One can never absolutely infer from the fact that genetic objects differ in gender anything except two series of events (male development and female development) needing to take place. Nor can one ever infer the realisation of two exclusive objects – man and woman – from two series of developmental events. Moreover, one will never obtain a definition of two intensive masculine and feminine values from these two distinct objects (man and woman), which are operations on the identity of man and woman and not consequences of this difference, as the naturalist would like to think.

Genders can be understood only if one understands the levels and relations between an objective difference and an evential difference within a big thing such as the human species.

6. Naturalist Ascent and Nominalist Descent

The two contemporary views which lead to a compact gender correspond to the naturalist ascent and the nominalist descent. These two interpretations of the stratification of gender levels of the human species do not divide up the long-standing relations of domination – such that, for example, naturalism would recommend a justification of the established masculine order and gender nominalism would strive towards feminist emancipation. In truth, since the concept of gender broke with early feminism's concept of it, naturalism has taken up the cause of emancipation. No interpretation of gender levels is on its own more apt to either defend or subvert the established order. A naturalist, who ascends from objective gendered difference to the difference between masculine and feminine characteristics, can just as well struggle against domination. Likewise, a nominalist, who descends from the cultural differentiation of roles to deconstructed gendered difference, can also challenge one sex's domination of the other, but without this stance being included in their descent of gender levels. One can imagine a nominalist starting from singular differences to construct their masculine or feminine or other gender, which would deconstruct the objective gendered differences, all the while leading back to a form of domination. For instance, they would consider 'active' gendered individuals superior to those who 'passively' accept their function. The nominalist is sometimes compelled to consider the individual who falls under a gendered category (who claims to naturally, normatively, or 'properly' be a woman or man) as being *lesser*, since this individual does not singularly adopt the singular, but singularly espouses the nonsingular. For this reason, the nominalist reintroduces a value judgement and a *more* or a *less*. On their view, all singular individuals are equal, but some are more equal than others, insofar as they realise and adopt this singularity (they are queer), in relation to those who 'banally' express it generically (they are straight).

The naturalist, who determines genders from the bottom up, and the nominalist, who determines them from the top down, are never safeguarded from processes of *domination*, that is, from rearticulating an equal inequality. But they can also struggle against inequality without these positions being included in their interpretation.

Both propose a unidirectional interpretation of genders, either in the sense of *being* (for the naturalist), or in the sense of *comprehension* (for the nominalist). They both arrive at some compact gender, even if both may considerably clarify the stratification of gender levels. The naturalist indexes masculine and feminine characteristics on objective genetic difference and the nominalist does the inverse; in both cases, gender self-compacts.

Debates about the future of feminism and criticisms of its tradition are held between these two interpretations of gender. Positions negotiated between the two are possible, but they all take place between the naturalist meaning and nominalist meaning.

A tradition which includes Beauvoir's phenomenology of sex, Michel Foucault's critical and genealogical nominalism, and Pierre Bourdieu's sociology of domination[10] understands the historical work of gender dehistoricisation in the form of contemporary gender studies in Judith Butler's work.[11] All these positions have something in common. They descend from the cultural constructions of gender differences to the reproductive functional level and to the genital and genetic levels, all the while contaminating all the objective differences through evential differences and differentiations, drawing on the source of what we make with what we are.

The other great, primarily Anglophone, tradition, which has its roots in David Hume's and Charles Darwin's naturalism, and includes Edward O. Wilson's sociobiology,[12] Leda Cosmides' evolutionary psychology,[13] Steven Pinker's[14] and David Buss's[15] studies on the sexes, and their popularisation in Helen Fisher's works on love,[16] also shares a common principle. This tradition begins from a Nature, in reaction to *tabula rasa* models of the individual, to understand how the human being is a natural, determined being, and to grasp how and why masculine and feminine roles are neither individual choices nor cultural combinations, but

an evolutionary or progressive expression of the species, expressing itself in individual organisms.

The two directions can neither be transferred into an interme-
diate truth, nor can they be overcome through dialectic. Quite
simply, they operate unilaterally, so that each ultimately ends up
where the other began. We can avoid compact thinking only if
we consider the two senses (being and comprehension) without
assimilating one into the other.

The nominalist will always stumble over a natural difference of
being or an unbearable specific limit at the end of their path. The
naturalist will always stumble over a gendered differentiation of
comprehension or an unbearable resistance to singular events at
the end of their path. Nothing will overcome these two senses of
human gender, but nothing will reduce them either; genders really
exist only if one conceives of them in two senses, from both sides.

Therefore, gender is the *minimal* objective or evential relation
comprehended in the same thing. When two objects or two events
are in the same identical thing (here, the human species), their
primary difference is their 'gender'. One can, like transgender
theorists, appeal to gender multiplication from the third to the
*n*th gender, but this would only amount to an operation trying
to dissolve gender in the individual and, ideally, to constitute the
nominalist's paradise, where as many genders exist as individuals. One can also, like the naturalist, index gender on a natural
objective difference which constitutes it, but this would be to
determine gender through the species and reduce objective gender
to species-effects.

In fact, gender subsists only insofar as one thinks of it in two
senses, between its singular dissolution and its specific determination. Gender is the primary difference between objects or events
which allows the stratification of objective accumulation. Gender
is neither purely inscribed in the nature of things nor purely
projected by the human mind, but exists as a minimal relation
between *that which is gender* and *that which comprehends gender*
– the primary relation which objects in the same thing maintain.

A single object is never in a thing. There are always at least two
objects in a thing, otherwise an object which is in a thing and a
thing in which an object is would be compact. Since at least two
objects (or two events) are always in a thing, the primary relation
which connects these two objects is a *gender* relation.

There can be three, four, or more objects, individuals, and as many new relations – but the primary relation always remains *twofold*, which explains how genders in the human species tend 'in most cases' towards duality, even if it is possible to imagine other, more particular genders.

Locally, in the human species, genders stratify into levels that are irreducible to each other. They are the primary mode of distinguishing human objects. But our lives are not human objects and events differentiating each other into genders. Rather, our lives differentiate each other internally as well – into *ages*.

Notes

1. 'The first class opposition that appears in history coincides with the development of the antagonism between man and woman in monogamous marriage, and the first class oppression coincides with that of the female sex by the male.' Friedrich Engels, *Origins of the Family, Private Property, and the State*, Chapter 2, Section 4.
2. Plato, *Timaeus*, 90e–91a. [Translation modified.]
3. Aristotle, *History of Animals*, IX, 608b1, p. 948.
4. Gentle or 'soft' is not a natural quality of females, but an adjective, an attribute connected to femininity and retroactively associated with different females, for a female lion or a female ant is certainly not gentle in itself.
5. In Galen's physiology, man is stronger and more complete insofar as he has external and fully-developed genital parts, whereas woman is inferior insofar as she has internal and atrophied genital parts.
6. Simone de Beauvoir, *The Second Sex*.
7. Émile Durkheim, *The Division of Labor in Society*.
8. Alexander H. Harcourt and Kelly J. Stewart, *Gorilla Society*.
9. Michèle Fonton, Évelyne Peyre, and Joëlle Wiels, 'Sexe biologique et sexe social'.
10. '[Psychologists] often let themselves be guided, in constructing and describing their object, by the principles of vision and division embedded in ordinary language, either seeking to measure differences identified in that language – such as the more 'aggressive' nature of men or the more 'timid' nature of women – or using ordinary, and therefore value-laden, terms to describe those differences', Pierre Bourdieu, *Masculine Domination*, pp. 3–4, n. 3.
11. 'Is "naturalness" constituted through discursively constrained performative acts that produce the body through and within the categories of sex?' Judith Butler, *Gender Trouble*, pp. xxviii–xxix.

12. Edward O. Wilson, *Sociobiology*.
13. Jerome H. Barkow, Leda Cosmides, and John Tooby, *The Adapted Mind*.
14. Steven Pinker, *The Blank Slate*.
15. David Buss, *The Evolution of Desire*. Buss understands and explains behavioural commonplaces which tend to be universal, such as a woman's desire for older men or financial resources and a higher social status, or a man's desire for younger, sexually attractive, and faithful women. He finds the key to these commonplaces among the relics of reproductive advantages, dating from the preagrarian era of human development.
16. Helen Fisher, *Anatomy of Love*.

Chapter XV

Ages of Life

1. Adolescence

An individual is an object in classes and in genders. However, an individual is neither the *terminus ad quem* nor the *terminus a quo* of the objectivisation of human life. An individuated life is itself divided into temporal objects commonly called 'ages'.

'Ages of life' are the primary objects that an individuated life comprehends, itself comprehended in classes and in genders. Today, among these ages, one in particular captivates, since it seems to be at the centre of ages, the heart of life, the object in the very middle of becoming: adolescence.

We are far from the time when humans thought that adulthood or maturity was the maximum of life. Today, adolescence is presented as the maximum of an individual.

The contemporary attraction to adolescence is both narcissistic and voyeuristic. It is narcissistic because it concerns adolescents themselves in television series, comic books, films, popular music, and all other artistic or non-artistic representations. It is voyeuristic because those who are not yet adolescents (who are called, by a symptomatic extension, 'preadolescents') and those who are no longer adolescents (adults) observe what they are not, separated from them by an invisible temporal line, with a mix of envy, contempt, and adoration.

Television series (*Buffy, Alias, Smallville, Veronica Mars*) establish the contemporary image of adolescence as a *double game*. An individual dependent on the adult world, but tormented by a desire for autonomy, an adolescent is two-faced, a wearer of masks, still a child for the parents, already an adult for her peers, a body tormented by metamorphoses, awakened to sexuality, one foot in the childlike imaginary of the uncanny, another in

385

adult social reality. Rock music, the adolescent art par excellence, expresses, through an unprecedented corpus of songs, attitudes, criticisms, gestures, voices, and machines, the frustration of the between-the-two – the joy and rage of considering the adult world from the outside, of being excluded from it, but of judging it as something insignificant which views itself as much more signifi-cant than it is. Cinematic representations oscillate between films *for* adolescents – comedy, horror, or melodrama, emotional initia-tions, banal humour subverting adult rules, and transformations of childhood's beautiful images into mordant horror and gore – and films *about* adolescents – the adventures of singular, obscure, elusive, or impossible characters.

Adolescence as the 'age par excellence' provokes enigmatic social emotions, producing fear as much as astonishment. Adolescence is completely different from, and must not be confounded with, the older concept of youth. Old fantasies of eternal youth, regret for the past, the fountain of youth, and the vampiric desire for fresh blood and living flesh do not directly correspond to adolescence. Adolescence is not the beginning of life, its commencement, but is situated *between-the-two*. Whereas youth is the commence-ment of life, adolescence is an intermediary figure. This is why adolescence, in contrast to youth, produces as much anxiety as veneration: fear of risky behaviours, talk of the age in crisis, drug or suicide prevention, fantasies about adolescent groups and gangs. From *The Wild One*, *Rebel Without a Cause*, *Splendor in the Grass*, and *Blackboard Jungle* to *Class of 1984*, the ambiva-lent image of adolescence, which eclipses that of youth, has been the object of sociological studies and hijacked by marketing strategists.

Adolescence's frustration and power, the conjoined feelings of absoluteness and degradation, of autonomy and dependence, is articulated around a mysterious stage of human life, both a natural age (marked by unparalleled physiological transforma-tions) and a social age (a relatively recent concept – in its current aspect at least). It is a recent fact that adolescence, apparently very natural, is only what it is for us. In 1904, the first complete study of the subject, G. Stanley Hall's *Adolescence*,[1] appears. Prior to that, there are only scattered remarks on the subject, such as in William Burnham's 'The Study of Psychology' in 1891.[2] During the first half of the twentieth century, the intermediary age became the age par excellence in our societies. But how can one explain that an age is both a clear expression of the human body's natural development and a conception of society's temporal division?

The adolescent age is often believed to be not only a compromise between a natural period and a cultural division of time, but the very expression of a contradiction between nature and culture. Following Rousseau's intuitions, Kant, in *Conjectures on the Beginning of Human History*, defines adolescence as a double between-the-two: between childhood and adulthood, and between natural age and social age:

> Nature has fixed the time at which human beings reach maturity – in terms of their urge and ability to reproduce their kind – at the age of approximately sixteen or seventeen. This is the age at which, in the raw state of nature, a youth literally becomes a man; for he then has the capacity to look after himself, to reproduce his kind, and to look after his children as well as his wife. The simplicity of his needs makes this an easy task. But in a civilised state, he requires numerous means of support, in terms both of skill and of favourable external circumstances, in order to perform these functions. In the context of civil society, the corresponding stage is therefore postponed – at least on average – by a further ten years. Nevertheless, nature has not altered the age of puberty to match the progressive refinement of society, but sticks stubbornly to the law which it has imposed on the survival of the human race as an animal species. As a result, the effect of social customs on the end of nature – and vice versa – is inevitably prejudicial. For in the state of nature, a human being is already a man at an age when civilised man (who nevertheless still retains his character as natural man) is merely a youth, or even only a child; for we may well describe as a child someone who, in the civil state, is unable because of his age to support even himself, let alone others of his kind, despite having the urge and capacity to produce offspring as called upon by nature.[3]

Neither cultural age nor natural age, but the 'prejudicial' gap between the finality of nature and the finality of social customs, adolescence is the relation, the latent period between puberty and civil autonomy. Determined by puberty, adolescence is prolonged and ends through the state of society, which hinders its access to autonomy.

2. The Time of Puberty

First hypothesis: if puberty *determines* adolescence as an age, then nothing is in adolescence that is not in puberty.

'Puberty' corresponds to a set of events affecting a body during a limited period. Its limits are variable, vague, and can expand or retract according to the era, culture, and educational or nutritional means, all the while remaining fixed between the end of childhood, more or less between the human individual's tenth and twentieth year, and the beginning of what Kant calls the adult 'social man'.

Three phenomena allow us to isolate the pubertal event, which affects *gender* in ways we saw in our discussion of 'sexual differentiation'. First, the acceleration of the speed of bodily growth begins. Second, morphological changes affect the whole person, especially in the development of secondary sexual characteristics. Third, the individual transforms into a sexually fertile being, dependent on the genital intensification analysed above. A great inter- and intra-individual variability marks these various processes, the supposed unity of which allows us to define something like 'puberty' in general. From one individual to another, and at the very core of a single individual's life, events can follow one another, overlap, shift direction, accelerate, persist, halt, vary in duration, change intensity, begin, or end. The growth of the bust, pilosity, the Adam's apple's protrusion, changes in relation between the hips and waist, and changes in the voice – all these events intersect with each other.

The beginning of growth changes appears fixed at around 11 years for young girls and 14 years for young boys. The maximal speed is attained one year later in both – this is obviously only a mean, and exceptions are so numerous that they transform the rule into a purely variable statistic. However, most of the time one observes a coincidence among girls between the developmental and pubertal processes of sexual organs, whereas development accelerates among boys, although the external, genital, reproductive organs are well formed after their maturation and development.

A young girl's 'menarche', her first menstrual cycle, the beginning of ovarian cyclical activity, is often irregular and at times anovulatory for two years, before the cycle stabilises. This event can occur between 8 and 14 years. A boy's 'spermarche', his first conscious ejaculation containing a large number of malformed spermatozoa with low fertility, is more difficult to date, though it is often dated between 10 and 16 years.

Differences between pubertal events are added to the differences between individuals and genders; physical growth rarely resonates entirely with the beginning of fertility. A strong disharmonic characteristic marks pubertal growth on its own. Increases in growth curves at around 10 or 11 years among girls and 12 or 13 years among boys express the passage from an annual growth of 4–5 cm to an annual growth of 6–7 cm, before a three-year rapid shift. The transformation of bodily proportions begins well before puberty: the size of the torso, which constitutes two-thirds of the body at birth and half of it at around 10 years; the size of the head goes from a fourth in the infant to a seventh five years later; the size of the neck increases by 8 mm at 15 or sixteen years, four more than in previous years. However, this acceleration accompanies formal and proportional changes which long precede puberty.

The real change results from endocrinal factors. At this age, growth hormones begin to play an important role – the anterior pituitary gland's active production of somatotropin is inhibited by somatostatin, preventing rare cases of gigantism. The relationship between growth and sexuality is remarkable insofar as the sexual glands often restrict growth; girls, generally more precocious than boys, are nonetheless often shorter than boys. The growth period and sexual period are more antagonistic than complementary, though they are both conditioned by dietary factors. In this way, the sexual period and growth period, disharmonic on their own (irregular, formed at different times), are also disharmonic between each other – from one individual to another, one gender to another, and one species to another.

What characterises pubertal change is therefore a many-sided temporal disharmony.

All these moments are relative to each other and correspond to a disconnected series of events; the body grows and becomes fertile without any preestablished harmony. For example, the differential response of glands to hormonal stimuli generally results in an interval of several weeks between the right breast's growth and the left breast's. The chest's growth, often experienced as the most sexualising event, and the pelvis' growth, often decelerated by the desire to lose weight, are unequal and discordant phenomena par excellence: continuous, irregular processes of an infinite variability from one individual to another.

Several times of puberty exist: the pubertal times of growth, sexuality, morphological transformation, and fertility. None of them *absolutely* determines the other, but all happen in the body when aged between 10 and 20 years, like so many discordant events which give individuals a disharmonic feeling with themselves and with the world, which delimit a variable age. For example, it is known that in around 1850 girls' first cycles began on average at 17 years in Europe. The four-year difference after a century and a half indicates the plasticity of these processes. Today, from one country to another, the average age of a girl's menarche varies by one to two years.

All pubertal times vary. They in no way constitute a solid, unchanging foundation for the natural determination of a cultural age: adolescence. By transforming the cultural conditions of life, adolescence, which is only the relation between childhood and adulthood, therefore determines pubertal times as much as pubertal times determine adolescence.

3. The Division of Ages

Instead of considering a series of determined natural events as the cause and condition of an age, let us consider the physiological transformations and cultural ages of life as two sides of the same coin: the organisation of human life into events and objects. Puberty does not *determine* adolescence, nor does adolescence *define* puberty. The best weapon against every reductionism consists in emphasising the different stages or levels in every objective or evential order: just as genital events are irreducible to genetic objects, the cultural object which adolescence is is irreducible to pubertal events.

Puberty, or rather pubertal times are bodily events which express a living individual's continuous identity transformations. Puberty is a constant becoming, accelerating and decelerating at certain times. Adolescence, on the other hand, resembles an 'age', that is, a part of life conceived as an object. It is a part of a human life which is discretely divided, between childhood and adulthood, through cultural determinations, rules, and customs.

Physiological time expresses an individual's life as a continuous change or a series of variable intensities. An 'age' projects onto an individual's life a series of divisions, of definite and divisible moments, which structure a lifetime as a sequence of objects contained in each other. Childhood is a container nested in the container of adolescence, nested in the container of adulthood, like Russian dolls.

An age is therefore a division of life into temporal objects. An age affects and is affected by the body's physiological becoming.

This division is the result of *rules*, contingent possibilities and impossibilities (as we saw throughout Chapter VIII), through which each human group, each era, and each culture defines some structure of life, 'childhood' and its end (its accomplishment), 'adulthood', which can persist, decline, or end in 'old age'.

Adulthood is commonly defined as that which, without terminating a life (which can end in old age), makes life obtain its highest point. Adulthood is the referent of life, and was for a long time the *maximal* moment of a life, without being its *terminal* moment. Societies give to adults the most rights, power, (physical or cognitive) force, civil responsibilities, and the establishment of the law. Recent history contrasts adulthood as a maximal social age with adolescence as a minority ideal of the greatest intensity in life. In our time, the maximal between-the-two is preferred.

But a culture's concise dividing into ages is the definite contingent relation between childhood, as the beginning of life, and adulthood, as the traditional maximum of life.

In several places, Plato describes the partitions of the soul – from the team of winged horses and their charioteer in the *Phaedrus*[4] to the three parts in the *Republic*:[5] desire or appetite, moral courage or enthusiasm, immortal spirit or intellect. He projects onto time the division of ages as the passage from the first level to the next. Ages are the geological strata of the soul, in which the child's appetite is covered by the adolescent's enthusiasm, which is topped by the adult's intellect. This stratification is also found in Aristotle: 'There are two periods of life with reference to which education has to be divided, from age 7 to the age of puberty, and onwards to the age of 21.'[6] Young children, at first dominated by their instincts, can willingly act, but they make irrational decisions. During adolescence, they acquire the capacity to decide, while still remaining subject to the passions, sexuality, impulses, and courage. For the ancient Greeks, the division of ages against the background of the body's physiological becoming is essentially the projection onto time of a spatial hierarchy, the expression of the human soul's partition, which progressively settles in the mind.

The ancient Romans had a considerably different perspective.

The individual's cognitive, sexual, and civil capacities establish the division of ages. The *infans* (up to 7 years) is one who is incapable of speaking (or of speaking well). The *puer* (up to 17 years) is one who has not yet completed puberty. The *adulescens* (up to 30 years), who is growing but not yet fully grown, owes their status to their civil incapacity to assume a number of civic functions. The *adultus* is clearly the maximal human being in terms of both physical strength and civic resources.

In this case, childhood and adolescence are both ages and functions. Childhood is the state of minority, divided into minorities of cognitive capacity (language), sexual capacity (fertility), and civil capacity (participation in the city's functions). Christianity, by placing the person's universality before God, progressively dissociates *age* and *function*. In the Middle Ages, a 'child' was anyone who was in a state of dependence: a servant or a slave. Later, childhood and adulthood are conceived as successive ages of the same life, rather than as different functions of human life. The child is a 'little person', less than an adult, who must become an adult. This is the emancipatory potential of rejecting the *function* 'child', which cannot apply to a being who would be a child without becoming a child, that is, without being destined to one day no longer be a child.

The traditional division of childhood reduces childhood to the maximal state of physical dependence – since the individual cannot walk alone and does not have the means to be self-sufficient. The individual is then quickly cast into the adult world. A child leaves his parents to become a young person, acquiring knowledge and values from guilds and apprenticeships, rather than from the family. A child was thought of as the representative of the first short-term age, who only differed in size and strength from those of the next age, adulthood; a child was a small adult.

In the West, the replacement of adult apprenticeship by the child's instruction and isolation in a scholarly milieu with other children of the same age led to the identification of the passage from childhood to adulthood with a qualitative leap, rather than with a quantitative progress. The Church's role was preoccupied with moralising behaviour and taking charge of the education of young individuals, and made possible a new division of ages determined by scholarisation, crystallising in the humanist project. When seventeenth-century Moravian bishop John Amos Comenius conceived of school programmes, the new division was based on the individual's changing faculties, rather than to an a priori partition of the soul or to cognitive, sexual, and civil status. Ages express human becoming. Education espouses the development of theoretical, moral, and practical capacities in order to encourage the individual to flourish. The sensory faculties are awakened at home from 1 to 6 years. The elementary education of speech, customs, and religion among individuals of the same generation, from 7 to 12 years, allows the development of memory and the imagination. Reason is perfected through mathematics, rhetoric, and ethics from 12 to 18 years. Travel, the exploration of the external world, and encounters with adults shape the individual's character from 18 to 24 years.

In this case, the ordered division – into six-year periods – again indicates the projection of a transcendental order onto the continuity of an individual's becoming. But – and this is the novelty of modern education – this order is increasingly at the service of the growing human being's spontaneous activity; age is there to express, encourage, and serve the natural becoming of humanity.

However, every division of ages is necessarily the imposition of a discontinuous order that is external to the continuity of an individual's temporal becoming. It is impossible to derive ages from the course of a life. It is always necessary to impose ages on a life when ordering what is suitable for it.

In the Renaissance, the age and status of childhood was conceived as the expression of natural human becoming, rather than as the imposition of an order on this becoming. But childhood's temporal location will only be weakened, since it is the result of an order which hides behind the appeal to the naturalness of childhood status, while it is the fruit of modern society's quadruple operation: the evaluation of intellectual faculties in reference to the adult model; the evaluation of physical faculties in comparison to adulthood as the maximal state of human life; the capacity to have sexual fertility; and the civil capacity to be a fully legal person.

Since childhood is presented as a natural age, inferred from human life's becoming from birth, and not as a transcendental order imposed on the continuous corporeal changes, its division was soon subject to important variations. The four criteria mentioned above developed in the seventeenth century. Childhood became solidified as an age-object apart from adulthood. Childhood was separated from adulthood by a difference of degree, which gradually led to the qualitative leap.

After educational reforms, the development of intellectual faculties led to the consideration of children as positive beings to educate, measured by their capacities rather than by the faculties that they are deprived of. The establishment of workers' rights encouraged this transformation – especially in Prussia where, in 1841, the minimum working age was fixed at 8 years and the maximum working day for those between 8 and 12 years was limited to eight hours. The transformation was accompanied by the development of marriage rights and religious pressure to protect minors sexually; sexual promiscuity between children and adults was curtailed, and paedophilia was strongly prohibited. The passage from the military criteria of majority (the right to bear arms) to political criteria (the right to vote) transformed childhood's civic status. While in the seventeenth century one could still serve in the King's army at 14 years, and while one can still do so today in some war zones in Eritrea or Nigeria, the determination of the legal limit between minority and majority no longer holds in most present-day countries through access to weapons, but, rather, through access to a legal status. In the courts, the age of legal responsibility went from 8 to 17 years in England over the course of a century, and from 7 to 18 or 21 years in the United States over the same period.

Generally, the prolonging of the time of childhood, the isolation of children from adults, the constitution of children as central figures within the family cell, and the construction of their fragility through affection and parental care led to the lengthening of childhood and to transforming it into a strengthened object, distinct from adulthood, temporally and legally circumscribed within familial and social space. In this way, the status of childhood became clearly separated from that of adulthood, towards which children must, however, strive. The modern paradox is thus that childhood must be isolated to define it, but it can never be defined *on its own*, only *for* the adulthood to which it must lead.

When this phenomenon became more pronounced, the gap between the 'childhood' object and the 'adult' object could no longer be filled except through an event which replaces the former with the latter and becomes of decisive importance: adolescence.

The widening historical gap between the childhood-object and the adult-object led to a reinforced elasticity of the gap between the time of puberty and the departure from the household, the access to civil autonomy, legal responsibility, the right to adult sexuality, and entrance into the working world. Between the two, a no man's land extends, widens, and in turn affects the time of puberty, moves the intermediary age forward, shifts and increases a child's status through nutritional and educational concerns. Little by little, the limit between the two objects, childhood and adulthood – the former comprehended in the latter, but both increasingly separated – itself became an age.

Adolescence is the limit between childhood and adulthood, reinforced until it clearly becomes *something* in turn. This is the objective consequence of the formal logic of limits that we described in the third part of Book I.

Modern adolescence is the transformation of *an event*, the passage between childhood and adulthood, into a third *object* through the solidification of the limit between childhood and adulthood.

Every age is a life within life, that is, a life-object on the inside of the universe of a whole life. Thus, the relation between two ages is always an event, the presence of one age in another, which marks a limit but which can become an object, another age. But until the twentieth century, 'adolescence' designated not the intermediary object between childhood and adulthood, but an event connecting one to the other, ritualised as a passage.

4. From the Threshold to the Enclosure

A rite of initiation, which makes an individual enter into a new space, should not be confused with a rite of passage, which makes an individual transit between two spaces. An initiate enters into a new space without ceasing to exist in the old space from which they came; an individual undergoing a rite of passage leaves a space behind and finds the same place transformed by their journey.

A ritual is a sequence of entirely predictable collective actions that in a number of human societies accompany the passage from childhood to adulthood – the passage par excellence, that is, the expression in social space of a time of natural transformation. Rites of passage are the primary human solution to the difficult problem of the articulation of ages, that is, the articulation between the continuous and ceaseless temporal becoming of a body between birth and death, and the spatialised division of the social world, organised into domains and discrete objects distinct from one another.

For most human peoples, there is not really any open conflict between natural becoming and social age, but a ritual articulation of the two through the transcription of time into space. In this way, adolescence, the between-the-two par excellence, is reduced to the staging of a passage, a social *threshold*. Adolescence is certainly not a modern age, a recent invention. Adolescence is an age, and thus an *object*, which is. Before, it was only an *event*.

In *The Rites of Passage*,[7] Arnold van Gennep provides the means to understanding 'passage' as a human metaphor of the division of time into a spatial division projected onto the social field. Van Gennep takes up Latin topological terms, and distinguishes *unde* (the place where one comes from), *quo* (where one goes), *ubi* (where one is), and *qua* (where one passes) in order to determine various ritual positions. On this view, a *limen* is a threshold or limit between two spaces, but which forms an intermediary space on its own, since every limit is a third thing between two objects. But, van Gennep claims, a limit is not a thing like the two objects that it separates, and a *limen* is also not a space like the spaces that it separates; it is a space where one passes. Van Gennep and his follower Victor Turner[8] delimit three stages in rites of passage: the *preliminary* stage, in the course of which the individual is separated from the group, the *liminary* stage, during which the efficacy of the ritual takes place in isolation – when the place one comes from is still visible and the place that one approaches takes shape – and the *postliminary* stage, which concerns the incorporation into the new group.

The known examples are innumerable: ancient Sparta's *crypteia*, which consisted in expelling the young man from his childhood space prior to reintegrating him into the space of armed citizens by letting him pass through a non-place where he is ignored by his own people and must provide for himself alone; the Amish *rumspringa*, which requires passing through the modern world outside the communal place prior to a possible return; the Japanese *genpuku*, a ceremony in the course of which the boy is first presented with his childhood clothes and hairstyle before passing through an isolated room, to return dressed in adult clothing and with an adult hairstyle. For most human peoples, whatever the division of ages of life may be, the ritualisation of pubertal passage is expressed through the liminary spatialisation of change. The continuous becoming of bodies is marked on the communal space or the individual body through a ceremony which materialises the limit as an event between two objects, two domains: the child domain and the adult domain. The evential and non-objective character of the passage derives from its rapid and predictable ritual execution. The passage is a moment, of course, but a ritual moment *different* from the two moments that it separates.

But what characterises modern adolescence as a new age of life between-the-two is its lengthening. Adolescence was not an age, but an evential limit. Adolescence thus went from being a *threshold* to being an *enclosure*. The time between childhood and adulthood became long, too long to merely be an event, an isolated ritual, because what separates childhood from adulthood became too important (education, workers' rights, sexual protection, legal minority) and too spread out (university scholarisation, creation of an adolescent culture). Adolescence, which was an event, became an object. It became autonomous, obtained a supposed 'in-itself' which challenged thinking about ages of life – a moment between-the-two which exists by and for itself, against everything else, an authentic *adolescent state within a state*.

An event of passage between the objective domains of childhood and adulthood does not ritualise intermediary adolescence any more. Intermediary adolescence becomes the age *against* ages, that is, the moment of life which refuses to be merely a moment, to serve individual, collective, social, and specific developments which go beyond it.

This 'third-age' accelerated in the post-war years in the United States, England, continental Europe, and Japan, before spreading to the whole world: the result of the democratisation of access to the university; economic prosperity; allowances; increases in individual buying power among those still dependent on the familial household; sexual maturation; cultural autonomy; economic heteronomy. The developments of the mass culture and leisure industries determined an adolescent culture, accelerated and realised in the 1960s. They marked the denial of the dialectic of ages of life – each age comprehending the previous age in order to go beyond it, before being comprehended by the next age which goes beyond that. The new adolescence was the source of an entirely different conception of human ages, through which every passage to the next age is a *betrayal* as much as an *overcoming*: whoever becomes an adult loses as much as they gain. Adolescence thus became the bad conscience of whoever grows and ages through life's progress.

5. Psychological Assimilation I: Synthesis and Denial of Synthesis

The fear of adolescence as a 'state within a state' gave rise to three types of responses – three attempts to assimilate adolescence into the framework of the harmonious development of ages of life and the construction of a temporal and social individual.

The first response was moral, and was expressed, beginning in the late nineteenth century, in the early studies of adolescent moral development. For Pierre Mendousse, an educator of the Third Republic in France and author of the major works *L'Âme de l'adolescent* and *L'Âme de l'adolescente*,[9] adolescence is not some vague 'youth', but the critical moment when one can lose a person. This period of life requires a sustained attention in order to not let the individual lose the possibility of their moral and social construction. In G. Stanley Hall,[10] the English precursor to Mendousse, the same moral concern is shown towards the pubescent person, contained in a series of personal contradictions which may prevent the person from assimilating into the adult milieu.

The second response, especially after the crystallisation of the counter-cultural adolescent state at the end of World War II, is sociological. People have a certain fascination for the formation of marginal adolescent communities, tribes apart from the dominant society, which can neither ritually exclude nor assimilate them through a single rite of passage. Sociology discussed adolescence as the margins of a society, dismissing adult social rules within the adult world. In this way, the problem of ages and the assimilation of the adolescent temporal moment shifts to the problem of the spatial assimilation, in the social domain, of the dismissal of all that this domain represents. Adolescence becomes social space's 'inside-out' object par excellence: apaches, hell's angels, Vespa-driving mods, Italian *vitelloni*, hippies, New York and London punks, skinheads, batcavers and goths, thugs, *otakus*, generation X, and geeks. All were made the object of sociological study.

The third response is the most important. While the moral response bore the stigma of an older way of thinking, and while the second response treated adolescence as a social space or domain rather than as an age of life, psychology constructed the new adolescent figure in crisis, and constructed itself as the new science of the development of individual life thanks to the adolescent figure.

Modern psychology – as well as post-Freudian psychoanalysis, Jean Piaget's genetic psychology, cognitivist and behaviouralist theories, and Lawrence Kohlberg's and John Coleman's theories – transforms a system of assimilating the ages of life into a theoretical totality thanks to the notion of 'adolescent crisis'. Whereas the old model of the passage of ages of life was ritual and organised through ceremonies and beliefs, the modern model of ages of life is psychological, organised by clinical studies and scholarly or popular scientific views of the psyche.

Adolescence was a threshold that became an age, a length of time where one remains (even though a threshold is only an instant through which one passes), the time of departure from social space, which is framed, brief, and ritualised through ceremonies; then it became a lasting, non-ritual time of exclusion from social space. It is therefore possible for the adolescent to consider the adult social world – where children are minorities and adults are majorities – from the outside, without taking part in it. The adolescent no longer passes through the inverse of the social world, but remains in it, and contemplates in it the constraints that govern it, discovering the negative of adult necessities in their radical contingency. Adult society's great fear mixed with fascination was that adolescence would reflect their negative image from the outside.

To avoid constructing an individual outside society, it was quite necessary to conceive of a new psychology, reconsidering adolescence as a moment. Thus adolescence was characterised as a necessary contradictory state, capable of being overcome, and as an inevitable life passage, all the while remaining a passage. Modern psychology constructed the idea that adolescence, the age par excellence, is a body of contradictions that must become an event of resolution; if the moment is in contradiction with the state, if the state prevented the moment, then there would be a 'crisis'.

G. Stanley Hall was the first to draw up a table of disparate and contradictory tendencies of the 'pubescent' age: alternation of overactivity and exhaustion; having fits of laughter and exuberant cheerfulness towards every real or imaginary object, but crying for no reason and having anxiety about death; egoism of the selfish boy who is proud of his figure and particular about his reputation, but who sees himself lacking virility and becoming effeminate or

careful; altruism and a passion for noble causes, but contempt
for the rights of others; oscillation between goodwill, a desire
to be moral, and the basest desires, a tendency to infringe upon
social constraints; a taste for solitude and natural beauty, but an
incapacity to think and speak except in the company of others, in
society; increase in sensitivity, but development of cruelty; successive states of curiosity and a natural or affected indifference; a
bookish attitude of the spectator and the desire to act; reformist
behaviour and the enemy of conventional forms, but conservative
when provoked; oscillation between the senses and the intellect;
wisdom made of intuitions and moments of madness or imbecil-
ity.[11] G. Stanley Hall's twelve famous contradictions make the
adolescent *immediately* what the adult is *successively*. The pubescent is immediately what the adult ought to embody mediately and
in an ordered fashion, in time.

Mendousse thought that these oppositions were too clear and
caricatured, but he also deciphers adolescence's 'anarchy of tendencies', their personality, which he thinks is inconsistent and
unstable, in the image of organic conflicts: growth in size and
weight between bones and muscles, cranium and face, dispropor-
tions between the general growth of the body and that of various
organs, lack of organic coordination, and so on. Mendousse finds
a mental image [*reflet*] in this bodily instability: the fluctuation
of tastes and intentions and 'the adolescent's inconsistency'. This
'inconsistency' is precisely the challenge of adolescence to psychology: an age which resists synthesis; a contradictory, incoherent,
maladjusted state, at times the anticipated mirror of madness,
which refuses to take part as an element in the growing whole of
a life.

> But at this age every law is provisional or at least meant to be com-
> pleted, if not supplanted, by other determinations. In this consists the
> principal difference which distinguishes the adolescent from the adult.
> While the adult almost always has its established place in the majority
> of questions, and while the adult is specialised in a career or nearly
> exclusive occupations, the most seemingly intransigent boy rarely
> persists in the same assertions. He makes in every way attempts that
> he will later only have a vague memory of, due to their imprecision.
> Whatever care that he tries to seek, he is condemned in advance to
> almost never find himself, since his personality characteristics which
> he finds most interesting today, may in tomorrow's synthesis only

occupy an insignificant place. Can one even speak of *synthesis* when it is a question of the adolescent?[12]

The idea of adolescent *pathology* arises in this way as a denial of 'synthesis', as a non-dialectical moment of life, refusing to be in order to become: a passage where one wants to remain, a contradiction that one wants to hold, a disequilibrium.

For psychology, this will be the key to the theoretical construction of personhood. Psychology – knowledge of the mind, consciousness, the psyche, behaviour – became in the twentieth century the discourse on persons as wholes, on a temporal individual life taken as a single object. Modern psychology makes of a temporal individual life an *object* from beginning to end. Yet, adolescence in crisis appeared as the very opposite figure: a part of life, an age, which refuses to be just one of them and to take part in the development of the whole, whose distinguishing feature was to not want to be a part of all of life as of the constituted society. An incoherent revelation of what is coherent in the adult, a contradictory revelation of all that is ordered in the adult person or which ought to be, modern adolescence, on the psychological view, is not simply the passage through an age, but the *simultaneous* proof of what will be *successive* in personhood.

Most psychological theories used the idea of crisis as both a solution to the illness and a peak of traumatism, whether they defended this concept or criticised it (for example, Coleman and Delaroche), to *assimilate* adolescent disorders. This idea permitted the construction of stages of life and the thinking of a rationality to a person's becoming, in which adolescence is the negative and necessary moment.

Maurice Debesse was among the first to describe through literary analysis what he called the 'crisis of juvenile originality'.[13] He distinguished three universal stages in an early model, to which the psychotherapist Pierre Mâle later added clinical experiment. To characterise the beginning of a crisis, he addressed doubts about bodily and self-authenticity and the entering into play of genital tension and masturbation. He distinguishes this pubertal crisis from the disharmonies of pubertal evolution, which fuel the crisis (a still-childlike body, genital development, conflicts, and so on), since the juvenile crisis follows the pubertal crisis, and can continue to the age of 25. Mâle distinguishes a *natural* [*simple*] crisis, in which a self-image is acquired, actions are laden with anxiety, and one's mind is receptive to others, from *severe* crisis, marked by neurotic inhibition, failure, and depressive moods. The crisis of adolescence is therefore the concept which permits the theoretical distinction between the *normal* and the *pathological*. The normal crisis is what one must pass through to be a temporally developing person; the pathological crisis is when one ceases to develop their personhood and remains stuck.

Psychoanalysis, especially, models this distinction into several stages through the concept of 'fixation'. Piaget's theories about social and moral judgement emphasise adolescence as a moment of personal assimilation, which is its negation, through the discovery of the transgression and contingency of rules, but which is negation made *dialectical* through personal development. One must therefore 'normally' pass through adolescence as through the negative moment of a life's whole and of a social whole, but one must not 'pathologically' remain there.

The crisis allows the idea that age as a 'moment' is *normal*, and that age as a 'state' is *pathological*.

6. Psychological Assimilation II: Crisis as a Developmental Model

In the 1960s, Kohlberg[14] developed a series of tests, inspired by Piaget's method, which made it possible to identify and hierarchise six stages of moral development, beginning with the form of justifications and arguments put forward by individuals of various ages to justify their attitude, rather than with the content of these judgements. Placing the subject before theoretical moral dilemmas, Kohlberg did not consider the solutions the subjects chose, but rather the form of arguments they used to justify their choices. Establishing a scale of these argumentative forms, he presented a picture of the ages of life as 'stages', within which adolescence represents only one level among others. Paradoxically, all the levels, all the ages are thought of as a body of contradictions to resolve the passage to the next age through a personal crisis. The passage assimilates the form of the previous arguments, in their cognitive and moral relationship to the world, within a higher form.

The first, pre-conventional stage of morality is based on the fear of punishment and blind respect to obedience. Only the consequences of one's action determine its value. The second pre-conventional stage – the stages are paired – directs the individual towards instrumental relativism: a right exists which must favour my individual action, my egocentric interests. The third, conventional stage of morality is directed towards the agreement with and concern for others: behaving in a certain way in order to satisfy the milieu's expectations. The fourth, conventional stage involves conforming to law and order and responding to social rules. The fifth, post-conventional stage marks the acknowledgement of a social contract and the search for the greatest good for the greatest number. The sixth, post-conventional stage is where the individual holds a universal ethical principle (justice, reciprocity, equality, and so on).

As in antiquity, the division of human ages is ordered through this transcendental series in the becoming of a temporally individuated life, but in this case by claiming that the division is based on their (cognitive and moral) development and inferring this series from it.

Kohlberg views adolescence, between 11 and 16 years, as one moment of cognitive and moral conflict among others, but an especially accelerated moment between the third and fourth stages. All individuals are supposed to pass through these stages in the indicated order. Childhood is identified with the development from the first to the second stage, and adolescence begins in the passage to the third. Adults reach the fourth stage. However, Kohlberg clarifies that only a minority of persons reach the last stage, identified with wisdom.

From one age to another, from one level to the next, on a line which never envelops itself (no regression exists without a degenerative illness), personhood is restructured and conflicts assimilate into a higher resolution. A normal person's life is a life which continues stage by stage, from age to age. A pathological life is a life which is curtailed at a particular stage.

Kohlberg's model assimilates adolescence as a *state*, which is in fact a *moment* – not a ritual passage, but a sum of cognitive and moral contradictions. These contradictions are necessary as long as they allow access to a higher stage, but pathological if they produce a fixation or blockage. There is a *normal* crisis if adolescence stops. There is a *pathological* crisis if it is the adolescent who stops.

But such a finalist psychological picture misses precisely what adolescence questions. Conceiving of personal life as a permanent synthesis, an experiential accumulation, directed towards the possibility of ultimate wisdom, it cannot conceive of adolescence as the denial and negation of the synthesis of ages towards wisdom.

In other words, the more one constructs a model of adolescence which assimilates a social individual's development, the more adolescence appears as the departure from this development, as 'the anti-moment' par excellence. But it is precisely this crisis of adolescence as a moment of the anti-moment in a person's life that psychology will stage in various models of identity, from the most erudite research to self-help guides. Erik Erikson is undoubtedly the best example of the way in which the crisis of adolescence became the means of considering all the passages from one age of life to another. The exceptional crisis of adolescence became the *rule* of psychological models. Erikson claims that the feeling of internal identity must be realised in adolescence by experiencing a progressive continuity between what we have become and what we think we become, between what we think we are and what others expect of us. Erikson assimilates both psychoanalytic stages and Piaget's cognitive-moral levels of development. Adolescence becomes the prototype of an age defined by contradictions, crystallised in an identity crisis, and overcome through the acquisition of 'virtue', which is not so much the solution to the contradiction as its acceptance and the acknowledgement of the equal importance of the two poles in conflict.

Erikson's eight stages of development[15] is one of the most successful accomplishments of twentieth-century psychology, not as a positive knowledge of consciousness or behaviour, but as a discourse producing an ideal totality of individual life and its temporal identity (which was also partially true of Freud's work). The first stage is born from the early childhood conflict between trust and mistrust, and allows one to acquire the virtue of 'hope'. The second stage gives birth to the virtue of 'will' through the recognition of the contradiction between the child's autonomy and shame. The third stage is connected to 'purpose' through the conflict, from 3 to 6 years, between initiative and guilt. The fourth stage allows one to access the virtue of 'competence', between 6 and 12 years, through the crisis that makes industry confront inferiority, in comparison with other children. The crisis of adolescence intervenes in the fifth stage: an identity crisis, between self-identity and role confusion, is resolved in the virtue of 'fidelity'. Erikson's model is the precursor to the psychological views of life which multiply the crises – of the 30-year-old, of the 40-year-old, of the 50-year-old, of 'middle-aged lust', and so on. The sixth crisis, occurring in adulthood, is the conflict between intimacy and isolation, which, once accepted, allows one to possess the virtue of 'love'. A seventh crisis follows, which like the previous crises is born from the departure from the previous one: generativity opposed to stagnation, from 40 years, is resolved in the virtue of 'care'. Lastly, the concern for the ego's integrity, in old age, faced with despair, is articulated around the classically terminal virtue of 'wisdom'.

In the last analysis, adolescence stages a crisis of assimilation, a contradiction and denial of synthesis. Psychology does not conceive of adolescence as an exceptional case, the problematic extension of the (formerly ritualised) passage from childhood to adulthood. Henceforth, adolescence appears as the model of passage from every age of life to the next, through a logic of crisis, which replaces ritual in the progressive construction of individual identity. It is the symptom of a transformation in our relation to the division of our life's duration into objects and events.

7. Critique of Crisis: Each Age's Chance and Price

Every critique of crisis refuses to consider a part of a temporal line as absolutely subordinate to the whole. There seems to be a crisis when every instant is viewed as a moment and when an instant which is valued on its own prevents the next moment, or the whole from being valued. But, we have said, every *object* comprehended in another object is also a *thing* formally equal to the thing that its whole constitutes. If a human life objectively comprehends moments, it is not formally valued more (or less) than one of its moments. An age is precisely a part of life which is worth as much as life itself. An age is what is irreducible to a moment. A stage of life is a *compact* age.

Modern psychology seizes the adolescent figure and the idea of crisis in order to reduce human ages to moments. Since passages cannot be articulated from one moment to another through rites, psychology produces discourses which articulate them through crises, with the symptoms of moments of life detailed in self-help books.

Modern adolescence, which is no longer an isolated event but a temporal object, is not pathological in itself. Bearing the idea of crisis, modern adolescence above all places the world which surrounds it in crisis, by denying the absoluteness of the assimilation of parts by a whole – of family members by the family, of individuals by society, of students by the school, of active adults by the working world.

Modern adolescence show us what an age of life really is: not a subordinate moment in the development of an individual life, but a part of life which is worth as much as life as a whole. Ages objectively accumulate: adolescence comprehends childhood as much as adulthood comprehends adolescence. Nonetheless, adolescence shows us what formally escapes 'experiential' accumulation. Unlike what all psychological models of life claim, being an adolescent implies losing all that is gained with age, and becoming an adult implies a loss equal to the consented gain. No dialectic exists between what is gained and lost from one age to another; all that I gain by growing, I lose by aging. Music or poetry cannot be understood without grasping – quite unlike the psychological models of a life's rational progress and experiential gains – the human consciousness of the loss which accompanies the passage from one age to another. This loss is called 'nostalgia' (which we have already mentioned in relation to history in Chapter X), the price to pay for the experiential blind spot of scientific psychology.

Adolescence is the *medium*, a modern age between the two, of the relationship between nostalgia and experience, between the formal equality of what is gained and lost and the objective augmentation of what is acquired through time. Since at least the seventeenth century, the *rhapsodic* adolescent has symbolised the contradiction between the body's natural development and the social division of ages: for example, Goethe's Werther, Friedrich Holderlin's 'When I was a boy', Arthur Rimbaud, Attila József, J. D. Salinger's Holden Caulfield, Sylvia Plath, James Dean, Elvis, the young Bob Dylan, Kurt Cobain's 'Serve the Servants' ('Teenage angst has paid off well . . .'). They split the image of the world and life, separated between childhood and adulthood, nature and culture, gods and men, past and future, nostalgia and experience, form and object. The *rhapsodic* adolescent, as opposed to psychology's adolescent in crisis, is the embodiment of the age against the stage and the moment.

Psychology gave new meaning to the idea of experience, which was until then the privilege of philosophical empiricism. Experience is henceforth what weighs down a life and makes us think that our ages are strictly *moments*, subordinate to each other, that we must know how to traverse. We accumulate our ages like so much credit for our ultimate passage to an imaginary cash register, where we are unsure of what it is that we are purchasing. By conceiving of life as the successive development of psychological, moral, cognitive moments, we attribute too much to its end and remove all consistency from the passage of life.

A life is the irregular order of ages, periods considered as wholes which are equivalent to an entire life, where we play out our entire lives, and that continuously short-circuit experience. Experience is the objective order of my life; I know more things and I comprehend all that I was, without being able to be it. When I encounter someone younger than myself, I also experience the limits of experience when I cannot communicate my experience to them, not only because it is *my* experience and not *theirs*, but because, like the adolescence that I believe I have overcome, adulthood also goes beyond me in its own way. I do not want an adolescent to commit the same errors as I did. So I speak to them, I recognise myself in them, I understand their ways of thinking. I understand that they may not want to listen to me, because I would not even listen to myself at that age. But I understand above all that they understand me, that they judge what I abandoned to acquire what I try to transmit to them in a higher way: wisdom, lucidity, distance.

Each age has its chance and its price to pay. What one acquires in comparison to the prior age is also what one loses, what one renounces in this subsequent age.

No *absolute experience* exists since no formal accumulative order of ages of life exists. The price that the adolescent pays is also the chance which belongs only to her, and which escapes adulthood. Adolescents provide for themselves naturally and are relieved of civil constraints by their civil status (education, family). Adolescents are not yet quite dependent on civil constraints ('autonomy', work). Society relieves them of the constraints of autonomy at the very moment when autonomy is acquired.

Adolescents have the *chance* to be autonomous from the state of social autonomy.

Adolescents are the soothsayers of contradictions. Adolescence is the gap or contact between our cultural customs and nature. What adolescents have less of is what allows them to acquire an additional quality, which modern society stages: a non-assimilated autonomy in the social domain, disclosing everything in which we are, our life's necessities disclosed from the outside as *contingencies*.

Adolescence is not primarily a moment. Rather, like childhood, it is something irreparably lost, and unassimilable.

To stop being an adolescent is to go outside adolescence and comprehend it – not simply to synthesise or assimilate adolescence into a higher development in order to reassure oneself, but to accept losing it. We *accumulate* experience and moments, but we *lose* a past age to gain a present age. The ages of a life are *things* of life, each age equal to life as a whole. And the moments of a life are *objects* of this life, durations comprehended in each other, which increase each other with time and increase our experience. We do not have an experience of our ages, only nostalgia. We only have an experience of the moments of our life, ordered in each other. All moments are in life and in a universe. On the other hand, all ages remain in a world.

Why is an age of life worth neither more nor less than life as a whole? Why is it unlikely that an age can be psychologically assimilated, like the moments that make up our experience? Because an age and a life as a whole are also comprehended in the form of their *death*.

Notes

1. G. Stanley Hall, *Adolescence*.
2. William H. Burnham, 'The Study of Psychology'.
3. Immanuel Kant, *Conjectures on the Beginning of Human History*, p. 228.
4. Plato, *Phaedrus*, 246a, p. 524.
5. Plato, *Republic*, 436a, p. 1067.
6. Aristotle, *Politics*, VII, 1336b38–40, p. 2121.
7. Arnold van Gennep, *The Rites of Passage*.
8. Victor Turner, *The Forest of Symbols*. Following van Gennep, Turner notes that in every liminal stage or transitional state the individual is 'betwixt and between', that is, 'between' and 'caught in the interval'.
9. Pierre Mendousse, *L'Âme de l'adolescent*. Pierre Mendousse, *L'Âme de l'adolescente*.
10. G. Stanley Hall, *Adolescence*.
11. Ibid.
12. Mendousse, *L'Âme de l'adolescent*.

13. Maurice Debesse, *La Crise d'originalité juvénile*.
14. See in particular Lawrence Kohlberg's 'Moral Stages and Moralization'.
15. Erik H. Erikson, *Identity and the Life Cycle*.

Chapter XVI

Death

1. Aging, Death of Others, and Death of Self

Death is the end of an individuated life's presence. Some parts of an organism can live or be maintained even though the individual is or will no longer be living. This end does not entail the destruction of what lived, which is still something as a body, as a memory, or as an author of residual traces in the physical universe. Rather, it denotes the absence without return of what lived.

What ends with death is not a life, but this life's presence. The being which was living and which is no longer living is absent from the world; the world comprehends it and it is not in the world. What dies stops being present.

However, all that lives does not die. Only individuated lives die. My hand will never die. One can certainly cut it off, in which case I will be missing a hand; it will cease to function, waste away, rot, and decompose, but one cannot say that it will be *dead*.

Death is therefore not the opposite or the end of life, but only the end of the presence of some organisational mode of a living thing: its individuation.

Two positions emerge from the incomprehension of this definition. The materialist or naturalist makes death the end of life. Death is thus easily reducible to a *function*. Death is inscribed in living things as a regulatory mechanism of the species' evolution, an internal clock, the organism's programming, the condition of possibility of a renewal, the very sign of the triumph of the logic of species-life over the logic of individual-life. Here, death is attributed to humans, other animals, and all living things, including cells.

Unlike the materialist or naturalist, the idealist makes death the end of being. Death no longer has anything to do with living things, but everything to do with the Idea. Death becomes the condition by which existent things, and not merely living things, can situate themselves outside their identity as human animals. Here, death belongs only to those who think about death, who are conscious of it, or who have an Idea of it. Other entities, like beasts, plants, and amoebas, merely 'perish' (according to Martin Heidegger[1]).

But whoever contrasts death with life or with subjective being forgets that death is neither the end of a life nor the end of an individuated subject, but the end of an individuated life's *presence*. Dying is irreducible to an operation of organised living things, which come undone, decompose, and recompose. Dying cannot be elevated to the idea of the end, nothingness, or the absolute. Neither a function of the living nor an ontological end, death is the event of an absence of life's presence.

Death is what can only be absent.

We can experience this absence in three ways: through aging, through the death of another, and through our own death. The first experience is immanent to living things, the second transcendent, and the third paradoxical.

The experience of death immanent to life is essentially that of aging and of illness. One cannot derive what death is from this experience, but one can understand how death happens, and at best what function it fulfils. In my life and another's life, I find signs of death: the partial malfunctioning of metabolism, fatigue, the loss of certain capacities, the withering of flesh, the fragility of organs, the lassitude of long life, the generational replacement, the increasing scarcity of first times, the accumulation of lived experience, the compression of vertebrae, and so on. None of this is logically necessary. They are merely a collection of more or less evident facts that anyone can interpret as they wish. One can derive from them a moral of death's unavoidability as well as a voluntary resistance to the power of negation, an affirmation of *conatus*, of vital force. But one never infers the necessity of a death outside life from the experience of life which exhausts itself in life. Nor can one understand death from the experience of life. If we could, death would be inscribed in our cellular nuclei, in an evolutionary mechanism, in the clogging up of my body, or in the slowing down of my becoming. Nothing can ever be extracted from the present life except tendencies: either a life which tends to resist death, or a life which tends to accompany a process realised in death.

The experience of a life's irreversible absence is never really apparent except through the death of another living being (whether vegetable, animal, or human). The death of another is the experience of the irruption of an absence from which there is no return within the presence of what lives. Here, death is not a *process* of weakening, of aging, or of illness, but an event which *suddenly* makes a thing necessarily absent. I can continue touching, questioning, and speaking to what lived – that is, continue presenting myself to this thing as if it were still a living being – but this thing is henceforth incapable of doing likewise to me.

The possibility that I am myself fated to die like any other appears to be the paradoxical experience of an experiential impossibility. Anyone may conceive of my death, my permanent absence, except me. My death has no meaning except outside me.

The experience of death as a life process immanent to life is a gradual *melancholic* experience. The experience of another's death is a *tragic* experience of an individual life that I can comprehend but that can no longer comprehend me. The 'unexperienceable' experience of my own death is ultimately *compact*; it is an event which only ever has the possibility of being impossible and whose only condition of possibility is its failure.

For each individuated living animal or human, death is shown to be a triple experience – melancholic, tragic, and impossible. And this triple experience relates the one who has it to a single object, death, in two ways: a *changing* death and an *equal* death.

Why 'change' and 'equality'?

The aging process, another's death, and my own death are each something insofar as they expose an absence in the world. Death is never a *departure* from the world. What dies, what is dead, and what will die exist in the world, since some mode of presence exists in this absence, a being of this non-being. Death is an object which contains nothing but absence, an empty something – an emptiness of individuated life. But this empty something remains present in the world, in the physical universe, in the human, animal, social, historical, and symbolic universe. Death does not exist outside the world, but only in the world, like an empty pocket in which human cultures put every possible, imaginable, and spatio-temporally variable form. *That which dies* is absent, but *that which death is* is always present. From this second objective side, death is changing. Death is certainly not presented and represented in the same way by different individuals, social classes, societies, cultures, eras, or species; the words, cults, attitudes, customs, roles, and meaning of death continually transform. This is 'changing death'.

However, death introduces a formal emptiness, an absence of determination and content, into the universe of historical, social, cultural, familial, and individual life. This is 'equal death'.

Let us begin by circumscribing the possible varieties of *changing* death, which various laws, customs, representations, and sciences contest, before coming back to *equal* death.

2. Changing Death I: Medical Definitions

The importance of a medical definition of death[2] follows from concerns not to consider as permanently absent what could still have a form of living presence. However, recent debates on the development of medical criteria for recognising the status of the deceased stem above all from legal requirements. Dying means passing from a subjective status to a legal objective status. In order to address old problems of inheritance and new problems raised by the possibility of organ transplants, it therefore appeared necessary to put forward a scientific definition of the moment when an individuated living being obtains the status of death.

Before the Renaissance, the decisive criterion was the 'last breath'. The definition of a respiratory death considered the loss of the capacity to breathe as the sign of the end of vital functions. The soul, frequently likened to the vital breath, abandoned the living body as soon as the organism failed to successively inhale and exhale air.

The objective progress in the medical knowledge of bodies allowed clarification of the definition, and marked the first step towards an increasingly greater predicament. When William Harvey and Descartes discovered the principle of the circulation of blood, it appeared that the cardiac function, bound to the respiratory function (which itself stops the cerebral function and leads to the irreversible decomposition of tissues), was primary. The heart's stopping, rather than the breath's, signified a body's death.

The technical advancements in medical equipment led to the determination of the status of 'cardiac death'. After World War II, direct clinical observations were made through the verification of the absence of a pulse, through the observation of blood pressure, or, when in doubt, through an arteriotomy (an incision of an artery) or Icard's fluorescein test (the non-colouring of connective tissues half an hour after the intravenous injection of fluorescein).

In the 1960s, the development of medical equipment made respiratory assistance and resuscitation possible. A prolonged absence of natural cerebral oxygenation could henceforth be artificially compensated for. Everything that medicine gained control of in the prolonging of vital functions was, little by little, lost in the definition of what a body's death was. Indeed, resuscitated patients whose circulation of blood was guaranteed could very well be in a state of cerebral death. The cardiac criteria, which replaced the respiratory criteria, were in turn made obsolete because of marginal though significant cases.

In 1959, brain death, grade four coma, was redefined as the decisive factor of death. The absence of relational brain functions – such as consciousness, sensory modalities, or reflexes – and of vegetative life functions also marked the status of legal death. The medical community's decision was clearly established to protect surgeons responsible for organ transplants from removing organs from living bodies (in the earlier sense) and from removing organs from dead bodies (in the new sense). Respiration and circulation could be guaranteed, even though the brain reached the point of no return. The first kidney transplant took place in France in 1954. In 1967, the first heart transplant was certainly facilitated by the medico-legal redefinition of cerebral death.

Encephalic death was measured through the absence of responses to external stimuli, the absence of spontaneous muscular activity, an entirely artificial respiration, and the observed absence of reflexes. Two thirty-minute electroencephalograms (EEGs) were carried out, accounting for the differences (or lack of them) in electric potentials and in activity in the cerebral cortex. Permissive hypercapnia (a test verifying the absence of spontaneous respiration) or angiography (an x-ray of blood vessels in the brain) could also be performed. The scientific community thought that they were capable of strongly ascertaining the status of death or the status of a body's life. However, the tests became increasingly complicated. Since an EEG could prove to be wrong in cases of toxic coma, revealing a momentary absence of activity even though a patient could later recover, it became necessary to undertake two successive EEGs four hours apart. Ad hoc hypotheses multiplied, and the definition of death lost in evidence and in simplicity what our medical control over the body gained in efficacy.

The idea of a cerebral death absolutely identifiable with the destruction of the brainstem diminished from the 1970s onward. The appearance of cases of vegetative coma – made possible precisely through the power of science and medical equipment, which artificially maintain vital functions that are unable to continue independently – split brain death, at the time the decisive criterion, in two. It seemed that the prefrontal cortex could be dead while the brainstem, guaranteeing the essential vegetative functions, was still in a functional state.

A patient could regain respiratory autonomy, open and close their eyes, and experience light–dark cycles, even if the destruction of the prefrontal regions of their brain prevented them from ever regaining something like consciousness. To determine this subjective status of presence in the world, medical science had to revive long-standing metaphysical concepts which nineteenth-century positivists thought they had made obsolete. The term 'vegetative' was thus borrowed from the Aristotelian stratification of the soul. Debates on the impossibility of the reappearance of consciousness in a patient immersed in an irreversible coma were all based on the definition of an internal something that remained inaccessible to measurements, x-rays, or technological observations.

The more medical science and technology progressed towards controlling the phenomenon of death, the less we knew precisely what death was. The price to pay for the human operation on living bodies, their support, and their care is the blurring of what was before a clear distinction between the living and the dead. By postponing natural death, medical science certainly postpones death, but also the *naturalness* of death.

Since it has become possible to artificially operate on bodies bordering on the end of their natural vital functions, the theoretical determination of what lives and of what lives no more seems increasingly thorny. More recent definitions of cortical and neocortical death appear as ad hoc theories faced with the accumulation of limit cases and problems outside of medical science's control. The identification of death with functions of the prefrontal cortex which refer to concepts debated in Western philosophy for millennia – especially the concept of 'consciousness' – attests to the fragility of observational testing. All the criteria can be falsified through particular cases of reawakening.

Whoever struggles against a phenomenon approaches it, mixes and confounds its means with those of the adversary, and in the process loses clear-sightedness of the identity of what it attacks. By technologically struggling against death, one loses the *absolute* theoretical notion of death. Death is no longer a natural or divine absolute, identifiable from afar through the absence of breathing or the circulation of blood, the sign of a deserted soul, but something relative, the sign of a technological relation maintained between living things and non-living things.

The autonomisation of functions which were connected through the human powerlessness to modify them, to affect them (respiration, circulation, brain functioning), fragmented the living body as much as death itself. Today, various limit states of death exist, which outline a continuous field between the clearly living and the clearly dead (the decomposed corpse), a between-life-and-death causing zombies and the living dead to resurface in books and on the screen.

The more we had control over death, the less we managed to distinguish what death could be on its own, independent of our activity as living beings who struggle against it.

3. Changing Death II: Biological Necessessity or Contigency

The growing difficulty of defining dead things at the medical limit of living things therefore accompanied the difficulty of identifying within living things a death which would be functionally inscribed in organisms or in their development.

Intersections between Darwinian evolution, biochemistry, and molecular biology consisted in removing death's imprint as a function of living things from lower and higher levels of living things. The usefulness of death in what composes each living organism (cells) as well as in what living organisms compose (species and an evolution through mutation and selection) was therefore sought. Death was no longer the negation of life's functions, which resist it, as in Xavier Bichat's apothegm,[3] but rather a positive function of living things.

By postponing accidental death, the increase in life expectancy and in the precision of medical technologies permitted the paradoxical appearance of a *denaturalised natural* death – a *natural* death since it is now easier than before to attain the extreme limit of a life untroubled by accidents, wounds, or illness; but also a *denaturalised* death, the result of the artificial maintenance of metabolism and vital functions, which blurs the frontiers between a death due to the organism's internal causes and a death caused by external factors.

The problem of death concerned the external infections and attacks slightly less and the internal mechanism of aging slightly more.

At the beginning of the twentieth century, when Alexis Carrel artificially kept a chicken's heart alive for thirty years – a chicken's life expectancy is normally five years – by removing it from its external environment, it was tempting to conceive of death as an external contingency: the more one isolates a living element from what surrounds it, the more it appears that it can live without limits, maintained and sheltered from every accident.

Biology led to the idea of a contingent, external death in the processes of living things, never occurring anywhere but on the outside. But in fact the history of death's conception does not cease oscillating between a contingent, external pole and a necessary, internal pole, internal to living things. In 1961, when Leonard Hayflick determined his famous 'limit', the biology of death appeared to turn towards the second pole. A kind of internal countdown of the organism's specialised cells, capable of dividing around fifty times, was thought to have been discovered. This phenomenon reveals an incomplete reproduction of the DNA strand's limits, the telomeres, and was thought to hold the agent programming the necessity of death in the order of living things, the necessity that DNA strands do not reproduce infinitely.

Shortly thereafter the balance again leaned to the other side. When the reproduction of non-specialised sexual cells is complete, it seems that the body provides both the problem and the solution to the problem – both the necessity of death inscribed in living things and the possibility of finding a solution in living things, thanks to the telomerases of sexual cells. But the use of these telomerases allowed a new problem to appear: how does one avoid the uncontrolled proliferation of cancerous cells?

Paralleling medical technical progress, the development of gerontology – which takes on metabolism – and of geriatrics – which treats successive illnesses in aging – contributed to the refocusing of research on the question of cellular aging. At the same time, no longer on a microscopic scale, but on a macroscopic scale of living things, neo-Darwinism examines death's function and seeks to prove that individual death constitutes an adaptive advantage, permitting generational replacement (an old argument), but also represents a kind of trial-and-error mechanism of the entire species.

This transversal line making death necessary at the microscopic and macroscopic scales of living things conflicts with a second voluntary scientific line, a concept of death culminating as an accidental event in the transhumanist promise of immortality. In the work of bioinformatics researcher, biogerontologist, and promoter of SENS, the project 'Strategies for Engineered Negligible Senescence', Aubrey de Grey writes of the contemporary desire to reduce death to something external to living things.[4] SENS identifies seven causes of aging, and refuses to treat metabolism or pathologies of aging, but promises to act directly on cellular damage caused by aging, with illnesses only considered consequences of this damage. This project is the very sign of a contemporary biological engineering replacing medical science and concerned with transforming a living body internally by caring for it, not against *that which is done to it*, but rather against *that which it is*.

Basing its claims on twentieth-century research, the project seeks to indefinitely postpone the age at which the accumulation of cellular damage reaches pathogen levels, and identifies seven causes of aging: atrophy and cell loss, cell senescence, nuclear mutations, mitochondrial mutations, intra- and extracellular junk, and aberrant crosslinks.

Some claim to resolve these malfunctions through the stimulation of the immune system, the use of enzymes destroying junk, the sealing of telomere elongation, the injection of growth factors, or the introduction of new stem cells. This programme presents a logic of permanent compensation, where each solution to problems of bodily disintegration and cancerous overflow marks the emergence of the next problem to resolve. By treating a body on its own, one heals it from a fatal illness through the promise of another fatal illness.

However, Aubrey de Grey claims that when human beings have the means to treat what causes death, they become passively *responsible* for death by not acting against it, and he is right to underline this fact. By becoming capable of healing – even if one has no desire to be healed – what in the past was a natural death, human beings transform *natural* death into *accidental* death, and therefore into contingent death. By postponing death as a set of symptoms, phenomena that one can always treat, contemporary biology transforms carelessness into murder by omission.

Either some individuals will make the radical choice of purity by refusing every human treatment of the natural body, in order to safeguard the possibility of a natural death, a self-evident death; or all human beings ought to confront the idea that death will never be natural for them.

By maintaining our body through the use of medications, going to extremes by obsessionally combating senescence, humanity makes obsolete the idea that death could exist *in itself*.

The consequence of the sciences and technologies linked to aging is that, while they extend life expectancy, they denaturalise death and leave humanity trapped in a dilemma. Either one must think that death is inscribed in the heart of living things at the microscopic cellular scale and at the macroscopic evolutionary scale, and fail to understand why all modern human efforts lead to combating and postponing this natural and necessary death. Or one must think that death remains external to the functioning of living things, is contingent and accidental, and can be willingly postponed through a technologically equipped living being; in this case there is no natural death, but only passively accepted deaths, through insufficient will, knowledge, or technology.

In the first case, humanity finds consolation by considering the individual's death as functional and necessary, but must think that all modern efforts against death are directed against nature. In the second case, humanity hopes to continuously postpone the prospect of death, but must think that death will never be more natural, that one ought to want it to be that way, that one ought to come to death, because death will not come to them.

Modern humanity is relieved through medicine and the biology of a fast-approaching death, but pays the price for it. Humanity takes up a historical responsibility vis-à-vis their own mortality, and makes death something against which they think can be active, something for which they feel responsible, since they think they are able to change it or slow it down. But can one live by attaching an excessive value to life? Insofar as one removes the possibility of dying naturally of old age, it is rational to fear that an accidental death could become intolerable in view of a death that one ought to be capable of postponing continuously.

Paradoxically, by *desocialising* changing death, humanity *denaturalised* death.

4. Changing Death III: Cultural Transformations

Human views on death espouse the spectre of different relations to an identical thing. What is identical – equal death, *that which is* death – is the occasion to change what can be different – *that which* death *is*, a 'dead' object in life.

The ancient Greek oscillation between the conception of a valued, heroic death and the dishonour of dreaded [*redoutée*] death opens up the field to an ambiguity between death as an activity regulated by and for the community and death as the *pathos* of the individual. Christianity is partly an attempt to synthesise death as a social *activity*, ritualised by the Church of believers, with the *pathos* of the individual who obtains with their end the meaning of what they had been.

Since Philippe Ariès's controversial work,[5] death is seen as socially domesticated by the Christian world, an accepted and expected death. The scenes of Gauvain's, Roland's, and Tristan's end of life testify to the idea that Christians confront death in a state of *active passivity*. The only action towards the feeling of approaching death is to know how to let it come, how to go *towards* death and not *against* it, when one recognises that it is there. This transformation was often discussed in the late Middle Ages and led to the apparent textual and behavioural acceptance of a natural order, in which society takes responsibility for an individualised death, conceived less and less as a collective fate. In the seventeenth century, the dying were often represented in their bedroom accompanied by an angel and a demon fighting over their soul, as if death were less the collective passage to a state of expectation – the dead's Resurrection and humanity's Last Judgement – but rather the decisive instant, the privileged moment when salvation and the truth of an individuated life are played out.

Attitudes towards a fast-approaching death come close to an *individual* heroism that Christianity paradoxically concealed at the moment of its institutional formation (except in martyrology). The pendulum of changing death again swung towards this individual heroism at the beginning of modernity. Following the certainty of regaining one's body at the moment of the Resurrection was the doubt about and fascination towards the dead body's subterranean life (the worms, humus, and putridity which haunted Gothic sensibility).

The novel configuration of a death at once heroic, the moment of internal truth, and assimilated into the movement of living things which come undone and decompose after the fact, contrasts an individual with the prospect of a double death: the uncertain life in death (fate of the spirit) and the indifferent life of what is dead (the decomposing body).

Yet, it is not the Western deritualisation of behaviour towards death which entailed the denaturalisation of death in medical science and in the biology of aging. But neither did the objective developments of the latter lead to the Western desocialisation of death, abandoned to personalised rites, words, and gestures. In reality, the two movements of denaturalisation and desocialisation both expressed a changing death, which fluctuated between several poles: activity and passivity, community and individuality, necessity and contingency.

Historically, our era experimented with new ways of making do with death, which all revived beyond the Christian moment something ancient or even pagan and invented something novel: a desocialised and denaturalised death. We relate to a death that we no longer feel coming, which no longer has a face, which no longer is inscribed in the natural order, but against which we continuously act, while losing the meaning of what death precisely is. Whereas a knight felt his death coming because he did not act against it, humans of our time make doctors, or those who have some knowledge or technologies at their disposal, those who know whether their own death will come or not.

One must neither look forward to it, for something is historically lost (a feeling against a knowledge, a body of rites, and collective ways of doing), nor lament it, for something is gained (a knowledge against a feeling, a duration of higher life). Death is simply the ultimate human experience of the articulation of the changing and the same.

Human death is the relation between itself and the relation that humanity maintains with it. Therefore, human death is an ever-changing relation with itself, which perpetually oscillates between contradictory possibilities. In this way, the way of taking on the individual who dies concerns both the desire to establish continuity[6] and the desire to provoke rupture.[7]

Nature is blamed for having broken the symmetric effect which connected it to society. Death, the interface of exchanges between nature and culture, resembles an error that one must correct or consolidate by recapturing something that nature appropriated from the community.

Jean-Pierre Vernant compares the ancient Mesopotamians', Indians', and Greeks' relations to death.[8] In ancient Mesopotamia, they buried the king with pomp and watched over him, thinking that he remained connected to living beings in the earth – the dead therefore ground culture and society. In Brahminical India, they cremated *sannyasi*, sages, and left no trace of them. They ascend towards purity, far beyond society. Each time a relationship is established, death seems to negotiate a contract between culture and nature. For the ancient Greeks, this contract is ambiguous. They hesitate between the horror of death[9] and the dream of beautiful death, such as Achilles's death. By ritualising good death (heroic death) or evil death (the soiled corpse) they add to death – as an interface between a natural outside and social inside – the ambiguity of a death between passivity and activity, between life's sublimation and life's decomposition.

Changing death is nothing but an equilibrium between *inside* and *outside*, between social life and natural life, between presence and absence. It marks both the possibility of this equilibrium, and the fear of disequilibrium.

Death is the changing sign of an individual's internal disharmony. Disharmony is provoked between humanity and nature, and must be compensated for through rituals and myths.

Claims that human relations to death are in no way death itself, and that the relations that we maintain with death are sufficient to think about death are equally although differently wrong. Underestimations of our knowledge, technology, beliefs, representations, historical changes, and cultural variations with respect to death lead to conceptions of death as always the same, a truth, or a reality transcending our customs relating to death in various ways, our views on the same unchanged thing. Overestimations of our death customs toss death into the scrapheap of metaphysical bric-a-brac; they hold that there is nothing other than variety in our ways of relating ourselves to death, which are relative to the period, class, culture, knowledge, or technology.

But death is both the presence of an absence and the absence of a presence. Positivists, materialists, and culturalists, who only consider the (symbolic, material, or cultural) modes of presence of this absence, merely take *changing* death into account. The religious, idealists, or spiritualists only really grasp the mode of absence of presence; they meditate on controversies, paradox, the 'empirico-metaempirical monster' (as Vladimir Jankélévitch calls it[10]) of *equal* death.

But death is nothing other than the relation between the two, each referring to the other, without any kind of dialectic.[11] Human cultures allow changing death to appear because death is an Archimedean point, the great fixity on which it is possible to rely in order to move the entire human cultural universe by testing the various possibilities of customs, of beliefs, of attitudes, of knowledge, of representations. And these varieties have meaning only with regard to a death which, whatever one makes of it, in whatever way one represents it, remains the same.

5. Equal Death I: Not to Think about Death

Where *changing* death ends, *equal* death and the work of the wise begin. Equal death is death that is indifferent to the relation that we maintain with it. It is death as an object not affected by what I think of it, what I believe of it, what I make of it, my identity, my age, the conditions of my extinction, my social class, my culture, my era, or my species.

Beneath the knowledge and technologies which concern changing death, equal death is the death that religions, philosophies, and wisdom seek. Equal death has no relation to the variety of relations that one can maintain with it. Against relativism, it is therefore the foundation of every doctrine of the absolute.

The wise, religious, and philosophical propose the adoption of an equal attitude to thinking about the prospect of death.

The problem of knowing whether or not one must think about death traverses both erudite reflections and human beings' spontaneous, everyday meditations on death's irruption and on the absence of once-present individuated lives around them. Those who do not think about death are irrational and let themselves be surprised at their or another's worst moments, deprived of all protection against that which snatches them from presence and from life. But those who do think about death are criticised for living their life to no avail; those who thought about death throughout their life are no less dead from doing so than another who does not devote a single second to it.

In the *Letter to Menoeceus*,[12] Epicurus claims that thinking about death is vacuous. For Epicurus, death is non-sensation and thus cannot be made the object of a sensation. His argument consists not in describing death as 'nothing' in itself, but in showing how death is – in two senses – *for* nothing. Death is not nothing, but is and has existence for nothing and in nothing. For living individuals, death cannot be something, since it is impossible to feel the absence of a sensation. Life is nothing for the dead, since they do not have sensation and nothing can be for them.

The strength of the Epicurean argument is to attribute being only in relation, and to think of death as the partnered dance between the living as a sensation – as a possibility of entering in relation with something – and the dead as an absence of sensation, and thus of relation. The relation between the possibility of relation (life) and its impossibility (death) allows one both to maintain the symmetric effect between life and death, and therefore to attribute being to death, which is not nothing, and to remove this being from it, since the relation is an unequal one. Only life allows one to enter into relation with the relation between life and death. Death is the impossibility of being in relation with this very relation.

Epicurus thinks that nothing is to fear in life, in the world of relations, since nothing is to fear on the outside, and there is no possible relation with the absence of relation. Epicurus constructs the figure par excellence of wisdom, which is an *equal* relation to the world. One must stand at an *equal* distance from the fear of death and from the desire to die. The sage desires neither to abandon life nor to maintain it, since the good life is worth more than long life. The sage knows that every life which is not saturated with its opposite, with death, is good.

The 'neither-nor' strategy, which grounds all wisdom, is implemented through the refusal to think about death. The good life is a meditation on life, and not on death, which either is nothing for me as long as I am something, or is something for me only when I shall not be anything any more. *Nothing* also exists, but differently, in death; either death is nothing for that which is living, or that for which death is something is nothing.

Nonetheless, Epicurean wisdom is not an *equally* wise wisdom. It is a self-wisdom insofar as I regularly experience the sensation of death in my life, the death of another whose remains I can see and touch. If I were the only mortal on earth, undoubtedly Epicurus's wisdom would be absolute. But not only does one's self die, others die – unless I refuse to remember what was, the dead as they were as living beings. To not think about death is necessarily to not think of the dead. It is to refuse to think of the relation between what they were, living beings, and what they are no more.

The death of others is not nothing for me. The wisdom of those who make themselves equal to their own deaths is also non-wisdom, the lack of consideration accorded to the death of others.

6. Equal Death II: To Think about Death

Although Michel de Montaigne cites and esteems Epicurus, the *Essays* implicitly demonstrate an entirely different wisdom of thinking about death. Michel Eyquem, a man whose life was so filled with deaths – his daughter's, his father's, Étienne de La Boétie's, his king's, his mother's – defends, in the famous Chapter XX of the *Essays*,[13] the possibility of an experience of death which is an experience of life and thought. Observing that common folk generally refuse to reflect on death, and fear what they refuse to contemplate, Montaigne proposes the idea that the preclusion of thinking about death is a political tool of domination, a way of instituting fear among the people. However, the body's life and its aging, without clearly denoting death, encourage the mind to account for the end of life. Montaigne insists on the fact that death can arise anywhere and in any way, by accumulating famous and anecdotal examples of historical deaths. He tries to remove the uncanny nature from death, to frequent it [*la pratiquer*], and to assimilate it into every form of life, including fairs and festivals. Freedom is nothing but the capacity to expect death everywhere and to never be caught by it.

'To learn to die' is both an *equal* and Epicurean wisdom; it is to be and to live while expecting death *equally* at every moment. The common folk's unequal attitude towards death is considered the opposite of wisdom. They enjoy themselves at festivals without thinking of the possibility of their end, and collapse into tears when they are overtaken by the fatal moment. But while Epicurus aims at this equality through the logical separation of life and death, which intersect and change roles without entering in relation, Montaigne incorporates death into life, in order to wisely make life equal through death and through its thinking.

Wisdom as the equality of life and death, not through their non-relation but through the incorporation of one in the other – until every moment of an intense life is penetrated by many thoughts about death – is an experiential wisdom. By rubbing shoulders with the deaths of others, it would be possible to prepare for one's own death.

However, one experiences and learns about death only through several occurrences. Yet, what recurs is the death of another. Never do these deaths themselves rehearse, like theatre actors before the premiere, my own death, which occurs only once and which I will never experience.

Montaigne's incorporation of death into life consists in de-singularising his own death by frequenting the deaths of others through thought. Unfortunately, his attempt to institute continuity into discontinuity makes sense only if I were the only immortal being on earth. If everyone dies without my ever dying, then I could, through a continuous exercise, wisely become used to the mortality of everyone but me. However, since I die neither more nor less than, but *different* from, others, Montaigne's wisdom will never prove to be an equal wisdom. Wisdom vis-à-vis others is for myself a kind of madness, a belief in the possibility of ironing out the differences between other deaths and my own, as if I could some day successfully identify them.

An unbridgeable gap exists between the decision not to think about death and the decision to think about it. By rejecting thoughts about death, one makes oneself equal to one's own death, but is unable to experience [*pris de court*] the death of others. By encouraging oneself to think about death, one makes oneself equal to the death of others, but one fails due to the inconceivability of one's own death.

Therefore, no wisdom exists. No equal relation exists between the death of one's self and the death of others. What calms me in one troubles me in the other. Instead, the 'price to pay' is that equal death, which is the same for me and for others, cannot be thought of equally. This price to pay precludes wisdom. Wisdom is a point of compactness: the illusion of an equal attitude towards equal death.

Since death is equal to me and to others, I cannot be equal to death.

7. No Wisdom Exists

Death is the elimination of the attitude, of the presence of what lives. It makes every attitude towards this elimination equal:[14] a good and true attitude will be neither more nor less when faced with death. Death formalises life. It transforms an individual's life into *something*; it is not merely an object, comprehended in other things, in the physical, social, and symbolic universe, with values and variable intensities. It is *something*, and it is something *equal* to another thing.

In this way, since we are mortal, we are led back to the flat and formal world, which is no metaphysical triviality, but which always captures us in the end, even though we considered it at the beginning of this work.

Since we live and die, our position in the material universe, our belonging to objects or events in other objects or other events, our status in time as living, animal, human beings, our representations, our rules, our culture, our history, our values and intensities, our classes, our gender, and our age are continuously short-circuited by our formal belonging to the world, since we are something.

Since each thing is equally in the world, each individuated life is equally in death. This formal equality of death responds to changing and objective death, and neutralises all intensities of life. To be true, to be good, and to be just are thoroughly meaningless when faced with death, but have an *equal* meaning, neither more nor less than the meaning of a false, bad, or unjust attitude.

And in this way any possible wisdom of a mortal is neutralised.

Equal death – and not the changing death of our representations and commemorations – is both a condition of wisdom and what makes all wisdom *compact*. No wise attitude exists, since all attitudes to death have a price, which is the chance of the opposite position. What true human beings lack when faced with equal death is what false human beings obtain – and vice versa. What good or just human beings fail at when faced with death is what bad or unjust human beings succeed at. And what belongs to the good or to the just before their end precisely escapes the bad or unjust.

The sage who does not think about death lacks wisdom about the death of others that occur in the sage's own life; this sage becomes a bastard, in the Sartrean sense of the term. But the sage who thinks about death, who experiences the death of others, lacks wisdom about her own death; this sage demonstrates the madness of considering her own death like the death of others.

Sages do not exist when confronted with death. Death is thus the revelation that no ultimate wisdom exists, that is, no position, attitude, thought, or belief which would allow us to remain equal to what is equal. Faced with equal death, like the world, which is the same for every true or false, beautiful or ugly, good or bad thing, nobody is equal. Whoever is *in this way*, and not otherwise, loses what they gain and gains what they lose. No good attitude towards death exists, since nobody will die less by having this attitude; no formally better or worse thing is in the world, since nothing will ever be either more or less in the world.

Wisdom rests on an absolute in order to disclose to us an equal attitude towards what is equal. Dialectics encompasses the loss and gain in a higher gain. In this way, wisdom and dialectics are always compact, that is, they obtain their failure in their very condition.

Since we are mortal and led back to the formally flat world, we will enter into the life from which we must depart without wisdom.

Death is to our individuated life what the world is to each thing: a principle of equality which precludes wisdom and the absolute, and attributes to every attitude and to each thing their *chance* and their *price*. And this is all that remains for us.

Notes

1. The animal, the merely 'living being', 'has death neither ahead of itself nor behind it': 'Only man dies. The animal perishes.' Martin Heidegger, 'The Thing', p. 178.
2. Paula La Marne, 'Mort'.
3. 'The definition of life is to be sought for in abstract considerations; it will be found, I believe, in this general perception: *life is the totality of those functions which resist death*.' Xavier Bichat, *Physiological Researches Upon Life and Death*, p. 1.
4. Aubrey de Grey with Michael Rae, *Ending Aging*.
5. Philippe Ariès, *Western Attitudes Toward Death*.
6. Through solace and company, Malagasy women caress the dying, encourage them to express their last wishes, recite legends of the beyond, and entrust them with messages addressed to their ancestors, explains Djénane Kareh Tager in *Vivre la mort*.
7. For the Beti of Cameroon, the death pangs are the occasion for a public settling of accounts, terminated through a collective, dramatised pardon. For the Mofu-Diamare, the dead person is first treated with respect, and then considered as a dangerous enemy

and banished from the community. See Louis-Vincent Thomas, *Anthropologie de la mort*.

8. Jean-Pierre Vernant, *L'Individu, la mort, l'amour*.

9. 'The atrocious Ker who wore clothing stained with the blood of men' on the shield of Achilles; the decomposition of cadavers on the Sirens' shores, 'completely whitened with human bones and remains, with decomposing flesh', Vernant, *L'Individu, la mort, l'amour*, p. 133.

10. 'Death is the extraordinary order par excellence', Vladimir Jankélévitch, *La Mort*, p. 8.

11. We have already mentioned in the debates between naturalism and gender studies that it is not a matter of making opposing positions dialectical, but of comprehending them as two possible senses of circulation in the same circulation of being. No possible synthesis exists between the two. Only a search for the 'chance' and the 'price' of each sense exists in a being's gender or death trajectory.

12. Epicurus, *Letter to Menoeceus*.

13. Michel de Montaigne, 'That to philosophize is to learn to die', *Essays*.

14. Suicide is the sign par excellence of the fact that we are never *equal* faced with death. 'Successful' suicide is often described as a failed suicide attempt; the individual remains alive, their eventual call for help can be heard, and it is still possible for them to act. Every suicide which succeeds, which ends in the death of the one who decided to do it, is a failure. The act culminates in a passivity from which there is no return, since anyone who wants to commit suicide destroys their very possibility of accepting death (and of making something of it) by eliminating themselves. Suicide is an attempt at self-reappropriation, through a self-gesture, but leads to dispossession, since I destroy the very condition of possibility of my success, which is my ability to act. Suicide is a chiasmus between success and failure, and never equal to itself; it succeeds when it fails, and it fails when it succeeds. It is compact – and the compact is theoretically suicidal.

Coda: Formally, Objectively

The Chance and the Price

To have one or many children and grandchildren. To succeed in what I do. To triumph in my sport or in my occupational field. To have money. To have financial, economic, or political power. To be desired. To enjoy a series of present moments. To be good, just, virtuous, and valued until the end. To be beautiful or to add beauty to this world. To be faithful to a truth or an idea, and to follow it, defend it, and give my body and my existence to it. To bind myself to something eternal. To be saved. To not be forgotten. To obtain genuine glory, honour, and renown. To remain conscious, lucid, critical, and without illusions. To be happy and to have been happy. To make the most of each instant. To love. To have loved. To produce an artwork. To give form to what I think.

Here are objects. Here are several ends that society and life present to the individual that I am, but none of them *holds*. For each solution is a way of including myself in something higher or transcendent which will outlive me, where I am captured, and through which I am supposed to obtain my ultimate meaning. Yet the thing that I am either dissolves into something larger, or remains a smaller thing in a more important thing.

There is neither a cumulative nor absolute meaning to what I am. I know this.

There is no salvation, because if it were real, then it does not concern me any more, and if it concerns me, then it is not real: it absorbs me as part of a whole.

Everything which comprehends me, and in which I remain, is only ever one sense of me. In another sense, I comprehend a number of things. This is clearly my tragedy and that of everything that is: if all I did was be, be comprehended, I could have aimed at, striven towards fusing with that which encompasses me and seems more important than me. I could only *be* in one sense, and I would

433

run towards my realisation, like the river that flows towards the sea, my resolution in what awaits me. I would be absolutely less than that in which I am, and which I am destined to fuse with. My existence would clearly be reduced to the path descending towards my end. Thus, my life would have meaning [*sens*].

However, my life has two meanings [*deux sens*].

Since things are in me and through me, and since I comprehend things no less than something comprehends me, I, like each thing, infinitely resist my dissolution or realisation, my being sublated through a salvation, a totality, an idea, a spirit, or an eternity that would envelop me. I am comprehended, but I comprehend. And never will I fuse with what is more than me.

This resistance is the tragedy of each thing which will not be saved, whose end cannot be its ultimate meaning, and which is not realised in what comprehends it. But this is also the *chance* of each thing.

The formally flat world ruins the universe of accumulated objects and events, with either more or less intensified values, but at the same time this formally flat world makes this universe possible.

I can belong to the universe, a body, living things, animality, humanity, culture, and history because I am in the world.

Within these Russian dolls, no one would be attributed these numerous identities, one after the other. Each one of them is assumed by all the others, and I, like each thing, am only comprehended in one, and comprehend the others. But each one of my identities, determined by all the others, is as solitary as I, who am their sum.

The fact of being alone in the world, like every thing, prevents me from spreading myself out or from raising myself absolutely in what comprehends me.

If I were not in the world, but merely in society, I would be wholly assimilated as an individual into this absolute totality, which would also embody my salvation.

If I existed only in the physical universe, this universe would comprehend everything that is within me: the matter of my body, the substrata of my emotions and thoughts, the materiality of my acts. I could die, and decompose in the material universe, with the certainty that nothing of me will escape it, that I am entirely its own. Flowing into it, I would be saved, both kept and fulfilled in the matter of which I would embody nothing but a tiny part.

And if I were only an individual, my individuality would save me. But I am so many other things.

Nothing, not even a god, could ever comprehend me or comprehend something, no matter what it is, without letting what resists it escape – the chance that stops both the salvation and the dissolution of each thing.

The world contains me, for I am alone. But the world contains me formally, for I am *equal* to each thing. I am no more in the world than the smallest dust particle, than a fraction of this dust particle, than the word 'dust', than language, than a galaxy, than a supergalaxy, than a contradiction, or than any part of me. The world undoubtedly maintains my chance – but there is a price. My chance is preserved as much as the chance of *that* or *this*, of a fraction of my life, or of a squeak of my voice. I am neither more nor less in the world than anything else.

In all likelihood, nothing and nobody will increase this chance very long after my death. I will disappear for all humans. My trace in the physical universe will completely fade away. No god will be there to save me, keep me, and preserve me in it. But it is not because nothing and nobody has my chance that it does not exist. Since I was in the world, I do not cease to be there, I do not go outside it; I will *be* dead, I will *be* forgotten, I will *be* lost.

Utility, excess, grace: everything is calculated. These accumulations are sometimes contrasted with wisdom; all wisdom replaces the calculation of accumulation by the 'neither more nor less'. Wisdom reveals to me, by comprehending things, that the world is equal. Then it teaches me that I must remain equal to the image of this flattened world. Since everything is equal, you are also equal, you can be neither more nor less, your character can be equal, you can seek out the flat world, and you can draw a single line on this plane and fold yourself over it. Wisdom articulates *being* and *comprehension*; it is necessary to be in the world in the image of what one comprehends of it.

All (Eastern and Western) wisdom is the illusion that it would be possible to bring what I am into accord with what I know. By some sleight of hand, wisdom attributes a unique and absolute meaning to what I comprehend of the world in me and to what I am myself in this world.

The world is equal, and because it is so it doesn't matter whether I am equal to it or not. Will the sage be more and better in the world than the one who has lived without wisdom? Since sages shape themselves in the image of the world, in the image of what really is, do they think that they will be *more*, that they will be *better* than the one who has comprehended nothing?

The consciousness of truth never makes something more true.

That one can be either more or less in the world, or that one can be either good or bad, either true or false, either wise or ignorant, or even indifferent, certainly does not mean that everything is trivial and that there is no morality. There is only objective morality and wisdom, that is, morality and wisdom relative to their comprehension by something. In this way, there is a social morality or wisdom, which allows one to be either more or less, either better or worse together, in a society; there are more or better social beings than others. There is even natural wisdom, which allows one to be either better or worse in nature, to assimilate oneself in it, to make do with and to respect other natural beings.

But no wisdom of the world exists.

Neither calculation nor wisdom: in the world, I only have a chance and a price to pay. And whether or not I pay it, I still pay it.

I know that I could err, do harm, or prove to be unworthy, and I know that I would not be less due to it. I live with this certainty. My morals are only local, attached to the fact of being objectively comprehended in a nature, a history, a society, a family, some class of ideas, even eternal ones.

So why not err, do harm, or prove to be unworthy? Perhaps I already am and have. I do not exactly know what I do.

I do not see any enemies of me.

Some will make themselves the enemies of what I say, but I do not know how to deal in advance with these enemies. In truth, I understand them, and I perceive their chance in advance. I try to be on their side by thinking.

If I had enemies, I would be jealous of them.

Seldom have I read in my enemies something they know and I do not. They understand me. I would like to prove them right, but I cannot do so.

I have no absolute wisdom, but I am not deprived of it; I cannot refuse others' claims to it, and I cannot impose my own on those who appear deprived of it.

Talk of the chance and the price is not wisdom. Whoever will not listen to it, whoever will criticise it, whoever will mock it will in no way diminish their proper chance, the primary and ultimate sense of what they are, their possibility of being in the world; and no more will whoever hears me increase their chance.

If *philosophers* thought that wisdom is likely to produce consciousness, a rational comprehension which would augment our being in the world, then philosophers have failed. Being a philosopher is only one way among others of being in this world. Being a philosopher does not make one more of a being, as many have often believed; being a philosopher does not make one less of a being, as those believe who only consider one's failure, rather than the equal success of all forms of failure.
Be charitable. Everything that is considered a failure is not less successful than what is considered successful.

Our work concludes with the consciousness of the fact that this consciousness is not more, and not less, than the relative unconscious from which it will have been torn.

Neither wisdom nor calculation, neither salvation nor indefinite augmentation; in the end, my chance and price alone hold. My chance is what I have, whether I find it or lose it. My price is what I pay, whether I accept or refuse it, whether I pay it in good or evil.

This work is a way of comprehending things and objects, in the world and in the universe. It ends as something more in this world; elevated as a whole, it fails in everything, but since everything equally concludes in things, only its way of being and of having been a thing will count. What this work is remains opaque so long as you are there. It will only become clearer, either more or less, for you and I, once finished and closed, once it is completely a thing.

Then its mistakes, its limits, the very price of its system, the Achilles heel offered to the theoretical enemies, will alone appear definitively; but its chance, the combination [*martingale*] particular to what was thought and said, which played out between these pages, will also appear.

I seek meaning, and I always find *two* meanings.

Where comprehension is fulfilled, being begins, and vice versa.

The greatest possibilities will have been *comprehended* here, but it is to you alone to know what those *are*.

Works Cited

Adorno, Theodor W., *Aesthetic Theory*, trans. Robert Hullot-Kentor, London: Continuum, 2004.

Amundson, Ron, 'The Hundredth Monkey Phenomenon', *Skeptical Inquirer* (1985), 9, pp. 348–56.

Ariès, Philippe, *Western Attitudes Toward Death: From the Middle Ages to the Present*, trans. Patricia M. Ranum, Baltimore: Johns Hopkins University Press, 1974.

Aristotle, *History of Animals*, trans. D'A. W. Thompson, in *The Complete Works of Aristotle: The Revised Oxford Translation, Volume One*, ed. Jonathan Barnes, Princeton, NJ: Princeton University Press, 1984.

Aristotle, *Metaphysics*, trans. W. D. Ross, in *The Complete Works of Aristotle: The Revised Oxford Translation, Volume Two*, ed. Jonathan Barnes, Princeton, NJ: Princeton University Press, 1984.

Aristotle, *Physics*, trans. R. P. Hardie and R. K. Gaye, in *The Complete Works of Aristotle: The Revised Oxford Translation, Volume One*, ed. Jonathan Barnes, Princeton, NJ: Princeton University Press, 1984.

Aristotle, *Politics*, trans. B. Jowett, in *The Complete Works of Aristotle: The Revised Oxford Translation, Volume Two*, ed. Jonathan Barnes, Princeton, NJ: Princeton University Press, 1984.

Aron, Raymond, *Le Marxisme de Marx*, ed. Jean-Claude Casanova and Christian Bachelier, Paris: Livre de Poche, 2002.

Augustine, *The Confessions of Saint Augustine*, trans. Edward B. Pusey, New York: Random House, 1949.

Barkow, Jerome H., Leda Cosmides, and John Tooby, *The Adapted Mind: Evolutionary Psychology and the Generation of Culture*, New York: Oxford University Press, 1992.

Bataille, Georges, 'The Notion of Expenditure', in *Visions of Excess: Selected Writings, 1927–1939*, trans. Allan Stoekl, Minneapolis: University of Minnesota Press, 1985.

Bateson, Gregory, *Steps to an Ecology of Mind*, Chicago: University of Chicago Press, 2000.

Beauvoir, Simone de, *The Second Sex*, trans. Constance Borde and Sheila Malovany-Chevallier, New York: Alfred A. Knopf, 2010.

Beck, Benjamin, *Animal Tool Behaviour: The Use and Manufacture of Tools by Animals*, New York: Garland STPM, 1980.

Benoist, Jocelyn, *Représentations sans objet: Aux origines de la phéno-ménologie et de la philosophie analytique*, Paris: Presses Universitaires de France, 2001.

Benoist, Jocelyn and Fabio Merlini, *Après la fin de l'Histoire: temps, monde, historicité*, Paris: J. Vrin, 1998.

Bentham, Jeremy, *An Introduction to the Principles of Morals and Legislation*, Oxford: Clarendon Press, 1876.

Bergson, Henri, *Creative Evolution*, trans. Arthur Mitchell, New York: Modern Library, 1944.

Bichat, Xavier, *Physiological Researches Upon Life and Death*, trans. Tobias Watkins, Philadelphia: Smith and Maxwell, 1809.

Binoche, Bertrand, *Les Trois Sources des philosophies de l'histoire (1764–1798)*, Paris: Presses Universitaires de France, 1994.

Boas, Franz, *Primitive Art*, Cambridge, MA: Harvard University Press, 1927.

Bodson, Liliane, 'Le Témoignage de Pline l'Ancien sur la conception romaine de l'animal', in Barbara Cassin and Jean-Louis Labarrière (eds), *L'Animal dans l'Antiquité*, Paris: J. Vrin, 1997, pp. 325–54.

Bolk, Louis, *Das Problem der Menschwerdung*, Jena: Fischer, 1926.

Bolzano, Bernhard, *Theory of Science*, trans. Burnham Terrell, Dordrecht: D. Reidel, 1973.

Bonnaud, Robert, *Le Système de l'Histoire*, Paris: Fayard, 1989.

Bouché-Leclercq, Auguste, *Histoire de la divination dans l'Antiquité*, Paris: Leroux, 1882.

Bourdieu, Pierre, *Masculine Domination*, trans. Richard Nice, Stanford, CA: Stanford University Press, 2001.

Bourne, Craig, 'When Am I? A Tense Time for Some Tense Theorists?', *Australasian Journal of Philosophy* (2002), 80:3, pp. 359–71.

Bowie, Andrew, *Schelling and Modern European Philosophy*, London: Routledge, 1994.

Bradley, F. H., *Appearance and Reality*, Oxford: Clarendon Press, 1930.

Brentano, Franz, *Psychology from an Empirical Standpoint*, trans. A. C. Rancurello, D. B. Terrell, and L. McAlister, London: Routledge, 1973.

Broad, C. D., *Scientific Thought*, New York: Harcourt, Brace and Co., 1923.

Brophy, Brigid, 'The Rights of Animals', *The Sunday Times*, 10 October 1965.

Burnham, William H., 'The Study of Psychology', *Pedagogical Seminary* (1891), 1, pp. 174–95.

Buss, David, *The Evolution of Desire: Strategies of Human Mating*, New York: Basic Books, 1994.

Butel-Dumont, Georges-Marie, *Théorie du luxe*, Paris: Bastien, 1771.

Butler, Judith, *Gender Trouble: Feminism and the Subversion of Identity*, New York: Routledge, 1999.

Campbell, Neil A. and Jane B. Reece, *Biology*, 6th edn, San Francisco: Benjamin Cummings, 2002.

Campbell, Neil A. and Jane B. Reece, *Biologie*, 2nd edn, French trans. Mathieu Richard, Brussels: De Boeck Université, 2004.

Carr, John Dickson, *The Burning Court*, New York: Harper, 1937.

Carr, John Dickson, 'The Grandest Game in the World', in John Dickson Carr, *The Door to Doom, and Other Detections*, New York: Harper & Row, 1980, pp. 308–25.

Christie, Agatha, *The Murder of Roger Ackroyd*, New York: Dodd, Mead and Co., 1926.

Close, Frank, 'The Quark Structure of Matter', in Paul Davies (ed.), *The New Physics*, Cambridge: Cambridge University Press, pp. 396–424.

Cogburn, Jon and Mark Allan Ohm, 'Actual Qualities of Imaginative Things: Notes Towards an Object-Oriented Literary Theory', *Speculations*, (forthcoming).

Cohen, Daniel, *Globalization and Its Enemies*, trans. Jessica B. Baker, Cambridge, MA: MIT Press, 2006.

Condorcet, Jean-Antoine Nicolas de Caritat, *Sketch for a Historical Picture of the Progress of the Human Mind*, trans. Stuart Hampshire, London: Weidenfeld and Nicolson, 1795.

Condorcet, Jean-Antoine Nicolas de Caritat, *Tableau historique des progrès de l'esprit humain (1772–1794)*, ed. Jean-Pierre Schandeler and Pierre Crépel, Paris: Ined, 2004.

Croft, Herbert, *The Abbey of Kilkhampton, or, Monumental Records for the Year 1980*, London: G. Kearsly, 1780.

Cuvier, Georges, *A Discourse on the Revolutions of the Surface of the Globe, and the Changes thereby Produced in the Animal Kingdom*, Philadelphia: Carey and Lea, 1931.

Dawkins, Richard, *The Selfish Gene*, New York: Oxford University Press, 1976.

De Gobineau, Arthur, *The Inequality of Human Races*, New York: Fertig, 1999.

Debesse, Maurice, *La Crise d'originalité juvénile*, Paris: Presses Universitaires de France, 1948.

Deguy, Michel, 'Paul Valery et la culture', *Bulletin des Études valéryennes* (2004), 96/97, pp. 241–60.

DeLanda, Manuel, *Intensive Science and Virtual Philosophy*, London: Continuum, 2002.

DeLong, J. Bradford and Michael Froomkin, 'Old Rules for the New Economy', (1995) November, <http://econ161.berkeley.edu/Comments/for_hudson.html> (last accessed 1 September 2012)

Descartes, René, *Discourse on the Method*, in *The Philosophical Writings of Descartes, Volume 1*, trans. Robert Stoothoff, Cambridge: Cambridge University Press, 1984.

Descartes, René, *Optics*, in *The Philosophical Writings of Descartes, Volume I*, trans. Robert Stoothoff, Cambridge: Cambridge University Press, 1984.

Descola, Philippe, *Beyond Nature and Culture*, trans. Janet Lloyd, Chicago: University of Chicago Press, 2013.

Dickie, Georges, *Art and the Aesthetic: An Institutional Analysis*, Ithaca, NY: Cornell University Press, 1974.

Dostoyevsky, Fyodor, *Notes from Underground*, trans. Michael R. Katz, New York: Norton, 2001.

Dubuffet, Jean, 'Notes pour les fins lettrés', in Jean Dubuffet, *Prospectus aux amateurs de tout genre*, Paris: Gallimard, 1946.

Dubuffet, Jean, *Asphyxiating Culture and Other Writings*, New York: Four Walls Eight Windows, 1988.

Dupuy, Jean-Pierre, *Pour un catastrophisme éclairé: quand l'impossible est certain*, Paris: Seuil, 2002.

Durkheim, Émile, *The Elementary Forms of Religious Life*, trans. J. W. Swain, London: George Allen & Unwin, 1915.

Durkheim, Émile, *The Division of Labor in Society*, New York: Free Press, 1984.

Eldredge, Niles and Stephen Jay Gould, 'Punctuated Equilibria: An Alternative to Phyletic Gradualism', in Thomas J. M. Schopf (ed.), *Models in Paleobiology*, San Francisco: Freeman, Cooper and Co., 1997.

Engels, Friedrich, *Origins of the Family, Private Property, and the State*, in *Marx-Engels Collected Works, Volume 26*, New York: International Publishers, 1990.

Epicurus, *Letter to Menoeceus*, in *Hellenistic Philosophy: Introductory Readings*, 2nd edn, trans. Brad Inwood and L. P. Gerson, Indianapolis: Hackett, 1997.

Erikson, Erik H., *Identity and the Life Cycle: Selected Papers*, New York: International Universities Press, 1959.

Ferguson, Adam, *An Essay on the History of Civil Society*, Cambridge: Cambridge University Press, 1995.

Ferguson, Adam, 'Of Man's Progressive Nature', in *Adam Ferguson: Selected Philosophical Writings*, Exeter: Imprint Academic, 2007.

Fisher, Helen E., *Anatomy of Love: The Natural History of Monogamy, Adultery, and Divorce*, New York: Norton, 1992.

Fonton, Michèle, Évelyne Peyre, and Joëlle Wiels, 'Sexe biologique et sexe social', in Marie-Claire Hurtig, Michèle Kail, and Hélène Rouch (eds), *Sexe et genre: De la hiérarchie entre les sexes*, Paris: CNRS, 1991.

Fouts, Roger and Stephen Tukel Mills, *Next of Kin: My Conversations with Chimpanzees*, New York: Harper, 1998.

France, Anatole, *The Garden of Epicurus*, trans. Alfred Allinson, New York: Dodd, Mead and Company, 1923.

Frege, Gottlob, *Écrits logiques et philosophiques (1882–1923)*, French trans. Claude Imbert, Paris: Le Seuil, 1971.

Fukuyama, Francis, *Our Posthuman Future: Consequences of the Biotechnology Revolution*, New York: Farrar, Straus and Giroux, 2002.

Garcia, Tristan, 'Arts anciens, arts nouveaux: Les formes de nos représentations de l'invention de la photographie à aujourd'hui', doctoral thesis, Amiens, 2008.

Garcia, Tristan, *Forme et objet: Un traité des choses*, Paris: Presses Universitaires de France, 2011.

Garcia, Tristan, *Nous, animaux et humains: Actualité de Jeremy Bentham*, Paris: François Bourin Éditeur, 2011.

Garcia, Tristan, 'Après Meinong. Une autre théorie de l'objet', *Atelier de métaphysique et d'ontologie contemporaines* (April 2012), <http://www.atmoc.fr/resources/handout23.pdf> (last accessed 27 September 2013).

Garcia, Tristan, 'Crossing Ways of Thinking: On Graham Harman's System and My Own', trans. Mark Allan Ohm, *Parrhesia* (2013), 16, pp. 14–25.

Gardner, Allen, Beatrix Gardner, and Thomas Van Cantfort, *Teaching Sign Language to Chimpanzees*, Albany, NY: State University of New York Press, 1989.

Geertz, Clifford, *The Interpretation of Cultures*, New York: Basic Books, 1973.

Gehlen, Arnold, *Man: His Nature and Place in the World*, trans. Clare

McMillan and Karl Pillemer, New York: Columbia University Press, 1988.

Gennep, Arnold van, *The Rites of Passage*, trans. Monika B. Vizedom and Gabrielle L. Caffee, Chicago: University of Chicago Press, 1960.

Goodman, Nelson, 'When is Art?', in David Perkins and Barbara Leondar (eds), *The Arts and Cognition*, Baltimore: Johns Hopkins University Press, 1977, pp. 11–19.

Goodman, Nelson, 'A Genuinely Intensional Set Theory', in Stewart Shapiro (ed.), *Intensional Mathematics*, Amsterdam: Elsevier, 1985, pp. 63–77.

Grant, Iain Hamilton, *Philosophies of Nature after Schelling*, London: Bloomsbury Academic, 2008.

Greene, Brian, *The Elegant Universe: Superstrings, Hidden Dimensions, and the Quest for the Ultimate Theory*, New York: W. W. Norton, 1999.

Grey, Aubrey de, with Michael Rae, *Ending Aging: The Rejuvenation Breakthroughs that could Reverse Human Aging in Our Lifetime*, New York: St Martin's Press, 2007.

Halais, Emmanuel, *Une autre vision du bien*, Paris: Presses Universitaires de France, 2008.

Hale, Matthew, *Contemplations, Moral and Divine*, Hartford, CT: Belknap and Hamersely, 1835.

Hall, G. Stanley, *Adolescence: Its Psychology and its Relation to Physiology, Anthropology, Sociology, Sex, Crime, Religion and Education*, New York: D. Appleton and Co., 1904.

Harcourt, Alexander H. and Kelly J. Stewart, *Gorilla Society: Conflict, Compromise, and Cooperation between the Sexes*, Chicago: University of Chicago Press, 2007.

Harman, Graham, *Tool-Being: Heidegger and the Metaphysics of Objects*, Chicago: Open Court, 2002.

Harman, Graham, *Prince of Networks: Bruno Latour and Metaphysics*, Melbourne: re.press, 2009.

Harman, Graham, *The Quadruple Object*, Washington: Zero Books, 2011.

Harman, Graham, 'Object-Oriented France: The Philosophy of Tristan Garcia', *Continent* (2013), <http://continentcontinent.cc/index.php/continent/article/viewArticle/74> (last accessed 27 September 2013).

Harrison, Ruth, *Animal Machines: The New Factory Farming Industry*, London: Vincent Stuart, 1964.

Hegel, Gottfried Wilhelm Friedrich, *Philosophy of Mind*, trans. William

Wallace and A. C. Millar, rev. ed. Michael Inwood, Oxford: Oxford University Press, 2010.

Heidegger, Martin, 'The Thing', in Martin Heidegger, *Poetry, Language, Thought*, trans. Albert Hofstadter, New York: Perennial Library, 1975.

Herder, Johann Gottfried von, *Outlines of a Philosophy of the History of Man*, London, 1800.

Hey, Jody, 'A Reduction of "Species" Resolves the Species Problem', Rutgers University, New Jersey (January 1997), <http://genfaculty. rutgers.edu/uploads/14/A_Reduction_of_Species_JHey_1997.pdf> (last accessed 27 September 2013).

Hjelmslev, Louis, 'The Basic Structure of Language', in Louis Hjelmslev, *Essais Linguistiques II*, Copenhagen: Nordisk Sprog- og Kulturforlag, 1973, pp. 119–53.

Home, Henry, *Sketches on the History of Man*, Edinburgh: W. Creech, W. Strahan, and T. Cadell, 1774.

Hume, David, 'Of Luxury', in David Hume, *Political Discourses*, Edinburgh: R. Fleming, 1752.

Husserl, Edmund, *Ideas Pertaining to a Pure Phenomenology and to a Phenomenological Philosophy: First Book: General Introduction to a Pure Phenomenology*, trans. F. Kersten, The Hague: Martinus Nijhoff, 1982.

Iselin, Isaak, *Über die Geschichte der Menschheit*, Frankfurt: J. H. Harscher, 1764.

Jankélévitch, Vladimir, *La Mort*, Paris: Flammarion, 1966.

Jevons, William Stanley, *The Theory of Political Economy*, 3rd edn, London: Macmillan, 1888.

Joyce, James, *Ulysses*, New York: Modern Library, 1961.

Kant, Immanuel, 'Conjectures on the Beginning of Human History', in Immanuel Kant, *Political Writings*, 2nd edn, trans. H. B. Nisbet, ed. Hans Reiss, Cambridge: Cambridge University Press, 1991, pp. 221–34.

Kant, Immanuel, 'Idea for a Universal History with a Cosmopolitan Purpose', in Immanuel Kant, *Political Writings*, 2nd edn, trans. H. B. Nisbet, ed. Hans Reiss, Cambridge: Cambridge University Press, 1991.

Kant, Immanuel, *Critique of Pure Reason*, trans. and ed. Paul Guyer and Allen W. Wood, Cambridge: Cambridge University Press, 1998.

Kant, Immanuel, *Groundwork of the Metaphysics of Morals*, Cambridge: Cambridge University Press, 1998.

Kant, Immanuel, *Critique of the Power of Judgment*, ed. Paul Guyer, Cambridge: Cambridge University Press, 2001.

Kawai, Masao, 'Newly-acquired Pre-cultural Behavior of the Natural Troop of Japanese Monkeys on Koshima Islet', *Primates* (1965), 6:1, pp. 1–30.

Kawamura, Syunzo, 'The process of sub-culture propagation among Japanese macaques', *Primates* (1959), 2:1, pp. 43–60.

Kohlberg, Lawrence, 'Moral Stages and Moralization: The Cognitive-Developmental Approach', in Thomas Lickona (ed.), *Moral Development and Behavior: Theory, Research, and Social Issues*, New York: Holt, Rinehart and Winston, 1976, pp. 31–53.

Kroeber, Alfred and Clyde Kluckhorn, *Culture: A Critical Review of Concepts and Definitions*, Cambridge, MA: Harvard University Press, 1952.

Kurzweil, Raymond, *The Singularity is Near: When Humans Transcend Biology*, New York: Viking, 2005.

La Marne, Paula, 'Mort', in Dominique Lecourt (ed.), *Dictionnaire de la pensée médicale*, Paris: Presses Universitaires de France, 2004, pp. 752–7.

Lachièze-Rey, Marc, *Cosmology: A First Course*, trans. John Simmons, Cambridge: Cambridge University Press, 1995.

Laertius, Diogenes, *Lives of Eminent Philosophers, Volume II*, trans. R. D. Hicks, Cambridge, MA: Harvard University Press, 1970.

Lasch, Christopher, 'Mass Culture Reconsidered', *Democracy* (1981), 1:4, pp. 7–22.

Le Bon, Gustave, *The Psychology of Peoples*, New York: Stechert, 1927.

Lecointre, Guillaume and Hervé Le Guyader, *The Tree of Life: A Phylogenetic Classification*, trans. Karen McCoy, Cambridge, MA: Belknap Press of Harvard University Press, 2006.

Leibniz, G. W., *Philosophical Essays*, trans. and ed. Roger Ariew and Dan Garber, Indianapolis: Hackett, 1989.

Lestel, Dominique, *Les Origines animales de la culture*, Paris: Flammarion, 2001.

Lewis, David K., *On the Plurality of Worlds*, Oxford: Blackwell, 1986.

Malaparte, Curzio, *The Skin*, trans. David Moore, Evanston, IL: Northwestern University Press, 1997.

Malebranche, Nicolas, *Elucidations of the Search After Truth*, in Nicolas Malebranche, *The Search After Truth*, trans. Thomas M. Lennon, Columbus, OH: Ohio State University Press, 1980.

Mallarmé, Stéphane, *Sonnet allégorique de lui-même*, in *Œuvres complètes, Tome I*, ed. Bertrand Marchal, Paris: Gallimard, 1998.

Mandeville, Bernard, *The Fable of the Bees, or Private Vices, Publick Benefits*, Indianapolis: Library Fund, 1988.

Maréchal, Sylvain, *Le Jugement dernier des rois*, Paris: C.-F. Patris, 1793.

Marx, Karl, *Capital, Volume III: The Process of Capitalist Production as a Whole*, New York: International Publishers, 1967.

Marx, Karl and Friedrich Engels, *The German Ideology*, in *Karl Marx, Friedrich Engels: Collected Works, Vol. 5*, New York: International Publishers, 1975.

Mauss, Marcel, *The Gift: The Form and Reason for Exchange in Archaic Societies*, trans. W. D. Halls, London: Routledge, 2001.

Mayr, Ernst, *Systematics and the Origin of Species from the Viewpoint of a Zoologist*, New York: Columbia University Press, 1942.

Mayr, Ernst, *The Growth of Biological Thought: Diversity, Evolution, and Inheritance*, Cambridge, MA: Belknap Press of Harvard University Press, 1982.

Maynard Smith, John and Eörs Szathmáry, *The Origins of Life: From the Birth of Life to the Origin of Language*, Oxford: Oxford University Press, 1999.

McCarthy, John, 'Programs with Common Sense', *Teddington Conference on the Mechanization of Thought Processes*, London: HMS Office, 1959.

McTaggart, J. M. E., 'The Unreality of Time', *Mind* (1908), 17:68, pp. 457–74.

Mehring, Daniel Gottlieb Gebhard, *Das Jahr 2500*, Berlin: Maurer, 1794.

Meillassoux, Quentin, *After Finitude: An Essay on the Necessity of Contingency*, trans. Ray Brassier, London: Continuum, 2008.

Meinong, Alexius, 'The Theory of Objects', trans. Isaac Levi, D. B. Terrell, and Roderick M. Chisholm, in Roderick M. Chisholm (ed.), *Realism and the Background of Phenomenology*, Glencoe: Free Press, 1960.

Mendousse, Pierre, *L'Âme de l'adolescent*, Paris: Alcan, 1909.

Mendousse, Pierre, *L'Âme de l'adolescente*, Paris: Presses Universitaires de France, 1928.

Mercier, Louis-Sébastien, *Memoirs of the Year Two Thousand Five Hundred*, trans. William Hooper, London: G. Robinson, 1772.

Merricks, Trenton, 'Goodbye Growing Block', *Oxford Studies in Metaphysics* (2006), 2, pp. 103–10.

Mill, John Stuart, *Autobiography*, in *The Collected Works of John Stuart Mill, Volume I*, ed. John M. Robson and Jack Stillinger, Toronto: University of Toronto Press, 1981.

Mill, John Stuart, *Bentham*, in *The Collected Works of John Stuart Mill,*

Volume X, ed. John M. Robson, Toronto: University of Toronto Press, 1985.

Minsky, Marvin, *Computation: Finite and Infinite Machines*, Englewood Cliffs, NJ: Prentice Hall, 1967.

Montaigne, Michel de, *Essays*, in *The Complete Works: Essays, Travel Journal, Letters*, trans. Donald M. Frame, New York: Everyman's Library, 2003.

Montesquiou, Robert de, *Roseaux pensants*, Paris: Bibliothèque-Charpentier, 1897.

Moore, George Edward, *Principia Ethica*, ed. Thomas Baldwin, Cambridge: Cambridge University Press, 1993.

Morin, Edgar, *L'Identité humaine*, Paris: Le Seuil, 2001.

Murdoch, Iris, *The Sovereignty of Good*, London: Routledge, 2001.

Nietzsche, Friedrich, *The Will to Power*, trans. Walter Kaufmann and R. J. Hollingdale, New York: Vintage, 1968.

Nietzsche, Friedrich, 'On the Uses and Disadvantages of History for Life', trans. R. J. Hollingdale, in Friedrich Nietzsche, *Untimely Meditations*, Cambridge: Cambridge University Press, 1997.

Nodé-Langlois, Michel, *Le Vocabulaire de saint Thomas*, Paris: Ellipses, 1999.

Oaklander, L. Nathan (ed.), *The Philosophy of Time*, London: Routledge, 2008.

Ohm, Mark Allan and Jon Cogburn, 'Garcia's Paradox', paper presented at the Notre Dame *Translating Realism* Conference, 2013.

Orwell, George, *Nineteen Eighty-Four*, New York: Harcourt, 1949.

Panofsky, Erwin, *Perspective as Symbolic Form*, trans. Christopher S. Wood, New York: Zone Books, 1997.

Pareto, Vilfredo, *Manual of Political Economy*, trans. Ann S. Schwier, New York: Augustus M. Kelley, 1971.

Pascal, Blaise, *Pensées*, ed. Louis Lafuma, Paris: Le Seuil, 1963.

Peirce, Charles Sanders, *Écrits sur le signe*, French trans. Gérard Deledalle, Paris: Le Seuil, 1978.

Penrose, Roger, *The Road to Reality: A Complete Guide to the Laws of the Universe*, New York: Alfred A. Knopf, 2005.

Pichot, André, 'Hérédité et évolution (l'inné et l'acquis en biologie)', *Esprit* (1996), 222, pp. 7–25.

Pigliucci, Massimo, 'Species as family resemblance concepts: the (dis-) solution of the species problem?', *BioEssays* (2003), 25:6, pp. 596–602.

Pinker, Steven, *The Blank Slate: The Modern Denial of Human Nature*, New York: Viking, 2002.

Plato, *Phaedrus*, trans. Alexander Nehamas and Paul Woodruffin, in

Plato: Complete Works, ed. John M. Cooper, Cambridge: Hackett, 1997.

Plato, *Republic*, trans. G. M. A. Grube, rev. C. D. C. Reeve, in *Plato: Complete Works*, ed. John M. Cooper, Cambridge: Hackett, 1997.

Plato, *Timaeus*, trans. Donald J. Zeyl, in *Plato: Complete Works*, ed. John M. Cooper, Cambridge: Hackett, 1997.

Pliny the Elder, *The Natural History*, trans. John Bostock, London: Taylor & Francis, 1855.

Poe, Edgar Allan, 'The Imp of the Perverse', in Edgar Allan Poe, *Poetry and Tales*, New York: Library of America, 1984.

Premack, Ann and David Premack, *The Mind of an Ape*, New York: Norton, 1983.

Priest, Graham, *Beyond the Limits of Thought*, Oxford: Oxford University Press, 2003.

Priest, Graham, *In Contradiction: A Study of the Transconsistent*, 2nd edn, Oxford: Oxford University Press, 2006.

Primatt, Humphrey, *A Dissertation on the Duty of Mercy and Sin of Cruelty to Brute Animals*, London: T. Cadell, 1776.

Quine, W. V. O., 'New Foundations for Mathematical Logic', *American Mathematical Monthly* (1937), 44, pp. 70–80.

Quine, W. V. O., *Ontological Relativity and Other Essays*, New York: Columbia University Press, 1969.

Regan, Tom, 'Animal Rights, Human Wrongs', *Environmental Ethics* (1980), 2:2, pp. 99–120.

Renan, Ernest, *The Future of Science: Ideas of 1848*, London: Chapman and Hall, 1891.

Restif de la Bretonne, *L'An deux-mille*, in Restif de la Bretonne, *Le thesmographe, ou idées d'un honnête homme sur un projet de réglement proposé à toutes les nations de l'Europe pour opérer une réforme générale des loix*, Paris: Maradan, 1789.

Ricœur, Paul, *Time and Narrative, Volume I*, trans. Kathleen McLaughlin and David Pellauer, Chicago: University of Chicago Press, 1984.

Rimbaud, Arthur, 'Letter to Paul Demeny, Charleville, 15 May 1871', in *Complete Works, Selected Letters: A Bilingual Edition*, trans. Wallace Fowlie, Chicago: University of Chicago Press, 2005.

Robertson, William, *The History of America, Volume I*, London: W. Strahan, 1777.

Rousseau, Jean-Jacques, *Discourse on the Origins of Inequality*, in *The Collected Writings of Rousseau, Volume 3*, ed. Roger D. Masters and Christopher Kelly, Hanover, NH: University Press of New England, 1992.

Russell, Bertrand, 'On Denoting', *Mind* (1905), 14, pp. 479–93.

Ryder, Richard, 'Experiments on Animals', in Stanley Godlovitch, Roslind Godlovitch, and John Harris (eds), *Animals, Men and Morals: Enquiry into the Maltreatment of Nonhumans*, London: Victor Gollancz, 1971.

Say, Jean-Baptiste, *Cours complet d'économie politique*, Paris: Guillaumin, 1840.

Schumpeter, Joseph A., *Capitalism, Socialism, and Democracy*, New York: Harper and Brothers, 1942.

Schumpeter, Joseph A., *History of Economic Analysis*, New York: Oxford University Press, 1954.

Schwitters, Kurt, *Ursonate*, [score], <http://www.ubu.com/historical/schwitters/ursonate.html> (last accessed 27 September 2013).

Segerdahl, Pår, William Fields, and Sue Savage-Rumbaugh, *Kanzi's Primal Language: The Cultural Initiation into Language*, Victoria: Palgrave Macmillan, 2006.

Simmel, Georg, 'The Concept and Tragedy of Culture', in David Frisby and Mike Featherstone (eds), *Simmel on Culture*, London: Sage, 1997.

Singer, Peter, *Animal Liberation*, New York: Avon Books, 1975.

Smith, Adam, *An Inquiry into the Nature and Causes of the Wealth of Nations, Volume III*, Edinburgh: S. Doig and A. Stirling, 1811.

Steeman, Stanislas-André, *L'Assassin habite au 21*, Paris: Librarie des Champs-Élysées, 1939.

Stern, Robert, *Hegel, Kant, and the Structure of the Object*, London: Routledge, 1990.

Stern, Robert, *Hegelian Metaphysics*, Oxford: Oxford University Press, 2012.

Tager, Djénane Kareh, *Vivre la mort: Voyages à travers les traditions*, Paris: P. Lebaud, 1999.

Taguieff, Pierre-André, *La Couleur et le Sang: Doctrines racistes à la française*, Paris: Mille et une nuits, 2002.

Teilhard de Chardin, Pierre, *Man's Place in Nature: The Human Zoological Group*, trans. René Hague, New York: Harper & Row, 1966.

Templeton, Alan R., 'The Meaning of Species and Speciation: A Genetic Perspective', in Daniel Otte and John A. Endler (eds), *Speciation and its Consequences*, Sunderland, MA: Sinauer Associates, 1989, pp. 3–27.

Terrace, Herbert, *Nim: A Chimpanzee who Learned Sign Language*, New York: Columbia University Press, 1987.

Thaler, Louis, 'L'espèce: type ou population?', *Sauve qui peut!* (1998), 10,

<http://www.inra.fr/dpenv/thales10.htm> (last accessed 27 September 2013).

Thomas, Louis-Vincent, *Anthropologie de la mort*, Paris: Payot, 1975.

Tipler, Frank J. and John D. Barrow, *The Anthropic Cosmological Principle*, Oxford: Oxford University Press, 1986.

Tooley, Michael, *Time, Tense and Causation*, Oxford: Clarendon Press, 1997.

Tort, Patrick (ed.), *Dictionnaire du darwinisme et de l'Évolution, tome I*, Paris: Presses Universitaires de France, 1996.

Trinh, Xuan Thuan, *The Secret Melody, and Man Created the Universe*, trans. Storm Dunlop, New York: Oxford University Press, 1995.

Tryon, Thomas, *Health's Grand Preservative; or the Women's Best Doctor*, London: Langley Curtis, 1682.

Turing, Alan, 'Computing Machinery and Intelligence', *Mind* (1950), LXI:236, pp. 433–60.

Turner, Victor, *The Forest of Symbols: Aspects of Ndembu Ritual*, Ithaca, NY: Cornell University Press, 1967.

Twardowski, Kazimierz, *On the Content and Object of Presentations: A Psychological Investigation*, trans. R. Grossmann, The Hague: M. Nijhoff, 1977.

Tylor, Edward B., *Primitive Culture: Researches into the Development of Mythology, Philosophy, Religion, Art, and Custom, Volume 1*, London: J. Murray, 1871.

Veblen, Thorstein, *The Theory of the Leisure Class*, New York: August M. Kelley, 1975.

Vernant, Jean-Pierre, *L'Individu, la mort, l'amour: soi-même et l'autre en Grèce ancienne*, Paris: Gallimard, 1989.

Vilmer, Jean-Baptiste Jeangène, *Éthique animale*, Paris: Presses Universitaires de France, 2008.

Vinge, Vernor, 'Technological Singularity', *Whole Earth Review* (1993), 81, pp. 88–95.

Viveiros de Castro, Eduardo, 'Cosmological Deixis and Amerindian Perspectivism', *The Journal of the Royal Anthropological Institute* (1998), 4:3, pp. 469–88.

Viveiros de Castro, Eduardo, *Métaphysiques cannibales*, Paris: Presses Universitaires de France, 2009.

Voltaire, *Essai général sur les moeurs et l'esprit des nations et sur les principaux faits de l'Histoire, depuis Charlemagne jusqu'à nos jours*, Paris: Garnier, 1963.

von Neumann, John, *The Computer and the Brain*, New Haven: Yale University Press, 1958.

Wachsmuth, Karl Heinrich, *Das Jahr Zweitausend vierhundert und vierzig: Zum zweitenmal geträumt*, Leipzig: Weygandsche Buchhandlung, 1783.

Wessel, Johan Herman, *Anno 7603*, Copenhagen: Trykt hos P. Horrebow, 1785.

Whitehead, Alfred North, *Process and Reality*, corr. ed. David Ray Griffin and Donald W. Sherburne, New York: Free Press, [1929] 1978.

[Wilde, Oscar], 'A Few Maxims for the Instruction of the Over-Educated', *Saturday Review of Politics, Literature, Science and Art* (17 November 1894), 78, pp. 533–4.

Wilson, Edward O., *Sociobiology: The New Synthesis*, Cambridge, MA: Belknap Press of Harvard University Press, 1975.

Wittgenstein, Ludwig, *Tractatus Logico-Philosophicus*, London: Routledge, [1922] 1968.

Wittgenstein, Ludwig, *Philosophical Investigations*, 4th edn, trans. and ed. P. M. S. Hacker and Joachim Schulte, Oxford: Wiley-Blackwell, 2009.

Wolff, Francis, *Dire le monde*, Paris: Presses Universitaires de France, 1997.

Index

453

Name Index